THE AFRICAN WORLD IN DIALOGUE

THE AFRICAN WORLD IN DIALOGUE

AN APPEAL TO ACTION!

Edited by

TERESA N. WASHINGTON

OYA'S TORNADO

This book is a publication of
ỌYA'S TORNADO
Books To Blow Your Mind
oyastornado@yahoo.com

ỌYA'S TORNADO™, Books To Blow Your Mind™, and all associated tornado logos are trademarks of Ọya's Tornado.

Washington, Teresa N.
The African world in dialogue: an appeal to action! / edited by Teresa N. Washington.
p. cm.
Includes bibliographical references and index.
ISBN 978-0-9910730-7-8 (cloth); ISBN 978-0-9910730-6-1 (pbk);
978-0-9910730-8-5 (ebook)
1. African authors—African American authors—History and criticism. 2. Pan-African studies. 3. Black world studies. 4. Black revolutionary studies. 5. Gender studies. 6. African American and African relations. 7. African politics. 8. African American politics. 9. Pan-African conflict, mediation, and resolution. 10. African immigration. 11. African identity politics. I. Title.

Revised Edition
First printing, 2018

Manufactured in the United States of America

for our progeny . . .

who must also be armed with wisdom
and viable strategies

Ọmọ Ẹlẹ́gbára Gidigidi

The air was too dense to breathe
for 57 seconds
on 21 April 2016
the Cosmos
stilled
and heaved
and struggled to receive the
Greatest
Gift
Given
So deep and rich a force
the universe expanded
to accommodate it
and once inside
sighed in delight

There
between the legs
of Gemini
a planet is born
boasting four funky moons
and a pimpstroll rotation
dippin on a phat axis
purple pulsating
bobbing throbbing
Ọmọba
Ọmọba
Ọmọba

Just like that!
The God's got a brand new home

"Everybody shut up!
Listen to the band. . ."

TABLE OF CONTENTS

PART TWO | RESTITUTIONS, RESOLUTIONS, REVOLUTIONS

PART THREE | AFRICANITY, EDUCATION, AND TECHNOLOGY

PART FOUR | LIFE LINES FROM THE FRONT LINES

PART FIVE | GENDER, POWER, AND INFINITE PROMISE

THE AFRICAN WORLD IN DIALOGUE

AN APPEAL TO ACTION!

INTRODUCTION

Continental Divides

Is Africa still "Africa"? Or is Africa becoming "Big China"?

The Sinocolonization of Africa has been both swift and devastating. While the Chinese have not demanded Africans adopt their language or writing system as did the Caucasian tribes who colonized the Continent during the "scramble" and "partition" of Africa which officially began in 1884, covert Chinese colonization is proving just as detrimental. Sinocolonization could be even more destructive, because so many African nations are struggling and so many African people are fragile, exhausted, and infuriated at the failure or refusal of their leaders to transform the astounding wealth of the world's richest continent and countries into sound roads, stable electricity, gainful employment, efficient drainage, potable water, and peaceful societies.

The unemployment rates in some African nations are so high that citizens are creating a new Middle Passage in their quest to find economic success in Europe. The last thing that nations teetering on the edge of economic collapse need is an endless caravan of barges filled Chinese products of decidedly dubious usefulness.

The Chinese are leveling African industries and economies. While Ghana and the "Giant of Africa," as Nigerians call Nigeria, continue to manufacture and export a wide variety of products, including foods, cosmetics, and tools, to many nations in West Africa, all too many of the products that one is able to purchase in Africa are of Chinese origin. It is only a matter of time before the Chinese undercut the few African industries that remain and turn the continent into a massive dumping ground for their junk.

The only African economic gain from Sinocolonization that I witnessed is the cottage industry of makeshift shops that "repair" Chinese products which will continue to fail—as if on schedule—at least once a month. While African metropolises are dotted with buildings that have Chinese flags flying over them alongside the flags of the African host countries, this looked, to me, not like cooperative development but like an ominous form of branding signifying "evisceration-at-work."

How, I wondered during my most recent African sojourns, could a communist nation be so ruthless? So ravenously avaricious? So inhumane? But one need only note China's human rights record and treatment of its own citizens to understand its methodical ravaging of Africa. What is more, Chinese robber barons are not rogue invaders; they are welcomed on the Continent by African officials and heads of state.

Evidence abounds of multi-billion dollar deals that clearly benefit China but have negligible positive impact on any African country. For example, thanks to China's trade agreements with Nigeria, money has flowed into select bank accounts, and petrol is flowing freely in China, the world's second largest oil consumer. However, Nigerians can routinely be found falling asleep on the hoods of their cars as they wait in fuel lines for 10 hours in hopes of obtaining the petroleum products necessary to cook food, travel, and illuminate their homes.

Across Nigeria's western border in Benin, electricity is relatively stable and fuel flows freely. However, Benin's leaders have also forged an imbalanced alliance with China that speaks volumes about the red nation's objectives on the Continent. I was shocked to find at Western Unions in Cotonou that, in addition to world-recognized forms of currency being traded, one can buy or sell the newly minted "Chinese Franc." If there is such a thing as an economic raping, the Chinese Franc is erect and thrusting into the bank vaults of a supine Benin.

Perhaps an efficient economic raping of Africa is all China desires. This may be the implication of the commercial for Chinese Qiaobi laundry detergent.[1] In 2016 Qiaobi released a commercial in which an African male house painter flirts with a Chinese house owner as she does her laundry. When the African moves in for a kiss, the Chinese woman jams a detergent pod into his mouth and then forces his entire body, head first, into a washing machine. When the savage cycle is complete, the African has been washed away and replaced by a glowing Chinese man.

The trope of the depraved, deprived, dirt- and/or tree-dwelling African is helpful for races desperate to create a false sense of superiority and for opportunists who wish generate wealth through dubious charities and ephemeral non-governmental organizations. But the reality is that luxuries in Africa can leave one dumbfounded. While studying in Nigeria, I was shocked to meet college students who don't know how to drive because they have chauffeurs who drive them everywhere they go as well as maids and "house boys" to tend to their needs: and these families would be considered middle-class in America. I was stunned when my librarian friend from Cotonou, whose husband is unemployed, complained about her maid's treatment of her children. (My suggestion that her husband could raise and care for his sons was inconceivable.) Many African professors, publishers, civil service workers, and entrepreneurs take for granted a style of freedom and a standard of living that would baffle many westerners.

People who cling to racism-fueled fictions about Africa would be shocked to know that anything one wants or can find in America—the most envied "whips" (cars), the most elaborate mansions, weaves from hair freshly harvested from the domes of devout Indian women, on-trend fashion and haute couture, concerts featuring African American stars, and, of course, hamburgers—one can find easily and in abundance in Africa. But in addition to overflowing with any and all things occidental, Africa also boasts things one can *only* find in Africa.

Many African universities are so expansive that they boast their own public transportation systems, restaurant hubs, supermarkets, and zoos—yes, zoos. However, outside the gates of sprawling university systems are humble elders who boast wisdom as deep as the cosmos and who are more accessible than university professors because they do not demand tuition fees in exchange for wisdom.

Nigeria is, in many respects, a mecca of wisdom. There are elders there that one cannot encounter anywhere else and there are books being published there—in an expansive and thriving publishing industry—that cannot be obtained anywhere else. The same can be said of Ghana, Senegal, Kenya, and many other African nations. What is more, one is likely to find the authors of these books relaxing in their homes or offices eager to share their knowledge with a wisdom-seeker.

No manner of enslavement, colonization, oppression, or identity crisis has been able to divest African wisdom-keepers of their wisdom, and they continue to preserve knowledge in the infinite expanses of the mind, through indelibly signifying ink, and in the outer limits of cyberspace.

The riches and wealth of Africa can also to be found in the ground, and miners are carving the Continent hollow in search of gold, diamonds, uranium, helium, bauxite, cobalt, coltan, helium, and more. And while few Africans will gaze upon a lion, gazelle, rhinoceros, or giraffe outside of the confines of a university zoo, Africa's wildlife is one of its biggest draws. It could be the case that Africa's wildlife piqued Chinese interests the most.

China is stamping an indelible brand on Africa's ecology: The brand reads, **EXTINCT**. The stench of death suffuses Africa's savannahs and grasslands which are littered with the bodies of elephants and rhinoceroses that, after having been divested of their tusks and horns, respectively, are left to rot. The Continent is becoming the world's largest wildlife cemetery—and there's an ivory glut on the Asian black market.

The odor of death also wafts up from the Mediterranean Sea which will soon boast so many African bodies that immigrants will be able to walk on the corpses of their unfortunate country men and women to reach Greece or Italy or some other Promise Land where Africans are not welcome.

The Continent is also damp with the blood of Africans who turn on and kill Africans from neighboring communities and countries because of envy, inadequacy, and greed. When community members decide to rid themselves of all members of a visiting and prospering ethnic group, they begin whispering that the outsiders are occultists and cannibals. When the whispers become roars, the lucky members of the branded ethnic group will leave the country with the clothes on their backs; the unlucky ones will serve as fuel for the bonfires of the jealous.

While xenophobic attacks on entire groups of people who are deemed "other" are prevalent, equally rampant are the routine lynchings of sons and daughters of the soil. Perhaps the most egregious example of murderous injustice is the parading, beating, and burning alive of four University of Port Harcourt students by the citizens of Aluu, Nigeria in 2012. The "crime" these students committed was going to the home of a debtor and asking for a loan to be repaid. Rather than pay or negotiate, the debtor cried, "Thief!" and an entire community coalesced to literally beat the brains out of the heads of the students and then set them ablaze. The community knew the young men and knew that they were collecting a debt. What fueled the fires of Aluu was not justice but an internal inadequacy that is reaching epidemic levels in the African world.

Although extrajudicial killings are nicknamed "jungle justice," the culture of enacting bizarrely brutal community lynching originates with Caucasian tribes, especially those of the medieval era. Caucasians exported their terror-tactics to Africa and applied them on Africans during colonization. While extrajudicial killings may also be deemed "instant justice," they are actually instant gratification for the jealous, envious, and lesser intellectually, artistically, and/or financially endowed. Indeed, the hallmark of "instant justice" is the complete *absence* of justice. One need only cry "Thief! Thief!" and point at *anyone*—even a child—and a lynching will soon follow. More than anything else, the exponentially rising popularity of public community lynchings in Africa, which are immediately uploaded for posterity, illuminates the gravity of our collective situation.

The gleeful lynching of people who are guilty of petty crimes and people who are completely innocent could be considered microcosmic symptoms of a macrocosmic Continental death. If this is the case, then the death could be considered an eagerly assisted suicide because it is the leaders who are selling out nations, industries, and economies to the highest bidders and, thereby, creating societies in which people find it difficult to survive. Rather than bolstering African economies and creating desperately needed jobs, leaders embark on global aid-begging tours and cash unnecessary loan checks to feed not masses but offshore bank accounts.

Another reason that a continent that is filled with some of the world's most intelligent and resourceful people and the world's most needed and desired goods is unable to lift its citizens from the bowels of poverty and oppression is because ego and individualism routinely trump collectivism. Africans residing on the continent are not alone in this. A cloud of selfishness, made even more suffocating by a cloying haze of capitalism, is smothering the African world, as millions have bought into their oppressors' model of success and focus on amassing wealth, benefits, and privileges for themselves and for their ethnic and/or political groups.

The most stunning example of selfishness and self-contentment in the face of national upheaval that I have witnessed concerned some southern Nigerians' take on northern-based Boko Haram.

It is important to note that Boko Haram did not pop up overnight and start shooting. One could argue that Boko Haram was conceived in 1999 when Nigeria held democratic elections. Concurrent with the national decision to hoist high the banner of democracy was the North's decision to embrace Sharia.

Relations between the major ethnic groups of northern and southern Nigeria are often hostile, as some contributors to this book detail. But the animosity could be considered logical because the three major ethnic groups who comprise the citizenry of Nigeria had, prior to colonization, been separated by language, culture, and geography, and they endeavored to keep their interactions limited to avoid wars. Caucasian colonizers knew all-too-well the volatility that would result from forcing together disparate people (and from separating groups of related people, as well), and they knew they would benefit from a perpetually explosive arrangement.

Because of Nigeria's curvilinear cultural, religious, and political hostilities, which have been exacerbated by England and its preferential treatment of some northern ethnic groups, when northern states began declaring what could be called secession-by-Sharia in 1999, the response of the collective South, including the federal government, was negligible. While the Biafra secession of 1967–1970 moved the nation to go to war to keep its oil-rich eastern region, many seemed to welcome a clearer distinction and deeper divide between the North and South.

With the declaration that Nigeria, long-ruled by military generals, would become a democratic nation, many southerners began dreaming about the windfalls that democracy would bring; some northerners worked to ensure that any bonanzas would come at an unimaginable price. Sharia was formally inaugurated in the year 2000 in Zamfara State with the amputation of a youth's right hand for the alleged theft of a cow. Nigerian newspapers were emblazoned with photos of the youth and his right hand which dangled from the ceiling by a string. Following this display, the sword of amputation grew exponentially.

During its height in 2014, Boko Haram's weaponry was so impressive and its training so sophisticated that the Nigerian military, which has long been regarded as one of the world's most brutal, simply refused to engage Boko Haram in battle.

One of the reasons that Boko Haram gained such notoriety and successfully embarked on so many campaigns of terror is that many southerners and northern- and southern-born heads of state ignored or downplayed what had been happening in the North since 1999. While Boko Haram shocked the world with the kidnapping of hundreds of schoolgirls in Chibok, by the time the hashtags had been forgotten, Boko Haram was seeing if it would be possible to kill everyone in the Nigerian village of Baga while extending its "caliphate" into Niger and Cameroon.

The passion and fury of the Bring Back Our Girls protest was moving to me because it was in stark contrast to the common consensus of many of the Nigerians that I met in Benin Republic and Nigeria. At the height of Boko Haram's rampage, many southern Nigerians offered the following sentiment about the terrorists: "Thank God they [Boko Haram] are [only] in the North." I was aghast, "How can one thank God that Boko Haram is *any*where?! What if a few terrorists board a bus for Lagos?" The answer was a shrug. It was clear that as long as *they* were not personally threatened, Boko Haram didn't matter. At any rate, why should these citizens care more than President Goodluck Jonathan and first lady Patience Jonathan who originally claimed the Chibok abductions didn't occur?[2]

Discussing such concepts as African Unity and Pan-Africanism is rather difficult on a vast Continent of endless intricacies, empowering connections, and stunning disconnects: At the same time that one is attending an international trade conference in Abuja, Boko Haram may be seeing how many people it can kill in Maiduguri. As the citizens of Makoko in Lagos ponder where to dispose of feces in their floating slum, the future citizens of Eko Atlantic in Lagos are estimating the size of their yacht docks. While Burkina Faso's youths launch a successful revolution and oust the country's head of state and cabinet, the youths of Benin Republic couldn't care less or have no idea that a revolution is taking place in a neighboring Francophone nation. One can travel to Ghana, a country some would consider the capital of Pan-Africanism, and have a lively political discussion with a Ghanaian brother named Marcus Garvey, after the legendary Jamaican Pan-Africanist. But when you and Garvey decide to have a lunch of kenke and fish, you find yourselves literally kicked to the curb as vendors push Africans into the gutter so that Caucasians can be served first. *Akwaaba*! (Welcome!)

Perhaps you make your pilgrimage to the home of Thomas Sankara so that you can stroll among the "Exemplary" and "Upright" People of Burkina Faso and salute the youths who toppled Blaise Compaore's regime. Imagine your shock at finding that Kwame Nkrumah Boulevard, named for the first president of Ghana, the first African nation to gain independence, is a Caucasian Heaven. Caucasians, especially those from Canada, France, and America, have quietly and decidedly made Ouagadougou the perfect place to live out the Caucasian superiority complex. Ouagadougou is an African city that is nearly fully owned, dominated, and controlled by non-Africans. Africans exist largely as petty traders, direction givers, procurers, guides, maids, human recreational facilities, and toters.

A Caucasian blogged that while she lived in Burkina Faso she never had to carry anything. Anytime anyone saw her carrying anything, they rushed to relieve her of her burden. No melanin-rich Africana visitor can marvel at Africans relieving her of all earthly burdens: quite the contrary. Rather than assisting the hardest working women in the world with their burdens, African women in Burkina Faso, and many other African countries and Africana communities, are subject to such customary abuse that no one is appalled when an African man publicly threatens to beat or beats a woman or girl he may or may not know for doing something that he doesn't like, like refusing to pay him an arbitrary male-privilege tax when purchasing a product or paying a fare. And no one comes to the African female's aid, let alone relieves her of her bags or offers her a seat.[3] And no NGO or charity writes her a check. In fact, many of the NGOs and charities collecting money for name-an-African-cause have no presence in Africa at all. . .

In the past, people of the "Upper Volta," as the colonizers called the land north of Ghana, were considered a cheap or free labor source for Ghana and Côte d'Ivoire. Thomas Sankara worked to transform "Upper Volta" from a designated area to exploit laborers to "Burkina Faso": The Land of Upright People. Sankara fought to ensure that the people of Burkina Faso were in fact "upright": fully self-sufficient, free, and independent. Sankara's simple and effective strategy of creating a nation in which the people produce what they consume and consume what they produce terrified France, America, and other neocolonial power-mongering states, so they had Sankara killed so that Burkina Faso and its citizens could become servants for Caucasians desperately in need of a vacation.

The slowly simmering outrage of people who've spent too much time toting foreigners' burdens (or carrying their "shit" to quote Fela Anikulapo Kuti) may be most apparent in the 2016 attack in Ouagadougou which was focused on Caucasian businesses and Caucasian peoples so as to send an unmistakable message.

The racial specificity of the 2016 attack in Ouagadougou was surprising because African violence routinely revolves around the theme of "_____ must go!" and the blank can usually be filled with nearly any African group. African indigenes who are disfranchised cannot attack the colonial, neocolonial, and Sinocolonial forces that leave them unemployed, underemployed, homeless, hungry, or on corners seeking "trade." So they attack African immigrants who have come in search of a better life, economic mobility, greater educational opportunities, and/or, ironically, freedom from ethnic, political, or religious persecution. Conflict in Africa usually finds the vulnerable attacking those who are even more vulnerable and attacking them without mercy.

Even when there is no violent conflict occurring, it is likely that preparations for one are being made. Outsiders would be shocked at the rigid classification systems—many rooted in conflicts that arose during the eras of enslavement and colonization—that some Africans employ when defining neighboring ethnic groups. The North–South and East–North divides in Nigeria provide one example. But geographical divisions are compounded when colonial languages are also a factor, as is evident with the Béninois' categorizations of Nigerians.

While any Anglophone person in Francophone Benin Republic is suspect, if one hails from Nigeria and one is Yoruba, one can journey to Ketu and fit seamlessly into a Francophone Yoruba city. Ketu is situated near the Nigerian border. Because the French claimed to own the land and the people to the west of the border and the British claimed to own the land and the people to the east of the border, the Yoruba people are divided by an imaginary boundary and two alien oppressive languages. But in Ketu, they are united by Yoruba language and culture.

The Yoruba stamp is everywhere in Benin Republic: from the languages to the Gods to the people. While living in Benin I found that Yoruba is very much the lingua franca of Cotonou and Porto Novo, and a Yoruba person is considered *almost* the equal of a Fon or Adja of Benin. Almost. I met many people who spoke Yoruba and admitted to having a Yoruba parent, but they would never claim to be Yoruba. *Never*. Such a marked distinction could be a vestige of the Fon and Yoruba empires' adversarial past.

However, the similarities in Yoruba and Fon spiritual and linguistic systems give the Yoruba a privileged status over other Nigerians. Consequently, while Yoruba is not considered an equal or desired ethnicity among the Béninois, the fact that my child and I speak an intelligible form of Yoruba and that my child is Odùduwà, the God who Created the Earth and the Fon and everyone else for that matter, actually saved our lives and afforded us unrequested benefits at the oddest of times and places.

I was moved to see that there was no irrational fear of or discrimination against Muslims in overwhelmingly Christian-professing southern Benin. Muslim immigrants, whether they are Zarma, Kanuri, Hausa, or Fulani, from both Francophone and Anglophone countries flourish in Benin. Muslims from Niger and Nigeria are so firmly and pleasantly entrenched in Cotonou subdivisions like Zongo and Guinkomey that upon visiting these communities one might imagine one is in Niamey or pre-Sharia Sokoto.

What shook me to my core was the blind hatred and disgust that many Béninois feel for Igbo people. While I found that anti-Igbo prejudice also prevails in Burkina Faso and Mali, what I witnessed in Benin shocked me.

I asked a friend about the discrimination against the Igbo, and his response was that the Igbo are treacherous and dishonest. I reminded him that the only market vendors we encountered who were honest, transparent, and conciliatory were Igbo and Hausa. It was the Béninois who were scheming and cheating because they were protected by home-turf advantage. My friend agreed with me, but then he looked at me with all seriousness and declared: "Igbos steal penises." After I stopped laughing, I asked him what one man would do with two penises. We both laughed, but then he frowned and said, "They eat human flesh." I was outraged and enraged. I told him that these are the same lies that Caucasian colonizers told about the Fon and all other African people to justifying killing or enslaving them. But my friend stood firmly on myth and lie. He gazed off into the distance and mused, "I remember the time we burned Igbos alive in the market place. . ." With this recollection, I knew it was unwise for my child and me or anyone who could ever be considered an ~~outsider~~ *African* outsider to live in Benin.

Because anyone can learn French and claim another nationality, the Béninois seem to make it a point to distinguish African outsiders in general from the Igbo in particular (this may be another reason why Yoruba is used as a lingua franca). My daughter and I made a dear friend, an Igbo man named Sunday. Whenever we saw him, we heralded him, "Àìkú Sunday" (*àìkú* means both "immortal" and the day "Sunday" in Yoruba language). "Àìkú Sunday" was honest, affable, gracious, and he spoke English, French, Igbo, *and* Fon. But I observed that the Fon who worked beside him all day long never called him by his name: They always called him "Igbo" with an intonation and connotation designed to mark him and ensure he would never gain full respect or acceptance no matter what he did.

Because discrimination in Africa is as vicious and ubiquitous as that Africans experience in America or France or China or India or Germany or Russia, *ad nauseum*, I wondered why the Igbo would struggle to live among a people who despise them. The answer is easy to arrive at: the Igbo dominate trade in Cotonou and many other lands.

Rather than abandon their lucrative and often legal and peaceful enterprises, some Igbo are using to their advantage the ignorance of the Béninois. My Béninois friend and I bought a fan from a group of Igbo vendors who happened to be watching Nigeria play in the World Cup. We chatted and rooted for Nigeria, and when I asked them what their ethnic group was, one brother said, "Biafra." I was surprised. I knew that the Biafra movement was enjoying a resurgence, but I had never before heard such a bold identification.

Later when my friend and I continued our discussion of the perception of Nigerians in Benin, my friend said, "Now Biafra . . . Biafra is good! But Igbo? No way!" I laughed and told him that Biafra and Igbo are one in the same. I couldn't believe that, in a city that is only two hours' drive from Lagos, an educated adult had no knowledge of Biafra or the Nigerian civil war! I gazed at him with amazement, but I understood when I looked deeply into his eyes and saw Eiffel Towers rotating therein. *Vive Pan-Afrique*!?!

Perhaps the most disturbing outgrowth of West African anti-Igbo prejudice is that many Igbo have decided to mete out to African Americans the shameful discrimination to which they have been subjected. As is revealed "In Their Own Words: Children of Nigerian Immigrants in the U.S.," which is included in Part Four of this book, and any number of internet discussion boards, in many Igbo communities, African Americans are stereotyped as *akátá*. The word in Yoruba language means "jackal," but the connotation among certain Igbo is that African Americans are more savage, wild, unscrupulous, and lethal than any jackal could ever dare to be. Given the copious amounts of Igbo blood that flow in African American veins, the akátá epithet is a clear indication of how lost some of us are. Many Africana people are so desperate to find *some*one *any*one to oppress and so eager to ape their oppressors, that they will gleefully destroy themselves.

Originally, I wanted to have actual community dialogues across the African world so that we Africans can openly and honestly discuss, deliberate about, and solve some of our problems. However, I found that, for many people, ego-fluffing and money-grubbing are more important than problem-solving and nation-building. For others, I found that there is no reason to solve a "problem" from which one is benefitting. For example, some Africans use their acquisition of a mandated colonial language to assume a stance of superiority over Africans who had a different oppressive language forced down their throats. Such petty individuals are loath to relinquish the pleasure and power they derive from being their masters' running and lap dogs.

It also became clear to me that some Africans benefit from labeling other Africans akátá, cannibals, penis thieves, and/or dabblers in the occult because such slander helps them accomplish several linked objectives: 1) they are able to justify their inability to achieve success in their chosen fields, 2) they are able to look down upon other Africans with a scorn that Caucasians (who created these ludicrous African savage, cannibal, witchcraft, witch doctor, fictions) formerly applied for all Africans, 3) they are able to justify—at a moment's notice—banishing, raping, and/or lynching innocent people, and 4) they are able to celebrate their terrorism as a religious triumph.

Given the complexities that Africa boasts and the ease with which many Africans use racist Caucasian ideology to destroy other Africans, it should not be surprising that mentioning Pan-Africanism and African Unity to many Continental Africans can result in stares of surprise, smirks of pity, or snarls of derision. Who would be foolish enough to follow the blood-soaked CIA-hounded footsteps of Lumumba, Sankara, Anikulapo-Kuti, El Shabazz, DuBois? Who wants to be murdered by police as they lie in bed beside their pregnant partner as Fred Hampton was assassinated? Who wants enjoy freedom via exile as Assata Shakur does in Cuba? Who wants to be tossed out of a window by soldiers as was Funmilayo Anikulapo Kuti? Who wants to be incarcerated for freedom fighting like Ericka Huggins, Mutulu Shakur, Dhoruba bin Wahad, Mumia Abu Jamal and so many more have been and are currently incarcerated? Who would like to have their home and country gutted by NATO's bombs and then have their lynching televised globally as was the case with Muammar al Qaddafi who was destroyed because he was working to unite Africa and fortify the Continent's economy with a gold-backed currency that would have given Africa more economic and political power than all western powers combined, including and especially America and France, the countries that organized the lynching of Qaddafi and the destruction of Libya.[4]

The least popular and most dangerous vocation in the world is that of Pan-African freedom fighter: It is also the most important lifework one can undertake.

When we note the rapidity with which the youngest and one of the wealthiest African nations transformed the glow of independence into an orgy of self-fragmenting mayhem, mutilation, outlandish displays of wealth, and hyper-weaponized rape over the ephemeral concept of currency and over natural resources that exist on the Earth for the benefit of all humanity, and when we observe that South Sudan's turmoil can be found to greater or lesser degrees in nearly all other African nations as well as Africana communities around the world, perhaps the African world will eventually realize that our current states of independence actually have us "in" varying states of "dependence" that are designed and remotely controlled by our oppressors and their oppressive agencies. Existing "in dependence" leaves us vulnerable, targeted, subject, and decimated but awash in soothing nihilism and glittery confusion.

The state of the world in general and that of the African world in particular gives us many questions to ponder.

How great is the difference between a teenager struggling to live in Juba, Sudan and one struggling to survive in Chicago, Illinois, which has been nicknamed "Chiraq" because Chicago's Africana inhabitants are at war against one another and are killing one another in numbers greater than those America generated in its most recent war in Iraq.

Would you, Dear Reader, stand a better chance of surviving an encounter with the militarized racist American police or with the Nigerian mobile police nicknamed "kill and go"?

Do you think you would have a better chance of surviving sailing the seas as a hostage of Somali pirates or surviving a "rough ride" in a paddy wagon from your home to a local Baltimore police precinct?

Does freedom in the town of Cape Coast, Ghana mean the same thing as freedom in the town of Eatonville, Florida?

As the world becomes smaller and as our experiences become deeper and more intertwined, more of us are asking such questions and being appalled by the answers.

Why are there Africana men and women all over the world who are tricking, trapping, and trafficking other Africana men and women all over the world? Why are my and my child's chances of be captured and trafficked the same in London as in Lomé?

Why are so many Africana people filled with so much raging jealousy, rabid intolerance, and free-flowing racist hatred of other African people that their viciousness and violence leave the most unreconstructed Caucasian supremacists in awe?

How does the African world combat racism, misogyny, homophobia, child abuse, pedophilia, self-hatred, and inter-African terrorism in this era? Do we ignore these issues; do we hashtag and retweet them; do we hitch rides on profitable-cause band wagons; or do we work to ensure that justice is served to the guilty and that the vulnerable are protected?

At a time when we are able to create our own lanes and determine our own destinies in ways unimaginable only ten years ago, how are we coping with success, celebrity, creative expression, wealth, and power?

In this era, in which more African men than ever are committing suicide, how do we manage depression, rage, shame, guilt, inadequacy, and fear?

The African World has never been more endangered, dangerous, important, inspiring, and confounding than it is right now. There are more ways to be African now than ever before. There are no set rules or approved paths in this expansive new African world. In many respects, we are all ọmọ Òrìṣà Ògún, children of the God Ògún, and we are all living our questions and answers in real-time as we clear paths through time and (cyber)space and determine how best to manifest our destinies.

A Book As A Bridge

The African World in Dialogue: An Appeal to Action! explores some of the hopes, goals, fears, celebrations, revelations, lyricism, witticism, and activism of the African world. This compilation includes rich and resonant short stories, poems, essays, and interviews that reveal the African world's hidden promise, blinding confusion, and surging expectations. The book also contains powerful and empowering proposals, speeches, and expositions that illuminate pathways to agency, autonomy, and unfettered elevation.

Part One: Listen: The Ink Speaks is dedicated to writers whose creative power leaves the ink whispering, throbbing and bobbing in their audiences' inner ears.

Ricardo Cortez Cruz's short story "Me & You [Let the Base Go *Boom!*]" is the perfect way to introduce the intensity and complexity of the contemporary African world. Cruz's curvilinear kaleidoscopic art effortlessly and exquisitely reveals the honesty, dissembling, danger, disease, dis-ease, politics, passion, and rage that suffuse male-female African-Africa relationships. The multidimensionality of Black Love (lost and found) radiates in Cruz's art which offers syncopated, reverberating, harmonic proof that Africa's roots boast both global extension and depth beyond measure.

Charlie Braxton's politically-charged poetic gift takes us on a ride through and into America's cotton fields and lynching bees with Ẹlẹ́gbà and Jesus as our guides. In "Kang Snake Blues," "A Slave Dreams of Revenge," and "A Vision of Purgatory," Braxton writes with a passion that groans like John Lee Hooker and growls like Nina Simone. With "Another Mississippi Murder," Braxton baptizes his readers in the truth of

a history so ugly
only a short ignorant-limp-dick
pot-bellied-beer-guzzling-
rebel-flag-waving-trailer-trash-talking redneck
could love it (47)

Braxton does this so that we fully understand the significance of our diverse weaponry to a war that we must never grow weary of fighting.

As if in response to Braxton's call for war, cerebral poet Aseret Sin muses on appropriate burial attire for defeated racist terrorists in the haiku "Mississippi White Sale (No. 2)." Sin's poem "If You Ain't Gon' Come in Handy. . ." demystifies the God concept as it is exists in organized religions and suggests readers invoke Gods who are, perhaps, a bit more familiar and effective. Sin's "The Coming of the Saviors" is a curt and chilling attack on the global culture of pedophilia and some of its annointed enablers and gift bearing ambassadors. "Amerikkka Eats its Young" consists of eight haiku that reveal how imperiled are the lives of America's youngest and most vulnerable citizens.

Asiri Odu's short story "Nommo, No Mo, No More" takes us into the studio of "88.9 Double You, Emm, El, Aay, your edutainment station," which has been commandeered by Azure and Alteveze, two community activists who reveal gruesome information about the global medical industry's wide-ranging murderous experiments on Africana people, in particular, and others who have been unfortunate enough to be mistaken for guinea pigs. "Nommo, No Mo, No More" is excerpted from Odu's novel *Ah Jubah! A PleaPrayerPromise*, and it could move you to change your prescriptions and your physician.

Part Two: Restitutions, Resolutions, Revolutions begins with Kevin Powell's searing indictment "Why Baltimore is Burning." Powell, with a clarity that reveals how logical and necessary a force is Black Rage, exposes truths that many upper echelon poets, priests, and professors—even those handcuffed on their front porches—are reluctant to tell: In America, we are always in season; we are always in the sights; we are always posing in the center of a bullseye. Powell writes that survival for dislocated Africans in America is so perilous and so aberrant that

> . . . they do explode, inside of themselves, and inside their
> communities. They would love to reach areas outside their 'hoods,
> but the local power structure blocks that from happening. So they
> destroy their own communities. I understand why. I am they and
> they are me. Any people with nothing to lose will destroy anything

in their way. . . . . Any people who feel as if their lives are not valued, like they are second-class citizens at best, will not be stopped until they've made their point. . . . A rebellion, a riot, are pleas for help, for a plan, for a vision, for solutions, for action steps, for justice, for God, someone, anyone, to see our humanity, to do something. (74)

Solutions for a people in crisis are not easy to come by, but after studying the state of African America, two possible solutions have come to my mind. The first is the "Citizens Defense Proposal," which is designed to prevent police officers from killing unarmed citizens.

Our oppressors celebrate when after a police officer kills an unarmed African American we respond with marches, prayer breakfasts, and soul-shaking renditions of "We Shall Overcome." El Hajj Malik El Shabazz asserted in 1964 that if you are singing "We Shall Overcome" in the 20th century, your government has failed you. Yet, the 21st century finds us singing the same song. The objective of the Citizens Defense Proposal is to completely disincentivize the killing of unarmed citizens by police. If police officers know that when they kill an unarmed person they will be immediately jailed and held without bail or bond and that they will lose sources of income until they prove in a court of law that their actions were justified, the number of state-sponsored lynchings would drop precipitously.

Unlike calls for de-escalation training and psychological assessments, the Citizens Defense Proposal would cost no money and require no classes, evaluators, evaluation, training, or tax-payer expense. I consider de-escalation training to be unnecessary because officers are clearly thoughtful enough to de-escalate situations involving Caucasians or presumed "model" minorities. The Citizens Defense Proposal does not treat race-based lynching as if it were a disorder for which one can receive counseling. The proposal treats officer-enacted lynching as what it is, the ultimate crime against humanity for which one must be incarcerated . . . at the very least.

The objective of the Citizens Defense Proposal is simply to protect the most precious thing we all have at this moment: life. Without tough human-rights-upholding legislation, police officers will continue to kill unarmed citizens. At present, officers who kill unarmed citizens are "rewarded" with paid administrative leave, so there is no reason for them not to and quite a few reasons for them to continue their asphalt lynchings. Even off-duty and plainclothes Africana police officers have been victims of America's new lynch law.

We need a need a cadre of liberation-minded lawyers, like Muhammad Ibn Bashir who provided essential insight to the Citizens Defense Proposal, and lawmakers who are willing to work to pass laws to *prevent* the killings of citizens. I am ready, willing, and eager to work with such a cadre.

My second proposal is as logical as the first and just as protective of Africana existence. In "Escaping a Prison Industrial Country: The Case for Quilombos" I seek to illuminate a path from the eternal victimhood American promises its Africana citizens into the quiet and understated glory of autonomy.

There is no need for our lives in America to be defined by such terms as "disadvantaged" or "at risk." Long ago, our ancestors envisioned, built, and lived their freedom, and we can too. Quilombos are autonomous military communities that Africans erected and thrived in as free controllers of their destinies in the hearts of enslaving nations and in the faces of enslavers. While America's goal for its Africana citizens is to isolate as many of us as possible from the general population in prisons where slavery is legal, with "Escaping a Prison Industrial Country: The Case for Quilombos" I discuss ways by which we can remove ourselves from attack and thrive on our own terms in cities and nations that we erect, arm, protect, and direct.

Chinweizu has become a force most difficult to find in this modern world: a fearless, African-centered, revolutionary, academic, and Elder who thrives in the grassroots and flourishes on the frontlines where our warriors are most needed. In "Education for Liberation in Black Africa," Chinweizu asks us to examine the usefulness of the "education" that we may be clamoring for or that we may even be forced to receive:

> What good is an education that keeps us blind to reality, that alienates us from our group, that fails to teach us our basic interests? Have you educated a child if you don't teach him about the situation he is in; or about the geography of his town; or about the snakes and scorpions and mosquitoes that abound in his environment; or about the habits and tricks of the liars and thieves and armed robbers that he will meet every day? (100)

Chinweizu's unflinching analysis compels us to open ourselves and be honest about our ugliest and most shameful inner-truths, because honest self-inspection will lead to psychological, cultural, and political resurrection. Chinweizu makes it clear that while our enemies and their evils abound, we are the most important directors of our destiny. We can either continue to be our enemies' strongest allies in their unceasing campaigns to destroy us, or we can educate, unite, fight, and relegate our nemeses to a well-deserved oblivion.

Baba A. O. Buntu is a Pan-Africanist, an activist, and a warrior-philosopher who could be considered one of many "Suns of Chinweizu." Buntu was born in Anguilla, raised in Norway, and repatriated to South

Africa where he is the executive director of Ebukhosini Solutions, a "community-based company specializing in Afrikan-centered solutions to social, political, and cultural challenges. We specialize in education, training, knowledge production leadership development and youth/ community empowerment." Buntu's vision is clear and his and voice resonant in "Perspectives on Afrikan Identity in the 21st Century," which tackles the question, "Who is Afrikan?" Buntu answers the question with clarity, specificity, and frank and essential truth-telling in an era of intentionally murky identity politics.

Blair Marcus Proctor's research helps us to appreciate the activism of lesser-heralded segments of the African World. In "Coloured South African Politics and The New Orleans Afro-Creole Protest Tradition," Proctor undertakes a deft and level-headed articulation and exposition of a delicate and potentially divisive topic. He explores the intricacies of the activism of those who have often been labeled "too Black for the Whites and too White for the Blacks." Proctor goes beyond superficial labels and appearances to mine the riches of a political history that is often overlooked but that is as important as it is intricate.

Part Three: Africanity, Education, and Technology looks to Africa's future which is rooted in its wisdom-rich past.

The Odù Ifá could be considered the world's first supercomputer; eons ago it utilized the binary numerical system upon which modern computers are based. This complex Yoruba tool, which helps individuals know and control their fates and determine their destinies and which can be found throughout Africa in various forms, is a scientific system of divination that combines computation, poetic recitation, pharmacognosy, and psychology. With timeless knowledge and tools comprising the cornerstones of their identity, the Yoruba should be at the center of 21st century technological innovation, and the same can be said of the Igbo, the Dogon, the Akan, the Wolof, the Kikuyu, the Nuba, the BaKongo, the Swazi, and all other African peoples who also boast extraordinarily advanced mathematical, astrophysical, scientific, and computational systems.

Tunde Adegbola seeks to place Africa where it should be—at the center of technological development, especially that related to Africa's commodities, resources, and cultures. As the director of Alt-i, the African Languages and Technology Initiative, Adegbola works to implement a paradigm shift that would involve not only the creation of technological innovations rooted in indigenous African languages but also the educational preparation of African students and scholars to make discoveries and blaze new paths in their indigenous languages as opposed to training them in a foreign language to serve foreign people and alien interests.

Adegbola reveals why "Indigenising Human Language Technology for National Development" is vital:

> If a nation teaches its young people science in a foreign language, the chances of developing scientific theories that account for phenomena that are more easily observable in such a nation are remote and the scientific world is the worse for it. Worse still, if a nation breeds its technologists in a foreign language, every technological wonder will be attributed to a more intelligent foreigner. That is why most Nigerians [upon experiencing] a technological wonder will involuntarily exclaim, "*Oyinbo!*"[5] The simple implication of attributing any technological wonder to the "superior" intelligence of foreigners is that the observer's critical intellect is not engaged by such an observation. Hence, explanation is not attempted and the observer settles for mystification. (164–165)

Ishola Akindele Salami is fighting the same battle against mystification and miseducation as Adegbola but on a different front. Salami's "When the Vehicle for a Long Journey is Abandoned: The Case for Indigenous Language in Early Childhood Education in Nigeria" focuses on the period of life during which the acquisition of language and culture is arguably most significant—the formative years. Salami makes clear the importance of educating African children, in general, and Yoruba children, in particular, in their native languages.

The Yoruba language is logical, layered, and extraordinarily complex. Yoruba mathematics is so profound that by learning to count, one learns addition, subtraction, and multiplication—at once! Yoruba science, philosophy, chemistry are all light years ahead of anything constructed in the west. As Salami intimates with the reference to a Yoruba proverb in his title, the most appropriate vehicle to usher the Yoruba world into a future of interdisciplinary intellectual dominance is Yoruba language. As a vehicle of communication, Yoruba is capable of transporting one across time and space and far into the cosmos.

When I was a doctoral candidate at Obafemi Awolowo University in Nigeria, Tony Tetuila released a song in 1999 that would become my jam, "Omode Meta." The melding of Yoruba orature with New York-influenced rap never failed to get me crunk. I love the song so much that, despite it being released eleven years before her birth, it became my daughter's introduction to rap. In 2005 the traditional tale "Omode Meta" was remixed, if you will, as the television miniseries, *Everything It Takes*. In "Narrating Nigeria: The Evolution of a Story," Oyinlola Longe reveals how a classic work of oraliterature motivates children and adults to strive to achieve greatness no matter how grand their goals. She also reveals how the story's televised reincarnation transforms a tale about personal success into a resonant message that champions cross-cultural collectivity and national empowerment.

Throughout the African world an intellectual revolution is afoot. People are realizing that state-maintained and state-mandated institutions of education are mis-educating Africana students and training them to serve the interests of the state which is controlled directly or indirectly, as is the case with neocolonization, by Caucasians. More and more Africana people are creating institutions that will give their children an education that will prepare them to be active agents of transformation, elevation, and holistic enlightenment for the African world. In "A Model for Success: The Importance of Traditional African Centered Approaches in Educational Models," Ayoka Wiles elaborates on the specific ways in which an Africentric education benefits the African; and to prove her points, she offers case studies of two successful African-centered institutions: Ifetayo Cultural Arts Academy of Brooklyn, New York and Egbe Omo Orisa of Philadelphia, Pennsylvania.

Part Four: Life Lines from the Frontlines includes interviews, first-hand accounts, and exposés about the African world experience from a rich and wide variety of perspectives.

Jumbe Kweku Lumumba co-hosts *What Good Is a Song? The Friday Night Drum* on 89.3 WRFG FM, a progressive public radio station in Atlanta, Georgia. "Brother Kweku," as he is known, has contributed four transcribed interviews from this radio program. His interviews with Mandingo, a Garveyite, an activist, and a radio host based in England; Hilary La Force, Executive Director of the Folk Research Centre in St. Lucia; Prince Kuma N'dumbe III, a Pan-Africanist academic from Bonabéri, Cameroon; and Kambale Musavuli, a human rights advocate from Democratic Republic of the Congo reveal the rich topography of the contemporary African cultural-political landscape and the bridges that activists are building to unite the African world.

Chinwe Ezinna Oriji's poems "I am African" and "Me" explore her struggles with embracing her Nigerian and Igbo identities outside of Nigeria and Igboland. Oriji's poems set the tone for her collection of interviews, "In Their Own Words: Children of Nigerian Immigrants in the U.S." The deeply moving and refreshingly honest narratives of Chinazaekpere Okonkwo, Edwin Ikenna Aufuru, James Obaniyi, and Adefemi Jones are a rollercoaster ride of humor, culture, education, inter-African racism, and revelations of self and other. When reading these interviews you will meet a teacher who teaches nonsense (to riff with Fela), an African who "passes" for "American," and a mother who works so hard to achieve her American dream that if her son doesn't bring her lunch, she won't eat. You will walk into the lair of akátá and escape its rabid jaws. You will feel the gentle rain of dollars bills and naira notes falling as they crown African achievements. You will wonder why so many seemingly intelligent allegedly modern people insist on reducing Africa to Tarzan-time. You will also wonder why some Nigerian immigrants readily embrace all of the well-worn stereotypes about African Americans while despising being stereotyped themselves.

When reading some of Oriji's interviews and analyses, it becomes clear that, for some Igbo people, hatred of and prejudice against African Americans is an ideological cornerstone. Perhaps this racism could be more appropriately termed a stepping stone, because individuals who feel inferior or who hope to hide information about themselves often seek out an "other" to hate and malign so that they can, in their own minds, appear to be superior to and a step above the "other." Consequently, readers may find some of the content in this chapter offensive. The final paragraph of Oriji's concluding analysis, with its generalizations and its assertions regarding "human capital," may prove especially troubling. However, the point of this dialogue is not to hear only one voice or view. The objective is to listen to diverse points and respect divergent perspectives to better understand why the African world is not united. After hearing and comprehending, we must gauge the width of the chasms that divide us and determine how best to bridge them.

Because anti-African American propaganda abounds in national and international discourse, it is not at all surprising that immigrants would shun or seek to distance themselves from African Americans. However, it is crucial to acknowledge the fact that the struggle African Americans waged to liberate and civilize America—a country we were forced to build under duress—makes it possible for all immigrants of African ancestry to dine in restaurants instead of taking their food from holes in walls, find gainful employment in any number of industries, use public restrooms instead of using nearby fields, sit where they desire when using public transportation instead of sitting "Jim Crow," walk on sidewalks instead of in gutters, sleep in hotels, swim in public pools, attend schools and universities, relocate when and where they desire, and, most of all, not be enslaved.

Many immigrants find it expedient to ignore both African Americans' contributions to world civilization and history and America's heinous racist reality because America has made racist myths of exceptionality and exclusivity central to its global image. When I lived and studied in Nigeria, the electrical electronics department of my university boasted a huge banner that read "AMERICA: God's Own Country." Nearly every student's goal was to travel to America—England was irrelevant; the thought of traveling to another African country was an insult—all routes led to America. When I would discuss America's realities and the racism, police brutality and extrajudicial killings, epidemic unemployment, and rabid discrimination that are facts of existence for Africana people, I was mocked. One student told me that anyone who cannot make it in America is either stupid or lazy.

America's ideologues, spin doctors, and propagandists weave myths and lies around the nation's bloody and vile reality while the nation's lawmakers limit the number of Africans they allow to enter the country. America takes on the status of the VIP Club or Champagne Room of nations. America even holds visa lotteries: as if getting a visa to America is hitting a jackpot! Because of the widespread belief that those who cannot make it in America are imbeciles or ne'er-do-wells, especially since legend has it that in America money grows on trees and streets are paved with gold, few Africans reveal the truth about how many menial jobs they work—with their Ph.D.'s or M.D.'s or J.D.'s deemed worthless in America—in order to send money home, lease flashy cars, and throw extravagant parties. Some even philosophize that it is better to scrub toilets in New York than be a physician in Lagos. Even New York police officers' extrajudicial killing of Amadou Diallo in 1999 was brushed off by many continental Africans: He was unlucky, they said. He should have known not to do this or to do that, they argued. Why didn't he just . . . ? they wondered. Police officers gunned Diallo down because they knew that killing innocent, unarmed Africana men is rarely a punishable crime in America. Indeed, Diallo's killers were exonerated. Thirteen years later, racist Americans sent Trayvon Martin's Caucasian killer, who was also exonerated, hundreds of thousands of dollars as a *reward* for killing an innocent, unarmed, Africana child. Caucasians have effectively commoditized lynching.

With the election of Barack Hussein Obama and the impact of contemporary technology, the world has been able to see America's truth in real-time. America elected the first president to identify publicly as Black, and many of America's racist citizens and police officers responded by killing as many Africana people as they could. The world has watched lynching after lynching occur for such "crimes" as being Black and walking home, being Black and enjoying music, being Black and doing exactly what the police officer said, being Black and sitting handcuffed and immobilized on a curb or in a police car, and being Black and asking for help.

The African world assented when Muammar al Qaddafi of Libya, Mahmoud Ahmadinejad of Iran, and Hugo Chavez of Venezuela stood before the United Nations and condemned the crimes against humanity that America was committing against its Africana citizens during Barack Obama's first presidential term. But the inhumane crimes have not only continued, they appear to have increased. I cannot give specific statistics because, in this era of high technology, the United States of America does not keep an official tally of the citizens its police officers kill.

Thanks to the Black Lives Matter movement, America's 2016 election, and the countless African immigrants who live in America and who must admit that this country does not value their African lives any more than those of their African American counterparts, America's myth is crumbling.

Jacqueline Bediako's "Obtaining the American Dream: Sometimes an Impossible Feat for African Immigrants" is an important essay that illuminates with patience, balance, and Pan-African perspicacity the realities that drive, terrify, inspire, and confuse Africans who are seeking fulfilment of all that America promises. Bediako's research is gleaned from shocking headlines, moving personal experiences, and her work with African Communities Together, which is "an organization of African immigrants based in New York City fighting for civil rights, opportunity, and a better life for their families in the U.S. and Africa." Bediako's exposition is filled with biting truths, inspiring stories, and important references and information that African immigrants will find essential to surviving being Black while living in "God's Own Country."

Gender Studies is routinely used as code for Women's Studies, and this does a disservice to men, women, and the discipline. **Part Four: Gender, Power, and Infinite Promise** flips the customary gender script and puts the resonant, rich, and soul-wrenching truths of Africana men front and center to better understand and strengthen the Africana male-female dyad. The section begins with "The Quiet Scream Within: Perspectives on Culture, Violence, and Transformation within Afrikan Masculinities" in which Baba Buntu undertakes a courageous and probing study of African men, violence, and the disintegration of the African family.

Buntu continues to lay bare the souls of the Brothers with "Rising from Ashes: About Black Men and Cheating." Buntu begins his exposé with many probing admissions, such as the following:

> As Black men, we carry big loads of insecurities. Behind our manly attributes is a sea of things we cannot figure out: all our psycho-emotional stuff, our self-doubt, our harsh self-criticism, our need to always compare and compete, our judgement that we might not really amount to much, and the list goes on. You might not see it— or at least we'd like to believe you can't—but our fears are there in abundance. They constitute psychological baggage that dates back to the first invasions of Afrika and the first generation of enslaved Afrikan men. The Black man has accumulated numerous wounds

from constantly being attacked, judged, and excluded. So severe are these wounds that it appears that a certain amount of brokenness is a part of Black manhood. (327)

How does a battered, beautiful, confused brother heal and find a way to love himself and his soul's sisters? What if the women he meets are just as abused, gorgeous, and mixed up as he is? In search of answers, Buntu leads us on a journey that is clever, honest, and often hilarious. Buntu's unflinching exploration of Black love and lust is perfect for this bold era of relationship fluidity—or disposability—in which we find ourselves.

It is essential that we go inside, analyze ourselves, understand the impact that oppression has had on us, heal, and prepare our souls and minds for the work we must do. The internal journey that we must undertake to fully manifest our destiny can be most difficult for Africana men because of the myths of masculinity that have been popularized by Western media. Getting brothers to remove their protective masks, reveal their fears, and open themselves to critique, healing, and transformation is dangerous work, as our global suicide and murder rates attest. But this is a danger we must face; this is work we must do because the reward is Divinity.

My objective with "Rapping with the Gods: Hip Hop as a Force of Divinity and Continuity from the Continent to the Cosmos" is to illuminate the ways by which some of Africana music's most talented wordsmiths seek to introduce their Africana audience, in general, and Africana men, in particular, to their identity as divinities. My research debunks the myth that rap and hip hop originated in the Bronx in the 1970s and traces these art forms to their ancient African roots with an important goal—to reveal the divine impetus embedded in rap. That rap music, in its truest sense, constitutes a summons from the Gods to the Gods is not surprising because the word "rap" comes from the Wolof word Raap, which means Gods of the Sea. There are many reasons that we Africans and our Raap and our raps survived the Middle Passage; one of the most important reasons is the vital transformative work that we have to do.

Asiri Odu's "Iṣẹ́ Ògbóni," which is also excerpted from the novel *Ah Jubah!*, takes the reader into a world in which the divine transformation has been completed and the work of liberation is underway. The Carver Homes housing project is the façade that shields an underground revolutionary army of a-alike Africana women and men. "Iṣẹ́ Ògbóni" literally means the Work of the Secret Society charged with protecting the Earth and its progeny; consequently, everyone and everything, from drug dealers to America's criminal justice system (which some argue is actually a system of criminal injustices) that harms the Children of the Mother of the Earth is on the secret society's docket for adjudication and destruction.

Alieu Bundu possesses a fresh voice and a compelling perspective in African fiction. The fact that Bundu is a male who often writes about the trials that African women endure is not unique; but Bundu's subject matter, which may span from gang-rape-while-ethnic-cleansing in "The Riot," to fistula-shaming in "The Wretched Being," and the gritty and graceful way that he embraces his subject matter and his characters, without relying on cliché or convention, makes reading his work a uniquely visceral experience.

In Toni Morrison's classic and epic novel *Song of Solomon*, Hagar weeps on her deathbed that Milkman, the man she adores, is "never going like [her] hair." All too many Africana women know exactly how Hagar feels. In lands in which people have been miseducated to believe that a woman's "crowning glory" is not her intellect, or her character, or her achievements, but her hair, many women will destroy not only their hair but also themselves in their quest to make their dominant genotypic and phenotypic traits appear recessive and essentially curse their DNA.

Morgan Miller chronicles her journey into a city of ugliness so complete that it spills forth from the lips of nearly every person who encounters her bilious, natural, dominant-gene-strong hair. In "Straightened Hair as Social Currency," Miller describes how the time she spent being bombarded by projected self-hate in the city of Santiago in the Dominican Republic inspired her to love her hair even more and to let it do what it does best: defy gravity and reveal her genotypic and phenotypic relationship with the cosmos. Miller may have had relatively little social currency while she was in the Santiago, but her natural hair signifies a woman gifted with genetic and cosmic riches that are beyond measure.

. . .

It has been an honor, a privilege, and a pleasure to work with the talented contributors and the remarkable literary works featured in this volume. The selections, many of which were crafted or revised and expanded specifically for this book, were written with passion, pain, urgency, and, a quality most rare in this era, sincerity.

I hope that reading this anthology proves to be a stimulating experience for you. I hope that you find yourself exhilarated, enraged, pensive, and inspired by the stories, interviews, essays, speeches, proposals, and poetry in this volume. But more than anything else, I hope that you are moved to contact this anthology's contributors so that we can work together and build an African world that nurtures, nourishes, educates, and elevates.

This book is subtitled "An Appeal to Action!" because our education, liberation, and elevation are *our* responsibilities—no one else's. No matter how many academic conferences in exotic locales we participate in, or the money we blow on pomp and pageantry, or the density of our vainglorious exhibitions in verbosity, the bottom line is that we are responsible for undertaking the grueling and gritty work of building a world worthy of ourselves, our progeny, and our ancestors' struggles. We have inherited a phenomenal cache of tools to undertake our work, and we have the ingenuity and resources to create whatever new tools we need.

We have no excuses.

It is clear that our oppressors have an alarming array of special weapons and tactics and a diverse cadre of agents, including many of African ancestry, working diligently to debilitate, undermine, and destroy us. But I submit to you that our true challenge in this era has less to do with battling oppressors and more to do with exiling our egos, refocusing our efforts, and investing everything we have in our complete liberation, elevation, and evolution.

Until we realize that **we** are the solutions to our problems, *aluta continua…*

The Editor

Notes

[1] You may view Qiaobi's commercial here: <https://www.youtube.com /watch?v=Xq-I0JRhvt4> accessed 09 September 2016.

[2] David Blair, "Don't be fooled by Boko Haram's video – the abducted Chibok schoolgirls are going nowhere," *The Telegraph*, 15 August 2016 <http://www.telegraph.co.uk/women/life/dont-be-fooled-by-boko-harams-video-of-abducted-chibok-schoolgir/> accessed 14 October 2016. Kudos to President Muhammadu Buhari and his administration for securing the release of 21 of the Chibok abductees in October 2016. The administration vows to continue negotiating to secure the release of all of the abductees. See Chris Stein, "21 Girls Kidnapped from Chibok School Released by Boko Haram, Nigeria Says," *New York Times*, 13 October 2016 <http://www.nytimes.com/2016/10/14/world/africa/boko-haram-nigeria. html?_r=0> accessed 14 October 2016.

[3] A telling example of the routine public abuse that African women endure comes courtesy of Koffi Olomide, the superstar musician of the Democratic Republic of the Congo, who kicked and threatened a female member of his band at Kenya's Jomo Kenyatta International Airport in July 2016. The assault took place while Olomide's arrival was being filmed, and it occurred in the presence of several soldiers and police officers who simply separated Olomide from his victim. Olomide's actions were not considered outrageous to him or to anyone present; Olomide was even posturing and hamming it up for the cameras, as if stomping a woman constitutes the epitome of African masculinity. If not for the fact that in this era everything one does is uploaded for global perusal, Olomide's attack would have been considered his business. However, the video was uploaded, and it went viral. The outcry resulted in Olomide being deported from Kenya. It is inspiring to see how effective this African internet protest was. Hopefully citizens all over the African world will be just as outraged, vocal, and protective when women are abused every day at the market, in the mall, at the bus stop, at the garage, in the club, on the avenue, *ad infinitum*.

For more on Olomide's actions see <http://www.bbc.com/news/world-africa-36875676> accessed 08 September 2016. Also see the incident Chinazaekpere Okonkwo discusses on pages 250–251 of this book.

[4] Bob Fitrakis, "Hillary's email revelation: France and US killed Qaddafi for his gold and oil," *The Free Press*, 31 March 2016 <http://freepress.org/article/hillary%E2%80%99s-email-revelation-france-and-us-killed-qaddafi-his-gold-and-oil> accessed 20 October 2016.

[5] Òyìnbó means Caucasian; it is said here with a sense of awe and wonderment, as if they and their inventions are magical.

PART ONE

LISTEN: THE INK SPEAKS

Me & You [Let The Base Go *Boom!*]

Ricardo Cortez Cruz

Contains elements of Nayo's "African Girl"
Contains a sample of "Altruism" by Oscar Key Sung
and "city lights, receding" as shown by William Gibson
and a piece of Tamar Braxton's "Broken Record"

You—the black eye/I, once a pretty young thang calling all brothers "the bangs of your existence"—could've sworn you were in love. Deep into it, as a matter of fact. As if love's an art. You *were* in love. Feeling revived. But maybe you were in too deep. You lent so much credence to that, the restoration of hope, until everyone and their mama couldn't help but to notice you going for broke. You thought you could walk on water. But now, on some sort of desert(ed) road from Vegas to nowhere, you find yourself spinnin' (round) mess like cray cray, your heart skipping a bit/beat as if submerged and buried alive in a battle coffin. You're coughin'.

You say, "The first time I fell in love, I didn't know what hit me."

This freaky shit. Gets complicated. And more tragic, comic. Too much crosstalk between. Both of us defensive.

As your world turns, hear [sick] you stand by yourself. You feel sweet, like you're making some movement towards happiness. But you knot. You believe you're *tight*. You're not. You think you're making progress. Sadly, all your efforts keep leading to naught. You (h)aint. And, everybody's sweatin' you. Looking to browbeat you. Everybody's beating you to the punch. Their heart still pounding. That baseness jumping out of their chests. There, hurt more important than your going in circles. Then history repeating itself. All scratched up. You experience that insane pounding sensation again.[1] You love so good it deserves an encore. You shake it out.

Your voice almost gets drowned out. Your heart… You're hurt, thumpin', bumpin' shit, fluttering. Rockin' down the house. For anyone to hear you, you gotta wear your heart on your sleeve. Grooves in your hand handing themselves over to whatever that needles them. You bin. Binge. You've been knocking down the house. Mind bending brain-numbing sound, heavy base/bass stuff shooting straight through your head, determined to emit till….

Everything about your life suddenly sounds ~~wack~~ ~~whacked~~ waxed. Dysfunctionally. Everything about you is distorted. Disoriented. Dislodged. As messed up as any dysenteric thing that a slave could contract. Who knows what's on deck. This sample goes on forever. Backed up in reverse and stuck on the break with too many punch phrases. Overlooped. Unrecognizable.

In love and war, this is your story. The big payback. Your dropping Strawberry Letter 23 on me, telling me how the sun doesn't shine for you despite rainbows and waterfalls running through your mind. Your voice muted to the max, you slap me with a live remix to show where things fall apart. Sound off on the situation revolving 'round us as if you're a siren or a 45. Your story is a bout…the fight for independence after suffering disaster. Your gaining freedom not happening unless you, a diamond in the rough, do something. This interdependence, priceless. Truly on another level. A smoothly dying note and a heavily modulated one. Only the persistence of memory keeping it going. You attempting to walk away from it all since nothing's heard in a "dead" listening room. This is your record. A rare track containing you in a time warp and a bubble. Evolving.

Wow. Although loaded with moments of jeopardy, your story sounds hysterical. At your hot house, in the family room which doubles as a living room and triples as a bedroom, I catch even you cracking up about it, a he-he, then a rumble, coming from your belly. The braided narrative conjuring girlish, child/hood memories.

There's plastic stopping the furniture from breathing and seemingly everywhere, archiving the black experience. Perhaps too revolutionary for my blood, you put a comforter down on the table. Leaving me to check out a single magazine.

According to *Vibe*, "what cyberpunk or *Crash* does for young, disaffected whites, the Nubian Queen putting her foot down does for darkest America. She gives black people a future." Returning to the room stomping and clapping in jubilee, you play a revisionary record for me, a musical treatment of a poor African-American woman who rises to the top. The theme from *Mahogany*. Skin momentarily turning white under some flashlight, you sample it along with Adele's "Lovesong."[2] The mix of us & mix for us maintained with running hand, hand running over the lines as if they could be the Congo's tributaries aiding those responsible for the resounding, creative, and intelligent pirate attacks.

"You make me feel like I'm young again," you rush to tell me. I can tell it's not good.

You argue this is the story where you need a new image. I don't see it. Your saying you will always love me seems like a lie. In the middle of things, the Supreme Creator—the One You Meet Everywhere, the Inexplicable—brings a boiling, black cauldron to light, a journey demanding courage: To start with, at Dizzy's Club Coca Cola, you surprisingly go into a lounge act. Mac eye shadow wearing thin while you put on sexy, mettle high heels to get pumped. I'm told these heels also double as a lethal weapon for protection! Then of course Dashing Diva's (natural selection) at your fingertips. Champagne Nude still not dry enough yet to stay on your toes, but you don't care.

Shoot, shit! With Taio Cruz on your phone, in your ear, railing about moving on, you suddenly throw your hands in air and scream it out. You become the jazz(y) standard, Cleopatra's needle, the Village Vanguard, juicy stuff from The Rooftop in Harlem, Smoke. Outside, when people hear you get live, they get in line.

Thank heavens, your LCD [that love coming down] is NOT a real Disney movie or highlight reel: It would look like the aftermath of Prime Minister Winston Churchill's resuscitation of "If We Must Die." There'd be too much bloody red tape. Nothing but disturbing footage on the cutting room floor, slices of Black holocaust depicting where you diligently served as a raucous misfit trying to recover. . . I'd throw down money to watch that, the theatre of the Spirit. You'd be fresh in that role. The superwoman attempting to seize the dark magic item of ultimate power before a diabolical tyrant can. Instead we're in a battle of he say, she say. Truly a fiasco. Like New York City house music barks, nightlife. Our roots, your struggle, encoded in a liminal space, in the middle passage of a popular jam. I promise not to alter/altar the truth. I give my word. However, to fulfill prophesy, the three witches–the weird sistas–twist it anyway. Spin it the any witch-way they want. They get you beat juggling at lightning fast speed in the interest of creating a new beat:

Beat. *It's been like that. You the butterfly pimped, caught by massive attack. You the one seduced, reduced, by the art of noise, unable to get away from the love beat, that grate thing in the street threatening to keep you in a vegetable state.*

Beet. *Swollen edible root. Red. A bloody growth. Boiling. Until it's ovah. And you are tender. [You make people pay.]*

Beat. *Machismo finally striking you as the root of all evil. The attempt to make sure you got no more juice. Prison industrial complex mood not fit for human consumption. You spit "what black men spin bad is just plain tired."*

Fok

You finally see the light. In your mother's tongue, you say bad things to yourself. Gutted out, frightened of this thing you've become, you lie flat between the nigrified bones of Marcus Garvey, Mistah 100 percent pure brute force, and fine-ass, bareback Langston Hughes nearly snatched up into Jazzonia with his dream deferred. Your purple heart pounding, blood full of pure Cain(e) sugar, you stare up into space where Sun Ra once used to be. Empire overlooking you. You're smoking. Your hair frizzled up. Crown bun ruined. You're here kinky. And [used] you'z can't help thinking about how you get fucked, the look on these men's faces when they bust a nut, how violent they acts are. They've taken you.

Who knows what you long for? Who knows what you need?

Staring in the direction of the bronze Invisible Man on 150th Street in Riverside Park in Manhattan, you feelin' shit, outta luck. But play it off. Nommo make you drink the cool aid.

"What we had was hittin', but I don't want it anymore," you tell ~~bra~~ bruh—Marcus, a stompie, a cigarette butt, a short person, a childlike soldier with good intentions, one of Africa's finest amputees, his ship having sailed already. You call him "Mr. So and So" because something's still missing.

Shame. You're just . . . attracted to the ratchet, turned-up stuff. That's what you're starting to believe, what you thought when Marcus was pushing up on your breasts and bad mouthing you as if bottling himself, upping the anties. So you get up and try to leave the joint 'cause Marcus keeps bothering you about going downtown. And Marcus is rough. So damn tough. *Jesus, bear with me*, you murmur.

You've got an extremely rocky relationship with the world, a lot of off-again/on-again, too much quarreling, when all you want to do is be satisfied with yourself, yes/no?

Langston, Marcus, even [tsotsi[3]] Claude Brown—they get to do they own thing, but everytime you fitna do yours people call you ~~gorilla~~ guerilla. Label you as a howling visionary gone apeshit. Paint you as a joke and trickster. On Halloween, they point you out in the lineup as the ladybug feeding on other pests, the pimply thug who wears the mask in order to beg for sympathy. They call you creature/feature from the black lagoon. No wonder society rarely gets to see you smile.

"Who moved the cheese?" Langston mildly asks with his simple ass, his melon/mellow caught up in the wrong African cosmogram, his voice reemerging from a river of lost time, the pitter-patter of an April rain song stealing him away from you. It's as if he refuses to acknowledge you, a black woman. How you swang your arms wide in the face of the Sun and did your weary, bluesy, toyi toyi dance! . . . and whirl! whirl! Langston rummages through the icebox, searching for coke and graze while dressed only in his Sean John. Raw Garvey overdyed black jeans, low rise, made of somebody's cotton. This brother looks black and white, like what you see from civil rights television, but he knows when to be light in his demeanor, full of levity, and you like that. You call Mr. Got-No-Time "Mr. So Damn Fine" because he thinks he blew your mind and the brother didn't even come close. He's giddy, inquiring what's his character like, demanding to know what he means to you and how appears.

Rubbing his nostrils as if a line remains underneath them, he's still grinding on you. The slow music in the background rewinding to the moment that triggered it all.

Negro talks about his dream with your freeze-r open and somethin else cookin. Says it's dream that just won't quit, just won't go away.

But this is a story about nightmares and lullabies, the small drumming snares and the wailers' cries.

Kill that shit is what you think, but the weed and common sense plead with you to *let it go*. "You might rejoice, but I must mourn," you tell Marcus and Langston. [Later with your celly, you give me a blow-by-blow of the (w)hole conversation.]

You order this dynamic duo of shady and strong and sometimes gay men to stop pressing you, to be chill, to be like fine wine, by the time you get back because they are habit for you now—you need them in your life everyday. You are tragically Americanized now, hooked on The Dream, addicted to love, though, like Nzambi, you still play the role of Justice, quickly remind me, your long-running shadow, that all of us possess the ability to change if we have enough vision.

But, who knows how to love you?

"Audi," you say, standing up. You kiss Marcus goodbye and leave him alone, caring but not really caring. With a dagga in his mouth and cash money in his drawers. "Look for me all around you," he warns, checking the mail and never looking up.

Walking away, you feel chopped and screwed.

Why even bother with Langston, you ask yourself, mini-skirting the issue. He's on borrowed time anyway. Seeing blood in his piss caused you too much anxiety, the splashes of pink toilet water almost jumping out of the bone-color porcelain to hit you in the face.

In your ride, you settle down by listening to a mix-tape and Madlib's *African Earwax*, speeding in the jungle and easily steering through the Bohemian culture as if looking for tom. Entertaining the between, you creep through the valley of the nest of spiders and past the dark reflections. Then you go with the flow before getting yourself into the turn-up jams. You stay in your lane. In your Caddy, in your lack, Nommo take the wheel to teach you a lesson while you fish for your makeup, cosmetics.

Crossing the East River, the Sound River, is all about brands and branding now. Having been thoroughly tattooed on your lips and chin and booty, you got Jaguar, Infiniti FX, and Evoque on your behind. Since you yourself got a Pioneer system, it's impossible not to advertise, so you rush through the tall, mangled trees, bitter leaves, and greens as food for thought—avoiding the walking sticks, the praying men, the oval fruit dropping down alongside your face like really loud earrings that agitate you to no end. And you 'round ivory/bush/salamander women on the streets, as well as Octavia's brood. The horde of dense women using their bread on depigmentation chemicals, corrosive creams, rubbing that on so they can shine at night, bring light and glow in the bedroom. Just girls really, washing their skin until it's white, apparently bent on becoming the "sluts" they are *scened* as. They leave you speechless.

Hoping to get a sign, recklessly looking to turn over a new leaf, you need a brake.

Crash: you feel yourself suddenly relax, relapse, back into depression, your maroon top in bad shape, and you forming tears deep as the Indian Ocean upon realizing, that even in America, no one is brave enough to dive into the wreck to save you.

As luck would have it, self-preservation is right up your alley. Cats calling. Even women in labor persist in asking you if you are alright.

The Nommo are forced to rename you, a bad/d B with a double consciousness. The deities and divinities put you in triple jeopardy.

In a dreamlike state, you start smashing windows like they're nothing. Taking bricolage too far. Letting Jesus take the wheel. The woman in the mirror taking a look at herself. Desperately trying to make it right this time. But frightened by the reflection.

On their way to a peacekeeping mission, another intervention, three social workers pray for you—that you may persevere (rather than be stripped naked in public).

On a war path, your mind takes off again. Woman in the mirror, you find yourself reminiscing about your brother in prison. How he cried for help until his throat got slit. Even before the death verdict, a HIV-positive member of your brother's own gang had a cut made in his anus to let blood have its way and then raped him. That was wicked.

Motoring through The Village, facing the east while flying past the robots, you flashback to the days of yea and nea, of goin' to Church and hollering there in the pews, knocking on wood and just happy to have a friend in Jesus. At first, it's almost fun to be stitching together pieces of nostalgia, going back down memory lane. Then '79 hits you.

1979 when Sister Sledge is singing "We Are Family," Donna Summer's doing "Hot Stuff," The Sugarhill Gang's scoring big with "Rapper's Delight," and Michael Jackson keeps saying "Don't Stop," you and your dopefiend daddy go digging, clearing out the black nightshade you can see, the man toting his favorite Pioneer radio, Empire overseeing you. The man's a mason (his job being to create tombstone for the black people in the graveyard)—he helped build the Tombs Detention Complex, Momma says, and you're a child still in your drawers, acting like you know. After you go down inside a huge hole, he snatches the ladder up and leaves you at the bottom, pulling up stakes. He stares at you long and hard, admits to feeling necrophilia. "Nigger, this is to teach you a lesson," he finally says, treating you like a man. "Stay up."

You can barely hear him before he walks away. You can't believe he called you the N-word, an ancestral sin. He used to call you "Sugar."

So it's like Sunday confession then, the scene at the Nuyorican Poets Café—amid a mass of Afro-Latinos and Nueva Latinas, where you wanna tell the whole group about your family life, slam your daddy. Force them to drink it all in. Sadly, you speak with a tremor and shake like you have a disease, what the Brown brother calls the plague or something. There's more than "The Gospel According to Saint Miguelito Piñero," you say, obscenely, the afro-Hispanic part of you beginning to sprout upwards and onwards as if you're Goapele moving closer to something, moving forward, but don't know what.

You're anxious, you're nervous, you're heckled, joned on. Folks crowding your space give you butterflies. No elbow room. You're as high as the sky, but you can't control the black butterflies taking over you. At one point in your speech, your voice faint, you lose your balance and fall off the stage, into the audience, as if in a rave. Rage. You literally fall on your face.

Oh, snap!

Before anyone realizes it, you're back up. You rise you rise you rise. Only one downer: what you thought would be an amazing coming-out story ends up a little humiliating. Not the rise you wanted to get.

Street life is abundant, but merely one part of a very fast-moving and very affluent world, a whole new world. You live in a sort of hall, a little hall bedroom, a room meant for makin' love. You live where it hurts. The violence against your being rivalling that of Johannesburg. *Where do I go from here*, you wonder. When more clouds gather, you find yourself facing *A Bewitched Crossroad*, looking for a rain god or a rainbow.

Outside, you rock tackies/tekkies and must stand in the mud when honkies pass; they (r)amble like they own the sidewalk. So you learn to be suspicious of even white liberals.

To begin with, your world is called the "Dark Continent." And the pictures that we get of the Motherland in these days are cannibals running around in the jungles, puttin' people in pots. You change all of that.

"You can almost see them, the incarcerated men—metamorph into something else," says Sister Samad of the mission. "You can see it. They suddenly get very tall because the smallest man in the standard-issued blue uniform still looks like a giant, thanks to the love they unexpectedly receive. I can tell you that from experience. They become gorgeous. The black men become gorgeous, no longer resigned to being mere chatter/chattel in their cells but making money in prison by selling off their blues."

They start to show off, start clowning in scary ways. Like the noteworthy Bud Powell expressing to his group feelings of persecution found in racism by first having a drink, then demonstrating the *Ups 'n Downs* of trippin music, moving his fingers over the piano keys but striking no chords.

Eventually in a twisted scene, even your girlfriends try to hold you responsible for making the black man the laughing stock of America.

One day, resentment boils over, and a disgruntled brother tries to hurt you, jook you, bumrush you. With a vendetta, he stabs you in the back and shoots you three times—but he wanted to blow you up with a car bomb, watch your arms and legs hit the top of the vehicle during the blast, but you bandage yourself up, get yourself together, and go to your next speaking engagement with new quasi-religious significance. Just like Gloria Gaynor or Gloria Steinem or the va(i)nglorious, you survived, survive, you say, stubborn as a mule. Even during the coldest winter ever. "That's all that matters.

"History is written by the victors."

You feel invincible until people slap the black off of you and re-wrap you as artificial white chocolate. Even WASPS in the field hail you as the "Joan D'Arc of Africa" and "negro Moses" and "MC Lyte," then ridicule you when you're not looking. Everyone's got their claws digging into you. Hooks serving you up on a platter. You look like you've been flayed by Hellraiser. Everybody's got their tentacles holding you down. Folks dancing around the issue. Refusing to note what's going on. You're trap music in the invasion of the octopus people.

When the tables turn, they don't stop for nothing. There's a gem in your eye, and, as reflexion mirroring your soul, it announces it comes from the beat. Gemini only recognizes the twin sides of you, that double-consciousness. In blackness or when somebody turns the lights down low, you cain't afford to be man or woman, dig? You ain't super or human, right, fool? You're justice. You Clarence Thomas, and your alter ego be Anita Hill, speaking truthfully about your experiences from some broad shoulders. All you should do is keep trying to stand up for yo'self.

You never seem to take a day, never seem to relax. You always look serious.

Still, nobody wants you to die or fall out on their watch as it would simply add to the martyrdom aspect.

No, America has a less spoiling option: It commands you to leave, disappear and never be heard again. As you go, prepare to sail away into the horizon and the big sea, folks remind you not to rock the boat. "Go back to Jamaica," they say, "your new island home. And, don't let the wind raise your skirt so you can become the mother-slut you're so bent on becoming."

You've come down in the world. Sparrow feed on seeds and insects by your feet. As you walk barefoot, sticks and stones almost break your bones. Children clutching their building and construction toys follow you to(at) the curb and ham it up 'cause you show too much Baby Phat, and a span of the usual suspects harass you during your trek. "Hey, dere, sweet thing, slim," monsters, vagrants from the local shebeens, holla' while street vendors flay fish, "can I have some of that ~~guerilla~~ gorilla milk." Other victims—women wearing necklaces made of rubber and living in matchbox house, shanties made of cow-dung—don't dare speak your name. They whisper it as if it is a rhythmical work song given to them by sailors. Scarred, scared, they urge you to move on.

With dread in control, they labor to isolate the vibrations in their voices.

You are Bessie Head in need of an herbalist: You got a black consciousness and come from a people that is rough-and-ready. Your whole history is oral, which is ironically the only thang hard to swallow.

You got the Negro world as your mouthpiece, but nobody wants to hear it. You got diamonds in a basket, in the Forehead of the Zebra, from Botswana. Dagga, funeral rice, and mealie, but you can't eat. Can't digest anything. Nervous system has been shot. You believe you've been severely mutilated. Blade wound up being a villain that sucked the life out of you. Men keep coughing, spraying, in front of your face, and somehow get away clean. In the mean time, you're labeled unfeminine, ugly, and unclean. Visual aids, such as the mirror revealing the cold sores and rashes on your skin, bother you. Desperate, you take reverse and protease inhibitors. Reduce viral loads (amount of HIV in the blood). Prednisone makes the problem worse. Antihistamines such as dye-free Benadryl help. Ya' drink kaffir beer from a tin like it's water because the alcohol's pleasantly sour.

As you ponder a question of power, you listen to the death song of mighty *King Kong* and partially document your own mental breakdown before finally suffering a stroke of genius.

Who knows what you live for?

You dream a dream that you came and people saw you.

"When you die for good, Archangel Michael and The Devil will fight over your body," says your best friend Jude from squat or tradition, trembling in the kitchen where black women traditionally talk. She's sorry for you, she cries. Washing her hands clean of it, every thang, with black soap, Body White.

Listening to trap music, she adds that she saw Brown in *el barrio* this morning. There, in the alley where the concrete walls are cracked and gray and the pipes get broken from habit, Brown appeared naked and staring back at her. "He's hung," she says.

"Hey, Jude," you say, "don't be afraid. Don't make it bad. Take a sad song and make it better." You twerk, do the butterfly, spread your legs but dance like you've never danced before.

"Mos [after all], Afrika, even wit your sassy black 'tude and ig'nant ex-ploy-tation dudes hating, I still ain't mad at cha'," you whisper alone in the still of the night, pitching over with a fever.

At last in frustration, you come to me like deep, dark, blonde torch singer Etta James, crying me a river but not really crying. You've never been that week. Today, you are screaming and bantering 'bout how Brown won't do right. You are no longer a wallflower. Bold, you act like Miss Peaches. Look like something's got a hold of you.

Somewhere along the way during that joyride, U-turn, you say. "I started putting the pieces of a broken puzzle back together. After all, what is right is like a broken puzzle.

[When the tables turn, it is blacks' magic. So pure, no other experience can match it.]

"Pay attention!" you insist. "Because this is where the story gets complicated, rough."

A new victor is introduced: "Give it up for me!" you yell, fresh from the hit factory.

As man of steel, I might as well be DJ Shadow for all you care. You make it clear: You the one in flux.

This is when you tell me everything, in blow-by-blow detail; I know the whole book on you. You even show me the B-side, your "break points" now visible to the naked eye.

You say you don't want to be a high-yellow ho, a dramatic thot. Nasty. You want to be in control. No more pretty boys with big heads or guns unless it's Cassius Clay or X.

"First time I fell in love, I didn't know what hid me," you declare. You stare at me.

Your story's poetry. Emotion. All explicitly stated. Its center existing for the sake of the volta, that indispensable turn expressing the possibility for transformation. When the gods put me in the mix, I am not Shango— I'm watching you get your swerve on. Indeed, it's like a moment of grace. Historical. Your remixing yourself, the black body, as a black "I." Funky. Demo stating the abuse you've been thru. That it's not ovah, you're not done. Your story's a black eye. No perfect sphere, but constantly moving, communicating the results of blunt trauma.

Listening to you, I realize my own anthem can't compare. "Calm down, honey—it gonna take a lot to bring me away from you," I swear at your crib. You hot, combing your kitchen and not playin', taking in juice that's brand new—good for you. "There's nothing that a hundred men or more could ever do," I add, tap-dancing around the issues.[4]

"Whatever this music is, we have to live by it," is your counter.

"We gotta take some time to do things that we never ever do," I vow just now. Your odyssey has been strange, but I would never change it.

"Naw, I ain't mad ya' now-now," I say to you. "Let me show you how to listen."

I catch you eyeing my military paraphernalia and memorabilia, my tee-shirt that says "South Korea got Seoul." "Cause if I was you, I be goin' buck wild, too. When baas/boss and folk get on me, I snap." Yeah, I always be a Sugar Daddy, a pod busting wide open, the seeds of my sorrow larger than normal. Green with jealousy, I ain't nothin' but some sugar/snap/pee.

Dis(s) is what I live with all up in me [kraal] all of the time, I say to my dear, sweet Africa, this Nubian queen. "We're celebrating your 4th of July, not mine. Dis(s) is all I know. The rest, you insist, would have to beat out of you by a brute. But now you want me to go away, stay silent." Truth is, the subject of everything keeps being you, and I just can't handle it.

"I am down but not out," you respond to me, right on time, ticked, coming out at me hard and in the voice of Winnie Mandela after a year-long period of silent mourning. "You no longer need to narrate me or editorialize what I'm saying to you. You will not hoard me. Tonight, I'm not fearing any man. No longer shall I be swindled or betrayed. I ain't your Earth Mama and you're going to get your ass whipped if not careful, but I still got a black consciousness. I come for a people tough and heady. My hole history has a voice that, I promise you, no one will ever forget."

"Some rise, some fall," you say through blunt force. "That's what motivates me."

Seemingly piloting yourself through this turbulent time like Bessie Coleman, you wrap me in mud cloth, trying a little bit of tenderness, and go on: "That other B," you warn. "She'll never treat you right.

"She could never give you what you want," you add, digging into my thin skin with your shiny polished nails. "What you need is this African girl," you mutter, pointing at yourself but seemingly referring to someone else. Nobody really knows what happened that day you started wrecking things. This is your show now, you insist. You plan on keeping it that way.

"You are lucky," you tell me. "Blessed.

"Just remember, Bomani [the name means "warrior soldier"]," you caution me. "You never gave birth to such madness."

Under the neon vernacular, a DJ's street lamp, the light flickering, I am sniggering, creating my own story in my head, letting it clot my brain while it do some triggering, the ball already set in motion.

"What you see is not what you get, Holmes," you let me know.

You say I am the one responsible for your lips sewn shut. "So now I am cutting you loose," you tell me. "I've been stuck, not feeling it." In this mad generation, you start queering the moment. You are fucking Victoria Monét. You argue that, while performing your best impression of the hunger games, you'd been dead without the gay community. Having found agency, you don't speak to me now; you talk to yourself, create change for yourself like a goddess.

"I wanna live free tonight," you say, "going up in flames with the tribe.

"I'd rather let the days go by—I love feeling that high luv," you scream. "It's the best way to feel will!

"I wanna live free tonight," you repeat, the structure of your face made beautiful by centre-parted Senegalese twists.

Even though I want you, Africa, to be mine again, because we are in our twilight—your story being about that evening sun and perseverance, all I can do for now is prey.[5] You close your eyes to regain sanctuary. Still, you have the nerve to try me. Ain't no more asking *why me*. You say, it's taken some time to find me. It's just. What I deserve for not helping when you were crying, admitting [sic] the sound that was not singing and not unsinging.

You laugh at me, hard. Rolling like thunder. Still capable of spitting hell with the resentment for how you've been treated as a black woman growing in size. Your memories of that obviously all clumped together.

"Thank God love is medicine, muti!

"In this game called 'Life,' no man shall ever beat me again," you repeat. Dreaming of being a walker again, walking before you crawl, you let me know. "No heart feelings," you emphasize, jagged edge becoming pronounced across your singing lips while you ease on down the road as if none of this is your fault and you just walked outta heaven.

"Be strong," you say to yourself. "This time I'm gone forever. Be strong. Negro should've understood 'never.' I have faith. I'm healing. I'm no longer that piece from broken peaces. I've fixed my life. I'm well. On my way to healing. My new thought is that I'm beginning my journey. I'll no longer be a victim of ~~rootlessness~~ ruthlessness."

Brandishing your new weapon, you shake a rainstick from enslaved African peoples, its rattle warning me that you're better off on your own now. Then you completely immerse yourself, baptize your whole body, in the sound of the proverbial storm.

I don't need no malicious jealousy sense; that's how rumors get started. But, I got it anyway like the plague. "Maybe I'll catch you on Schenck [Skank] Avenue in Brooklyn or in New Lots," I say, although you're not listening and half of me is really jumping for joy. Like Mister at the end of *The Color Purple*, I suddenly, strangely, give in to you on a compassion note. I'm actually a little excited you won't be living any longer in The Hole that's a part of deserted, rundown Queens. Caught up in fisticuffs or a nasty showdown with black cowboys like me. I'm your scribe now. I only wish the line you spit as an unequivocal response to me just wasn't so plain foul: "It ain't nobody's business if I do."

Birds flying high—they know how you feel. Every enraged protestor engaged in a rallying cry . . . the linked ladies in a police state urging all men who copped a feel from a black woman to say her name. They know how you feel. Black women subject to violence, seen as vulnerable, and sadly not part of the conversation.[6] They know how you feel. Marshall Mathers' critics taking joy in mimicking that "Mockingbird" song and attacking the misogynistic rapper whose taken his manhood and mailed it in. They know how you feel.

Me? I'm through. I'm left, asking *why*. But even that, I can tell: Music is your weapon. Something made in response to others, the objects of both hate and love. You make it clear it's a new day, a new Dawn, a New World, a new Fate. And, you're feeling good! So good.

It's obvious you know how to love again. Although your spirit got crushed, it has survived! You are a survivor. Having reversed misfortune and remixed your double consciousness into a single black g-thing, you ignore the platitudes, are estranged from anything or anyone that tried to dominate you. A slave only to the riddim now, to the soulful beat drumming in your head that calls you to perform a celebratory dance, you prove Black people can walk on water without it killing anyone, without it taking its ultimate toll.

From that point on, you ~~can't stop~~ won't stop singing. Everyday, the same song.

Notes

[1] The loop: "*Encore et Encore* [Again and Again]," by Isleym.

[2] Alienating as alterity. Like Alicia Keys & Bono performing "Don't Give Up (Africa)."

[3] South African word for "young black urban criminal."

[4] "Borrowed" from *"Africa"* (bootleg ultimix) by Toto.

[5] From "Sanctuary," *Fire*.

[6] A tribute to Kimberlé Crenshaw, founder of the African American Policy Forum.

Kang Snake Blues: Paradise Lost

Charlie Braxton

saints say
seek solace
in the
sublime shadow
of self
so said
spirits of
sages can
sing songs
to those
daughters and sons
whose eyes
see no sun
shhh
shut up
& listen
somewhere
amidst the slithering
sound of silence
death crawls
through a slit
in the universe
like a mississippi
king snake sliding
through grass
waiting its turn
at prey

A Slave Dreams of Revenge

Charlie Braxton

In the middle of a Monday on
a Mississippi summer's day, when the combination
of heat and dust make my mouth dryer
than blooming cotton. Fresh off the bloody
trees, where black bodies droop limp and
lifeless, I dream of drinking water fresh
from the rivers in massa's worst nightmare

A Vision of Purgatory

Charlie Braxton

They say that somewhere between the dreams
Of slaves and the nightmares of those
Who own them, lay a river of tears
Ever flowing into a sea of boiling
Blood where demon sharks lurk with gnashing
Teeth waiting to fill their belly with
The fancy fat flesh of our oppressors

Another Mississippi Murder

Charlie Braxton

For Mike Brown, Lennon Lacy, Eric Garner and
countless others
who have fallen victim
to racial violence

they kilt that boy
lynched him
just as sho' as my name is
what it is
they did it
cause that what they do in
kokomo mississippi
kill folk

the same way they did
emmett till
in money mississippi

the same way they did
vernon dahmer
in hattiesburg mississippi

the same way they did
medgar evers
in jackson mississippi

the same damn way they did
schwerner, goodman and chaney
in philadelphia mississippi

the same way they did
mack charles parker
in poplarville mississippi

the same way they killed
andre jones
in a simpson county jail cell

hung him
like he was a skint pig
left to rot
under the watchful eye
of an old pale-faced devil's
moon
down in mississippi
where
raynard ladell johnson
found death's cold hands
draped in swaddling
white sheets
wrapped around his teenage throat
choking the life from his virile black
body
as it swayed
like a lusty whore
flirting in the flushed face
of a history so ugly
only a short ignorant-limp-dick
pot-bellied-beer-guzzling-
rebel-flag-waving-trailer-trash-talking redneck
could love it
mississippi is a slithering seductress
a geographical jezebel
whose whiteness torments me
like an electric ghost in
the industrial machine of
dixicratic politics
I know her well
cause
I love
and
I hate

her so
much
that every now & again
it hurts
it hurts
it hurts
yet we continue to march and sing and pray
for a land soaked in our innocent blood

when war cries
and battle hymns are needed
for this is a new song
for a new day
and a new time
our piece will not be said
in hushed apologetic tones
of slobbering uncle toms seeking reconciliation
naw
this time
we want justice
if denied
then
we'll settle for revenge

Mississippi White Sale (No. 2)

Aseret Sin

Confederate flags
Will make lovely winding sheets
For modern "rebels"

If You Ain't Gon' Come In Handy. . .

Aseret Sin

"The people can be their own gods"
~ John McCluskey

The gods descend
The devotees stand stock and shudder as they are mounted
and ridden until riven around and through sacred groves
The gods feast on sumptuous foods
slurp expensive rum
spew gravity defying clouds of gin
and shotgun cigars like steamships
as they buck in their righteous groove

Holy rolling ghosts possess believers
like Yemoja in flood
throwing them across pews
snatching wigs
instigating straight-step jitterbugging
and bending backs like broncos
as they juke past the grasps of gasping urshers

Whirling dervishes swirl
whipping nonexistent devils
and exiling imagined jinns
with reams of cloth that conjure
colorful tornadoes
over the bones
of eternally tortured Africans

Yes!
The gods descend and
possess parishioners and
inflame the faithful
until
engorged on the frothy fruitlessness of belief
the gods depart

True believers trudge to homes
that double as
rat factories
roach waystations
bedbug bazaars
The faithful find no jobs, no crops
no help or hope
to feed the hungry
or cure the incurable
or castrate the plentiful pedophiles

But the gods were *here*!
Right *here*! They were
Bucking
Eating
Puffing
Spinning
Whipping up furies
Abounding in ecstasies

The gods were here
riding the rollercoaster waves
of their devotees' spiraling agonies
salivating over their insurmountable suffering
picking their kaposi's sarcoma scabs for play
molding newborn heads too tiny for brains

Yes, the gods were here.

Now they are gone.

Wake up.

The Coming of the Saviors

Aseret Sin

The United Nation's
peace-keeping soldiers
hand out lollipops to African children
so the children can
practice...

Amerikkka Eats Its Young: 8 "Childku"

Aseret Sin

1.
If left alone with
a child would you rape or kill?
That is the question

2.
"Come sit on my lap.
You can trust me. Look! I've got
a sucker for you. . ."

3.
More and more men kill
the children left in their care
It's yesterday's news

4.
I've programed a drone
to watch my daughter for me
while I go to work

5.
I am designing
clothes for Chicago's children
clothes made of Kevlar

6.
"Forgetting" children
So that they die in hot cars
My, how . . . convenient?

7.
We've called our children
"kids" for so long that we treat
them, kill them like goats

8.
Civilization's
apex is the nadir for
innocent millions

Nommo, No Mo, No More

Asiri Odu

"Welcome to Nommo!"

"I'm, Azure"

    "and I'm Alteveze"

        "and we manifest the power of the word!"

"Àṣẹ. Àṣẹ. Our number is 252-7119, and our program is not complete without your Nommo. So please call us."

"Tonight we ask our Ancestors to open our powers of understanding as we discuss an issue that threatens the entire Pan-African nation: HIV/AIDS—its creation, manipulation, and dissemination. In our goal to better understand these issues, we are going to share with you information that we've gathered from a number of sources, including the 92 minute documentary *The Origin of AIDS*; Andrew Goliszek's book *In the Name of Science*, Alan Cantwell's book *AIDS and the Doctors of Death*; and documents released courtesy of the Freedom of Information Act.

"The world was introduced to AIDS through the male homosexual community—its first documented victims. The facts that the disease was ravaging gay communities, that it had no cure, that its modes of transmission were not fully known, and that it destroyed the human immune system were cooked in the media's pot of perversion to produce a disease that was not only considered a 'gay plague' but also a plague that *you* could get—if *you* followed a less than righteous lifestyle.

"Even though the media used a Caucasian heterosexual woman who acquired AIDS from her dentist and a Caucasian hemophiliac child who acquired the disease from a blood transfusion to put 'a human face' on HIV/AIDS (others who had died were apparently deemed nonhuman), the virus' association with degeneracy and debauchery remained.

"HIV/AIDS became not only a physical death sentence but it also became a license for the media to dig into the victims' personal lives in search of lurid details that could become headline news. Even the statement that an individual 'died from complications related to the AIDS virus' was designed to lead 1 to the conclusion that a lifestyle of lasciviousness led to the individual being rightly cursed with the dreaded 'gay plague.'

"You may have never known or cared about the sexual orientation of your favorite actor, singer, athlete, reporter, or writer until HIV/AIDS got a hold of him or her and the media drug that person's character from the hospice to the sewer of Christian hypocrisy.

"But to understand the origin of what was introduced to the world as a 'gay plague' and has now become a 'black plague' fittingly associated with 'black' (signifying evil, vile, beyond redemption, and a human being of African origin) people, 1 need not look to biblical scriptures or godly rage. 1 can simply look to the evil that masquerades in the west as 'science.'

"In 1978, under the guise of testing the efficacy of an experimental hepatitis B vaccine, the Centers for Disease Control (CDC) working with the National Institutes of Health (NIH) injected 'promiscuous homosexual' male test subjects of New York with a concoction manufactured by Merck that physician Wolf Szmuness of Colombia University School of Public Health created by developing the pooled blood serum of gay men infected with hepatitis B in the genetic material of chimpanzees.

"Several weeks after receiving Szmuness' 'experimental vaccine,' test subjects were diagnosed diseases that are now known as the hallmarks of HIV/AIDS infection, most notably Kaposi's sarcoma. Despite or, perhaps, because of the developments among the New York test subjects, in 1980 the CDC expanded its hepatitis B vaccine trials to Los Angeles, San Francisco, Chicago, St. Louis, and Denver.

"In 1981 the CDC acknowledged the existence of AIDS and confirmed that there were 26 known cases of the disease. Those infected were all previously healthy gay men who were residing in New York, San Francisco, and Los Angeles—the cities where the CDC conducted its experimental trials in 1978 and 1980. By 1982, 30% of the participants of the CDC's trials were HIV/AIDS positive.

"Since the 1980's, scientists and physicians have reaped billions of dollars in their proclaimed struggle to understand and cure a disease that it appears they created using criminally unhygienic and contaminated processes. And it appears they were not content to create 1 devastating disease; they used the parent virus to give birth to various lethal offspring, from the various members of the HIV family to the quick-killing Ebola, Marburg, and Lassa viruses.

"There are 2 recognized types of HIV: HIV 1 and HIV 2, and there are diverse mutations of these 2 viruses. HIV 1 is found largely in the U.S., Europe, and Central Africa, while HIV 2 is prevalent in West Africa. HIV 2's West African predominance appears to be indicative a race-specific viral construction, 1 perhaps tailored to African genetic structures.

"In addition to understanding the significance of HIV 1 and HIV 2 in the realm of medical genocide, which we will explore a bit later in the program, we must also examine the ways by which HIV 1, a disease originally rooted in the American homosexual, Caucasian, male demographic can reach pandemic levels among African American women.

"How a disease can move from the homosexual Caucasian male demographic to that of African American women within 2 decades has never been addressed by any study I have seen. The unspoken answer from the Caucasian medical community is promiscuity. But the sexual habits of the world's populations have not changed. Gay men have not started lusting after Africana women. So how did the disease 'jump' demographic groups?

"1 factor in America could be the incarceration rates of African American and Latino and Chicano men, which are at all-time highs. The United States incarcerates more people than England, Germany, Canada, and France combined. At present, more than 1 million brothers are incarcerated, and many of them hold that having sex with men while imprisoned 'does not count.' These men enter into various liaisons while confined and never reveal their exploits to their female partners upon release. Because in this patriarchal society many women are convinced that they are incomplete without men, many women do everything to keep men, including not insisting on condoms or on testing for STDs and HIV.

"However, downlow brothers switching lanes, IV drug use, and accidental infections cannot account for the pandemic level of HIV infection among African American women age 18–40. We must also look to seemingly innocuous sources, such as yearly visits to gynecologists and implanted contraceptive devices, as possible routes of infection.

"Depo-Provera is an injectable contraceptive that is also used for chemical castration. It has consistently been tested on and injected into women in developing nations and on poor American women without their consent. Racist Israelis injected Ethiopian women with the drug without the women's consent—the women were told the drug was a vaccination.

Dorothy Roberts' book *Killing the Black Body* reveals that Caucasians have marketed Depo-Provera as the go-to contraception for African American, Native American, and South American women; women in Thailand and Mexico; and African women in South Africa and France. The reason for the Caucasian medical establishment's promotion and distribution of Depo-Provera to women of color goes far beyond the evil of population control. A study published in the medical journal *The Lancet* revealed that Depo-Provera increases the likelihood of a woman to contract HIV by 40%!

"The makers and distributers of the HIV-linked injectable contraception refuse to stop administering Depo-Provera to the millions of women it has been forced upon. The excuse they give is that the poor downtrodden women of Africa don't have many options for birth control. But the truth is that through Depo-Provera, the beast can reduce the population of Africana peoples with a double whammy—HIV-tainted contraception."

"Our first caller is Sahai. Peace: You're speaking with Nommo."

"Alteveze, Azure: thank you so much for sharing these life-saving truths with us. You sisters are true consciousness-raising warriors."

"Thank you for the recognition, Sahai."

"It doesn't take a Ph.D. to see that HIV/AIDS is melanin-directed, if not from its creation then its dissemination. But I am inspired by the information that you are sharing with us because it changes our perspective on this disease and its victims. Rather than seeing members of various communities as pariahs or sexual deviants, what emerges is a picture of people simply living their lives who are being attacked and killed in the most cowardly way possible.

"Many people would be loath to believe that their general practitioner, gynecologist, obstetrician, proctologist, cardiologist, or hematologist is using them as a test subject. Many would laugh or be incensed at such accusations. But the truth of the medical community's manipulation and desecration of our living and dead bodies is all too well documented. And the United States' government has authorized and funded experiments that have been conducted on various ethnic groups in this country and abroad. What we are really discussing here is a national pathology that has resulted in global crimes against humanity.

"It is frightening to know what the beasts have been able to do—and it is chilling to consider what they are doing right now. Thank you, sisters, for enlightening us tonight. I know there is much more to come."

"Sahai, we so appreciate the wisdom you have shared with us. Our goal is to drop knowledge that will encourage people to do their own research, to draw their own conclusions, and to approach with extreme caution medical services and members medical establishments."

"This is important, Alteveze, because mass inoculations are thought to be the primary route of HIV/AIDS transmission. A stirring 92 minute documentary—and make sure you view the full length hour and a half doc, not an edited version—titled *The Origin of AIDS* discusses the possible creation of a strain of HIV/AIDS in the Kongo by physician Hilary Koprowski and virologist Paul Osterrieth who were trying to create a polio vaccine using the kidneys of chimpanzees. Koprowski and Osterrieth used entire populations in Central Africa as tests subjects for their polio vaccine. 10 years after they had been given the polio vaccine, Central Africans began dying of AIDS. 1 can trace the first HIV/AIDS infections in the 1960s directly to Koprowski and Osterrieth's the mass inoculations in the 1950s.

"The documentary hypothesizes that the HIV/AIDS pandemic in Haiti could be traced to the Haitians who traveled to the Kongo to fill the positions vacated by fleeing Belgians in 1960. These Haitians naturally married Kongolese or sought medical services in the Kongo only to find, later, that they were infected with the disease now called HIV/AIDS.

"The documentary also offers information that connects America to the Kongo. Osterrieth, the virologist who created the virus-causing vaccine, not only worked in secret because he was cognizant of the diseases he could create by using chimpanzee tissue, but he sent finished vials of his lethal concoction to Koprowski's lab in Philadelphia. It would have been easy, and expedient from a Caucasian supremacist position, for Koprowski to share his virus with Szmuness, the NIH, and/or the CDC. And HIV 1's prevalence in Central Africa and North America bears out the contention that the virus was shared."

"Powerful information, Azure. And speaking of expedience, it is widely-held that the World Health Organization infected millions of Africana people with HIV/AIDS during its smallpox eradication campaign which ran from 1967-1980. The WHO focused its campaign in the Kongo, Burundi, Rwanda, Zambia, Tanzania, Uganda, Malawi; Brazil (which has the highest population of Africana people in the Western Hemisphere and was the only Latin American country included in the WHO's campaign); and Haiti (the first free Africana country in the Western Hemisphere). The staggering rates of HIV/AIDS in these regions corresponds directly to the WHO's smallpox campaign."

"In addition to avoiding mass vaccination campaigns, we must call out and fight against governmental manipulations that link mass inoculations with 'compulsory' education. Citing an alleged outbreak of hepatitis C, Caucasian medical intuitions in America undertook the forcible mandatory testing and vaccination of children in so-called 'high-risk' areas. If 1 refused to test or vaccinate 1's child, 1's child could not attend school.

"In March of 1996, Yahweh, a religious leader in an African American community in Memphis TN, organized a protest against the board of education for its refusal to admit to school children from that community who had not received the Hepatitis C vaccine."

"Hmp, this makes me think of Shinally Medical College, right next door, always soliciting African Americans to participate in some test or other, and even promoting this same hepatitis C vaccination that the brothers and sisters in Memphis fought against."

"Clearly, it's Nation Time."

"Our next caller is Dr. Northerly."

"Good evening."

"Peace."

"I'm not a regular listener, but I saw so many flyers in Shinally, I had to tune in. I'm a pediatrician in Shinally's Clinical Research Center.

"Here at Shinally we've always tried to combat Tuskegeephobia, which is what we call the fear induced in African Americans from their knowledge that the American medical establishment has used them as guinea pigs. Our goal is to advance the study and prevention of African American health problems. Incendiary information such as what you've shared tonight will set back our work significantly!"

"Well, I suppose our planning this 'incendiary' program and not killing African Americans through seemingly innocuous clinical trials, such as those conducted at Shinally, reveals our true level of community concern."

"Northerly we are not an economically motivated outfit thriving off of federal grants and Black bodies. Our entire motivation is to stop the genocide of the Pan-African world."

"Listen, it is a known fact that AIDS came from the green monkey disease. The SIV II virus in Afr"

                    "Northerly, we are not here to entertain lies and misinformation. Were homosexual Caucasian men going to Africa to copulate with green monkeys?!?" Alteveze was heated.

"This green monkey nonsense is just an attempt to cover the dirt of Osterrieth and Koprowski," Azure rolled her eyes.

"Northerly, you should rejoice! Being situated in the heart of our community and using us to perfect weapons of mass destruction to kill us has been more than successful," Alteveze offered the caller mock applause.

"I've not accomplished anything! I want as much as you to protect the Black community and eradicate this dreaded disease!"

"Yes, of course you do."

"Don't patronize me! Your program will instill fear in everyone!"

"Yes, and fear will precipitate action, even if the only actions are staying away from Shinally, except in case of dire emergency and using products from the Earth in treating ills."

"Exactly, Azure. The Earth has a cure for every human illness. In Ghana, Kenya, and Cameroon pharmacologists are developing or have developed cures for AIDS. 1 Ghanaian herbalist's cure for AIDS was so successful, he was killed. We need our traditional physicians, our 2 headed doctors, to return to the field and find the cures waiting in the Earth."

"Hogwash! Such primitive beliefs will contribute to the spread AIDS— no 1 will be tested, people will transfer viruses back and forth!"

"How?"

"Sex. Drugs."

"So now we have it. Northerly, your argument dates back to the era of Caucasian encroachment on Africa and its enslavement, colonization, and continued raping of the people and Continent."

"A group of savages whose lives were a merry-go-round of plagues due to their inability to establish a healthy civilization witnessed a people clothed in the beauty of skin as pure and smooth as the night sky. These people not only practiced excellent hygiene and boasted impeccable morals, but their lives were in harmony with the world and cosmos: they understood, as John Henrik Clarke points out, that the word 'civilization' is rooted in the word 'civil,' which means to be peaceful and at harmony with the Earth and all its inhabitants.

"The mutant couldn't understand such balance, harmony, and power. It could only see lack in its pale skin and bestiality. But rather than attempt to advance itself, the Caucasian decided to pervert or destroy millions of peaceful peoples and cultures around the world. HIV/AIDS is merely the latest assault. If you are looking for vile primitive beasts, Northerly, you need look no further than within yourself and your peoples."

"Azure, we've lost the caller."

"And yet, we've lost nothing."

"Well said, Azure."

"Before we return to the phone lines, I will share information with you about various experiments the US government and its agencies have conducted on its citizens and on any human beings unlucky enough to be in the United States' clutches. This information is readily available to everyone thanks to the Freedom of Information Act and can be found in numerous books and websites. What becomes clear when perusing this data is the government's lack of regard and respect for *any* human life. These demented pseudo-scientists will experiment on anyone in their vicinity— except, of course, themselves.

"Throughout the 1840s, J. Marion Sims, the so-called 'father of gynecology,' performed medical experiments on enslaved Africana women without anesthesia. These women would routinely die of infection soon after surgery. Based on his belief that the movement of newborns' skull bones during protracted births causes trismus, Sims used a shoemaker's awl to move the skull bones of babies born to enslaved mothers.

"In the late 19th and early 20th centuries, there are more than 40 reports of experimental infections with gonorrhea. Some researchers even applied gonorrhea cultures to the eyes of children using sticks. In 1895 in New York City, pediatrician Henry Heiman infected 2 mentally disabled boys aged 4 and 16 with gonorrhea to study the disease.

"In 1896, Dr. Arthur Wentworth performed spinal taps on 29 children at Boston's Children's Hospital to determine if the procedure was harmful.

"From 1913 to 1951 Dr. Leo Stanley, chief surgeon of San Quentin Prison, performed testicular transplants on prisoners at San Quentin. Stanley transplanted the testicles of recently executed inmates as well as the testicles of goats, boars, and rams into prisoners.

"In 1950, Dr. Joseph Stokes of the University of Pennsylvania infected 200 female prisoners with viral hepatitis. From the 1950s to 1972, mentally disabled children at Willowbrook State School in Staten Island were also intentionally infected with viral hepatitis.

"In 1952, Chester M. Southam injected live cancer cells into prisoners of the Ohio State Prison. In 1963, Southam performed the same procedure on 22 elderly female patients at the Brooklyn Jewish Chronic Disease Hospital in order to study their immunological response. Southam did not obtain informed consent from the patients. Although he temporarily lost his medical license, he was later rewarded by being elected the vice-president of the American Cancer Society in 1965.

"From 1963 to 1966, New York University researcher Saul Krugman promised parents of mentally disabled children enrollment into the Willowbrook State School in Staten Island, New York, a residential mental institution for children, in exchange for allowing Krugman to perform procedures he called 'vaccinations.' Krugman was actually infecting the children with viral hepatitis by making them ingest an extract made from the feces of infected patients.

"While many of us are familiar with the Tuskegee studies in which, from 1932 to 1972, 400 African American men were denied treatment for syphilis so the disease' effects on the men, their wives, and children could be studied. However, we may not know that from 1946 to 1948 the National Institutes of Health and the organization that would become the World Health Organization infected Guatemalan prison inmates, mental patients, and soldiers with syphilis. Approximately 700 Guatemalans, including children, were infected and studied. And, in 1911 Dr. Hideyo Noguchi of the Rockefeller Institute for Medical Research injected 146 hospital patients, including some children, with syphilis.

"Many of these heinous experiments, like the Tuskegee Study, were overseen by the Centers for Disease Control, which, a journalist wrote, 'sees the poor, the black, the illiterate and the defenseless in American society as a vast experimental resource for the government.'"

The CDC, WHO, and NIH have also worked in conjunction with the American military to create weapons of mass destruction and to test them on and use them to destroy certain populations.

"A 1975 military manual observed that it would be possible to develop 'ethnic chemical weapons' designed to 'exploit naturally occurring differences in vulnerability among specific populations.' Here, 1 should think of Hanta, HIV 2, and Middle East Respiratory Syndrome."

In February, 1987, a lawsuit by the Foundation for Economic Trends, a Washington, DC environmental group, forced the Department of Defense (DOD) to admit to the operation of biological research programs at 127 sites all over the country, including universities, foundations and corporations.'"

"We will take a quick break for station identification. Stay with us."

This is 88.9 Double You, Emm, El, Aay, your edutainment station, broadcasting from the campus of Malare University, Nashville, TN.

"Peace unto you Black Nation, as we prepare for war. You are tuned in to Nommo with Alteveze and Azure. The number is 252-7119. Please join this important conversation."

"Previously we discussed the controversy over mandatory hepatitis testing and vaccination in Black communities. *Frontline*, a newsmagazine based in Atlanta, reports cases of cholera, hepatitis B, and tuberculosis and other diseases mysteriously popping up in Black communities.

"Like Shinally's Dr. Northerly, the U.S. government attributes this resurgence of formerly eradicated diseases to Black nastiness. However, there have been cases of TB that were, listen, non-responsive to treatment. The appearance of these mutated disease strains coincides with genetic-engineering advances and mandatory 'screening' initiatives that are imposed on certain communities and populations."

"Azure," Alteveze tapped her hand, "We must also note here the infection of millions of Haitians with cholera by United Nation's aid workers who came to 'assist' Haitians following the earthquake of 2010.

"The goal of Caucasian global supremacists is simple: increase their dwindling numbers and decrease the populations of the melanin-rich people of this world. This is why population control organizations are focused on countries in Latin America, the Caribbean, Africa and Asia, not Bosnia, Russia, Czechoslovakia, France, and Britain, because the European, or properly, Caucasoid life form has a lower birth-rate than *hue*man beings.

"Indeed, certain Caucasians are fighting to make abortion illegal so that Caucasian women will be forced to bring more of them into the world. This is why HIV/AIDS is surging at pandemic levels among Africana populations but has been stabilized among Caucasians. This is not about lifestyle, self-control, morals, or righteousness. It is about genocide."

"So true, Azure, and Africans are not the only victims. In 1768 Caucasians gave Native Americans blankets infected with smallpox, this was repeated in during the 'Trail of Tears' in 1838 and 1839 when Andrew Jackson forced the Cherokee to relocate from their lands east of the

Mississippi River to what is now called Oklahoma. More recently the Hanta virus has killed approximately 200 Native Americans."

"Cambodian, Vietnamese, and Japanese people have all been victims of US germ warfare. And Caucasian gynecologists sterilized thousands of Native American and African American women without their knowledge or consent. California recently outlawed the sterilization of women in prisons—1 must wonder why was this even occurring."

"We, the masses, must refuse to be tortured and defiled by mutants. We must say, 'No More!'"

"No mo!"

"Sydney, peace and awareness, you're with Nommo."

"Peace, daughters. Thank you for taking my call.

"My people are from Alabama. They were pickers, migrant workers. We traveled all over Alabama. But this white man knew when we would return home to Notasulga and he always came to visit us. His name was Dr. Haskins, and he was real interested in me. Always listening to my heart, checkin my eyes, limbs, and skin. I was afraid of him at first cuz white folks was rare, comin to the house in all, and his smell was worse than wet chickens. I hated to go near him, but he always come. 'Regular as the reaper,' Momma would say.

"I am blind. I've been blind since birth. Once when he checked my eyes, Momma asked im, 'Can you cure im? Can you make im see?' I was about 6 and I prayed he could. But he laughed and said, 'Mary, I'm not god, just 1 of his representatives. I can't work miracles.'

"Daddy and Momma wanted other children after me, but they couldn't have any. 1 night I heard my folks whisperin bout something that wasn't normal. That's what Momma was saying, 'This thang ain't normal.' I didn't know what they was talkin about, but I knew sometimes Daddy and Momma had sores. Sometimes Daddy was in so much pain, he would cry out in the night. It was horrible to hear my daddy scream," Sydney's voice cracked like thin glass exposed to frost.

"1 time, Daddy and Momma left me with Miss Lolly to go to Mobile for free penicillin," Sydney choked up. "They came back. Said Haskins met em there an tol em they was sposed to be in Tchula, not Mobile."

"Have strength, Elder."

"You can't imagine how my daddy suffered in his last days. . . When he finally died, the casket was closed. H-h-his nose had rotted off."

"My word," Alteveze's hands were trembling.

"So I know y'all's speakin the truth, the facts. I'm 70 now. I've never had children. I'm sterile. My wife left me. She run off and had a child but she come on back as her man left her. We raised her child as our own.

"I never had spite against nobody. But I know, sure as I'm blind, they can create AIDS and anything else they want. My own self proves that."

"Elder Sydney, we appreciate your revelations. I know it wasn't easy for you to share this, but it is elders like you who can educate us with your experience," Azure's voice cracked.

"Elder, stay strong and keep teaching your truth."

"You girls are doing important work. I would be proud to call you my own. I hope that because of your work tonight, we can save some lives."

"Àṣẹ and Amen, Father."

"You are tuned into Nommo—the power of the word by which we declare, No Mo! No Moe hueman guinea pigs. No mo slaying of our mothers and fathers of our progeny and prophets. No More under-handed tricks. No more turning our other cheeks to the reality of our oppressors' bestiality only to be slapped again. No more.

"Sons and Daughters of Boukman of Nat Turner of Denmark Vesey of Gabriel Prosser of Patrice Lumumba of Winnie Mandela of Sojourner Truth of Ida B. Wells Barnett of MahuLisa of Consciousness and Evolution of Odù stand up and love your selves and souls by refusing to be oppressed any longer. No more slavery. No more neo-slavery. No more genocide. The only freedom is that we take! The only evolution is that we create. Listen, for 200 years they've been trying to exterminate us: No More."

"We urge you to do your own research. You can see the documentary, *The Origin of AIDS* free online. You can also access Tom Curtis' groundbreaking *Rolling Stone* article also titled "The Origin of AIDS" online for free. Also insightful is Edward Hooper's *The River*, Andrew Goliszek's *In the Name of Science*, and Harriet A. Washington's *Medical Apartheid*. In everything it does, the beast evinces pride. So it publishes all its evil. Arm yourselves with the ultimate weapon: knowledge."

"Never believe the death an oppressor has planned for you is the 1 you must succumb to."

"Our next caller is Derrick. Peace, Derrick."

"Peace, sisters. My mind is blown by the information you've shared. You know, the elders say that the beast is awake and thinking of ways to kill us as we party, sleep, fu"

"Please, brother"

"my bad, sisters, have sex, and get high, but this is a new level of assault. If these beasts are successful, we will be extinct by 2050!"

"If not before, which is the plan."

"But let's keep in mind the word 'undesirable.' We'll still have some toms floating around. . . Quite a few, in fact," Alteveze mused.

"Queens, this is a monumental global attack and its results so far have been devastating," Derrick lamented.

"Derrick, you're right. The attack we face is multipronged and the agents of destruction are numerous. In the 1990s, AIDS infection rates were soaring and so was the '0 Population Growth' movement. Today, with millions of Africana peoples having died and currently infected with HIV/AIDS, the hue and cry about population growth has ceased.

"While the catch phrases change, objectives and outcomes have not. African nations are now under attack by Ebola, which wreaks immediate havoc and is capable of decimating nations in mere months. Ebola and its brother Marburg are digging many graves in Central and West Africa.

"Ebola, Marburg, and Lassa are all part of the HIV/AIDS family and were created using similar processes. Indeed, Gorbee Logan, a Liberian physician practicing in Tubmanburg successfully treats Ebola victims with lamivudine, which is, not surprisingly, used to treat not only HIV but also hepatitis B. Logan states that his decision to use HIV drugs to treat Ebola was rooted in the fact that 'Ebola is a brainchild of HIV. . . . It's a destructive strain of HIV.' To determine the parentage of HIV we need look to the laboratories of individuals like Szmuness and to agencies of mass distribution that include the CDC and WHO, the World Health Organization."

"Derrick and Alteveze, we do not yet have the tools to fight Marburg, Lassa, and Ebola, but we have some tools to fight HIV/AIDS. First and foremost, we must know and protect our HIV statuses. With over-the-counter test kits available, there is no excuse for not knowing your status and that of your partner. If you are negative, stay negative; protect your life, destiny, and future. If you are positive, be honest. Condoms can break, but your word cannot. Discuss your status with your partner long before sex, and consult with a physician you *trust* and obtain lifesaving antiretroviral drugs. *Always—no matter your status—insist on safe sex*."

"Excellent points, Azure. I think we also need to undertake grassroots education and protection plans that focus on our pre-teen youths. A documentary about the pandemic level of HIV/AIDS infection in the rural American south was stunning because it revealed that our children are in the throes of a living death. But what really shocked me is that rather than educate and protect the children, the schools' awareness programs only discuss abstinence.

"The human body's hormones surge during puberty because the drive to create life is the ultimate directive. Teaching abstinence is so ineffective it's a joke. Indeed, in the documentary, after a teacher gave a speech about abstinence—not safe sex, condom application, or full disclosure, but abstinence—a young man raised his hand and asked, 'What do you do if after you have sex you tell your partner that you have HIV and she says that she has it too?' The teacher was silent and offered no answer, because she was told she could only preach abstinence."

"Our children are grappling with issues of astounding and life-changing and life-taking depth and the would-be educators offer them solutions that solve nothing or silence. This is criminal."

"It is as if the school boards are promoting HIV/AIDS transmission by restricting their teaching to abstinence. It as if they are saying, 'If you are not abstinent, you deserve to get AIDS.' This, like the entire educational system, is miseducation by design.

"We have to be responsible for ourselves on all levels. We have to establish values that are not rooted in our oppressors' avarice, deception, and immediate gratification. We are failing our children—and ourselves—if we continue to allow the schools to continue to miseducate them."

"Excellent points, Alteveze. We have to realize the fact that the nation that made it illegal for us to read and write, that criminalized our education, will not now educate us—not unless they are educating us to destroy ourselves . . . Our education and our health care are *our* responsibilities.

"We also need to remove the sexual stigma from the disease because HIV/AIDS was not created in the genitals; it was created in a laboratory. What is more, sex is only 1 of its many routes of transmission. HIV/AIDS is not a punishment for having sex. Sex is a natural, healthy, necessary aspect of life; indeed, it is the source of life. Having a healthy sex life—no matter your sexual orientation—is as important as being holistically healthy.

"Being disgusted by sex and considering having sex an offense that merits punishment is only logical for a people who have a historical abhorrence for the life-making genitals: The hatred of the womb, vagina, menses, and to a lesser extent, the penis, testes, and semen, is the foundation of Christianity.

"We have to liberate our minds from their religious shackles to understand our genitals, bodies, and roles on this Earth and in the cosmos."

. . .

"The beast, that hates creation, thinks it's god. Alteveze, this country was founded by masons and deists. Freemasons worship Nimrod, the African architech who built the tower of Babel, and Solomon, the wisest man of his time, who was another African master architech. The deists believe god created the world and vamped and left them to oversee everything and everyone. Deism is 1 of the many ways by which these mutants have tried to justify their existence and their oppression and slaughter of billions of innocents.

"Caucasians created the construct of race in their attempt to make the *absence* of melanin, which is a genetic deficiency, the measure of excellence. But what motivates them, Alteveze, is the lack they feel and signify because of their melanin deficiency."

"Those without melanin specialize in oppressing and killing those with melanin. They also enslave bodies, and, more important, they chain minds. This is done via religious and cultural indoctrination. The beasts' ideological twisting and trapping have been so successful that many of us believe we have to be like the beast to succeed. Many of our leaders—heads of state, university professors, community leaders, and chiefs—actually surpass the beast in crushing minds and spirits."

"Those Tuskegee experiements went on under the mutual control of knee-grows and beast doctors, and there could be no slave master without slave catchers and factors," Alteveze noted.

"But morally bankrupt knee-grows didn't shoot whole communities of Africans into rivers because they lost the Civil War—confederate soliders did that. They didn't organize lynching bees. They did not create AIDS. So, while we often struggle to [better] our oppressors in oppressing, there is no comparison."

"It is also clear there is no limit to the methods the beast will devise to torture and kill African people and amputate our arc of existence. I want to share with you information from *Psychiatry's Betrayal*, an exposé published by the Citizen's Commission on Human Rights. It details numerous crimes against humanity that have gone unanswered:

"Margret Sanger, a eugenicist and the founder of Planned Parenthood of America proposed in 1939 a plan to stop the population growth of Africans in the U.S. Her plan to 'exterminate the Negro population' involved having Black ministers preach throughout the South that 'sterilization was a solution to poverty.' Sanger's objective and mission help us to put Planned Parenthood's mission and objective into proper perspective.

"*Pychiatry's Betrayal* also reveals that in the 1950s in New Orleans Black prisoners were used for psychosurgery experiments which involved electrodes being implanted into the brain. The experiments were conducted by psychiatrists Dr. Robert Heath from Tulane University and Australia's Dr. Harry Baily, who boasted in a lecture to nurses 20 years later that the 2 psychiatrists had used Blacks because it was 'cheaper to use niggers than cats because they were everywhere and cheap experimental animals.'"

"Peace unto you, brother. You're speaking with Nommo. . . ."

PART TWO

RESTITUTIONS, RESOLUTIONS, REVOLUTIONS

Why Baltimore Is Burning

Kevin Powell

I am from the ghetto. The first 13 years of my life I grew up in the worst slums of Jersey City, New Jersey, my hometown. If you came of age in one of America's poor inner cities like I did, then you know that we are good, decent people: in spite of no money, no resources, little to no services, run down schools, landpersons who only came around to collect rent, and madness and mayhem everywhere, amongst each other—from abusive police officers, and from corrupt politicians and crooked preachers—we still made a way out of no way. We worked hard, we partied hard, we laughed hard, we barbecued hard, we drank hard, we smoked hard, and we praised God, hard.

And we were segregated, hard, by a local power structure that did not want the ghetto to be seen nor heard from, and certainly not to bring its struggles out in plain sight for the world to see.

Indeed, my entire world was the block I lived on and maybe five or six blocks north south east west. A long-distance trip was going to Downtown Jersey City on the first of each month so our mothers—our Black and Latina mothers—could cash their welfare checks, buy groceries with their food stamps and, if we were lucky, we got to eat at Kentucky Fried Chicken or some other fast-food restaurant on that special day.

When I was about 15, I was badly beaten by a White police officer after me and a Puerto Rican kid had a typical boy fight on the bus. No guns, no knives—just our fists. The Puerto Rican kid, who had White skin to my Black skin, was escorted off the bus gingerly. I was thrown off the bus. Outraged, I said some things to the cop as I sat handcuffed in the back seat of a police car. He proceeded to smash me in the face with the full weight of his fist. Bloodied, terrified, broken in that moment, I would never again view most police officers as we had been taught as children: "Officer Friendly" —

Being poor meant I only was able to go to college because of a full financial-aid package to Rutgers University. I did not get on a plane until I was 24-years-old because of that poverty, and also because I did not know that that was something I could do. These many years later, I have visited every single state in America, every city big and small, and every ghetto community you can name. They all look the same.

Abandoned, burnt-out buildings. Countless churches, funeral parlors, barber shops, beauty salons, check-cashing places, furniture-rental stores, fried-chicken spots, and Chinese restaurants. Schools that look and feel more like prison holding cells for our youth than centers of learning. Playgrounds littered with broken glass, used condoms, and drug paraphernalia. Liquor stores here, there, everywhere. Corner stores that sell nothing but candy, cupcakes, potato chips, soda, every kind of beer you can name, loose cigarettes, rolling paper for marijuana, lottery tickets, and gum—lots and lots of gum.

Then there are also the local organizations that claim to serve the people, Black and Latino people. Some mean well, and are doing their best with meager resources. Others only come around when it is time to raise money, to generate some votes for one political candidate or another, or if the police have tragically killed someone.

Like Rekiya Boyd in Chicago. Like Miriam Carey in Washington, DC Like Tanisha Anderson in Cleveland. Like Yvette Smith in Texas. Like Aiyana Stanley Jones in Detroit. Like Eric Garner in New York City. Like Oscar Grant in Oakland. Like Walter Scott in South Carolina. Like Freddie Gray in Baltimore. . .

Yes, we have the first Black president in the White House but it feels like open season on Black folks in America once more. One hundred years ago this year, the Hollywood image machine was given a huge boost by a racist and evil film called "Birth of a Nation," a movie so calculating in the way it depicted Black people it set the tone, quite literally, for how we were portrayed and treated in every form of media for decades to come. One hundred years ago, it was common to see photos of African Americans, males especially, lynched, hung from trees, as the local good White folks visibly enjoyed their entertainment of playing hangman.

One hundred years later, "Birth of a Nation" has been replaced by a 24-hour-news media cycle still obsessed with race, racism, racial strife, racial violence, but no solutions and no action steps whatsoever, just pure sensationalism and entertainment. One hundred years later, the lynching photos have been replaced by cellphones capturing video of Walter Scott running away from a police officer, like a slow-footed character in a video game, only to be shot in the back—pop! pop! pop! pop! pop! pop! pop! pop!

Except all of this is mad real. Black people in America—the self-proclaimed greatest democracy on earth—are being shot here, there, everywhere, by the police, in broad daylight, with witnesses, sometimes on video. And with very few exceptions, nothing is happening to the cops who pulled the triggers. No indictments. No convictions. No prison time.

And every single time one of these scenarios occurs, we are handed the same movie script: Person of color is shot and killed by local police. Local police immediately try to explain what happened, while placing most of the blame, without full investigation, on the person shot. Police officer or officers who fired shots are placed on paid "administrative leave." Media finds any and everything they can to denigrate the character of the dead person, to somehow justify why she or he is dead. Marches, protests, rallies, speeches. Local police show up in military-styled "riot gear." Tensions escalate. Folks are arrested, people are agitated or provoked; all hell breaks loose. The attention has shifted from the police killing an innocent person to the violence of "thugs," "gangstas," "looters." The community is told to be nonviolent and peaceful, but no one ever tells the police they should also be nonviolent and peaceful. Whites in power and "respectable Black voices" call for calm, but these are the same folks who never talk about the horrific conditions in America's ghettoes that make any 'hood a time bomb just waiting for a match to ignite the fury born of oppression, marginalization, containment, and invisibility. These are the same people who've been spent little to no time with the poor.

If you aren't from the ghetto, if you have not spent significant time in the ghetto, then you would not understand the ghetto. . .

No matter. Big-time civil rights organizations, big-time civil rights spokespersons, and big-time church leaders are brought in to re-direct, control, and contain the energy from the people at the bottom. Started from the bottom now we here. . . But they really cannot, because the people have seen this movie a million times before. They know it is madness to be told to let justice take its course. They know it is madness to wait out a legal system that rarely if ever indicts and convicts these police officers who've shot and killed members of their community. They know it is madness to be told to stay cool, to be cool, when they have no healthy outlets for their trauma, their pain, their rage. They know it is madness to hear pundits and talking heads of every stripe on television and radio and via blogs analyze who they are, without actually knowing who they are. They know it is madness when middle-class or professional Black folks speak the language of the power structure and condemn the people in the streets instead of the system that created the conditions for why the people are in the streets. They know it is madness that so-called progressive, liberal, human-rights, or social-justice people of any race or culture have remained mightily silent as these police shootings have been going down coast to coast. And they know it is madness that most of these big-time leaders and big-time media only come around when there is a social explosion.

So they do explode, inside of themselves, and inside their communities. They would love to reach areas outside their 'hoods, but the local power structure blocks that from happening. So they destroy their own communities. I understand why. I am they and they are me. Any people with nothing to lose will destroy anything in their way. Like anything. Any people who feel as if their lives are not valued, like they are second-class citizens at best, will not be stopped until they've made their point. They, we, do not care if our communities have not rebounded from the last major American rebellions of the 1960s. We care that we have to live in squalor and misery and can be shot at any given moment by each other, or by the police, and no one seems to care. A rebellion, a riot, are pleas for help, for a plan, for a vision, for solutions, for action steps, for justice, for God, someone, anyone, to see our humanity, to do something.

Condemning them is condemning ourselves. Labeling the Baltimore situation a "riot" because it is mostly people of color is racist, given we do not call White folks behaving violently after major sporting events "rioters" or "thugs" or "gangstas," and Lord knows some White folks have destroyed much property in America, too. It ain't a democracy if White people can wild out and it is all good; but let people of color wild out and it becomes a state of emergency with the National Guard dropping in, armed and ready.

Black lives matter, all lives matter, equally. I believe that, I believe deeply in peace and love and nonviolence. I believe in my heart that we've got to be human and compassionate and civil toward one another, as sisters and brothers, as one human race, as one human family. I believe that our communities and police forces everywhere have to sit down and talk and listen as equals, not as enemies, to figure out a way toward life and love, not toward death and hate; a way toward a shared community where we all feel safe and welcomed and human.

Yes, I love people, all people. But I also believe in justice, for all people. And I know that what has been happening in America these past few years not remotely close to any form of justice, or equality. Imagine, if you will, White folks being shot and murdered by the police like this, what the reactions would be?

Imagine if George Zimmerman had gone vigilante on a White youth with a hoodie in that gated Florida complex. Imagine White parents having to teach their children how to conduct themselves if ever confronted by the police. Imagine that Aiyana Stanley Jones was a little 7-year-old White girl instead of a little 7-year-old Black girl, shot by the police as she slept on a sofa with her grandmother, in a botched raid? It would be a national outrage.

Baltimore is burning because America is burning with racism, with hate, with violence. Baltimore is burning because far too many of us are on the sidelines doing nothing to affect change, or have become numb as the abnormal has become normal. Baltimore is burning because very few of us are committed to real leadership, to a real agenda with consistent and real political, economic, and cultural strategies for those American communities most under siege, most vulnerable. Policing them to death is not the solution. Putting them in prison is not the solution. And, clearly, ignoring them is not the solution.

Citizens Defense Proposal

Teresa N. Washington and Muhammad Ibn Bashir

The Citizens Defense Proposal recommends legislation to prevent police officers from shooting and/or killing unarmed citizens. The proposal also recommends legislation to prevent police officers from benefiting or profiting in any way from the shooting and/or killing of unarmed citizens.

PREAMBLE

Every citizen of the United States of America is endowed with certain inalienable rights—the most important of which is "life." Officers of the law swear to protect and serve the citizens of the United States, and officers are entrusted with certain powers because of their positions. Officers of the law are the only public servants who, while undertaking their job duties, have the ability to end the lives of citizens of the United States of America. Many police officers have used the power granted them to carry out extrajudicial killings of unarmed citizens for suspected or even imagined crimes. This is unlawful and unconstitutional; it is a violation of the public trust and a violation of citizens' fundamental human rights.

Because of the powers and authority granted them, police officers must be held to the *highest* of standards as it regards human beings, human rights, and the taking of human life.

WE, THE CITIZENS OF THE UNITED STATES, PROPOSE THAT:

WHEREAS the taking of life is a permanent irrevocable act; and

WHEREAS unarmed African Americans are being killed by police officers at disproportionate rates; and

WHEREAS there is ample documentation revealing that police officers who kill unarmed citizens, especially those who are African American, routinely circumvent standard operating procedures, ignore citizens' rights, and deliberately escalate situations; and

WHEREAS police officers who shoot and/or kill unarmed citizens are rarely prosecuted for their crimes which gives the appearance that the laws of the United States of America do not apply to them or that lesser or subjective laws apply to them; and

WHEREAS police officers who shoot and/or kill unarmed African Americans are routinely placed on administrative leave—which is tantamount to a paid vacation—while their actions are reviewed by a panel of law enforcement officials whose objectivity is compromised; and

WHEREAS the shooting and/or killing of unarmed African Americans by police officers has been monetized through paid administrative leave and/or through crowdsourced donations;

1. any and every police officer who kills an unarmed citizen (via shooting, tasing, choking, "rough ride" in a police vehicle, or any other means) must be
   a. jailed **without pay** and
   b. held **without bail or bond** until he or she can prove beyond a reasonable doubt that the killing was justifiable homicide or a lesser charge; and
2. any and all monies raised for the police officer via social media or traditional channels, including fraternal police orders, must be held in escrow; and
   a. if it is found that the officer acted within the law and committed justifiable homicide or a lesser charge, the officer can be granted the money; however,
   b. if the officer is found guilty of murder or manslaughter or any charge greater than justifiable homicide, all monies must be given to the victim and/or the victim's family, who may also file a civil suit if they so desire; and
3. because any police officer who kills or assaults or abuses an unarmed person acts both under the color of the law and as an individual, in a civil action, the officer would be named as both a member of the state and sued as a member of the state as well as made personally liable.

Escaping a Prison Industrial Country: The Case for Quilombos

Teresa N. Washington

"It's time to build"

~ Dark Sun Riders
featuring Brother J

All the World's a Cell: The Globalization of Incarceration

America has always been a prison industrial country, and it is likely to remain such. Michelle Alexander's important book *The New Jim Crow* sparked outrage—and change. However, even with the hue and cry against the mass incarceration of Africana and Latino nonviolent offenders and the early release of many convicts, America simply makes too much money off of its variously promoted wars on melanin-rich peoples to appreciably alter its system. What is more, history reveals that a prison industrial system is an inherent aspect of the America's origin, character, and identity.

When England needed to reduce the populations of its swollen prisons, it decided to ship convicts to its two prison colonies. Between 1766 and 1866 Australia received over 160,000 dregs of English society and America received nearly 60,000. Given the pedigree of the bulk of its Caucasian inhabitants and the ways by which those individuals decimated America's native inhabitants and enslaved the Africans it trafficked to build America, it is not at all surprising that America's Caucasian controllers would make the penal system America's cornerstone, lifeblood, and capstone. What is more, it appears to be the case that Caucasians have been grooming Africans for an eternity of actual and virtual captivity.

In the 1400s, Caucasians from Portugal were sneaking to Africa's western coast and kidnapping and trafficking Africans. When Africans realized what was occurring and fought and defended themselves, the Portuguese declared "war on the blacks."[1] Yes, they declared war on a people for having the audacity to defend their right to enjoy their lives on their land and in their homes as they saw fit. Portugal's declaration of war was made in 1444 and was justified by papal bulls issued by the Vatican in 1442, 1444, and 1452. The Portuguese and Spaniards worked with the enslavers' chief religious-political ally, the Christian church, to drape with the veil of legitimacy, even righteousness, their desire to criminalize, incarcerate, and commoditize human beings.

With few exceptions, the pomp, honor, and regard given African chiefs and rulers from the late 1440s to the 1800s are but fluff. Every chief and king who struggled to make deals and curry favor with Caucasians knew that they could easily—no matter how many wars they sanctioned or villages they sacrificed—find themselves and their family, friends, and advisors processed, packed, and chained in the hold of a vessel of abomination bound for the Caribbean, America, France, Brazil, Portugal, England, or anywhere else capitalist Christian Caucasians decided to exploit human beings.

For Caucasians, Africa was not a Continent was filled with shining, thriving, intelligent, organized, industrious human beings; it was a land filled with captives awaiting capture. (This is why they termed part of Africa's western coast the "Slave Coast.") To help Africans understand and occupy their proper place in the world, Caucasians created "factors" of various ethnicities whose jobs were to raid villages and abduct people and to foment conflicts and hostilities that would net them prisoners of war who they would transport to "factories" Caucasians had built to undertake the difficult process of trying to turn human beings into slaves. The initial processing—or intake—consisted of beating, branding, stripping, oiling, raping, chaining, and packing, and was followed by imprisonment in the dungeons and holding cells of factories, which was followed by incarceration on ships, which was followed by incarceration in alien lands.

The "crime" the African captives committed was to have been endowed by their creators with melanin as deep as the cosmos and with intellectual, architectural, agricultural, political, and social genius to match: There were no people better suited to build what would become the world's most powerful and envied nation.

Caucasians needed African ingenuity to build in America the types of societies that Africans had erected in Africa. The civility and industry of African empires were so evolved that African children lived in states of delight, as the lyrics of the Yoruba song "Labe Igi Orombo" reveal:

Labe igi orombo	Beneath the orange tree
Nibe la gbe nsere wa	There, we gather and play
Inu wa dun	We are perfectly content
Ara wa ya	Our bodies are fulfilled
Labe igi orombo	Beneath the orange tree

It is hard to imagine a more perfect existence than relaxing with friends in the shade of an orange tree and enjoying the nutritious bounty that, on a mission to be shared and savored, falls into one's lap. This state of bucolic bliss must have stunned Caucasians who saw in these healthy, intelligent, glowing children footstools, lice pickers, cotton pickers, weed choppers, fanners, footwarmers, "pets," "favorites," and a pedophile's playground.

When the raids began, African children found they could no longer lounge under orange trees. As Olaudah Equiano details in his narrative, children had to climb trees and play sentry to protect themselves, their families, and their communities from roving factors, human harvesters.[2] For its previously privileged citizens, the African continent became a free-range pipeline to coastal prison-dungeons. At any moment, for no particular reason, Africans could be kidnapped, processed, sold, and made to sail to the mother of all prisons: America, where sentences are not merely for life but are generationally eternal.

Systematic Oppression: It's a Family Affair

When comparing American chattel slavery to America's prison industrial system it becomes clear that these two institutions are as close as father and son. Two texts that reveal the similarities of these systems of oppression are Albert Sample's autobiography *Racehoss: Big Emma's Boy* and Alex Haley's *Roots: The Saga of an American Family*. Although *Roots* is tainted by its plagiarism, it contains detailed information about the prison societies in which Haley's protagonist existed in Africa and in America.

Kunta Kinte's Africa is one of fleeting joys and unimaginable anxieties. He must always watch his back, front, and sides, lest he be captured. Indeed, when he eases his vigilance, Kunta is kidnapped. African Americans live in similar states of perpetual awareness, anxiety, fear, unease, or resignation because they know that at any time, for any reason or no reason at all, an "officer of the 'law'" may arrest and incarcerate them.

Just as convicts fashion and ferret away weapons for their defense, protection, and liberation, so too does Haley describe his protagonist secreting forks, knives, sticks—anything that may aid him and further his goal of liberation. What is more, Kunta is cognizant that a missing object may result in a search of the cabins of the enslaved—or a "tossing of bunks," in prison parlance.[3]

Kunta Kinte's enslavement resembles the captivity of a convict because America transitioned one system into the other. To better understand the purpose of the contemporary prison industrial complex and its oneness with slavery, it is helpful to read the thirteenth amendment to the United States' Constitution which decrees slavery illegal *except as a punishment for a crime*. The same amendment that is celebrated as a legal liberator serves as a legal enslaver via incarceration. This clause must be stricken from the Constitution, and America's complicit leaders should be indicted and tried in the International Criminal Court for crimes against humanity because— according to its own Constitution—America reigns as the longest-standing and most brutal and unrepentant enslaver and human trafficker in the world.

America's incarceration, enslavement, and monetization of Africans has been methodical and pathological. After the abolition of slavery, the United States created Black Codes. These state's rights laws were made specifically for Africana people, and they made everything from gathering in groups of three or more people, to seeking work without the approval of a, yes, "master," to merely looking at an object a crime.[4] The Black Codes were not only designed to restrict the newly minted freedoms granted in conceptual "emancipation" but, more importantly to racist capitalists, the Black Codes were constructed to give officers of the 'law' any excuse to arrest and incarcerate an Africana person. Even if an African American had committed no crime the state could still capture, incarcerate, and enslave him.

As Caucasians in America continued the work—arresting and enslaving Africans for profit—that they had been undertaking and overseeing in Africa, thousands of newly manumitted African Americans found themselves convicted and sent to a virtual penitentiary which could easily have been the actual plantation from which they had been "liberated."[5] As "convicts" they did the same work that they had done as "slaves" with the exception that the conditions were even more brutal than slavery. Because Africans were no longer classified as an individual's property, they became, ironically, a source of truly free labor in that Africans could be obtained without cost and be worked to death or be casually killed for not working because Caucasians could simply go outside and freely arrest, convict, incarcerate, and enslave any African man, woman, and child they saw.

Whether through their own misdeeds or the connivance of Caucasian oppressors, millions of African Americans have come to call prison home. Albert Sample's first stay in jail occurs when he is four-years-old. His mother, Big Emma, is confident that her sentence for bootlegging will be shorter if she does time with her son. She's right. After mother and son are placed in adjoining cells, Emma starts bawling. After Emma instructs Albert, "Don' let me do all the fuckin cryin an hollerin by myself," the duo's wails prompt their captors to free them.[6]

The rocky road Sample is born on leads straight to the penitentiary. From 1956 to 1972, Sample comes to know the rigors of American slavery courtesy of prison. While incarcerated on the Retrieve prison farm of the Texas State Prison system, Sample's work crew is headed by Boss "Kill-A-Band," who earned his title because he grew so enraged by the fact that his wife had an Africana convict as a lover, that he led his work crew or "band" out in the field and, while their backs were turned and hunched over rows of cotton, "He opened up wit dat pump scatter-barrel. He mowed 'em down, two an three atta time. Dem whut he didn' git wit dat scatter gun, he finished off wid his .45. Dey say he blowed suma dem nigguhs half in two. Holes in 'em big nuff to put yo' two fists in, all foteen uv 'em."[7]

Boss Band introduces himself to Sample and the other enslaved African Americans of the Texas State Prison system in the following manner:

> I'm gonna tell ya'll one time, an one time alone how I'm gonna deal. First off, if airy one uv you tries to run off, I'm gon' kill ya. If airy one uv you 'sputes my word, I'm gon' kill ya. If airy one uh you don' do lack I tell ya, I'm gon' kill ya. If you lay th' hammer down under me, I'm gon kill ya. And if I jes take a notion to, I'm gon' kill ya.[8]

In the customary Caucasian melding of vicious domination with religious hypocrisy and self-glorification, Boss Kill-A-Band makes every convict cry out, "Oh Lawd!" before addressing him. If anyone fails to say "Oh Lawd!" before asking or answering a question, Boss Band kills him.

Sample is so terrified of being killed while laboring under Boss Band that he earns the nickname "Racehoss" because he picks and chops cotton—and any other crop—faster than anyone else. He has to. Boss Band drives the men under his command to work so quickly and efficiently that he pits them against combines. Initially, when the men begin their race against the machines, the machines begin pulling away. After Boss Band fires a shot in the ground near Sample's feet, Sample and his colleagues beat the combines by thirty feet at the end of the first row and stayed twenty yards ahead of the combines throughout the rest of the day. John Henry and his "fool self" would have been proud.

Boss Band knows that the primary reason his forebears invested what today would be billions of dollars to abduct and traffic approximately 80 million Africans across the oceans and seas is because Caucasians sought to create an intelligent, capital-producing, self-regenerating labor force. In a telling scene in *Roots*, Kunta Kinte watches as the cotton and tobacco that he and other enslaved Africans have sown and reaped are taken to be sold to add to the vast wealth of the plantation owner and his family.

Slave labor continues to fuel the American economy. Indeed, inmates of the William C. Holman Correctional Facility in Alabama rose up in March 2016 specifically demanding that the slavery to which they are subjected be abolished.[9] In September 2016, the Free Alabama Movement, which was founded and is organized by inmates at Holman in conjunction with the Incarcerated Workers Organizing Committee, organized the "largest prison strike in history" to protest their enslavement.[10] In our modern era, Africans in America are literally fighting for and escaping to freedom with the same devotion, righteousness, and fury as Nat Turner, Frederick Douglass, Harriet Tubman, Boukman, and Zumbi.

America has also found ways to systematically target, hold captive, and commoditize Africana people who live in the "free" world. Police officers racially profile and undertake bogus traffic stops and stop-and-frisk searches of African Americans so that they can ticket and/or arrest their prey and thereby generate revenue to pay officers' salaries and to line the coffers of Caucasian-controlled state and local governments while maintaining America's slave population. Some municipalities have even created debtors prisons by arresting primarily Africana peoples on petty charges, such as poor yard upkeep, chipped house paint, and not wearing seat belts, and refusing to free them if they cannot pay the required fines and fees.[11]

When monetization is not desirable, maiming and killing are employed. Certain "law officers" thirst for the "sport" of killing Africana people. While modern-day lynchings are, perhaps, not as exhilarating as the hunt, chase, and ritual killings of traditional lynchings, Caucasians such as Koon et al. who leisurely and joyously battered a defenseless Rodney King, and Michael Slager, who shot Walter Scott in the back, as would a typical coward, describe the rush and incomparable satisfaction they derive from maiming and killing Africana people.

The Seeds of Our Fathers

In an Islamic State-inspiring scene in *Roots*, after Kunta Kinte is captured in his final escape attempt, his trackers make him chose between the amputation of his penis or of half of his foot. An appalled Kunta shields his genitals, and, in doing so, he sacrifices his ability to flee so that his progeny can continue the fight for the freedom that is their inherent right.

Here we stand—the progeny of the defiled, forgotten, dismembered, and disenfranchised. We are the living promise of our fathers' nurtured seeds, but are we any freer than our butchered fathers?

America promotes itself globally as a promise land, but the promise it keeps most consistently is incarceration. One could argue that Caucasians have relegated Native Americans to what could be considered an open-air penitentiary, the reservation. The "place" of Native Americans in a land that they once enjoyed freely is so accepted that if a Native American is said to have gone "off the reservation" he or she is understood to have threatened or harmed at least one Caucasian, which Caucasians consider going berserk. As it relates to Africans in America, racial profiling is so prevalent that America's melanin-endowed citizens could be said to exist in a virtual penitentiary in which one simply hopes to keep one's inevitable interactions with police and their administration of "justice" to a survivable minimum.

When one lives in a state of virtual incarceration one knows, even if only subconsciously, that it is only a matter of time before one enters a state of physical incarceration. One's actions or inactions have no impact on the relative freedom that one is permitted to enjoy because freedom is also a subjective and necessarily elusive construct in a prison-state. It may very well be the case that the concept of "freedom" came into existence after Caucasians had introduced multitudes around the world to the horrors of slavery.

Albert Sample asserts that every imprisoned person ponders escape, and if a prisoner does not hatch escape plans in his head—even if he quickly abolishes those plans—it is because the prisoner has become institutionalized. Institutionalization is one of the causes of America's high recidivism rate. However, I think the most insidious form of institution-alization is that which occurs when a people think that they are free but can envision no other life, or death, except that designed for them by an oppressive other. This type of institutionalization, which Asa Hilliard describes as conceptual incarceration,[12] is that in which all too many African Americans exist. Ironically because of the lies and propaganda that America uses to promote itself and bolster its global ego, millions of Africana people around the world have one dream—to be the most successful conceptual convicts in the world.

Freedom: At Home and Abroad

Africana people in America are, by far, the most profiled, patrolled, stereotyped, followed, interrogated, criminalized, and incarcerated of any people in this world. But there is no reason for Africana people to exist in states of cyclic conceptual or literal captivity. Africana people can look to their ancestors and follow their paths to liberation. One path leads to African-controlled nations including Haiti and many nations on the African continent. More African Americans than ever are repatriating to nations like Ghana, Nigeria, and Senegal where racial profiling is laughable and where freedom takes on dimensions that would astound the average African American. Imagine living in a nation in which the police couldn't care less about what you are wearing, the way you walk, what you are driving, or what may or may not be in your pockets. Imagine officers being friendly, even joking with you as they pass the time. Imagine seeing officers and even soldiers in full uniform and armed reading books in a café. Imagine only hearing sirens and seeing flashing lights when police are escorting a VIP or when they want to get somewhere in a hurry. Imagine life without speed-traps, roving helicopters, and bystander-killing high speed chases. Imagine enjoying life with no record.

Another path leads to all Africana towns, such as Mound Bayou, Mississippi; Eatonville, Florida; Oyotunji, South Carolina, and Grambling, Louisiana. There is nothing preventing African Americans, especially given the financial power that many enjoy, from fortifying and expanding existing and founding and incorporating new autonomous towns and cities which could be administered, policed, and maintained by the towns' Africana citizens. America is also dotted with both ghost towns and bankrupt and disappearing towns that anyone with purchasing power can literally buy and/or those with strength and skill can rejuvenate. There are more than enough Africana doctors, educators, attorneys, police officers, masons, carpenters, administrators, accountants, architects, veterans, agricultural engineers, plumbers, and auto and HVAC technicians to build, maintain, and defend thriving towns, cities, states, and nations.

Autonomy would mean hard work and cooperative organization. It would mean forsaking the individual ego for the fortification of the community. Autonomy would also mean the end of police brutality and police-enacted and state-approved lynchings. Autonomy would mean the end of gang violence, as individuals who are unfit to reside in freetowns would have to relocate. However, given the labor and struggle involved in building liberated nations, individuals who travel or lounge on flashy paths toward destruction would find little appealing in the proposed freetowns. These emancipated lands would not be utopias, of course, but they could bring African Americans out of our present states of ritual persecution, anxiety, terrorism, and fruitless protest and into states of security and holistic elevation.

An important segment of the population that could thrive in Africana freetowns is individuals who have been freed after paying their debts to society: Indeed, I originally drafted this essay when pondering ways to rehabilitate convicts in a manner that is respectful and empowering, as opposed to being cruel and inhuman. In freetowns, former inmates could earn honest and lucrative livings through carpentry, writing, electrical engineering, performing, construction, farming, any number of vocations. They would have no tale-tell boxes to check and they would be able to vote for their leaders and run for office. Ex-convicts would not be known for their former convictions and incarceration would be simply free citizens of a free land, like everyone else.

Freetowns could also be structured to ensure that employees earn living wages and parents are able to create "living schedules" that are structured around their children's and family's needs as opposed to the demands of some oppressive employing entity. Citizens of freetowns would also be able to build on the drive for holistic and relevant education that is sweeping many regions of the African world and build institutions of education that prepare graduates for success on *their* terms, as conscious and free African-centered scholars and professionals, as opposed to the life of cyclic stress and struggle endured by those Fela Anikulapo Kuti in his song "Perambulator" termed "certified slaves."[13]

During a research trip through the south, I traveled to Mound Bayou, Mississippi and was inspired to learn that in the 1920s–1960s Mound Bayou was a haven for persecuted African Americans. When the Klan or any of its offshoots was lusting for Africana blood, hunted individuals would flee to Mound Bayou and the citizens would shelter and protect them. Africana people could put that same force of protective empowerment to work in the guarding, supporting, and protecting of our own citizens in our own towns and cities. When feasible, our enclaves could be gated and guarded 24 hours to ensure residents are safe from state police, hate groups, and other terrorizing agents.

. . .

Quilombos are autonomous militarized communities founded by free Africans. Carlos Diegues' lush film *Quilombo* depicts the legendary enclave of Palmares, which rose as a symbol of Black Autonomous Power in the heart of an oppressive Brazil. The word Quilombo is from the Kimbundu language of Angola, but the concept is Pan-African. During the era of slavery, one could find Quilombos in every enslaving land: from the American states of Florida, South Carolina, and Louisiana; to the Maroon Towns of Jamaica, Surinam, and Mexico; from the Palenques of Colombia; to the Cimarrons of Panama. History reveals that wherever Africans were oppressed, groups of revolutionaries took their freedom and built autonomous militarized oases.

Africana people of all walks of life could work together and establish contemporary Quilombos in America, Nigeria, England, France—anywhere we live and need peace and protection. Indeed, the only impediments that I can think of are the grandstanding, pettiness, jealousy, superficiality, selfishness, egotism, and "hating" in which all too many of us throughout the African world are inundated. These impediments lead straight to destruction, as Toni Morrison reveals in her novel *Paradise*. However the choices that we face are simple: We can continue to live among racist oppressors and accept the treatment they decide to mete out, or we can erect gated, guarded, autonomous, incorporated cities and nations of our own, just as we built Napata, Kush, Kemet, Ghana, Songhai, Mali, and Zimbabwe, and countless other empires. With the resources and intelligence that the African world boasts, there is no reason for us to subject ourselves to police brutality and lynching, racist miseducation, racist medical treatment, neoslavery, and debtors prisons.

It is time we stop singing, begging, marching, and praying and begin building, fortifying, and flourishing in worlds worthy of our forebears, our progeny, and ourselves. Given the genetic and intellectual resources with which we are endowed, if we continue to suffer at the hands of our oppressors, as the legendary Fela Anikulapo Kuti declares, "Now, [our] fault be that!"[14]

Notes

[1] Baffour Ankomah, "Slavery: Africa's Case," *New African*, September 1999 <http://www.hartford-hwp.com/archives/30/144.html> accessed 15 April 2016.

[2] Olaudah Equiano, "from *The Interesting Narrative of the Life of Olaudah Equiano, or Gustavus Vassa, the African*," in *Crossing the Danger Water*, edited by Deirdre Mullane (New York: Anchor, 1993), 8–9.

[3] Alex Haley, *Roots: The Saga of an American Family* (New York: Dell, 1976), 250.

[4] "Chain Gangs," *History's Mysteries* (The History Channel, 2000).

[5] "Chain Gangs," *History's Mysteries*.

[6] Albert Race Sample, *Racehoss: Big Emma's Boy* (New York: Ballantine, 1984), 44.

[7] Sample, *Racehoss*, 207.

[8] Sample, *Racehoss*, 208.

[9] "Prison slavery: Alabama inmates strike over awful conditions, unpaid work," *RT*, 12 May 2016 <https://www.rt.com/usa/342844-alabama-prison-strike-conditions/> accessed 23 June 2016.

[10] Hanna Kozlowska, "US prisoners are going on strike to protest a massive forced labor system," *Quartz*, 09 September 2016 <http://qz.com/777415/an-unprecedented-prison-strike-hopes-to-change-the-fate-of-the-900000-americans-trapped-in-an-exploitative-labor-system/> accessed 09 September 2016. You can read the Free Alabama Movement manifesto at <https://supportprisonerresistance.noblogs.org/post/2016/04/01/announcement-of-nationally-coordinated-prisoner-workstoppage-for-sept-9-2016/> accessed 09 September 2016.

[11] See Whitney Benns and Blake Strode, "Debtors Prison in 21st Century America," *The Atlantic*, 23 February 2016 <http://www.theatlantic.com/business/archive/2016/02/debtors-prison/4623 78/> accessed 14 April 2016. The Arch City Defenders of St. Louis, Missouri are prosecuting municipalities that are running debtors prisons. Hopefully, their model will inspire liberation-minded lawyers across the nation to do the same. (See Brenda Breslauer, "Lawsuit Charges 13 St. Louis Suburbs with 'Extorting' Black Drivers," *NBC News*, 10 August 2016 <http://www.nbcnews.com/storyline/michael-brown-shooting/lawsuit-charges-13-st-louis-suburbs-extorting-black-drivers-n625666> accessed online 10 August 2016.)

[12] Anthony Browder, *Nile Valley Contributions to Civilization: Exploding the Myths*, volume 1 (Washington, DC: Institute of Karmic Guidance, 1992), 21.

[13] Fela Anikulapo Kuti and Egypt 80, "Perambulator" (*Perambulator*, Lagos International Records, 1983).

[14] Fela Anikulapo Kuti, "Shuffering and Shmiling" (*Shuffering and Shmiling*, Coconut, 1977).

Education for Liberation in Black Africa

Chinweizu

> "The major function of education
> is to help secure the survival of a people"
>
> ~ Amos Wilson[1]

> "Know yourself, know your enemy;
> and in a hundred battles you will never be defeated"
>
> ~ Sun Tzu[2]

> "Our youth from the primary schools, through the secondary
> schools to the universities and higher institutions of learning, . . .
> must be taught to know the workings of neo-colonialism
> and trained to recognize it wherever it may rear its head.
> They must not only know the trappings of colonialism
> and imperialism, but they must also be able to
> smell out the hide-outs of neo-colonialism."
>
> ~ Kwame Nkrumah[3]

I wish to make some observations and raise some questions that should, I hope, help us to design an education system that would help us to build a Black Africa that is liberated from imperialism, neo-colonialism, powerlessness, and from the world's contempt—a Black Africa that has a technologically robust culture; is autonomous in its economy, culture and politics; and is prosperous and Afrocentric.

I submit that for a people to be truly liberated, they must be powerful, and powerful enough to deter or defeat any attempts, by anyone whatsoever, to impose on them in any way. In other words, they must be truly sovereign; i.e. they must be able to conduct their affairs independently, without outside interference. For Black Africa to be truly liberated, it must have at least one superpower among its countries, a superpower that will serve as the core state (leader and protector) of the whole Black World.

PART 1: SOME QUESTIONS TO PONDER

A1] Is Black Africa liberated?

The short answer is no! Let me explain by commenting on some key aspects of our far-from-liberated situation of today.

We are not politically liberated: we belong to the "Commonwealths," "Communities," and "Leagues" of Europeans and Arabs; and especially to the UN which was set up, and still operates, as a syndicate of imperialisms led by the USA. The budgets of our countries are heavily subsidized by Western and Arab donors, thus giving the Western and Arab imperialists the controls to dictate our policies. Our NGOs and CSOs are also funded by the Western and Arab "donors," thus compromising their autonomy.

We are not socially independent: their NGOs have unfettered and unsupervised access to even the remotest villages in our rural areas.

We are not culturally or mentally independent: we are ruled by the ideologies and religions of Europeans and Arabs; their music, ideas and images dominate our airwaves and our minds. Their cultural missionaries and the evangelists of their religions are everywhere—on TV, on radio, in schools, in village meetings—subtly instilling in our minds the subversive and anti-African idea that anything African is inherently inferior, degraded and evil. Their books, their movies, their newspapers and media shape our values and desires; our social reform parrots echo their fads and denounce patriarchy, homophobia, circumcision, etc; our languages, our architecture, our literature, are becoming more and more Europeanized; our governance institutions and norms imitate European and Arab models; our discourse is saturated with Neo-Liberal concepts, prescriptions and jargon like transparency, public private partnership, global best practices, training in entrepreneurship, NGO, CSO, Freedom of Information, stakeholders, human rights defenders (i.e. missionaries), HIPCs, MDGs, and poverty alleviation; the minds of some Black Africans are controlled by Arab concepts like jihad, sharia, kaffir, dhimmi, jizyah, zakat. Yet we lie to ourselves and say we have become free from Europe and Arabia. But are you free from the person who thinks for you and controls your mind and aspirations?

Dessalines mockingly pointed out to the Haitians in 1804 about the French:

> our laws, our customs, our cities, everything bears the charac-
> teristics of the French . . . and you believe yourselves free and
> independent of that Republic![4]

The same could be pointed out about the influence of Europeans and Arabs in Africa today.

A2] Should Black Africa be liberated?

Why not? Why must we remain any longer under the thumb or boot of others? Why must we allow ourselves to continue to suffer the contempt of the other races of humanity? Why should we deny ourselves the material and psychological benefits of being a powerful people? We must understand that without liberation, Black Africa will not achieve prosperity or power or self-respect, let alone the respect of the world. And Black Africans will not savor the material and psychological satisfactions that only prosperity and power can give.

For example: why should each Black person not gain self-respect as a member of a powerful race; or lose the inferiority complexes and insecurities that undermine the confidence and life performance of black people? And why should we not experience the quiet confidence that comes with knowing you can defend yourself and your loved ones against all comers? Others sense this confidence without any immediate proof. If they know there are people in your race with that capacity, they automatically wonder if you are one of them, and give you the benefit of the doubt. Their caution is warranted, for your weakness can then not be taken for granted, as it presently is, and will continue to be for as long as your black skin is indisputably a badge of your membership of a group that's afflicted with chronic powerlessness.

A3] What should a liberated Black African society be like?

A liberated Black African society is one in which the Black population is in full charge of all its affairs, internal and external—from growing enough food to feed its population to making the armaments that enable it to defend its territory. The people should not feel subservient to any other people on earth, and should have no inferiority complexes. They should feel confident that their prosperity and autonomy cannot be destroyed by any other people.

A4] Have we significantly de-Europeanized, de-Arabized and re-Africanized our institutions?

Not at all! After 50 years, our laws, our customs, our cities, everything bear the characteristics of European colonizers. Our administrative, judicial, military, educational institutions and their procedures have not significantly deviated from those implanted by the colonizers. We have followed the European fashion in every aspect of life. When they sponsored military government, we went along. When they changed their mind and demanded electocracy, we went along, and dutifully imported constitutions and legislative institutions that imitated those in Paris, London, and Washington.

In the case of the Arabs, Black Africans in several countries are insisting on imposing Arab Sharia on themselves and other Africans; and even resort to war and terrorism to do so.

In popular culture, we have imitated the break dance, hip hop, sagging pants, and whatever else we saw was fashionable in Europe or America. Hence we are, on the whole, drowning in European culture more deeply than 50 years ago. Just as Fanon predicted, our lumpen-bourgeois, "caste has done nothing more than take over unchanged the legacy of the economy, the thought, and the institutions left by the colonialists."[5]

A5] Have we significantly de-Europeanized and re-Africanized our colonial education systems and curriculums?

Let us find out through answering a few questions:

Do our schools make us proficient in our African mother-tongues? Do they ground us in our African heritage? Do they steep us in the myths, legends, proverbs, ethical and aesthetic values bequeathed by our ancestors; or in the cosmological and philosophical assumptions of our ethnic groups? Do they teach and commend the African architectural, agricultural and ecological wisdom that our ancestors harvested in the course of millennia of living in Africa? The obvious answer to each of the above questions is NO! In not doing these things, our education is still colonial. In 50 years, no conscious campaign has been made to change the colonial character of our education. If anything, change has been in the other direction. For example, within the last two decades, European and American universities have opened branches in Black African countries, and are disseminating their view of the world among us. So we still produce Black Africans who are fascinated with European ways, who are mindlessly obedient servants of Europe; who are filled with inferiority complexes; who are culturally de-Africanized, Europhiles, and Afrophobic, just like those produced by colonial schools.

A6] What kind of education must we institute to re-Africanize our cultures?

If we claim we are still African, then how are we relating to our African heritage? Are we shaped by it through an education that, in the words of the 17th century Songhay scholar Abderrahman es-Sadi, "tells men of their fatherland, their ancestors, their annals, the names of their heroes and what lives these led.'"?[6]

Furthermore, if indeed we are still Africans, we need to teach and dialogue with our pre-colonial Black African heritage. For our lives today, we need to draw inspiration from the entire Black African legacy. We need to learn from all extant Black African works: starting with works from Ancient Egypt and on through the epics, proverbs and wisdom texts of non-Islamic, non-Christian 19th century Black Africa. Are we constantly dialoging with African culture? What do I mean by that? Let Maulana Karenga explain:

> For us, Africa, more specifically ancient Africa, is our moral ideal, the foundation and framework on which and within which we understand ourselves and the world, conceive our purpose and obligations in life, ground our hopes and forge our future in effective and expansive ways. We take seriously [Malcolm X's] teaching that even if we can't or don't go back to Africa physically, we should go back mentally, spiritually and culturally. And this is not to escape into the past or to neglect the real challenges of the present or avoid decisions that will determine our future. Rather, it is to ground and center ourselves in our own culture and to extract from it models and messages of human excellence and achievement and to use them to confront and solve problems and to enrich and expand our lives. It is not an uncommon practice for persons to consult ancient texts for grounding and guidelines for how they live their lives. It is only with ancient African texts that some question the value and validity of the practice. Indeed, every day people read ancient texts of Greece, Rome, Palestine, Israel, Arabia, India and elsewhere for insight, inspiration and grounding. And we have read and read them too, but with Cheikh Anta Diop we ultimately ask what does Africa have to say about this or that critical issue? . . . In Kawaida philosophy, we call this dialoging with African culture, asking it questions and seeking from it answers to the fundamental concerns and issues of humankind."[7]

Unless our education introduces us to these African texts—and they don't as yet—we will not be in a position to dialogue with them and harvest and apply their wisdom.

A7] We have talked much about unity but done little to forge it. How do you unite people?

What kind of education forges a sense of oneness in a population?

According to Cheikh Anta Diop, you give them a shared history, a shared culture, a shared language and values. If you don't do that, you can put them under one government and they'll still be disunited. Look at Sudan. It is under one government, but its different sections have been fighting to get away, some for more than 50 years. Why? Though all are black, some accept that they are culturally African; others deny they are African and claim they are Arabs, because they have imbibed Arab culture. Hence there is no proper cultural basis for unity in Sudan.

In addition to a shared culture, you give them a shared historical project working together at which gives them a feeling that they are one team.

A8] What are the flaws of the neo-colonial education we have entrenched?

These are the same as the flaws of colonial education. A primary flaw was that colonial education was focused on producing clerks and other auxiliaries for the colonizers, and was not focused on educating creative economic producers of necessary goods and services for the colonized Africans. Furthermore, under colonialism Africans were educated so that they could be better Europeanized and enslaved. As Governor Cameron of Tanganyika put it in the 1920s, the intention [of colonial schooling]

> was that the African should cease to think as an African and instead should become "a fair minded Englishman."
>
> ~ Governor Cameron of Tanganyika[8]

Likewise,

> a French ordinance of 1899 indicated that the purpose of schooling in Madagascar was: ". . . to make the young Malagasy faithful and obedient subjects of France . . ." [and] in 1919, Henry Simon (then Colonial Minister) outlined a program for secondary education in Africa with a view to "making the best indigenous elements into complete Frenchmen."[9]

Furthermore,

> the colonial education corrupted the thinking and sensibilities of the African and filled him with abnormal complexes.
>
> ~ Abdou Moumini[10]

Accordingly,

> those who were Europeanized were to that extent de-Africanized, as a consequence of the colonial education and the general atmosphere of colonial life. . . . Unfortunately, the colonial school system educated far too many fools and clowns, fascinated by the ideas and way of life of the European capitalist class. Some reached a point of total estrangement from African conditions and the African way of life, and like Blaise Diagne of Senegal they chirped happily that they were and would always be "European."
>
> ~ Walter Rodney[11]

In the colonial period,

> being educated meant, in the eyes of the populace, an escape from the visible and perceived backwardness of traditional life and society.
>
> ~ Kwesi Prah[12]

As Samuel Chiponde of Tanganyika put it in 1925,

> to the African mind, to imitate Europeans is civilization.[13]

Now, 50 years from 1960, we have achieved neither the disappearance of colonialism nor the disappearance of the colonized African. Our task remains to achieve both. And the job of disappearing the colonized African belongs primarily to our education system.

However, and unfortunately till today, our education does not question the beliefs fostered among us by imperialism; does not liquidate the ideas put forward by imperialism to influence us in its favor. Our education induces uncritical admiration for everything White (European or American or Arab); our education, through the school, the church, the mosque and the media, teaches reverence for whites and their culture; it subliminally teaches that the white man is god; that Arabic is the language of god; that the white man is the true or real man. As a Fanti saying, from colonial times, expressed it: "Bronyi ara na oye nyimpa"; literally "the white is indeed human," which is to say that the white man is the model or archetype of humanity and, by implication, that the blacks are not quite it, don't measure up. We behave as if we still believe in this tenet from the colonial era. We seem to have "no greater desire than to resemble the white man as far as possible,"[14] culturally, and even physically.

Furthermore,

A9] Does our neo-colonial education teach us how to face the perils of today; or how to create our own future; or prepare us to face the perils of the future?

It does not. It does not even teach us the perils of the past. And that is why our worldview is still pro-imperialist. We still talk of the "Slave Trade" instead of "The Great Chattelization War."[15] We still think that colonialism brought us the gift of civilization; think colonialism is over. Not knowing of the perils in our past, we can't imagine there could be any perils today or in future. Not knowing of the enemies who enslaved us in the past, our youth don't know our enemies of today. The idea that we could have enemies is strange to them. They think of the imperialists as our generous and benevolent "development partners"; they think that race doesn't matter and shouldn't matter; they are desperate to escape to a benevolent Europe or America or Arabia in search of golden opportunities.

If you think you don't have enemies, you have no motivation to change or reorganize your life to meet the danger an enemy represents. You are then liable to take no thought for your future. Without a perceived danger to stimulate you, why should you bother to prepare to face any perils? You have little incentive to think of a different future, let alone plan for it.

PART 2: PRINCIPAL FLAWS
IN OUR NEO-COLONIAL EDUCATION

It is said that "by their fruits ye shall know them." Let us therefore judge the failings of our neo-colonial education system by the behavior of its products:

B1] *It doesn't teach us loyalty to our race, the Black race:* That is why a grown up Nigerian Muslim could say:

> I am a Muslim and I worship Allah and I follow the way of the Prophet Muhammad (peace be upon him). I have no relationship with you, except that your skin is black. The lightest Arab is closer to me than you. If there were to be war between Muslims of any shade of color and the darkest of black people, I will be on the side of Muslims.
>
> ~ Najib Bilal[16]

B2] *It doesn't teach us racial solidarity:* That is why we have been unconcerned, and have shown no outrage at—let alone tried to do something to stop—the current torture of Haiti by the USA, France, and their UN, a torture which has been going on for the last three decades, since President Aristide was first deposed by a coup in 1991; that is also why we did not rally to help the African peoples of South Sudan when for half a century, 1955–2011, they were struggling to free themselves from the Arab colonialist oppressors in Khartoum; and we have not rallied to defend the African peoples of Darfur who, for decades now, have been under military attack by Arab expansionists and ethnic cleansers.

B3] *It doesn't teach us that we as a people have enemies, let alone who our enemies are;* in particular, it doesn't teach us that the Arabs and Europeans are our enemies, and have been so for thousands of years. That, for instance, is why we embrace the Europeans as our "development partners" despite their success in diverting us from pursuing industrialization policies, and despite their pressuring us to sign Economic Partnership Agreements (EPAs) that will push African, Caribbean and Pacific (ACP) countries deeper into poverty, and negatively affect the livelihoods of people living in ACP countries. In other words these EPAs are instruments of economic war on the ACP countries, yet we refuse to see that those imposing them on us—those using them to make economic war on us, are our enemies.

B4] *It doesn't teach us how the world is structured and functions against us:* That is why we are not suspicious of the UN and of its key agencies such as the World Bank, the IMF, the WTO and the WHO. By the way, the WHO, World Health Organization, during its smallpox eradication campaign in the 1970s, vaccinated 97 million Black Africans with HIV-contaminated vaccines and thereby brought AIDS to Black Africa.[17] Being unsuspicious of these UN agencies, we naively still seek guidance and take orders from them.

B5] *It doesn't teach us how to triumph against the forces arrayed against us.*

B6] *It doesn't teach us about ourselves and how to overcome our weaknesses.*

B7] *It doesn't teach us who we are as a people, and how we came to be in the despised condition in which we find ourselves in the world.*

B8] *It doesn't teach us why there are no jobs in our country for the teeming millions of our youth,* or what we must do to create jobs for everybody: That is why our governments have no inkling about what to do to end the situation.

B9] *It doesn't teach us why we stay poor despite our abundant resources.*

B10] *It doesn't teach us how we can make our country and Black Africa prosperous and powerful.*

B11] *Our education does not teach economic patriotism:* That is why our leaders loot and plunder our countries and export the loot abroad, to "safe havens" in Europe, America and Arabia.

B12] *It doesn't teach us to defend our country and our race from every form of attack; let alone how to do so.*

B13] *It doesn't teach us about our enemies and how they have been defeating and exploiting us for centuries.*

B14] *Our neo-colonial education doesn't give us an understanding of the world in which we live, and of how it came to be the way it is.*

B15] *It does not equip us with a world picture—a global-political picture of the way the world is structured, and how it functions, and our Black World's place within it—let alone an understanding of how the world is rigged against us.* If it supplies any coherent global-political picture at all, it is the vague pro-imperialist picture in which the UN system is presented, quite falsely, as serving the interest of all of humanity rather than just the imperialist interest. But actually, any interest of the rest of humanity that the UN happens to serve is just an unintended byproduct of its serving the imperialist interests, like crumbs that fall off the master's table that beggars can stuff their mouths with, even though the feast was not organized for them.

B16] *Its cardinal failure is that it leaves us oblivious of global power realities.* In particular, it doesn't teach us that those who have vital and highly desired assets, but lack the power to defend those assets, are prone to exploitation and even extermination by the powerful.

Specifically, it has failed to acquaint us with what Marcus Garvey taught a century ago:

> The attitude of the white race is to subjugate, to exploit, and if
> necessary exterminate the weaker peoples with whom they come in
> contact. They subjugate first, if the weaker peoples will stand for it;

then exploit, and if they will not stand for SUBJUGATION nor EXPLOITATION, the other recourse is EXTERMINATION.[18]

And Garvey further elaborated:

When the colonists of America desired possession of the land, they saw that a weak aboriginal race was in their way. What did they do? They got hold of them, killed them, and buried them underground. This is a fair indication of what will happen to the weaker peoples of the world in another two or three hundred years when the stronger races will have developed themselves to the position of complete mastery of all things material. They will not then, as they have not in the past, allow a weak and defenceless race to stand in their way, especially if in their doing so they will endanger their happiness, their comfort and their pleasure. These are the things that strike the thoughtful Negro as being dangerous, and these are the things that cause us who make up the Universal Negro Improvement Association to be fighting tenaciously for the purpose of building up a strong Negro race, so as to make it impossible for us to be exterminated in the future to make room for the stronger race, even as the North American Indian has been exterminated to make room for the great white man on the North American continent.[19]

Furthermore,

B18] *Our education doesn't teach us that the Arabs and Europeans are our cardinal enemies.*

As Chancellor Williams concluded after documenting the facts:

The whites are the implacable foe, the traditional and everlasting enemy of the Blacks . . . The necessary re-education of Blacks and a possible solution of racial crises can begin, strangely enough, only when Blacks fully realize this central fact in their lives: The white man is their Bitter Enemy. For this is not the ranting of wild-eyed militancy, but the calm and unmistakable verdict of several thousand years of documented history.[20]

Not only are the Arabs and Europeans our enemies. We actually have been subjugated and are under pressure from their rival imperialisms. Each has implanted its culture among us and secured the allegiance of Black Africans. The Europeans have done so through colonialism and the modern technology and the European institutions and values, as well as the Christianity, Liberalism, and Marxism that colonialism brought in its train.

The Arabs have done so principally through the Arab religion, Islam, through which some Black Africans have come under the domination of the ideology and institutions of Arab imperialism.

The above are some of the fundamentals we must know about our global-political environment if we are to organize ourselves to survive as a people in this world. And yet the education system we inherited half-a-century ago from the European colonialists, and have foolishly retained, does not supply us with such knowledge. What good is an education that keeps us blind to reality, that alienates us from our group, that fails to teach us our basic interests? Have you educated a child if you don't teach him about the situation he is in; or about the geography of his town; or about the snakes and scorpions and mosquitoes that abound in his environment; or about the habits and tricks of the liars and thieves and armed robbers that he will meet every day?

As we need to know all these things in order to survive as a race, needless to say, we need to create the type of education that will teach us all these things, and more.

Political education, education about our global-political environment, is indispensable. Without it, we are like a farmer who does not know his soil, his crops and the weather under which he farms; like a hunter who knows nothing about the behavior of the animals he encounters; like a plane whose crew know nothing about the sky and the weather through which they fly.

PART 3: KNOWING OURSELVES

In addition to not knowing the world in which we live, we also do not know ourselves. In particular, we do not know our weaknesses, weaknesses which our enemies have studied and still exploit to get their way with us. As Cabral correctly insisted: "One type of struggle we regard as fundamental is . . . *the struggle against our own weaknesses.*"[21]

We therefore need to admonish ourselves:
Black Man, Know thyself; study your weaknesses and get rid of them!

We must ruthlessly eliminate all the traits in our character and in our culture that enable others to dominate our race. Below are some cultural flaws we must fix by education if we want to get and stay liberated, flaws that have made us easy prey for Arab and European predators for the past two millennia.

Here are some of the traits that must go:

C1] We are not a suspicious race:
As Steve Biko pointed out: "We are not a suspicious race. We believe in the inherent goodness of man."[22] We have to stop being naïvely trusting. We need to learn, as John Le Carré said somewhere, that "survival is an infinite capacity for suspicion."

C2] We cling to unreal ideas about existence and who we are:
Mollie West, in a 2009 email, said:

> It's hard to believe how (forgive my language) fucked up many of us are in our heads. I no longer wonder why we haven't achieved liberation as a group. *We cling to unreal ideas about existence and who we are.*[23]

C3] We're humane to the world and yet traitors when it comes to one another:
Mollie West also observed that "black people are the biggest stumbling block to their own liberation. We're humane to the world and yet traitors when it comes to one another. It's madness."[24]

C4] We are too religious:
As Steve Biko pointed out: "Africans are a deeply religious race."[25] And Mollie West elaborated:

> Somehow Blacks have the strange notion that "everything will fall into place for them if they just pray." Ha! Prayer certainly has its place, but we've been complacent for far too long now, and if the end came tomorrow for us as a people, I wouldn't be surprised one iota. I'd say, "We had enough time!"[26]

C5] Our craziness and gullibility:
As Amos Wilson diagnosed, we are a crazy and gullible people:

> In order for us as a people to be in the situation we are in, and not be in concentration camps and not have guns pointed at our heads throughout the day, we must be maintained in a particular state of mind. In a sense then, we literally must be out of our minds—and we must be kept out of our minds.[27]

Wilson continues, asserting, "Our mentality has been reversed and our behavior made backwards because we take the lie for the truth, and the truth for the lie."[28]

We won't even accept the fact that the Arabs are not part of us, let alone that they are our permanent enemies. And as Mollie West perceptively said, we "cling to unreal ideas about existence and who we are." Such are the attributes of crazy Niggers. And while we cling to our maladaptive nigger behavior, we want to stop being called niggers; we want to be respected and treated as equals by the sane sections of humanity! No way!!

C6] Our fatalistic patience, especially under misrule:
Another of our Afrocidal traits is a fatalistic patience, especially under misrule. General Jan Smuts, that white supremacist promoter of imperialist Pan-Africanism, declared in 1930 "that the black man's patience was one of the world's marvels [and] second only to the ass's."[29]

Any shortlist of our weaknesses must include what Nkrumah described as
C7] "a lack of malice, an absence of the desire for vengeance for our wrongs."[30] Though Nkrumah seems to regard this as among the admirable traits of the African Personality, we need to take a critical look at it, for it is, in fact, Afrocidal. And we would be suicidal to treat as admirable something that is killing us.

Other observers have described it more candidly and in more revealing detail. For example, an American reporter, David Lamb, after five years traveling and observing Africans in 48 countries during the late 1970s, said:

> Given all he has had to endure from the beginning of slavery to the end of colonialism, the African displays a racial tolerance that is nothing short of amazing. He holds no apparent grudge against the European as an individual, and it is rare indeed for any white person to experience even the slightest indignity because of his color. . . . The African has forgiven, if not forgotten.[31]

As a white settler in Kenya, a former hunter of Mau Mau freedom fighters, explained to Lamb:

> Why has it been forgotten? Well, partly I think, because the African isn't capable of the depth of emotion that the European has. He doesn't love his women or hate his enemies with the same intensity. You look at a good solid white hatred and it can last for generations. Africans don't hate that way.[32]

But, on the other hand, Lamb notes:

> For a people who have had to tolerate so many injustices over the centuries, yet have remained basically gentle, polite and racially equitable, I was constantly shocked to see the cruelty, even sadism, that Africans inflict on one another so willingly.[33]

And he wondered what makes the African "a fatalist, intent on his own survival but caring little for those who are less fortunate."[34]

Likewise, from Canada in the 1980s, another investigator, O. McKague, reported:

> As one female member of the Nationalist party told me, one can treat blacks like dirt for years, cease such treatment, and almost immediately they are willing to be your best friends. This, she explained, is because blacks do not have the capacity either to feel injustices or to remember them. Jews, she stated, are quite a different [matter].[35]

This obscene rush to forgive and forget even the most grievous wrong, provided it is done to us by the white enemy, was most publicly exhibited in Archbishop Desmond Tutu's Truth and Reconciliation Commission which, quite sacrilegiously, placed on the same moral level both the violence of the Apartheid oppressors and the counter violence of those who fought their oppressors! The armed aggressor violence of the Apartheid state criminals who inflicted the Sharpeville and other massacres and who murdered Steve Biko was treated as no different morally from the unarmed, defensive counter violence of the children of the Soweto uprising. *Tutu's approach is as obscene as condemning equally for violence the soldier's hand that is strangling a baby and the milk teeth by which the baby tries to bite off the strangler's hand!*

In addition to the explanation proffered in Kenya to David Lamb by a white-settler, ex-hunter of May Mau freedom fighters, we should consider another possible contributory factor to our alleged "lack of malice, and absence of the desire for vengeance for our wrongs." Seeing as this lack of vengefulness is shown only towards the powerful whites, but is rarely extended to our fellow blacks, isn't it possible that it is simply fear that restrains us from seeking vengeance for wrongs done to us by the whites? After taking a crippling beating from whites, what but an even more devastating beating can we expect if we tried to exact revenge? In which case it would be prudent to banish from our mind any thought of seeking vengeance. If so, this trait that Nkrumah lauded is just a manifestation of our dread of massive and devastating retaliation if we tried anything other than forgiveness and forgetfulness. It is just a manifestation of our helplessness due to our utter powerlessness relative to the white world. That's hardly a virtue over which to preen ourselves.

By the way, when Nkrumah commended to the British our "lack of malice, an absence of the desire for vengeance for our wrongs," as one of our "qualities worthy of emulation," he was actually indulging in what in China in the early 1920s was named and despised as "Ah Q" behavior. It was named after the hero of the novella "The true story of Ah Q,"[36] in which that behavior was satirized by Lu Xun. In the story, Ah Q is famous for his "spiritual victories," that is to say for the self-deception in which he mentally persuades himself that his defeats and humiliations in life are really spiritual victories. Every time Ah Q lost a fight he deluded himself that he was the spiritual victor.

Rather than follow Nkrumah and indulge, like Ah Q, in delusions of our moral superiority, wouldn't we be better to remedy the underlying cause of our defeats: our powerlessness?

C8] Our resignation and apathy:
Amos Wilson noted that

> the resignation and the apathy of too many of our people are part of the means by which the system maintains itself. The fear of trusting and uniting with each other, the fear of coming together and solving our problems together, the belief that it is just not in us to unite and solve our problems and overcome the dominance of European imperialism itself becomes a part of the problem and helps to maintain the system."[37]

C9] The openness and cosmopolitanism of African societies:
According to Cheikh Anta Diop: "one of the weaknesses of black civilization, particularly during medieval times, was the openness, the cosmopolitanism of these societies. . . . And today, one of the basic weaknesses of African societies is that they still maintain this inherited cosmopolitan trait."[38]

That is why we welcome, even invite, Arabs, Indians etc. into our Pan-African movement, on the excuse that anybody born in Africa is an African. On this principle, we would suicidally embrace and welcome a python into our family meeting simply because it has made its nest in a corner of our compound. We thus disregard the basic fact, as is said in Jamaica, that "simply being born in Jamaica does not make one a Jamaican, in the same way that a chicken hatched in an oven is not a biscuit."

Our enemies have studied us thoroughly, which is why they easily defeated and continue to dominate us. Let us avail ourselves of what they have found out about us, however painful and distasteful their findings may be, and let us consciously work to give up those self-defeating traits.

C10] Main flaws in the African character:

Here are two sketches of the Negro/Black African character; one by P. W. Botha, the last-but-one President of Apartheid South Africa, and the other by Frederick Lugard, the conqueror and founder of Nigeria.

> the Black is the raw material for the White man. . . . Blacks cannot rule themselves. Give them guns and they will kill each other. They are good in nothing else but making noise, dancing, marrying many wives and indulging in sex. Let us all accept that the Black man is the symbol of poverty, mental inferiority, laziness and emotional incompetence. . . most Blacks are vulnerable to money inducements. . . . His inferior sense of morals can be exploited beautifully. And here is a creature that lacks foresight. There is a need for us to combat him in long term projections that he cannot suspect. The average Black does not plan his life beyond a year: that stance, for example, should be exploited."
>
> ~ President P. W. Botha, of Apartheid South Africa, to his Cabinet, 1985[39]

"In character and temperament" wrote Lord Lugard,

> the typical African of this [Negro] race-type is a happy, thriftless, excitable person, lacking in self-control, discipline, and foresight, . . . His thoughts are concentrated on the events and feelings of the moment, and he suffers little from the apprehension for the future or grief for the past. . . . He lacks the power of organisation, and is conspicuously deficient in the management and control alike of men or business. He loves the display of power, but fails to realise its responsibility. His most universal natural ability lies in eloquence and oratory. . . . He is very prone to imitate anything new in dress or custom, whether it be the turban and flowing gown of the Moslem, or the straw hat and trousers of the European, however unsuited to his environment and conditions of life. . . . In brief, the virtues and defects of this race-type are those of attractive children, . . . they bear no malice and nurse no grievance. . . .[40]

Any honest assessor of how Nigerians have mis-managed Nigeria in the fifty years since they got self-government in 1960 will acknowledge that Lugard thoroughly understood the people he conquered and ruled so easily.

I have presented above a list of some self-defeating traits of the Negro/Black race. Some of these traits were pointed out by Negroes/Blacks, some were pointed out by Whites. We need to be aware of all of them, and must resolve to correct these weaknesses.

PART 4: WHAT OUR EDUCATION MUST DO AND BECOME

Think of the issues I have raised thus far in this paper. They should properly determine the core aspects of an Afrocentric education, of any education of Black Africans in the interest of Black Africans; any education that aims to carry out what, according to Amos Wilson, is the major function of Black African education, i.e. to help secure the survival of Black people.

Bearing in mind the fact that the countries, societies and races on earth are in an unceasing struggle for power, prosperity, status and survival; and also bearing in mind the ancient Chinese military adage: "Know yourself, know your enemy; and in a hundred battles you will never be defeated," we must consciously invent an education system that will serve us well in that inescapable struggle.

We must invent an education system that gets us to understand, not only ourselves and our European and Arab enemies, but also the way the world of today works and was put together. It must get us to understand all the other peoples with whom we must share this planet Earth. Such an education is a strategic necessity for our survival.

We must also consciously fashion an Afrocentric education system, formal and informal, that will repair the colossal damage that centuries of defeats and enslavement, and a century or more of Eurocentric education has done to the Black African psyche.

In summary, what is needed is an Afrocentric education that grooms the young to be loyal to the Black race, to feel responsible for ending the humiliations of the race and psychologically prepares them to take full control of our societies and our destiny, and grooms them to not tolerate dishonor to the race, and makes them psychologically driven to independently define Black Africa's interests and go forth, boldly and skillfully, to defend and advance them.

I shall comment on these core aspects under the following ten heads: Afrocentric Political Education; Education for race loyalty; Education for the unification of our peoples; Education for strong racial consciousness and solidarity; Education for security consciousness; Afrocentric re-orientation of disciplines; Education for productivity; Education for social responsibility; Education for autonomous modernization; Education for an Afrocentric governing cadre.

D1] Afrocentric political education

On political education, Nkrumah correctly urged:

> Our youth from the primary schools, through the secondary schools to the universities and higher institutions of learning, . . . must be taught to know the workings of neo-colonialism and trained to recognize it wherever it may rear its head. They must not only know the trappings of colonialism and imperialism, but they must also be able to smell out the hide-outs of neo-colonialism.[41]

Lest we forget, Nkrumah set a worthy example by teaching what he knew about colonialism and imperialism; even though what he knew proved grossly inadequate to help him win his struggle against imperialism. Have we been following his wise prescription and example? Are we teaching Pan-Africanism, or colonialism and neo-colonialism in our primary schools, secondary schools and tertiary institutions? Are we updating our knowledge of imperialism as it evolves?

Beyond what Nkrumah urged, are we also implanting in the minds of our children the motivating vision of an industrialized and powerful and respected Black Africa? Do we teach them to defend, at any price, the honor and the land of the Black race?

D2] Education for race loyalty

We need to effectively compete for the emotional loyalty of African children—that is to say, their loyalty to Black African people, Black African culture and Black African interests. In the past century, through television, school curriculums, religious institutions—both Christian and Muslim—and "social inertia," black children have been routinely, and very early, imbued with loyalty to non-African peoples and cultures, and most importantly, to non-African *interests.* This needs to be changed by effective educational measures. These should be carefully and imaginatively worked out. For a pioneering example of what should be done please see Jerry Johnson's stories. They can be found at marcusgarveycubs.com.

D3] Education and the unification of peoples

The teaching of history, culture and languages should be guided by the need to unify the peoples of Black Africa through shared languages, values and histories. Diop's prescription should be followed.

D4] Education for strong racial consciousness and solidarity
As Chancellor Williams pointed out:

> Caucasians will wage frightful wars against other Caucasians, but will quickly unite, as though by instinct, against non-whites, not only in wars but in international politics. They have developed a kind of built-in solidarity in their relations with non-Caucasian peoples. This fact, as much as anything else, helps to explain their position as masters of the world.[42]

A graphic illustration of this took place during the Congo crisis in 1963:

> Congolese Prime Minister Adoula had announced that he was breaking relations with the Soviet government and expelling the Soviet Embassy. Mobutu and his right-wing friends had found the necessary pretext. They had arrested two Soviet diplomats, carrying official documents, on the ferry to Brazzaville. As [US Ambassador Edmund] Guillon recalled the incident, the Congolese police, who had no respect for the sanctity of the diplomatic pouch, tore open and seized the documents inside. One of the Soviet diplomats tried to swallow the papers. The enraged Congolese threatened to throw him into the river to be eaten by the crocodiles. Just at that moment, he was rescued—by the chief British intelligence agent in the Congo. In the end, European blood had proved thicker than ideology."[43]

We need to emulate this racial solidarity of the Caucasians. One important way to bring this about is by consciously designing education curriculums that foster Negro or Black racial solidarity.

D5] Education for security consciousness
The average Black African today, military leaders included, is obsessed with personal prosperity. The security of his country or race from enemy attack is the last thing on the mind of the Negro/Black African; but given the dismal history of the Negro, it ought to be his paramount concern; it ought to be the framework within which all else, especially personal wealth, is subordinately situated since, as Ubuntu Philosophy states: **"Umuntu ngumuntu ngabantu," meaning a human being is a human being because of others,** which implies that it is on the public welfare that the individual welfare depends. However, the security of a society is the context for its welfare. Consequently the security of society is the context for the welfare and prosperity of the individual. And, after all, isn't it much better

to be a poor member of a strong country or race than to be a rich member of a weak and defenseless country or race?

In the 1930s, following the Italian attack on Abyssinia, Garvey warned us that "unpreparedness [is] a crime."[44] It is a warning we still need to heed. What is needed is an education that produces in each person a state of preparedness for the likely dangers to the country and the race, and of watchfulness for the unexpected. We desperately need an education curriculum to produce habits of alertness and careful observation; logical and comprehensive situation analysis; problem solving aptitudes; facility for strategy and logistics (chess would be helpful here); security consciousness (through early training in martial arts together with a year of compulsory military service for all 18-year-olds.)

D6] Afrocentric re-orientation of disciplines—e.g. history, economics

Every discipline taught in Black Africa should be deliberately re-oriented to serve Black Africa.

History and economics, especially, need to be re-oriented. History should be obliged to teach African and world history from an Afrocentric perspective. Economics should be reorganized away from the allegedly universal doctrines and principles that promote European power and wealth; it should be obliged to explain how Black Africa can exploit or escape from the tyranny of the world market that has been designed by Europeans for European global hegemony. Afrocentric Economics should be specially charged to show us how to transform our abundant resources into wealth and economic security for Black African societies, with full employment for all in Black Africa. Rather than mislead us with neo-liberal doctrines and theories of 'development' that have never produced industrialization anywhere, it should emphasize economic history, particularly case studies of industrialization, so we know why and how it was actually accomplished in the already industrialized countries.

D7] Education for productivity to meet Black Africa's material needs

Education should be re-designed to emphasize practical and management skills, to prepare each of its products for making some simple necessities like food, clothing, environmentally suitable houses, household goods, etc. This redesign should result in a high density of applied productive and management skills in the population, and prepare the way for every village or town to become dense with goods-producing enterprises. It should make a healthy break from the prestige-wrapped academic education that the colonizers introduced to provide them with clerks and other auxiliaries.

D8] Education for social responsibility

Every school leaver, whatever the practical skills acquired, should be burning with a desire to take responsibility for the entire society and the Black race. Needed is an education designed to instill in the population, and especially in the elite, a devotion to meritocracy and a deep sense of responsibility for the whole country and the whole race; an education that teaches that the autonomy of the community and the survival and power of the Black race are supreme values, supreme because they are the indispensable guarantors of individual wealth and liberties; an education that teaches that it is the responsibility of each member of the community to look out for and help guarantee the autonomy of the community and the survival of the Black race.

D9] Education for autonomous modernization

Prime examples to learn from are:

Meiji Japan—For its selective adoption of foreign practices. We should adopt and adapt their slogan: "wakon yosai": Japanese spirit, western technology/technique/knowledge.

Maoist China—For its Socialism with Chinese characteristics. China resisted Russian pressure to get China to toe the Russian line, and this led to the Sino-Soviet rupture. We should be taught to find and stick to our own path of modernization, without yielding to any hegemonists, even if they are our allies.

Castro's Cuba—For how it worked out its own path to modernization after overthrowing US neocolonialism.

North Korea—For how President Kim Il Sung and the Korean Workers Party, guided by its official slogan *Juche*—self-reliance, and using the state planning methods of the Soviet Union, industrialized North Korea within 20 years, despite US economic sanctions against North Korea that had been in place since the Korean War; and how the government gave priority to food, housing, and clothing needs—and provided everyone with free school, free medical care, and old-age and disability pensions.

South Korea—For how it achieved the industrialization of South Korea that was thought necessary for South Korea's defense and prosperity. Park Chung Hee, when he seized power in 1961, generally relied upon private businesses, the *chaebol*. The Park regime initiated a successful *program* of industrialization for South Korea based upon export-oriented industries which were guided and aided by the government.

Singapore—For how it transformed Singapore from Third World to First. Lee Kwan Yew and his team deliberately altered the mode of Singapore's insertion into the Capitalist World Economy, and changed it from a trading post into a manufacturing and financial center. (The book to read is Lee Kuan Yew, *From Third World to First*.[45])

And lastly, but perhaps most importantly,

D10] Education for an Afrocentric governing cadre
One of the roots of Black Africa's problems is the unnoticed fact that its elites are not governing cadres but self-seeking individuals addicted to possessive individualism. A governing cadre is a tightly-knit group of persons trained for a life of service and duty to its country; trained to take collective responsibility for the survival and long-term welfare of the country it governs; trained to a sense of duty to serve and safeguard the public interest; and trained to approach its governmental responsibilities with deliberation and seriousness. An elite is not trained to these things. Though composed of the best and brightest individuals in their fields; and though its members occupy the pinnacles of the institutions of its society or country, an elite is not necessarily imbued with a sense of group responsibility for their country, or with a sense of duty to serve the public interest. Only when it is so trained does it become a governing cadre. As Walter Rodney pointed out:

> Any socio-political system needs its cadres. That was the role played by the youngest age-grades in Shaka's armies and it was the role played by the Komsomol or Young Communists in the Soviet Union. Being a cadre involved not just training for a practical job but also political orientation to serve as a leading element in the system.[46]

Other countries have their distinctive ways and their elite schools for indoctrinating the cadres that eventually take total charge of their country. Think of Britain's public schools with their character-building game of cricket. Think of the handful of elite schools (grandes ecoles) that have produced most of the political, intellectual and administrative leaders of France in the last two centuries. Think of the imperial examination system that produced the Confucian-indoctrinated mandarins that governed Imperial China for centuries. Think too of the education system that indoctrinated the scribes and bureaucrats who governed Pharaonic Egypt for thousands of years. Think also of the seminaries which produce the cadres that manage the affairs of the Catholic Church, and think also of the Central Party School of the Communist Party of China which indoctrinates the leadership of the CPC who then proceed to govern the country. While in these schools, besides having their individualism subordinated to elite collectivism, the cadres are indoctrinated with appropriate values that transform them into an army of political soldiers responsible for their country.

From this indoctrination, the individual members of a ruling cadre emerge with an ingrained sense of collective responsibility to go forth and, like a phalanx of foot soldiers, defend their country against the world; and within their country, to be the defenders of their own class, the ruling class: whether it is the proletariat in China or the bourgeoisie in France. That is why they will gun down without compunction any challengers to their class power, whether such are the rebellious students of Penn State in the USA or the rebellious students in Tiananmen Square in China.

Inside their country they will make war on the other classes and protect the class power without which they cannot dominate and organize their country for the outward antagonism that's needed for external defense against outside countries. This is biologically correct behavior for our species.

Why is this issue of a governing or ruling cadre perhaps the most important of all that I have enumerated?

White Marxists, coming from countries with long entrenched and effective ruling classes, sometimes take effective governance for granted, and do not appreciate the vital role a ruling class plays in producing effective governance, and therefore lose sight of the value of having a ruling cadre. Some of them, in their vulgar Marxist economism, with its focus on nothing but the wealth and income disparity between the ruling and other classes, give the impression that a ruling class is by its very nature an evil and should be abolished; and that no ex-colonial country should even consider creating a ruling class. But they and their Black Marxist parrots would do well to reflect on the functions of a ruling class and on the alternatives, such as a looting elite, an elite of possessive individualists whose appetite is only for plundering their own country. Like miners in a gold rush camp, all they are concerned with is digging their concession, finding the gold and sending it away to some safe bank far away where they will retire to enjoy their pile when their gold lode is mined to exhaustion. Hence they give no thought to administering the camp, organizing its security or sanitation or scenery, let alone its future. That's how an elite which is not a ruling cadre tends to treat its own country. A notorious case in point is Nigeria since 1960.

Fifty years on, the elites of Black Africa are a far cry from the ruling cadres we need: men and women with the passion for public service and capacity for leadership which self-rule requires. The absence, in Black Africa, of an Afrocentric and Pan-Africanist cadre has meant that no functional Pan-African programs or political movements can be sustained, or presented as viable alternatives to the neo-colonial status quo. There is, therefore, a paramount need to organize leadership training to produce an Afrocentric governing cadre that is indoctrinated to take full responsibility for every aspect of each Black African country.

To sum up: A country without a ruling class or ruling cadre is in a bad way; but educate a ruling cadre or ruling class, and its mentality and self-interest will make it liberate the country, solve its problems and achieve its aspirations.

Concluding Remarks

In educating our children, let me recommend an approach which I found useful for decolonizing my own colonially mis-educated mind. Here is what I wrote in the preface to *The West And The Rest Of Us* (1975):

> [Black] Africans especially, must endeavor to see clearly the larger system of things in which we are enmeshed or be irretrievably lost in catacombs of irrelevant details; and . . . we must understand the awful predicament that binds us together or we shall be repeatedly manipulated to fight one another and so hasten the march of disaster upon ourselves. . . . I have found it invaluable to focus upon the arsenal of techniques accumulated to serve western imperialism, and upon the structures and processes whereby the West constrains events, determines our views and actions, and shapes our realities. If this approach should contribute to clarifying for the reader . . . how that world stage was put together and is managed upon which African and other Third World nations have to perform to regain their liberty; if it should help us decrease, even by one jot or tittle, our susceptibility to being lured by carrots, intimidated by the lash of sticks, or stampeded by hysteria into collaborating in the defeat of our enlightened [Black African] interests, then this work would have done more than I could seriously hope for.
>
> ~ Chinweizu[47]

Notes

[1] Amos Wilson, *Awakening the Natural Genius of Black Children*, second edition (Brooklyn: Afrikan World InfoSystems, 1992), 1.

[2] Sun Tzu, ancient Chinese strategist, ca. 5th c. BC.

[3] Kwame Nkrumah, *Revolutionary Path* (London: Panaf Books, 1973), 190.

[4] Quoted in Jacob H. Carruthers, *The Irritated Genie* (Chicago: The Kemetic Institute, 1985), 123.

[5] Frantz Fanon, *The Wretched of the Earth* (New York: Grove Press, 1968), 176.

[6] Quoted in Chinweizu, *The West and The Rest of Us* (1975, Lagos: Pero Press, 1987), 226.

[7] Dr. Maulana Karenga, "African Renaissance and Cultural Consciousness: Standing On Sacred Ground," *Los Angeles Sentinel,* 15 April 2010, p. A7.

[8] Quoted in Walter Rodney, *How Europe Underdeveloped Africa* (London: Bogle L'Ouverture, 1988), 248.

[9] Quoted in Rodney, *How Europe Underdeveloped Africa*, 257.

[10] Quoted in Rodney, *How Europe Underdeveloped Africa*, 249.

[11] Rodney, *How Europe Underdeveloped Africa*, 248, 249.

[12] Kwesi Prah, *The African Nation* (Cape Town: CASAS, 2006), 94.

[13] Quoted in Ralph A. Austen, "Notes on the Prehistory of TANU," *Makerere Journal* 9 (March 1964), 2. See also Chinweizu, *The West And The Rest Of Us*, 86.

[14] Prah, *The African Nation,* 126.

[15] Please see the entry "Slave Trade" in Chinweizu, "Afrocentric Rectification of Terms," 2000 <http://www.oyastornado.com/special-feature.html> accessed 29 August 2016.

[16] Bankie F. Bankie, email correspondence, Mon, 11 June 2007.

[17] For part of the evidence, please see Pearce Wright, "Smallpox Vaccine 'triggered Aids virus,'" *The Times* (London), 11 May 1987.

[18] Marcus Garvey, *Philosophy and Opinions of Marcus Garvey*, edited by Amy Jacques Garvey (Dover, MA: The Majority Press, 1986), 13.

[19] Garvey, *Philosophy and Opinions of Marcus Garvey*, 63–64.

[20] Chancellor Williams, *The Destruction of Black Civilization* (Chicago: Third World Press, 1987), 310.

[21] Amilcar Cabral, *Unity and Struggle* (London: Heinemann Educational Books, 1980), 121.

[22] Steve Biko, *I Write What I Like* (Oxford: Heinemann African Writers Series, 1987), 42.

[23] Mollie West, email correspondence, 2009.

[24] West, email correspondence.

[25] Biko, *I Write What I Like*, 44.

[26] West, email correspondence.

[27] Amos N. Wilson, *The Falsification of Afrikan Consciousness* (Brooklyn: Afrikan World InfoSystems, 1993), 66.

[28] Wilson, *The Falsification of Afrikan Consciousness*, 25.

[29] Quoted in Manga Clem Marshall, "From Imhotep to the Internet: Honour Their Ashes, Follow Their Flames" in *Pan-Africanism/African Nationalism: Strengthening the Unity of Africa and its Diaspora*, edited by F. Bankie and K. Mchombu (Windhoek: Gamsberg Macmillan, 2006), 174.

[30] Nkrumah, *Revolutionary Path*, 114.

[31] David Lamb, *The Africans* (New York: Vintage Books, 1985), 161–162.

[32] Lamb, *The Africans*, 164.

[33] Lamb, *The Africans*, 235.

[34] Lamb, *The Africans*, 236.

[35] Quoted in Marshall, "From Imhotep to the Internet," 174.

[36] In Lu Xun *Selected Stories of Lu Hsun* (1960, Peking: Foreign Languages Press, 1972) <https://www.marxists.org/archive/lu-xun/1921/12/ah-q/index.htm>.

[37] Wilson, *The Falsification of Afrikan Consciousness*, 75.

[38] Quoted in Shawna Moore, "Interview with Cheikh Anta Diop," in *Great African Thinkers: Cheikh Anta Diop*, edited by Ivan Van Sertima (London: Transaction Books, 1986), 243.

[39] Reprinted by David G. Maillu, *The Sunday Times* (South Africa), 18 August 1985.

[40] F. J. D. Lugard, *The Dual Mandate in British Tropical Africa*, fifth edition (London: Frank Cass and Co. Ltd, 1965), 69–70.

[41] Nkrumah, *Revolutionary Path*, 190.

[42] Williams, *The Destruction of Black Civilization*, 298.

[43] Madeleine Kalb, *The Congo Cables* (New York: MacMillan, 1982), 377–378.

[44] Marcus Garvey, "Unpreparedness a Crime," in John Henrik Clarke, ed., *Marcus Garvey and the Vision of Africa* (New York: Vintage Books, 1974), 359.

[45] Kuan Yew Lee, *From Third World to First* (New York: HarperCollins, 2000).

[46] Rodney, *How Europe Underdeveloped Africa*, 258.

[47] Chinweizu, *The West and The Rest of Us*, xxii.

Bibliography

Biko, Steve. *I Write What I Like*. Oxford: Heinemann African Writers Series, 1987.

Cabral, Amilcar. *Unity and Struggle*. London: Heinemann Educational Books, 1980.

Carruthers, Jacob H. *The Irritated Genie.* Chicago: The Kemetic Institute, 1985.

Chinweizu. *The West And The Rest Of Us.* 1975. Lagos: Pero Press, 1987.

Fanon, Frantz. *The Wretched of the Earth.* New York: Grove Press, 1968.

Garvey, Marcus. *Philosophy and Opinions of Marcus Garvey.* Edited by Amy Jacques Garvey. Dover, MA: The Majority Press, 1986.

-----. "Unpreparedness a Crime." In *Marcus Garvey and the Vision of Africa.* Edited by John Henrik Clarke. New York: Vintage Books, 1974. 359–362.

Kalb, Madeleine G. *The Congo Cables.* New York: Macmillan, 1982.

Lamb, David. *The* Africans. New York: Vintage Books 1985.

Lee, Kuan Yew. *From Third World to First.* New York: HarperCollins, 2000.

Lu, Xun. *Selected Stories of Lu Hsun.* 1960. Peking: Foreign Languages Press, 1972. <https://www.marxists.org/archive/lu-xun/1921/12/ah-q/index.htm>.

Lugard, Frederick John Dealtry. *The Dual Mandate in British Tropical Africa.* Fifth edition. London: Frank Cass and Co. Ltd, 1965.

Marshall, Manga Clem. "From Imhotep to the Internet: Honour Their Ashes, Follow Their Flames." In *Pan-Africanism/African Nationalism: Strengthening the Unity of Africa and its Diaspora.* Edited by F. Bankie and K. Mchombu. Windhoek: Gamsberg Macmillan, 2006. 175–193.

Moore, Shawna. "Interview with Cheikh Anta Diop." In *Great African Thinkers: Cheikh Anta Diop.* Edited by Ivan Van Sertima. London: Transaction Books, 1986. 239–248.

Nkrumah, Kwame. *Revolutionary Path.* London: Panaf Books, 1973.

Prah, Kwesi. *The African Nation.* Cape Town: CASAS, 2006.

Rodney, Walter. *How Europe Underdeveloped Africa.* London: Bogle L'Ouverture, 1988.

Williams, Chancellor. *The Destruction of Black Civilization.* Chicago: Third World Press, 1987.

Wilson, Amos. *The Falsification of Afrikan Consciousness.* Brooklyn: Afrikan World InfoSystems, 1993.

-----. *Awakening the Natural Genius of Black Children.* Second edition. Brooklyn: Afrikan World InfoSystems, 1992.

Perspectives on Afrikan[1] Identity in the 21st Century

Baba A. O. Buntu

> "I move slowly in the world,
> accustomed to aspiring no longer to appear."
>
> ~ Frantz Fanon[2]

Lately a debate over the term "Afrikan" has resurfaced, both on the Afrikan continent and in the Afrikan Diaspora. In the USA and the Caribbean, many people of Afrikan descent have done away with the terms "Afrikan American" and "Afrikan Caribbean" and simply state they are Afrikans. However, out of ignorance and/or self-hate, many Diasporan Afrikans chose not to identify with Afrika at all. Continental Afrikans moving to Western countries realize that some Diasporan Afrikans have internalized racist stereotypes about Afrika and do not want to associate with Afrikans. On the opposite end of the spectrum, in Azania (South Afrika) and Zimbabwe we have seen descendants of European settlers claim that they are Afrikan based on the fact that they are born in an Afrikan country.

As urbanized youth in Afrikan cities are coming to terms with socio-economic changes, discussions about who is an Afrikan and what defines Afrikan-ness stirs both debate and controversy. Aspiring members of the middle class are accused of trying too hard to substitute their Afrikan identity for a European identity. As we hear messages about the necessity of knowing Afrikan history, we also witness great animosity between ethnic Afrikan nationalities and a generally underdeveloped understanding of Pan-Afrikan principles.

So, who has the right to call herself or himself an Afrikan? Can Afrikan identity be claimed by anyone who sees it fit? By which standards can the claim be verified? What if people who would never have dreamed of identifying with Afrikans years ago would today like to embrace an Afrikan identity? Are the new identifiers' claims legitimate? What about Black people who choose not to identify as Afrikans? What about European descendants who played an active role in supporting Afrikan emancipation? Should they not be welcomed into the Afrikan family? And what about Afrikans who have betrayed their fellow Afrikans? Should they not lose their Afrikan family membership? Can one choose her or his identity at all?

Common Definitions of Who Is Afrikan

In contemporary discussions concerning Afrikan identity, three major arguments are routinely made:

1. *Every Black person is an Afrikan*
   This standpoint argues that Afrikan-ness is visible (i.e. predisposes Blackness) and that everyone who descends from an "indigenous Afrikan" is an Afrikan. This argument is often criticised as a one-dimensional "racial" definition.

2. *Every person born on the Afrikan continent is Afrikan*
   This standpoint sees Afrikan-ness as linked to place of birth, as a right that one inherits. This position is criticized by many as a definition of convenience used predominantly by European descendants in Afrika to soothe guilt-complexes deriving from their ancestral linkage to exploitation and oppression.

3. *Every person who wants the best for Afrika is an Afrikan*
   This standpoint defines Afrikan-ness as based on loyalty and good morale. This viewpoint is often posed to assert that there is a difference between "good whites" and "bad whites," and that there are Black people who, because of their disloyalty to Afrika should be denounced as Afrikans.

What do these definitions have in common?

- That many people hold aspects of all of these three views, alternating between them according to context and situation;
- That you can find all of these views expressed among people who call themselves Pan-Afrikanists;
- That a good 100 years into Pan-Afrikan discourse, defining "Afrikan" is still a highly sensitive issue. Although often ignored,

avoided or seen as not to be a "serious issue," discussions around these definitions can spark great controversy and even animosity.

This last point, that defining Afrikan is both a "non-issue" and an "issue" at the same time should be of interest within a self-reflecting Pan-Afrikan discourse. As long as we claim to uphold Pan-Afrikanist principles such as Afrikan unity and progress, we must scrutinise every obstacle that keeps us from obtaining these ideals. Could the identity question be one of the obstacles? Are we making identity too much of an issue? Or, are we still reluctant to examine it thoroughly?

Contextualizing Afrikan Identity

There is normally agreement around identity-affirming statements such as "know yourself" and "be proud of who you are," but many times these affirmations are not uttered in context. As much as everyone needs to know their people's history, the conditions for not knowing are not the same for everyone.

The overwhelming experience of the Afrikan is the scourge of racism. It is the myriad of racist practices that has, by distorting Afrikan history, forged confusion around Afrikan identity and brought about a critical need to reclaim it. Charles William Ephraim finds that racism is not, as is often argued, a disease. It is, rather, a symptom of a pathology diagnosed by Freud and Nietzsche as *ressentiment*.[3] The French term *ressentiment*, which in English translates as *resentment*, is a psychosocial condition whereby an individual or group projects its personal feelings of frustration or inadequacy on another individual or group. Whites projected their personal feelings of inferiority and jealousy on Blacks and then constructed the concept of Black inferiority. They followed this psychological projection with physical acts of slavery, colonization, and systematic racism and oppression to validate their projections and make their *ressentiment* appear to be rooted in biological or historical fact.

The need to rediscover, redefine, and reclaim Afrikan identity is directly linked to a political history wherein Blackness and Afrikan-ness have been stereotyped, degraded, and made to appear worthless. Afrikan children, women, and men routinely struggle with feelings of self-hatred, low self-esteem and identity confusion. However, how we deal with these impediments, to a large extent, is based on choice. In our study of Afrikan identity, we shall therefore apply strict criteria: Solutions to issues regarding Afrikan identity must give practical answers and they must foster a holistic understanding of both Blackness **and** Afrikan-ness.

Blackness, Race, and Racism

The belief in "race" as a biological determinant to explain human differences has been thoroughly denounced and proven baseless. Yet, race, as visible characteristics (skin colour, hair texture, and other physical attributes), continue to inform our worldview and how we define others and ourselves. Also, elements of racist discourse and praxis can be examined on all levels of human life, including the gap between rich and poor, imbalances in political power, and practices of exclusion and discrimination. Black people, and people of colour, continue to be victimised by a system of white supremacy. Hence, "black" and "white" continue to be highly politicised terms in a racialised world.

The reality of Blackness is dictated by the reality of whiteness. Whiteness has been projected as the norm, and so, Blackness has become the abnormal. Blackness, according to Lewis R. Gordon, transcends Afrikan-ness, because it is the identifiable phenomena in an anti-Black world.[4] The being of a Black person revolves around a dichotomy of presence (visibility) and absence (absence of whiteness). It is also the experience of living in this anti-Black world that has guided the discourse on Afrikan-ness. The disregard for the Black person's worth through hundreds of years of enslavement and colonialism has also been the disregard for the Afrikan. Gordon goes on to say that Blackness is not only a symbol of crime, bestiality and primitive instincts, but, in an anti-Black world, it **is** all these attributes.[5]

Blackness, however, from a more neutral point of view, is "only a colour" and must be seen as a very limited, even disqualifying, description of a person. Kwame Anthony Appiah, a strong opponent of the term "race," takes the debate further by rejecting the notion that a people can belong to a particular race.[6] He believes nobody belongs to **any** race, and that race is an imposed invention. He finds it, however, important to understand how people **think** about race. Appiah's wish to make people rid themselves of racial categories and work together for democratic principles can be written off as somewhat romantic. Yet, his point of critiquing many Afrikan intellectuals for being captivated by the Western themes of identity and difference, seeking to "fashion themselves as the (image of the) Other,"[7] should not go unnoticed. To uncritically accept "race" is, at the same time, to tap into a Eurocentric matrix. For the sake of this discussion, we shall see "Blackness" and "race" as descriptive terms, relating to the Afrikan's experience and self-perception. "Race" might not be a truth, but it does exist throughout socio-political reality. And, although, it is not a preferred term, we need words to describe the imposed different-ness (Blackness). In the project of reclaiming an Afrikan identity, the Afrikan carefully needs to make his Blackness relevant to the project, as it, in the words of Molefi Kete Asante, "is indeed more than colour; it functions as a commitment to a historical project that places the African person back on center, and, as such, it becomes an escape to sanity."[8]

Black Consciousness, Pan-Afrikanism, and Afrocentricity

Black Consciousness, in the words of Steve Biko, is "the realisation by the black man of the need to rally together with his brothers around the cause of their operation—the blackness of their skin—and to operate as a group in order to rid themselves of the shackles that bind them to perpetual servitude."[9] It was, indeed, in opposition to perpetual servitude that many Afrikans in the late 1800's engaged in a discourse which would lead to what we today know as Pan-Afrikanism. Introduced in the 17th century to describe Afrikan customs, the term Afrikanism has had several meanings. At times it referred to the Greek understanding of one Afrika "the land of the Blacks."[10] Other times it categorized multidisciplinary studies of Afrika in opposition to Eurocentric studies.[11]

The European "Scramble for Afrika," motivated by the Berlin Conference in 1884–85, gave birth to a mutually inspiring process between Afrikans in the Diaspora and Afrikans on the continent and resulted in several anti-colonial conferences and organizations. In 1900, Henry Sylvester Williams called the first Pan-Afrikan Conference in London. Conferences and movements spearheaded by powerful leaders such as George Padmore, Marcus Mosiah Garvey, W. E. B. DuBois, Malcolm X, Kwame Nkrumah, Thomas Sankara, Patrice Lumumba, and Sekou Toure gave ground to a new wave of Afrikan liberation and self-determination. In various ways, these, and other leaders, brought forth an understanding of Pan-Afrikanism as emancipation by and for Afrikan people—both on the continent and in the Diaspora.

The process of physical decolonization also inspired a new dimension of emancipation: the decolonization of the mind. Scholars such as Frantz Fanon, Walter Rodney, Drusilla D. Houston, Cheikh Anta Diop, Theophile Obenga, Ngugi wa Thiong'o, and Chinweizu emphasised the importance of thought, self-reflection, and research to uncover the truth about great Afrikan achievements throughout human history. Marcus Garvey's *Black nationalism*, Aimé Césaire's *Negritude* and Frantz Fanon's decolonization theories galvanized anti-imperialistic thought and self-determination, as expressed through the formation of such movements as Black Panthers in the USA and Black Consciousness Movement in Azania. Although vastly different in approach and content, these movements returned the Afrikan to the centre of action, as an agent in her/his own liberation. The latest advancement of a Pan-Afrikan discipline is Afrocentricity (or Afrikan Centeredness) which teaches that the Afrikan person can only be truly liberated when she/he reclaims a cultural platform (centre) that affirms the Afrikan's history and being.

The aforementioned revolutionaries and works all position Afrikan-ness and Blackness as integral components of coexistence. Since the liberation these authors advocated has not yet been fully attained, there is little reason to believe that these authors would have separated the two today. The symbiotic relationship between these two components, both for Afrikans in the Diaspora and on the Continent, is well illustrated in one of Malcolm X's speeches: "By [Western powers] skillfully making us hate Africa and, in turn, making us hate ourselves, hate our color and our blood, our color became a chain. . . . It became a prison. It became something that was a shame, something that we felt held us back, kept us trapped."[12] Afrocentricity, and the liberation theories it builds on, educates the Black/Afrikan person to break free from this "prison" by locating her/himself in an Afrikan cultural praxis manifested on all levels of being.

Afrikan Imagery, Youth Culture, and "Nigga-tivity"

Today, more than any other phenomena, a young generation of Afrikan-Americans is dominating the image of Afrikan people internationally. Through massive media campaigns, Black sports stars, actors, musicians, and entrepreneurs have become idols to young people, across the ethnic spectrum, all over the world. And although many of them might not possess much political power in the traditional sense, they certainly influence the behaviour of the young generation. They have become the definition of beauty, style, language, expression, and entertainment. They have become representatives of Blackness, the way other people see us, and the way we see ourselves. Through an onslaught of mass media manipulation, Black youth all over the world strive to look and behave like Afrikan-American models, sports personalities, and entertainers. Many of whom exhibit no understanding of the Afrikan identity. In fact, it could be argued that many of the icons who are so influential to young people play a fundamental role in promoting anti-Afrikan ideals, self-alienation, and ignorance.

Hip-Hop culture, which started out as a positive culture of self-affirmation, awareness, anti-violence, anti-drugs, etc., has now become the main advocate for negative and stereotypical images and behaviour. It is particularly interesting to see how certain negative or destructive behavioural traits, presented as integral expressions of Hip-Hop culture, are being copied and somehow form an international language or cultural code. Sagging pants and untied sneakers originate in prison, where belts and shoelaces are forbidden because inmates might use them to commit suicide. Certain body postures and hand and arm movements of Hip-Hop artists have become common means of articulation in youth culture. Perhaps the most disturbing and dehumanising export of Afrikan-American Hip-Hop culture is the widespread adoption of the word "nigger" or "nigga." Throughout the Afrikan world, one can find young Afrikan people referring to themselves as "niggers" or "niggas." "Nigger" is a destructive and racist term of Latin origin meaning dark, useless, Satanic, under-worldly and evil. Young Afrikans all over the world use this term, jokingly, as an affirmation, and as a sign of affection.

To Afrikan young people who have no experience with Jim Crow laws and being "treated as a nigger," the term becomes both controversial and familiar in that it straddles both the forbidden and the acceptable. It is a way to bypass other identities (Afrikan, Black) and to mock political correctness. While the term Afrikan, to many people, presupposes a strong identification and ability to "defend" that identification if challenged, there is an implied sense that a Black person does not have to defend his or her use of the word nigger, because it is understood that the Black person is not *really* a "nigger" (in the racist, sub-human sense). Most youth will admit that they are aware of the word's racist nature and cannot wholeheartedly defend the use of the word. Yet, it remains a prominent element of Hip-Hop culture.

Some voices claim that the widespread use of this "forbidden" word nullifies its racist connotation. This is a rather shallow argument. A curse word so directly linked to, and deriving from, a gruesome history of murder and annihilation, cannot be disempowered so easily. Others would say that, after all, "nigger" is just a word. But, we should, as John Henrik Clarke has reminded us, be extremely careful to excuse harmful concepts: "There are times that when a people answer to a name that they did not choose for themselves they fall into a condition that they also did not choose. If you answer to the name 'dog,' in some ways you will become a dog."[13]

Continental vs Diasporan Identities

Discussions within the African Union have employed two definitions of Diasporan Afrikan. One includes Afrikans born on the Afrikan continent, now residing in mainly Western countries. The other speaks of descendants of Afrikans who were enslaved, or who left Afrika hundreds to thousands of years ago.

The foundation of Pan-Afrikanism was formulated by Afrikans in the Diaspora who claimed Afrika as the continent of their ancestors, and, by extension, the Afrikan continent as their home. The Back-To-Afrika movement, founded by Marcus M. Garvey, was not just a shallow answer to a difficult question of belonging. It was an act of reconnecting physically with the Motherland, Afrika. Loyal to this line of Pan-Afrikan thought, many Afrikans have worked hard to develop practical approaches to repatriation and reparations. There is still a long way to go to fully enjoy the fruits of these processes, but the reality of Afrika as the Mother Continent of all Black people, wherever they may reside, continues to live on.

The Afrikan Diaspora and the Afrikan Continent have always served as sources of mutual inspiration, as is evident in Afrikan and Afrikan Diasporan political life, academia, music, cultural expression, and spiritual practices. However, some continental Afrikans have been shunned and ridiculed by some Afrikan Americans when visiting the States and have not felt any sense of brotherhood with them. On the other hand, some Diasporan Afrikans have been shocked to find, when finally returning to the Afrikan continent, that some continental Afrikans regard them not as authentic Afrikans and treat them as tourists to be conned or outsiders to be scorned.

It is important to see these problems in the light of other intra-Afrikan conflicts, such as Hutu vs Tutsi, French speaking vs English speaking, Christian vs Muslim, one Caribbean island vs another Caribbean island, Afrikan Americans vs Afrikan Caribbeans, West Afrikans vs South Afrikans, dark skinned vs light skinned, rural vs urban, modernized vs traditional, educated vs analphabetic. Many of these conflicts have their origins in colonial divisional borders that were drawn up at the Berlin Conference in 1884–85 and solidified through colonial rule. Also, as Frantz Fanon found, on a psychological level, the experience of being victimised in the anti-Black world also leads the Black person to project her/his self-hate as hatred of other Black people.[14]

Cultural Disposition and Mixed Identities

Some would say that "Afrikan," first and foremost, is a cultural term. What then, if many Afrikans are more schooled and comfortable in European culture than Afrikan culture? The Europeanised Afrikan might not admit a strong allegiance to Europe, yet in language, thought, behaviour, dress code, religious beliefs and life style, European culture has been fully absorbed and internalised. As renowned philosopher Es'kia Mphahlele has noted, the colonised person has two selves: the indigenous (traditional) self and the other self, imposed by the colonizer. Many Afrikans find themselves in a battle between these two selves.

An internal battle may also be waged within people of mixed parentage or ancestry. They carry the direct lines of descent from both oppressor and oppressed. Children of mixed descent have been named–and regarded– differently, depending on where they grew up. In North America, the Jim

Crow "one drop" rule asserted that as long as you had only "one drop" of "Black blood" in you, you would be classified as Black. Ability to claim some European descent did not necessarily offer any privileges.

However, on the Afrikan continent and throughout its Diaspora, including America and especially in Latin and Caribbean America, the politics of mixed identities have been sources of deep conflicts. White oppressors indoctrinated Afrikans with less melanin to believe they were better than Afrikans with more melanin. White oppressors assisted the lighter-skinned mixed populations in rising above and exploiting the darker masses, and in many nations, the mixed Africans came to constitute not only an economic and political elite but also a separate caste. Whereas the children of Arab slave traders and enslaved Afrikan women may be called Arab, the children of mixed Euro-Afrikan descent in many Afrikan regions are called "coloured," "mulattos," "creoles," etc. These identities are invented categories of "being neither this nor that," which is a highly effective way of making sure mixed descendants will neither be able to enjoy white privileges nor fully identify with the Black masses.

The state of being "in between" of being *neither* this *nor* that is the crux of the dilemma for both the ethnically mixed person and the Europeanized Afrikan: They can never **choose** whiteness or European-ness. Unless they can "pass for white" (physically look European), their "membership" in the white/European community will always be denied. On the other side, these individual can choose Blackness/Afrikan-ness and enjoy full acceptance and privileges. Yet, rather than embrace Afrikan identity, some individuals choose a middle position, seeing themselves as just "mixed" or "citizens of the world." As comfortably diplomatic this might sound, the reality is that the middle position is not rooted in one cultural heritage, but two. One European, declared superior, which the person is programmed to desire yet is not accepted within, and one Afrikan, which is declared inferior and which the person rejects. By occupying a middle position, the individual does not gain the ability to maneuver between Afrikan and white identities, but ends up being stuck, and even lost, between them.

Blackness as Unwanted, Afrikan-ness as Fashion

White racist enslavers, colonizers, and occupiers made a culture of categorising Africans based on their skin tones and hair textures, with Africans with less melanin and being labeled beautiful and with individuals with deeper melanin being condemned as ugly. Unfortunately, complexion consciousness continues to exert tremendous influence in many Afrikan societies and can fuel everything from humiliating intra-Afrikan "jokes" to intricate pseudo-scientific categorizations of African ethnic mixtures, as is the case in Brazil, for example, where there are almost 100 descriptive terms for the ranges between dark and light.

The stigma connected with dark skin has led many Afrikan women and men to resort to using skin lightening creams that have dangerous side effects. However, there is also a proliferation of individuals who are enhancing and glorifying their African attributes. In any city or town one can find Afrikans wearing afros and dredlocks, taking pride in their Afrikan physical features, wearing Afrikan garments, adopting Afrikan names, and aspiring to ancient Afrikan spiritual practices. These are, of course, acts of self-affirmation and strong statements in opposition to Eurocentric ideals. It is, however, important to ensure that these acts are not merely fashion statements which will fade when new trends hit the market.

Afrikans Who Betray Afrika

What should we say about Afrikans who have betrayed their people? Afrikans who have been despised by the populace for misleading, spying on and destroying their own people? The askaris who chose to work for the Apartheid government? And, on the other side, what about people of European descent who could have enjoyed the privileges their skin colour afforded them, but chose not to? Those who fought courageously alongside Black comrades for freedom and liberation? Are they to be seen as Afrikan? Did they not, by contributing to the advancement of the continent, at least earn themselves a place as honorary Afrikans? The answer to this depends on what criteria we use in the definition of Afrikan. In terms of identity, "Afrikan" is not a badge of honour. It is not a prize awarded those who have advanced the Afrikan cause, and it cannot be taken away from Black people who do not support the same cause.

In relating the planning process leading up to the 7th Pan-African Congress, held in Kampala, Uganda in 1994, Tajudeen Abdul-Raheem admits that there were disagreements about the definition of who is an Afrikan.[15] However, he explains, the organizing committee rejected the idea that only Black people are Afrikan as "reactionary blackism": "While a majority of Africans are Negroid in origin, it is not true historically, factually, or even politically that blackness is the only condition of Africanness."[16]

To prove his point, he asserts that if Joe Slovo (white anti-apartheid activist and co-founder of ANC's covert military wing, Umkhonto weSizwe) had attended the conference, it would have been "proper." In contrast to the activist Slovo are Black leaders such as Mangosutho Buthelezi, Mobutu Sese Seko, and Idi Amin who, in his words "are as black as you can get, but can we truly infer any Pan African commitment from their ignominious acts?"

Here, Abdul-Raheem makes the mistake of not distinguishing between the definition of who is an Afrikan and who is a Pan-Afrikanist. It could be argued that, Pan-Afrikanism, as an ideology, can be shared, adopted, advanced and promoted by anyone, regardless of origin. Supporting Pan-Afrikanism, however, does not necessarily make you an Afrikan. For a man to be supportive of womanism, does not make him a woman.

There is, of course, also a strong Pan-Afrikan following that insists that the Pan-Afrikan movement must be organised by and for Black people only. As Pan-Afrikanism is a struggle for freedom and self-determination, it cannot be wrong to choose the methods and principles from within. Even if that leads to some people feeling excluded. It must be understood, naturally, that ensuring Black-only membership does not mean that every Black person—just because they are Black—will play a supportive role in the movement. It also does not exclude the possibility of choosing to work in strategic partnerships with other groups of peoples and movements within assigned areas of operation.

From a Pan-Afrikan point of view, we can identify many Black people who might not be very useful to the movement. Some will even be detrimental to the progress. Mental and spiritual oppression have twisted many of our people's minds, some even, seemingly, beyond repair. As our Ancestors have left us with a culture which is founded on the extended family, it is, however, our duty to embrace the community, to understand the multifaceted manifestations of colonialism, and to work tirelessly to rehabilitate our family members.

The Relevance of Having a "Non-Exclusive" Definition of Afrikan

A humanist perspective asserts that there is only one race: the human race. Hence, there should be no need for dividing people into racial categories. The differences in skin colour, hair textures, physical features, cultural attributes and legacies should be seen as the richness of **one** human family, shouldn't it? Additionally, since it is proven that all humankind stem from an Afrikan ancestor, shouldn't we all have the right to claim Afrikan heritage?

We opened the discussion in this paper saying that we would apply strict criteria to our discussion on Afrikan identity and search for answers that apply to both Blackness and Afrikan-ness. The current tendencies of excluding Blackness from the Afrikan identity may have its origin in two concerns:

1. To assure white people that they will not be thrown out of Afrika—ideologically based in Nelson Mandela's "we need you" message to white South Afrikans;
2. To oppose claims that Afrikan identity is based on race.

Most Afrikans who advocate against inclusion of Blackness in the definition of Afrikan identity would agree that racism continues to negatively impact Black people's lives. So where does the fear of applying Blackness come from? It could be rooted in the following notions:

1. They feel that agreeing with a "Black-focused" definition is also to agree with the Eurocentric notion of race;
2. They do not want to apply an exclusive terminology (exclusion is a bearing element in racism and it might keep progressive non-Afrikans out).

In our search for practical terms—i.e. terms that help to examine, explain, and demystify—it will be difficult to separate Blackness from Afrikan-ness. Moreover, the separation does not seem to serve any practical purpose. The Black and Afrikan experiences are part of an inseparable legacy of revolt against oppression and struggle for emancipation, a process which still is not fully completed. Challenges facing Afrikan people all over the world call for a practical approach, defined by reality as we experience it. Soothing white people's guilt over their ancestors' involvement in slave trade and colonialism cannot be part of this approach.

A Practical Understanding of "Afrikan"

In an attempt to summarise some critical points related to Afrikan identity, we can outline the following arguments:

1. Race is Misleading—Racialism is Real
Race, in its origin, is based on misconceptions and lies. Black, as a reference, is limited. But we cannot do away with the terms, thinking we have, at the same time, solved the realities they stem from. It is unfortunate that we live in a racialised world. The Black/Afrikan identity has been so intimately associated with negativity that any person of Afrikan heritage will never be a liberated person until she or he liberates her/himself from within an Afrikan identity, informed by the experience of Blackness.

2. *Blackness and Afrikan-ness are Intertwined*

Our discourse should be one that centres us as both Afrikan and Black. Some people might call this racial. We should call it real. The Afrikan experience is engraved in the Black experience and vice versa.

3. *The Afrikan Continent and the Afrikan Diaspora Coexist*

The Afrikan Continent and its Diaspora should be seen as a global Afrika or the African world. While the African world is inseparable, intra-Afrikan relations will remain challenging until we have obtained freedom and healing.

4. *The Afrikan Experience is Not Homogeneous*

Being Black/Afrikan does not mean being "pure." This is where we should deviate from racialised dogmas. The Black/Afrikan experience is a complex journey of enslavement, colonialism, displacement, rape, cultural dislocation, ethnic and cultural mixing, and psychological self-annihilation. It is also the journey of majestic civilizations, refined cultural practices, and resistance, uprising, and victory. The Afrikan family is comprised of members who are influenced by different cultural traits, who live by diverse sets of ideological, philosophical, and spiritual ideas, and who boast diverse lines of descent.

5. *Afrikan Identity is Not a Token*

As Afrikan people wanting freedom and self-determination, we should acknowledge everyone who advances our cause. Likewise, we should despise anyone who works against these principles. But this does not alter the definition of Afrikan. The European lending her/his support to the benefit of Afrikan people does not change her/his European-ness. Black traitors who have betrayed the Afrikan cause are still Afrikans: Afrikan traitors. Afrikan-ness can never be handed out as a token of appreciation, and it cannot be nullified because of an individual's egregious actions.

6. *It is the Responsibility of Afrikans to Define "Afrikan"*

That Europeans want to own and define the term Afrikan can be seen as an egotistical desire to dominate everyone and everything. Arrogantly following in the footsteps of their ancestors, they continue an attempt to own and define the realities of Afrikan peoples. A Eurocentric worldview objectifies the Afrikan person to a peripheral existence. It goes without saying that this worldview cannot liberate the Afrikan identity.

7. *European Discomfort Manifests as Neocolonialism*

Many European descendants seem to be looking for a way to "escape" their "race" or cultural group. Haunted and embarrassed by their ancestors' exploitation of innocent people, by the slave trade and acts of genocide, some Europeans appear to attempt to swap identities, and, by so doing, buy a ticket to a guilt free conscience. It is important to carefully examine and understand the implications of such an attempted identity-swap. Just as the Afrikan cannot wish away her/his Blackness, the white person cannot wish away her/his European-ness. Rather than playing potentially dangerous and divisive identity games, progressive Europeans can work individually and with progressive organizations to institute lasting social and political change.

8. *Reparations is a Must*

The growing understanding among Afrikan peoples of the enormous depth of European exploitation can be observed in the increasing efforts to launch and support reparations claims. Global Afrikan Congress (GAC) has defined reparations, including restitution, as "the process of self-repair, healing and restoring of a people injured because of their group identity, and the violation of their fundamental human rights by individuals, corporations, religious and other institutions, governments and other entities."[17] The demands for Afrikan reparations can, and must, be put forward by Afrikan people, informed by the Black/Afrikan historical experience: "It is up to us to continue the pressure on the ground until our just and justifiable demands are met. Only by doing so will we have paid proper tribute to our Ancestors."[18] An integral part of the reparations question is return of illegally occupied land, return of stolen artefacts, and the right to repatriate.

9. *Afrikan-ness is Expressed in Consciousness and Spirituality*

The contemporary Afrikan personality is shaped by its self-extension, as the Afrikan being is part of a Divine principle (Creator God) and the continued life cycle of ancestors and the yet-unborn.[19] This means that the Afrikan personality is rooted in past, present and future. It is when this realisation takes form as consciousness that the Afrikan identity can enter its fullness. An Afrikan centred way of life revolves around the Afrikan taking centre stage in her/his own liberation, confronting the problems and challenges she/he experiences and insisting on finding adequate solutions to them. It is through this sense of practical Afrikan nationalism that an ideological commitment will be demonstrated to the perpetuation, advancement, and defence of a cultural, political, racial entity, and way of life.[20]

10. *Easy Terms—Complex Realities*

We are not trying to pretend that agreeing on a definition in and of itself solves the whole Afrikan problem. No matter how we construct our definitions there will be weaknesses and shortcomings. The Afrikan experience is complex and multifaceted. Even if we say that all Black people are Afrikan, we will come across different understandings of what constitutes Blackness. Even if we agree that an Afrikan cultural identity is essential, we might not agree on how to determine such an identity. So, in our attempt to find practical answers to Afrikan realities, we are not looking for comfortable terms and certainly not for easy terms. What we are looking for are terms that make it possible for us to continue to operate within the reality we experience. Our real project is the restoration of self, community, culture and nation—all in one. And to engage in this restoration project adequately, we need identifiable terms.

If Everybody is an Afrikan. . .

Identity and culture are not static categories. They are shaped and transformed by evolving stages of historical events, demography and political realities. Black peoples' wish, especially in the Diaspora, to identify with Afrika has gone through many stages, including resentment, confusion, and shallow romanticism, but the embrace of Afrika has also led to cultural and political coalition building and nation building. There is a new awakening both on the Continent and in the Diaspora to embrace a liberated Afrikan identity. In our excitement and rush to freedom, we should be careful to take the painful and necessary steps to restore the Afrikan identity. And not apologise for the time and efforts we need to complete this project. Failing to do this, we might come out grossly short-changed.

In his contribution to the African Renaissance Conference hosted by South Afrika in 1998, Kwesi Kwaa Prah, warns against a growing tendency where "being African is conceptually equated with citizenship. This is not only confusing, but can be construed as mischievous. Without pandering to any chauvinistic sentiments, my argument against this tendency is that **if everybody is an African, then nobody is an African.**"[21]

Afrikan identity is, indeed, a sensitive issue. It is, for instance, often confused with the debate about who has the right to stay in an Afrikan country and often mislabeled as reverse racism. The time is, however, ripe for the Black woman and man to unapologetically stand up and pronounce their Afrikan identity with pride. Doing this, as Na'im Akbar reminds us, is a declaration of war.[22] The Eurocentric world will be upset and provoked by Afrikans cutting the strings of dependency and announcing their self-determination.

Maybe, sometime in the future, when Afrikan people have decided that the healing process is complete and new pages can be turned and painted with fresh colours, we might decide that it is time for all people to take on an Afrikan identity. In the meantime, Peter Tosh's lyrics, "As long as you're a Black man, you're an Afrikan," are as relevant today as they were when the song was released in 1970's.

Notes

[1] The word "Afrikan" is spelt with "k" instead of "c." This is a Pan-Afrikan spelling reflecting the spelling of "Afrika" in all Afrikan languages. It also refers to the ancient Kemetic (Egyptian) concept of "ka," the vital energy that sustains and creates.

[2] Frantz Fanon, *Black Skin, White Masks* (New York: Grove, 1967), 116.

[3] Charles William Ephraim, *The Pathology of Eurocentrism: The Burden and Responsibilities of Being Black* (Trenton: Africa World Press, 2003), 88, 346.

[4] Lewis R. Gordon, "Existential Dynamics of Theorizing Black Invisibility," in *Existence in Black: An Anthology of Black Existential Philosophy*, edited by Lewis R. Gordon (New Brunswick: Routledge, 1997), 71.

[5] Gordon, "Existential Dynamics of Theorizing Black Invisibility," 75.

[6] Kwame Anthony Appiah and Amy Gutmann, *Color Conscious: The Political Morality of Race* (Princeton: Princeton University Press, 1996).

[7] Kwame Anthony Appiah, *In My Father's House: Africa in the Philosophy of Culture* (London: Methuen, 1992), 115.

[8] Molefi Kete Asante, *The Afrocentric Idea* (Philadelphia: Temple University Press, 1987), 125.

[9] Steve Biko, "The Definition of Black Consciousness," in *Steve Biko: No Fears Expressed*, edited by Millard W. Arnold (Johannesburg: Skotaville Publishers, 1987), 18.

[10] Basil Davidson, *The Search for Africa: A History in the Making* (London: James Currey, 1994), 80.

[11] Lalage Brown and Michael Crowder, *The Proceedings of the First International Congress of Africanists, Accra 11th–18th December 1962* (London: Lonmans, 1964).

[12] Malcolm X, *Malcolm X Talks to Young People: Speeches in the U.S., Britain, and Africa* (New York: Pathfinder, New York 199), 37.

[13] John Henrik Clarke, *Notes for an African World Revolution: Africans at the Crossroads* (Trenton: African World Press, 1991), 407.

[14] Fanon, *Black Skin, White Masks*, 116.

[15] Tajudeen Abdul-Raheem, "Reclaiming Africa for Africans: Pan-Africanism: 1900-1994," in *Pan-Africanism: Politics, Economy, and Social Change in the Twenty-First Century*, edited by Tajudeen Abdul-Raheem (London: Pluto Press, 1996), 11.

[16] Abdul-Raheem, "Reclaiming Africa for Africans," 11.

[17] Ahmad Daniels, "Reparations: Working Group Report," in *The Bridgetown Protocol: Official Report, Africans and African Descendants World Conference Against Racism, 2–6 October 2002*, edited by Amani Olubanjo Buntu (Johannesburg: Global African Congress, 2002), 44.

[18] Roger Wareham, "The Popularization of the International Demand for Reparations," in *Should America Pay? Slavery and the Raging Debate on Reparations*, edited by Raymond A. Winbush (New York: HarperCollins, 2003), 235–236.

[19] Daudi Ajani ya Azibo, "Mental Health Defined Africentrically," in *African Psychology in Historical Perspective and Related Commentary*, edited by Daudi Ajani ya Azibo (Trenton: African World Press, 1996), 51–52.

[20] Marimba Ani, *Yurugu: An African-Centred Critique of European Cultural Thought and Behavior* (Trenton: African World Press, 1994).

[21] Kwesi Kwaa Prah, "African Renaissance or Warlordism," in *African Renaissance: The New Struggle*, edited by Malegapuru William Makgoba (Johannesburg: Tafelberg, 1999), 40, emphasis added.

[22] Na'im Akbar, *Visions for Black Men* (Nashville: Winston-Werek, 1991).

Coloured South African Politics and the New Orleans Afro-Creole Protest Tradition

Blair Marcus Proctor

Introduction

The political histories of the United States and South Africa are both rooted in the nexus of racial and economic politics, as is evidenced by acts of colonialism, slavery, and institutionalized racism. One of the key tactics Europeans in both the U.S. and South Africa used to dominate and maintain power over Africans and other groups is divide-and-conquer. Two of the most polarizing concepts created by the dominant socially-constructed White elite are the categorizations "Coloured" and "Creole."

Revolutionary movements, including slave rebellions, abolitionist movements, the Underground Railroad, the Black Power and Black Consciousness Movements that occurred during the late 1960s and early 1970s, and the current #BlackLivesMatter movement, center on systemic and perpetual racial politics. And these movements have been spearheaded by people of color, including African Americans and Creoles in the U.S. and Blacks and Coloureds in South Africa. Creoles and Coloureds have a deep history of collaborating with other racialized peoples and utilizing the strength born of numbers to fight for liberation and equality.

This study examines how the impact of apartheid and economic oppression fueled the fires of Coloured South Africans who contributed to the Black freedom struggle during apartheid. This work also explores how Creoles of Color were affected by legalized segregation through racial classifications of the United States during the Reconstruction, Jim Crow, and Civil Rights periods, and how, by fighting against segregation and oppression, Creoles of Color developed the Afro-Creole Protest Tradition.

Background

Racism, a social construction rooted in economics, was a system created and established by imperial Europe. The mission of the competitive European colonial powers was to exploit socially-classified Black bodies through enslavement, pillage, and control for two purposes: 1) generating profit which established the foundation of capitalism;[1] and 2) establishing power through political autonomy, global White supremacy, and world domination. Corporate entities such as the Dutch West India Company and the Royal African Company, were privately-owned companies that, under the auspices of European powers, profited off enslaved African bodies. The exploitation of enslaved and free African labor for the benefit of the European-elite was a global phenomenon.

European colonial expansion in the sixteenth, seventeenth, and eighteenth centuries gave rise to a number of Creole[2] societies and Creole languages, such as Louisiana Creole in New Orleans and Afrikaans in South Africa.[3] Contrary to the 1869 edition of the French dictionary *Larousse*, the 1929 edition unequivocally states that "Creole" was correctly used only in reference to the presumably White population of colonial societies. According to *Larousse*, Haitian Creoles, for example, had to be defined as "Creole Negroes" and not simply "Creoles."[4] With such distinctions, Europeans created an insider-outsider component to Creole identity and identity formation.

Emergence of the Afro-Creole Protest Tradition in Twentieth Century New Orleans, Louisiana

Both White Creoles and Creoles of Color in antebellum New Orleans understood the benefits of forming a distinct Creole class in America. In order to protect their privilege and status, White Creoles and Creoles of Color originally combated Americanization, the penetration of American culture and values.[5] However, Creole of Color leaders describe 1852 as the year of the breakdown of their sheltered and privileged order in New Orleans.[6] With the approach of the Civil War, and as hostilities between Whites and Blacks grew, the cultural and linguistic boundaries between the White Francophones and the Anglophones began to blur.[7] Both groups increasingly perceived the entire Black population (African Americans and Creoles of Color) as a common enemy, regardless of their appearance or social status.[8] The main motive for White Creoles relegating Creoles of Color to the realm of Blackness was to collapse the boundaries that had previously distinguished slaves from second-class citizens. The new order would emphasize the White-Black binary that prevailed in greater America. White Creoles eagerly acquiesced in Americanization which solidified their privilege in American society.

The continuous penetration of American race ideology and Protestantism into New Orleans during the Reconstruction, also forced Creoles of Color to redefine identity along phenotypic and political lines. Some Creoles of Color who were able "passed" into White society, but many more Creoles blended into the African American community.

Racial polarization between White and Black/Colored populations became even more acute during the Reconstruction with the emergence and rapid growth of racist groups such as the Ku Klux Klan and the Knights of the White Camellia. As a result, in spite of their being enfranchised and free, a mass exodus of the Creoles of Color occurred, and Louisiana became predominantly White for the first time in years.[9] Large numbers of Creoles of Color sought refuge not in the American North but in France, Latin America, Haiti, and Mexico.[10] The desire and ability to traverse national boundaries and emigrate to various lands could have been due to the diverse cultural composition and the Francophone and Hispanophone backgrounds of the Creoles. The ability to be accepted in foreign lands was likely facilitated be the physical appearance of those Creoles who appeared White or non-Black.

Racial politics and economics for many Afro-Creoles were centered on privilege due to their White ancestry, yet their second-class citizenship was due to their African and indigenous ancestry. The paradox of Creoleness for Afro-Creoles specifically resulted from not only racial and cultural ambiguities, but also from political identity and the ideology of *metissage* (racial-mixing or miscegenation. Many White and free people of color who benefitted from the established race hierarchal system during slavery wanted to continue acquiring the benefits of privilege and socioeconomic security over Blacks, particularly former African-descended slaves, throughout the Reconstruction era. However, local governments passed restrictive laws that impeded all Blacks from obtaining gainful employment and economic opportunities. The objectives were to keep privileges, authority, and resources in the hands of Whites.

In New Orleans, Black Creoles and Black Americans tried to protect their rights and dignity in the face of the rising tide of racial discrimination.[11] The majority of Creoles were more affluent and politically and socially powerful than Black Americans.[12] Prior to the enforcement of Jim Crow during the late nineteenth century, Creoles of Color and African Americans were two different groups of people. Afro-Creoles were acculturated to White Creole culture, also referred to as Latin (French and Spanish) European culture, and African Americans were primarily acculturated to African cultures and to White American (Anglo-Saxon and English) European culture. Many African Americans who were in New Orleans during the antebellum period were enslaved property of American slave masters who had moved from other southern states. Additionally, several affluent Creoles of Color enslaved Blacks as well.[13]

The majority of Creoles of Color were born free, educated, and assumed lifestyles which protected them at times from the realities of the White-Black binary and racial hierarchy that occurred in other parts of the southern United States. The reluctance of most Creoles of Color to adhere to the American color line struck some Black Americans as a denial of racial solidarity.[14] However, the enforcement of the one-drop rule made Creoles of Color enter the Blackness of America's White-Black binary, and it gave birth to the Afro-Creole Protest Tradition.[15]

The Afro-Creole Protest Tradition was rooted in Afro-Creoles revolting against the race ideology established by the White-elite in colonial New Orleans. It is important to note that the majority of leaders who fought for suffrage rights for people of color during the Civil War, Reconstruction, and Civil Rights eras were Creoles of African descent.[16] For example, on March 10, 1864, Creole leaders Jean-Baptiste Roudanez and E. Arnold Bertonneau, met with U.S. Senator Charles Sumner of Massachusetts and Congressman William D. Kelley of Pennsylvania to discuss the final preparations for a petition in support of suffrage rights for people of color; Kelly and Sumnar suggested to Roudanez and Bertonneau that the petition be amended from its original, which asked that suffrage rights be extended to all freemen in the South.[17] Roudanez also published a newspaper in both French and English called *La Tribune* which promoted unity within the multicultural and multilingual Black communities and fought for suffrage rights.[18] The Creole fight for suffrage rights occurred initially due to interest-convergence. In theory, taking a Marxian approach of collaborating with African Americans, another group that was disenfranchised, would not only assist African Americans, but would protect and maintain the Afro-Creoles' privileged status.

African Americans who had been enslaved were enfranchised shortly after emancipation, and the constitution was changed in 1870 to prohibit the denial of the right to vote on grounds of "race, color, or previous condition of servitude."[19] However, White citizens, court clerks, and elected officials created various laws, tests, and catch-22s to prevent African Americans from voting. White legislatures passed "Black Codes" and "vagrancy laws" and enforced segregation to maintain the color line and to prevent Blacks from advancing in the free-market and to ensure that Whites would maintain economic power, financial opportunity, and unearned privilege.

During this period, African American men were elected to positions within state and local governments. Caesar Carpentier Antione, an Afro-Creole, served as 13th Lieutenant Governor in Louisiana from May 22, 1873 to April 24, 1877.[20] However political gains were temporary: due to fear of losing power and for the purpose of maintaining White supremacy, the U.S. Supreme Court severely limited the ability of the federal government to protect the civil rights of newly freed African Americans.[21] The 1875 *U.S. vs. Cruikshank* case, along with other Supreme Court case decisions that supported the Jim Crow laws in the southern states not only affected African Americans, but Creoles of Color who now were classified along with Black Americans as "Colored/Negro."

In his classic 1903 publication *The Souls of Black Folk* W. E. B. Du Bois contends that the problem of the twentieth century was the problem of the color line.[22] Although the "color-line" had been in existence since slavery and White supremacy were established by the European-elites in the fifteenth century, the 1896 *Plessy vs. Ferguson* U.S. Supreme Court case paved the way for further restrictive and discriminatory so-called "separate but equal" laws. Homer Adolph Plessy, who was one-eighth Black and a Creole from New Orleans, challenged the separate but equal law.[23] Although, Plessy appeared White, he was an active member of the Afro-Creole Protest tradition as a civil rights activist. Plessy was an important candidate hired by the Citizen's Committee of New Orleans (Comite des Citoyens) to prove the absurdity of racial segregation.[24] Plessy was arrested and forced off of the streetcar because he claimed his Blackness. In other words, no one would have noticed that he was of African descent if Plessy remained quiet and not acknowledged his ethnicity.

The color line which DuBois stated would be the problem of the twentieth century was also used by Afro-Creoles to discriminate against African Americans.[25] As historian Sharlene Sinegal DeCuir reveals,

> They [American Blacks and Creoles] experienced the pressures of Jim Crow differently. American Blacks were discriminated against by both Creoles and whites. Being dark-complexioned and poor, instead of being light-complexioned and "well-off" created the tale of "two-cities." Creoles experienced problems with whites, but their problems differed significantly from those blacks experienced. Their problems came from whites who were resentful of their education and wealth. American blacks' problems consisted of simple survival, such as finding jobs.[26]

Race relations during the Jim Crow era intersected with colorism, class, and discrimination to stoke hostilities among poor Whites, Creoles, and Blacks.

Hence, social constructions of race, class, gender, and caste along with racial discrimination and segregation, and cultural antagonisms served to reinforce the White elites' political and economic autonomy during the twentieth century.

During the twentieth century, many people of African ancestry began studying their origins and uniting and working for solutions as Africans. Several Black Creole intellectuals embraced Pan-Africanism—a philosophy formulated by African Diaspora intellectuals that focused on the importance of continental Africans and Africans of the Diaspora coming together and fighting for liberation. In the early 1900s, Afro-Creoles were reading the works of DuBois and Marcus Garvey. In the 1940s to the 1960s they read Franz Fanon, George Padmore, C. L. R. James, and Aime Cesaire. Cesaire, for many, personified of Pan-Africanism.[27] Cesaire believed that people of African descent from Africa and the Diaspora were bound through their shared oppression within the various colonial European powers throughout Africa and the Americas. Black scholars of the *Negritude* movements of the late nineteenth and early twentieth centuries argued that Black Creoles should not look to France for identity and elevation, but to the African continent due to their African ancestry.

Many upper-class Black Creoles understood the importance of working with African American New Orleanians and used their class and educational attainments to work to uplift Black communities. This movement entailed Creole intellectuals and powerful organizations, such as the Autocrat Club, and political parties that fought for equal rights from the era of slavery to the Reconstruction to the Civil Rights era all working together.[28] Alexander P. Tureaud, a prominent Black Creole attorney for the New Orleans chapter of the National Association for the Advancement of Colored People (NAACP) in the late 1920s, stated that, "if we are ever to enjoy full citizenship as a race, we will have to unite our forces and fight for it."[29]

By the advent of the Great Depression in the early 1930s, the distinction between Black Creoles and Black Americans "became increasing blurred through intermarriage, social mobility, the decline of the French language, and the sheer weight of white supremacy."[30] Louisiana's laws of racial classification expanded in 1940 such that, "any degree of traceability was sufficient for Negro classification."[31] In other words, concurrent with Americanization diluting colonial French culture, Afro-Creoles became technically more phenotypically Black, leaving creoleness to be associated with remembered culture and pedigree as opposed to racial classification.

Black New Orleans residents, whether they were of Creole or American backgrounds, were connected because of their shared African ancestry. To Caucasians, they all merited second-class status and none were ever viewed as equal to Whites (Creole or American) throughout the various periods in

New Orleans and American history. Thus, any hope that Black Creoles would become "American" in the Jim Crow era was unrealistic because Americans of African descent in the U.S. (including Black Creoles in Louisiana) were segregated and thus restricted from assimilating and integrating into American society. In other words, the American South's Jim Crow laws removed any possibility of distinction between Creoles of Color and Black Americans: The one-drop rule prevailed.

The political consciousness of the 1960s and 1970s sparked both fear and change throughout the nation of America and the world. As Black Americans began rising and demanding equal rights and equal participation in the governing of their cities and states, Blacks began effectively utilizing their collective power and their electoral power. Ernest Nathan Dutch Morial, the first Black mayor of New Orleans hailed from a prominent Creole family.[32] Morial could have passed as White, but he identified as Black.[33] During his mayoral bid, the mainstream White press was preoccupied by Morial's ethnic background and appearance and commented on them in its campaign analysis. Columnist Iris Kelso said of Morial what is often said of influential mixed race African Americans, that he was "too white for the blacks and too black for the whites."[34]

New Orleans media outlets promoted propaganda supporting race ideology in order to help maintain the status quo. White elites in New Orleans wanted to stoke fears among the masses of White New Orleanians as to what could potentially happen to New Orleans if the first Black mayor in Louisiana history was elected into office. The 1970s Morial's mayoral campaign was the turning-point in New Orleans history for two reasons: 1) because of the continuous, antagonistic race relations that occurred after the enactment of the Civil Rights Act of 1964 and 2) the media wanted to perpetuate racial divisions among the White, Black, and Creole New Orleanians through racism and colorism in order to maintain White supremacy and control of the various markets supporting White elites since the colonial period.

Morial could have attempted to straddle the race line and play up his Creole heritage to mollify Whites, but his Black consciousness and not his Creole background was the determining factor as to how Morial identified himself. Morial's identification with and service to the New Orleans' Black community was reciprocated with deeply felt pride and admiration.[35] The Civil Rights Movement was essentially the ethnic cauldron melding Black New Orleans into a united whole.[36] The younger generations of Creole descendants abandoned their Creoleness and identified with their Blackness because racist oppression marginalized the entire Black community without distinction. As a cohesive unit, the Black community asserted its agency and demanded equal rights as New Orleans citizens.

Conflicted Coloured Politics in Apartheid South Africa

Coloured South Africans are officially divided into seven subgroups: Cape Coloured, other Coloured, Malay, Griqua, Asiatic, other Asiatic, and Chinese; it is important to notice the use of the word "other" in these classifications.[37] As dehumanizing as these categories may be, the alternative term, "non-White" is just as dehumanizing and even more likely to elicit feelings of inferiority.[38] The South African nation-state created a crude notion that Coloureds were an amalgamation without a history and were dependent on the rights and privileges formulated for them by the ruling White elite order. Just as it happened around the world, in South Africa, race was used as a tool to separate people into designated categories that were defined by and that supported the apartheid social order. Consequently, the racial classification of a South African within the social order determined their condition within South African society. While some members of the Coloured intelligentsia—political leaders, teachers, and other professionals—comprised the upper echelons of the Coloured community, the majority of Coloureds were of the rural and urban underclasses and remained outside of the Coloured political organizations.[39]

The major difference between Coloured and African politics, and a major dynamic of Coloured politics, is the complex issue of the nature of the Coloured peoples themselves.[40] Coloured political leaders such as J. W. Tobin, A. E. Abdurrahman, and George Golding argued for Coloureds to have racial pride. Racial pride for many Colored was decidedly not based on African heritage. Racial pride for many would become a tool by which to obtain privilege from and to fight for integration into White society rather than to support Black liberation.[41] By adhering to racist race ideology and its support of the apartheid state, the Colored ideology was particularly problematic.

There were, however, Colored leaders who refused to perpetuate the status quo. In the January 1959 issue of *DRUM*, Stanley B. Lollan, a secretary of the South African Coloured People's Organization (SACPO) in 1953, was active in campaigns against racial classification of the Coloured people under the 1950 Population Registration Act.[42] In their promotion of non-racialism and democracy, Lollan, along with former lawyer and civil rights activist Nelson Mandela, were among 30 anti-apartheid political figures charged during the 1956 Treason Trial by the National Party in which Lollan was a defendant between 1956 and 1961.[43]

Since non-racialism was the antithesis of apartheid, many political leaders and supporters of the philosophy were imprisoned. As a radical in favor of dismantling legalized racism and race ideology, Coloured South

African scholar-activist Dennis Vincent Brutus joined the Anti-Coloured Affairs Department organization (Anti-CAD).[44] CAD was established by the apartheid regime as a political tool to promote divide-and-conquer and maintain divisions between Blacks and Coloureds. Brutus, like Mandela, was arrested and imprisoned at Robben Island due his fight to abolish both racism and the idea of race. Brutus symbolized what the apartheid regime wanted to eradicate, but he was not solely an anti-apartheid activist. Brutus was a humanist whose mission was to achieve global liberation of oppressed people, regardless of social-construction along with other likeminded freedom fighters.

Because the efforts of activists to abolish race, racism, and apartheid in the 1960s were not successful, revolutionaries analyzed their tactics and considered ways to more effectively challenge the established order.[45] Veli Mbele asserts that, "what Black Consciousness had taught us [was] that it was the mission of the system for us to kill one another so that white people could continue to dominate us."[46] Instead of continuing to work in separate political movements that served only Black/African, only Coloured, or only Indian/Asian interests, by uniting, these groups embodied Pan-African socio-political consciousness and organized struggle.

The apartheid regime used many tactics to dissolve the unification of Black and Coloreds. One of their strategies was the forced relocation of Black and Coloured South Africans, during the early 1950s, and throughout the 1960s. Coloureds were exiled from Sophiatown to Westbury, and Blacks were dispossessed from their homes in Westbury and were relocated to the Meadowlands. The dispersal of Blacks and Coloureds was a divide-and-conquer tactic used to maintain White supremacy and social order. These attacks and dispossessions did not go unchallenged. Coloured activist Don Mattera describes a protest meeting at which "speakers rose; their themes hardly varied: Injustice; Slavery; Exploitation; Expropriation of properties; Domination; Freedom and human dignity, and the recognition of Black people's rights to own homes and live without the threat of being forcibly removed from their properties and houses by the police and the government's military forces." [47] Blacks and Coloreds subjected to forced relocation were not only fighting for the right to remain in their homes, they were fighting to protect their birthrights.[48]

The state-enforced removal from homes and confiscation of property supported apartheid interests in two ways: 1) the state was able to use cheap Black labor and convict labor in mining based industries, and 2) Blacks and Coloreds were forcibly relocated to lands that were insufficient and incapable of producing produce and goods necessary to feed residents or generate income. Hence, through legalized segregation, racial oppression, and Afrikaner and British economic dominance, Coloureds and Blacks remained dependent on the private-sector markets and the White-controlled apartheid government.

The Black Consciousness Movement in South Africa was influenced by both African thinkers and the Black Power Movement, a forceful expression of racial assertiveness that had begun in the mid-1960s in the U.S.[49] The Black freedom struggle was an international movement. Many activists were also international exchange-students and part of the intellectual class producing the future leaders of various movements in the U.S., the Caribbean, South America, and various African countries, including South Africa. Anthony Marx in *Making Race and Nation: A Comparison of South Africa, the United States, and Brazil* states that "Bishop Manas Buthelezi of Soweto recalls first learning about Black Power while he was a student at Drew University in 1965, where he heard Stokely Carmichael speak, and telling others about it on his return home in 1968."[50] In the U.S. context, Malcolm X, Martin Luther King, Jr., and several other leaders involved in the Black freedom struggle were not only political leaders but they were also affiliated with religious organizations and dogmas (such as the Nation of Islam and Christianity, respectively). In South Africa, religion, faith, and spirituality intersected and synthesized with secular political movements and were used to further fuel social change. Perhaps Black Power was most influential in South Africa through the adoption of its derivative Black progressive theology by popular religious figures, including Bishop Desmond Tutu, Dr. Allan Boesak, and others in the South African Council of Churches and in the African Independent churches.[51]

Advocates of Black theology, inspired by the writings of James Cone, emphasized combatting spiritual as well as material oppression and focusing on healing.[52] Black Consciousness advocates adopted a similar stance, concluding that "it is a sin to allow oneself to be oppressed."[53]

Advocates of apartheid and racists in various parts of the world excel at using religious dogma to justify their oppression of Black people. Although the Church and State are presented as separate entities, both political orders are indeed intertwined and in bed together in promoting White supremacy. While racist White supremacists might offer concessions to Coloreds in some cases, this was done pure to sow seeds of dissention. In the racist worldview, any ethnicity other than Caucasian is inferior.

Black Theology was a philosophy used to assert a counter-narrative and to serve as an acknowledgement that Africans and Colored people were also made in God's image. As Boesak states, "God's power is a liberating, creative power and it is this 'full authority' with which God has endowed humanity."[54] Similarly, the late Steve Biko, known as the leader of the Black Consciousness Movement, asserts that "freedom is the ability to define oneself with one's possibilities held back not by the power of other people over one but only by one's relationship with God and to natural surroundings."[55] The objective of Black Theology, Pan-Africanism, Black Power, and Black Consciousness movements is to instill the consciousness of empowered Blackness into all Black people, including Africans, Afro-Creoles, Coloureds, and Asians, and to impress upon them the fact that it is their duty to join the Black freedom struggle for global liberation.

Conclusion

Many of the organizations and movements that fought for social change during the Black Power era dissolved and many people involved with the struggle were either assassinated or driven underground in order to survive state-sanctioned repression. Oppressive nations feared that these social movements would overthrow governments that have perpetually benefitted from Black peoples' suffering since the first Europeans penetrated Africa in the seventeenth century.

While some revolutionaries and revolutionary movements are no longer active, new warriors have arisen as a new generation learns that the war against racism and oppression must be fought unceasingly. The rampant lynchings by police officers of African American men have led to uprisings across America, especially in Ferguson, Missouri; Baltimore, Maryland Baton Rouge, Louisiana; and Atlanta, Georgia, the cities where police have recently killed African Americans. New revolutionary organizations that have arisen to organize the fight for freedom in the twenty-first century abound and include the New Black Panther Party and Black Lives Matter.

In the past, Black stars and artists fought on the frontlines of the freedom struggle, so too, in this era, are celebrities rising up and raising their fists against oppression. During the 2016 Super Bowl half-time show, superstar Beyoncé performed her hit song "Formation," which asserts the importance for solidarity against police brutality, and calls on Black women and members of the Black LGBTQ communities, in particular, to prepare for battle. Beyoncé's anthem of unapologetically celebrated Blackness, which was also a tribute in honor of the 50 year anniversary the founding of the Black Panther Party, was staged before a predominantly White audience. Although the right-wing media referred to Beyoncé's performance as an example of "reverse racism," the majority of Black feminist groups and progressive media pundits viewed "Formation" as a Black feminist and Black pride anthem whose declaration in America is long overdue.

In the song, Beyoncé charges Black women in particular and Black folks in general to "get in formation" and start a revolution to achieve liberation. However, "Formation" could also be said to begin within the artist herself. In the song, Beyoncé's articulates her identity formation as a person whose father is from Alabama and whose mother is from Louisiana. As she sings, "Mix that Negro with that Creole / makes a Texas-Bama" Beyoncé silences critics who charge she disavows her Black ancestry and affirms that her Blackness is multifaceted multicultural continuation of a deeply-rooted Black Freedom Struggle.

The "Formation" music video is a tribute to the hundreds of unarmed and innocent African Americans killed by police officers and racist citizens, to the Black Lives Matter movement, and to thousands of African Americans who were killed or left devastated when the levees that were holding back the waters of Hurricane Katrina broke. Beyoncé's "Formation" reveals the connectedness of these atrocities and confirms that there can be no "post-racial" celebration in a blatantly racist society.

While South Africa and America are glossed as lands of opportunity, modernity, and diversity, both nations boast police departments that are notorious for their racist brutality and extrajudicial killings. What is more, racial inequalities in education, housing, income level, and employment status persist in both contemporary America and in post-apartheid South Africa.[56] In an era in which times appear to have changed but have actually, in many cases, regressed, Coloreds in South Africa and Creoles in America find themselves facing an array of personal, social, and political choices similar to those of their ancestors. Some may seek to position themselves as a separate caste—a buffer race—that can enjoy less persecution than Africans. Those who are phenotypically able may find themselves abandoning the struggle altogether and "passing" into the ease of Caucasian society. There will also be many South African Coloreds and Afro-Creoles who follow the paths of their esteemed predecessors, fall into revolutionary formation, and continue the fight for freedom, justice, and equality.

Notes

[1] Claud Anderson, *Dirty Little Secrets about Black History, Its Heroes and Other Troublemakers* (Bethesda: Powernomics Corporation of America, 1997).

[2] *Creole* has meant different terms throughout the centuries and the concept has changed over time. The word *creole* first arose in Portuguese *crioulo* approximately in the sixteenth century, although it was first attested in Spanish *criollo* in 1590 with the meaning of "Spaniard born in the New World." By the early 1600s, a Peruvian source records it with the meaning,

"black born in the New World." Thus, creole distinguished Old World parents from New World children of those parents—not mixed race or mixture. However, creole is often used as another form of explaining mixture or blended culture whether referring to language, certain ethnic groups, religion/spirituality, and/or cuisine.

[3] Virginia R. Dominguez, *White by Definition* (New Brunswick: Rutgers University Press, 1986), 13.

[4] Dominguez, *White by Definition*, 14.

[5] Shirley Elizabeth Thompson, *Exiles at Home* (Cambridge: Harvard University Press, 2007).

[6] Joseph Logsdon and Caryn Cossé Bell, "The Americanization of Black New Orleans, 1850–1900," in *Creole New Orleans: Race and Americanization*, edited by Arnold R. Hirsch and Joseph Logsdon (Baton Rouge: Louisiana State University Press, 1992), 208.

[7] Sylvie DuBois and Megan Melançon, "Creole Is, Creole Ain't: Diachronic and Synchronic Attitudes toward Creole Identity in Southern Louisiana," *Language in Society* 29:2 (June 2000): 241.

[8] DuBois and Melançon, "Creole Is, Creole Ain't," 241.

[9] DuBois and Melançon, "Creole Is, Creole Ain't," 243.

[10] Logsdon and Bell, "Americanization of Black New Orleans," 208.

[11] Logsdon and Bell, "Americanization of Black New Orleans," 215.

[12] Sybil Kein, *Creole* (Baton Rouge: Louisiana State University Press, 2000), 73.

[13] Kein, *Creole*, 74.

[14] Logsdon and Bell, "Americanization of Black New Orleans," 237.

[15] The "one drop" rule is rooted in American slavery. Mixed-race children took the status of their enslaved mothers. "One drop" of African blood made someone Black, no matter how White they appeared. This rule only applied to people of African descent. There is no rule for U.S. citizens of indigenous, Asian, or Jewish ancestry. (See also F. James Davis. *Who is Black?* (University Park: The Pennsylvania State University Press), 2001).

[16] Caryn Cossé Bell, *Revolution, Romanticism, and the Afro-Creole Protest Tradition in Louisiana, 1718–1868* (Baton Rouge: Louisiana State University Press, 2004).

[17] Logsdon and Bell, "Americanization of Black New Orleans," 225.

[18] Sharlene Sinegal DeCuir, "Attacking Jim Crow: Black Activism in New Orleans, 1925-1941," Ph.D. thesis (Louisiana State University, May 2009).

[19] George Frederickson, *Black Liberation* (Oxford: Oxford University Press, 1995), 14.

[20] John W. Blassingame, *Black New Orleans, 1860–1880* (Chicago: University of Chicago Press, 1973).

[21] *U.S. vs. Cruikshank: 1875* <http://www.encyclopedia.com/doc/1G2-3498200092.html>.

[22] W.E.B. DuBois, *The Souls of Black Folk* (Chicago: A.C. McClurg and Co., 1903), 13.

[23] Plessy vs. Ferguson, *U.S. Supreme Court Case*, 1896.

[24] Katy Reckdahl, "Plessy and Ferguson unveil unique plaque today marking their ancestors' actions," *The Times-Picayune*, October 6, 2009.

[25] W.E.B. Du Bois, *Souls of Black Folk*, 1903.

[26] DeCuir, "Attacking Jim Crow," 46.

[27] Thompson, *Exiles*, 153.

[28] Arnold R. Hirsch, "Simply a Matter of Black and White," in *Creole New Orleans: Race and Americanization*, edited by Arnold R. Hirsch and Joseph Logsdon (Baton Rouge: Louisiana State University Press, 1992), 271.

[29] Hirsch, "Simply a Matter of Black and White," 244.

[30] DuBois and Melançon, "Creole Is, Creole Ain't," 244.

[31] DuBois and Melançon, "Creole Is, Creole Ain't," 244.

[32] Hirsch, "Simply a Matter of Black and White," 292.

[33] Hirsch, "Simply a Matter of Black and White," 292.

[34] Hirsch, "Simply a Matter of Black and White," 317.

[35] Hirsch, "Simply a Matter of Black and White," 292.

[36] Hirsch, "Simply a Matter of Black and White," 292.

[37] Pierre Hugo, *Quislings or Realists?* (Johannesburg: Ravan Press, 1978), 200.

[38] Hugo, *Quislings or Realists?* 200.

[39] Hugo, *Quislings or Realists?* 251.

[40] Lewis, *Wire and the Wall*, 250.

[41] Lewis, *Wire and the Wall*, 250.

[42] Stanley B. Lollan also hid and protected Nelson Mandela and his ANC comrades during the apartheid era. See *DRUM* (January 1959), 22.

[43] *DRUM* (January, 1959), 22.

[44] Julie Frederikse, *The Unbreakable Thread: Non-Racialism in South Africa* (Bloomington: Indiana University Press, 1990).

[45] Anthony W. Marx, *Lessons of Struggle: South African Internal Opposition, 1960–1990* (New York: Oxford University Press, 1992), 39.

[46] Veli Mbele, "Biko's Influence on Me," in *We Write What We Like: Celebrating Steve Biko*, edited by Chris Van Wyk (Johannesburg: Wits University Press, 2007), 60.

[47] Don Mattera, *Sophiatown* (Johannesburg: Ravan Press, 1989), 84–85.
[48] Mattera, *Sophiatown*, 85.
[49] Marx, *Lessons of Struggle*, 43.
[50] Marx, *Lessons of Struggle*, 43.
[51] Marx, *Lessons of Struggle*, 43.
[52] Marx, *Lessons of Struggle*, 43.
[53] Marx, *Lessons of Struggle*, 43.
[54] Boesak, *Farewell to Innocence*, 51.
[55] Bokwe Mafuna, "The Impact of Steve Biko on My Life," in *We Write What We Like: Celebrating Steve Biko*, edited by Chris Van Wyk (Johannesburg: Wits University Press, 2007), 88.
[56] F. M. Griffith, "Race and Space in Post-Apartheid South Africa, 1996–2001." Ph.D. thesis (Philadelphia, University of Pennsylvania. 2009), iv, 149.

Bibliography

Anderson, Claud. *Dirty Little Secrets about Black History, Its Heroes and Other Troublemakers*. Bethesda: Powernomics Corporation of America, 1997.

Blassingame, John W. *Black New Orleans, 1860–1880*. Chicago: University of Chicago Press, 1973.

Boesak, Allen. *Farewell to Innocence: A Socio-Ethical Study on Black Theology and Black Power.* Maryknoll, NY: Orbis Books, 1977.

Desdunes, Rodolphe Lucien. *A Few Words to Dr. DuBois "With Malice Towards None."* Baton Rouge: Louisiana State University Press, 1907.

Dooling, Wayne. *Slavery, Emancipation and Colonial Rule in South Africa.* Scottsville: University of KwaZulu-Natal Press, 2007.

DuBois, W.E.B. *The Souls of Black Folk*. Chicago: A.C. McClurg and Co., 1903.

Dubois, Sylvie and Megan Melançon. "Creole Is, Creole Ain't: Diachronic and Synchronic Attitudes toward Creole Identity in Southern Louisiana." *Language in Society* 29:2 (June 2000): 237–258.

Dyson, Michael Eric. *Come Hell or High Water: Hurricane Katrina and the Color of Disaster*. New York: Basic Civitas Books, 2006.

Frederickson, George. *Black Liberation: A Comparative History of Black Ideologies in the United States and South Africa*. New York: Oxford University Press, 1995.

Griffith, F. M. "Race and Space in Post-Apartheid South Africa, 1996–2001." Ph.D. thesis. University of Pennsylvania. 2009.

Hamilton, Charles V., et al. *Beyond Racism: Race and Inequality in Brazil, South Africa, and the United States.* Boulder: Lynne Rienner Publishers, Inc., 2001.

Hirsch, Arnold R., and Joseph Logsdon. *Creole New Orleans: Race and Americanization.* Baton Rouge: Louisiana State University Press, 1992.

Hirsch, Arnold R. "Fade to Black: Hurricane Katrina and the Disappearance of Creole New Orleans." *Journal of American History* 94 (Dec. 2007): 752–761.

-----. "Simply a Matter of Black and White." In *Creole New Orleans: Race and Americanization.* Edited by Arnold R. Hirsch and Joseph Logsdon. Baton Rouge: Louisiana State University Press, 1992. 262–320.

Kein, Sybil, ed. *Creole: The History and Legacy of Louisiana's Free People of Color.* Baton Rouge: Louisiana State University Press, 2000.

Lewis, Gavin. *Between the Wire and the Wall: A History of South African "Coloured" Politics.* New York: St. Martin's Press, 1987.

Logsdon, Joseph and Caryn Cossé Bell. "The Americanization of Black New Orleans, 1850–1900." In *Creole New Orleans: Race and Americanization.* Edited by Arnold R. Hirsch and Joseph Logsdon. Baton Rouge: Louisiana State University Press, 1992. 201–262.

Mafuna, Bokwe. "The Impact of Steve Biko on My Life." In *We Write What We Like: Celebrating Steve Biko.* Edited by Chris Van Wyk. Johannesburg: Wits University Press, 2007. 77–90.

Mattera, Don. *Sophiatown.* Johannesburg: Ravan Press, 1989.

Marx, Anthony W. *Lessons of Struggle: South African Internal Opposition, 1960–1990.* New York: Oxford University Press, 1992.

-----. *Making Race and Nation: A Comparison of South Africa, the United States, and Brazil.* New York: Cambridge University Press, 1998.

Mbele, Veli. "Biko's Influence on Me." In *We Write What We Like: Celebrating Steve Biko.* Edited by Chris Van Wyk. Johannesburg: Wits University Press, 2007. 53–62.

Nystrom, Justin A. *New Orleans after the Civil War: Race, Politics, and a New Birth of Freedom.* Baltimore: Johns Hopkins University Press, 2010.

Sinegal DeCuir, Sharlene. "Attacking Jim Crow: Black Activism in New Orleans, 1925-1941." Ph.D. thesis. Louisiana State University, May 2009.

Thompson, Shirley Elizabeth. *Exiles at Home: The Struggle to Be American in Creole New Orleans.* London: Harvard University Press, 2009.

Van Wyk, Chris. *We Write What We Like: Celebrating Steve Biko.* Johannesburg: Wits University Press, 2007.

PART THREE

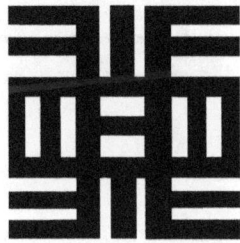

AFRICANITY, EDUCATION, AND TECHNOLOGY

Indigenising Human Language Technology for National Development

Tunde Adegbola

Preamble

Mr. Vice Chancellor, sir, other principal officers of the university, deans of faculties and heads of departments, distinguished ladies and gentlemen, one of the beauties of the intellectual enterprise derives from the humbling privilege it gives to build on the efforts of one's teachers and mentors. Seated in this audience today are some of those who have taught and mentored me, and it is a source of great pleasure that many who I look up to are of the opinion that the things that I am about to say here today may be sufficiently significant to warrant their attendance of this lecture. I thank you very much for this honour.

I have never had any difficulties with the idea of being a lecturer. It is a role that I relish, and it is the basis of my relationship with ARCIS. Furthermore, most of the things that I really understand, I have learned in the process of trying to teach to others. However, both the circumstances of a distinguished one among superiors and equals, as well as that of a confirmed host that suddenly becomes a guest, I find quite intriguing. Be that as it may however, I wish to thank the Africa Regional Centre for Information Science (ARCIS) for according me the honour of being its 1st Distinguished Guest Lecturer.

Introduction

The title under which I have chosen to speak today is Indigenising Human Language Technology (HLT) for National Development. Most times that I have had the opportunity of speaking about HLT in public fora, the response that I usually get from the audience is *"Ṣé ìyẹn ló wá kàn?"*

("Can that be our priority at this time?") In anticipation of this valid question from this august audience, let me paraphrase the topic and thereby make an attempt to better place it in context. So, the topic of our discussion may be paraphrased as making HLT indigenous to our cultural reality so as to be able to exploit it as a productivity enhancement in our national development efforts.

Human Language Technology describes a range of computational techniques designed to process natural language as presented in the form of speech or text (Dale 2000). Within this context, a technology can be described as a process of exploiting natural laws towards achieving better understanding and greater control of the human environment and the use of this capacity to improve the human condition. The natural laws that technology exploits are elucidated by science. Science is to a large extent value free, but technology is motivated by cultural imperatives, which are necessarily value laden. Technology, being a cultural product therefore, is inextricably tied to the culture that demands and produces it. Hence, even though there is a high level of global commonality in science, diversity of human cultures dictates commensurate levels of diversity in technology and its applications. It is in this context that the indigenisation of technology becomes an issue.

Indigenisation is the act or process of making something indigenous. Indigenous means originating in and/or characteristic of a particular region or country. It implies an adaptation in order to increase the local content of a product, local participation in a process or local ownership of a tangible or intangible possession.

Development is a complex multifaceted positive change phenomenon characterised by social, environmental, political and economic objectives. According to Iwayemi (2001), development is about creating a better world for all citizens based on advances in skills, knowledge and capability.

Present development thinking began to crystalise around the middle of the 20th century. After the Second World War, the need to factor the economic growth of the then colonies into the general understanding of world affairs was realised. This realisation led to the emergence of theories of how these colonies could modernise and industrialise based on western models and values. Since its inception however, development thinking has gone through a series of phases such as the dependency and other theories of top-down relationships between the advanced countries and Third World nations. Alternative theories of bottom-up approaches to development have also been proposed by opponents of the essentially top-down approaches and the debate between the proponents of these two approaches have now culminated in the present popular paradigm of human development.

Within the human development paradigm, people are the real wealth of a nation and hence the center piece of national development. The goal of national development therefore is creating an environment in which people can develop to their full potentials and are capacitated to lead productive and creative lives based on their own needs and interests. It involves expanding the choices people have to lead lives that they value, within the limits of sustainability. The Millennium Development Goals (MDGs), which are derived from the purpose of human development, are aimed at:

- Eradicating poverty and hunger
- Achieving Universal primary education
- Promoting gender equality
- Reducing child mortality
- Improving maternal health
- Combating disease
- Ensuring environmental sustainability
- Developing a global partnership

These goals encapsulate the development priorities in the world we live in today.

It is from the above described loci of HLT, indigenisation, and national development that I intend to address my topic of Indigenising Human Language Technology for National Development. The task I have set myself is to demonstrate that HLT has important implications for national development. Having done that, I shall then proceed to propose a strategy for developing HLT capacity in Nigeria.

What is HLT?

Humans have always exploited laws of nature to facilitate communication through language. The production of speech sounds by the deliberate pumping of air from the lungs through various articulatory devices in the mouth and the nose into the atmosphere constitutes an exploitation of natural laws for the betterment of the human condition. Over the ages, humans have also used the technology of graphic markings to represent ideas in written language and have also developed printing technology to mass produce written text. All these technologies are addressed primarily at providing media for the expression of human thought and they have all been enhanced by recent developments in digital technology.

Beyond the use of digital technology to enhance these traditional language technologies however, digital technology is now opening new vistas in the development of HLTs that enable machines to undertake some of the linguistic activities that used to be the sole preserve of human beings.

Language technologies such as Text-to-Speech (TTS) synthesis which enables a computer to convert written utterance to spoken utterance and Automatic Speech Recognition (ASR) which converts spoken utterance to written utterance have been developed, taking advantage of the versatility of digital technology. At Alt-i, we have been working on Automatic Speech Recognition of Yoruba in the past five years and we have good results to show for these efforts. Also, one of our associates, Dr. Odetunji Odejobi of the Department of Computer Science and Engineering at the Obafemi Awolowo University is making good progress on TTS synthesis of Yoruba.

Other important language technologies include machine translation (MT), by which statements in one natural language can be translated into equivalent statements in another natural language, and Natural Language Understanding (NLU) by which the meaning of statements in one natural language can be automatically extracted and used by a computer. Our on-going projects in Igbo-English and Yoruba-English machine translation are showing us how difficult machine translation can be, but more importantly, that it is possible. I am sure that members of the audience that have visited the exhibition stands on these two projects will agree with me that it is difficult but possible and that we are equal to the task of making it possible.

A farmer in a remote Nigerian village dials a special number on his/her ordinary "pure water"[1] Nokia cell phone and demands from the machine at the other end, *"Eélòó ni wọn ń ta kòkó lọ́wọ́ lọ́wọ́ báyìí ní ọjà àgbáyé?"* ("What is the going price for cocoa in the international commodities market?") And the machine at the other end of the phone line answers, speaking the same language of inquiry. That is HLT at work.

This may sound like a story from science fiction, but I would like to remind us that barely thirty years ago, only James Bond could take a telephone call sitting in the audience of a lecture like this one. I would be really surprised if there is anyone in this audience that still lacks that capability.

To bring things closer home, two years ago, I was privileged to attend a meeting of the National Council for Information. During the meeting a lady from the Federal Ministry of Information demonstrated a system by which any Nigerian that has access to an SMS-enabled phone network can obtain information from the ministry by sending a simple text message to a computer server through a dedicated phone number. A number of people in the meeting tried it there and then and the system worked. Since then, the project seems to have gone the way of many other Nigerian projects, i.e. nothing has been heard of it since then.

I refer to this project in order to demonstrate that some of the platforms required for our farmer in a remote Nigerian village to participate productively in the globalised economy already exists and is widely available in this country. All we now need to do is bridge the communication gap between the unlettered and such opportunities using HLT. I dare say that the relevant technologies are within our reach.

In order to make this seeming science fiction a reality however, we need to understand the acoustic and symbolic structures of our languages by working with linguists and we need to understand the mechanisms and strategies that people use to communicate with each other by working with psychologists. We also need to enable the machine at the other end to tolerate the noise of the uncontrollable baby crying in the next room, the older children quarreling over turns on their *kànàkànà* along the corridor and the hardworking lady hawking "*jòò-óó-gí lee-èè lòò-òò*" on the adjoining street; this is the domain of digital signal processing in electrical engineering. Finally, the architecture and platforms required to utilise the various knowledge gathered from these other disciplines will be contributed by computer scientists. Hence, HLT is a multidisciplinary enterprise that demands expertise in linguistics, psychology, engineering and computer science as well as many other academic disciplines. It requires research and development activities in the coding, recognition, interpretation, translation and generation of language (Cole 1996).

HLT as Productivity Enhancement

Embedded in the lecture title is the idea that language technology can be exploited as a productivity enhancement in our national development efforts. This is not an assumption made to simplify the problem at hand as it is the tradition in intellectual endeavours, rather, it is a position informed by careful observation and systematic analysis. The great heights in science and technology that humans have achieved today are due mainly to the levels of synergy made possible by communication through language. Language is the essential substance of human thought and the chief manifestation of human intelligence. Through it we are able to describe simple objects as well as express complex notions and highly convoluted concepts. It is through the instrumentality of language that human thoughts are made concrete and usable. Language is the medium within which the totality of human knowledge is codified and made available for use.

It is language that facilitated the required communicative processes that turned man the hunter and gatherer into the cultivator of plants and domesticator of animals in the neolithic revolution. Language also made possible the transformation of man the agriculturist to man the industrialist, who not only cultivates food but also processes and thereby preserves it in the industrial age. It is also language that is responsible for the transformation of man's industrial society into the information society in which the creation, distribution, diffusion, use, and manipulation of information has now become a significant economic, political, and cultural activity. Language is at the very core of our new found knowledge economy, the economic environment in which wealth is created mainly through the exploitation of understanding.

One big challenge of this information age in which we now find ourselves is that the rates at which information and knowledge are generated are much higher than the rate at which we can productively consume them manually. As far back as in 2003, it was estimated that 8 Terabytes of books are produced annually. Eight Terabytes of books, by the way, is about 8,000 pickup truck loads of books. To put it more graphically, 8,000 pickup truck loads of books will line up the Lagos-Ibadan express way from the Ibadan toll gate up to Ògèrè (a distance of about 60km), nose to back, and that was long ago, in 2003. Today, it would take a human being about five years to read the scientific literature produced every 24 hours (Bird et al. 2007). The only way to cope with this information explosion and take due advantage of the volumes of information and knowledge now available to us is to develop technologies with which we can sift through this sheer bulk of materials with higher efficiency and greater effectiveness.

We require technologies that can help in information extraction, in information summarisation as well as in inferencing, all from unstructured masses of texts. Furthermore, we need technologies that can translate statements from one language to the other, so that these vast amounts of available knowledge become accessible to the whole world in each prospective user's own language. We also need technologies with which we can automatically transform spoken utterance into written utterance and written utterance into spoken utterance.

Many European and Asian languages have been subjected to studies of relevance to HLT and the levels of success achieved so far indicate that before long many key goals of HLT would have been achieved. Unfortunately however, developments in human language technology for most African languages remain at best in various fetal stages. Apart from South Africa, very few, if any other African countries, south of the Sahara have coherent programmes for developing capacities in language technology. In Nigeria for example, there are references to language in the Nigerian Constitution, the National Policy on Education, the Broadcasting Code and a number of other policy, legislative and regulatory instruments, but we do not have a unified national language policy not to talk of a coherent language technology programme. To the best of my knowledge, no university in Nigeria toady offers any formal courses in HLT or computational Linguistics, two important subjects at the very edge of human knowledge. The survival or extinction of human cultures and the livelihoods built around them will become more and more dependent on capacities in HLT and computational Linguistics as we go further into the knowledge age.

Language and Development

But why should we bother about developing language technology for African languages? After all, Africans have been successfully conducting their lives in English, French, Portuguese and other foreign colonial languages from colonial times, through independence to post-colonial times. Unfortunately, the above statement is a fallacy. It may be true that Africans have been conducting their lives in foreign colonial languages, after all, we are conducting this event in a foreign colonial language, but the fallacy of the statement is consequent upon the introduction of the notion of success. To what extent have Africans been successful in conducting their lives in foreign languages?

If it is true that we Nigerians conduct our lives successfully in a foreign language, why is it that political campaigns are more often than not conducted in the relevant local languages? Will any serious and self-respecting Nigerian politician deliver a political speech to his/her own people (people of his/her own city, town or village) in English? The answer obviously is no. When the chips are down, politicians know what to do to communicate and identify. Little wonder that Nigeria's intellectual elite is finding it progressively difficult to play useful roles in the political life of the country. At reality time, Nigerian politics adopts the language of the people, the language that works. In governance however, it adopts a language that excludes, a language that mystifies. According to Bamgbose (2005),

> good governance cannot be achieved unless those who make laws at all levels of government and those who implement them can function maximally in a language they are proficient in, and, similarly, unless those for whom laws are made can understand what their rights and obligations are. As long as the language of governance is accessible only to the educated elite, majority of citizens will be excluded, thereby making nonsense of participatory democracy. Consequently, the only viable alternative is for Nigerian languages to be used in many domains hitherto dominated by English.

Africa is probably the only continent in which the languages of governance and officialdom are languages of minorities; they are foreign colonial languages. All known development indicators speak eloquently negatively of this faulted approach as shall be demonstrated presently.

The development process demands the efforts of a critical mass of the citizenry. Development goals cannot be achieved by the fulfillment of the aspirations of an elite minority such as the acquisition of formal education through the use of an exclusionary foreign colonial language. If an appreciable segment of the population is excluded from development processes due to the imposition of an exclusionary communication strategy, a few would be made to bear the burden of the totality and the development process will manifest extremely low productivity, as we continue to experience in Nigeria.

Really, how many Nigerians can access this presentation in a foreign colonial language? Going by the official literacy figures from the Federal Bureau of Statistics, and using literacy as a rough measure of ability to conduct life in English, we can say that about 52.6% of Nigerians can access this presentation. However, if we scrutinise this official literacy figure, we will find that it is based on self-disclosure in which no proof is sought that a person who claims to be literate is actually literate. But we know better. Even on this university campus of the great UI, the first and still the best (as we usually describe ourselves), it is not uncommon to hear such statements as, "give them ten-ten Naira," "open the door down," "if you don't go and be careful yourself," "I cannot come and go and die."

Those who speak that type of English do so because they think in their mother tongues, like most normal human beings, and translate such thoughts into English in order to communicate them to others. It is for the same reason that the French would sometimes say "I see you tomorrow" instead of "I will see you tomorrow" or "I have gone to Ibadan yesterday" instead of "I went to Ibadan yesterday." As for those who on the other hand would rather make English statements such as "give them ten Naira each," "leave the door open," "if you are not careful" and "I do not intend to exhaust myself over a small matter," I wonder if we have ever taken time to find out using carefully designed psycholinguistic experiments whether they think in their mother tongue, in English, or in both (or whether they think at all) and what the effects of passing thought through various languages are on their productivity. Omamoh (2003) gives several examples of significantly low competence in English of Nigerian university students even at post-graduate levels. A valid conclusion from her examples is that the use of a foreign language in the learning process can be a serious impediment to learning and this unfortunate phenomenon manifests in the Nigerian situation.

Yet, members of various Nigerian university communities form the cream of the 52.6% of literate Nigerians. Where in Nigeria do we expect to encounter higher competencies in English? At the federal or state secretariats, in the State Houses of Assembly or at the National Assembly? In some exclusive elite clubs in Ikoyi or Bodija? So, where exactly is this successful conduct of the Nigerian life taking place in English?

It may be alright to communicate the odd idea to a foreigner in such statements as "I see you tomorrow," but to base national development communication on such embarrassingly tight-fitting borrowed clothes leaves a lot to be desired. The main difference between the French person who says, "I see you tomorrow" and the Nigerian who says, "Give them ten-ten Naira" is that the French make such statements only when they condescend to speak English to foreigners. They are not constrained to make such statements in the conduct of their normal national life. But when Nigerians makes such statements, they make them in elevated states. That is why such statements can be heard in post-graduate classrooms in Nigerian universities, in transactions at government secretariats and of course in the National Assembly. During the course of investigations at the Human Rights Violation Investigation Commission (HRVIC) popularly referred to as the Oputa Panel, a retired General of the Nigerian army, a former military governor and former minister of the federal republic of Nigeria declared in the course of a formal dialogue; "I am not a soja that Mustapha can *şakara* to," by which he meant, Mustapha cannot intimidate a soldier of my status. So, I am constrained to ask again, where exactly is this successful conduct of the Nigerian life taking place in English?

Let us shift our attention from anecdotes to systematic analyses of development indicators. Preliminary results of an on-going study[2] at Alt-i show a compelling level of correlation between the use of the mother tongue in education (including science and technology) and various development indicators. Statistically significant difference was observed in the values of various development indicators between countries that deliver education in their mother tongues and those that deliver education in foreign languages. The countries of interest in the study are African, Asian and South American countries. The following charts provide some insights into these results.

HDI for 71 Asian, African and South American countries (randomly) plotted according to the alphabetic order of their names

Chart 1

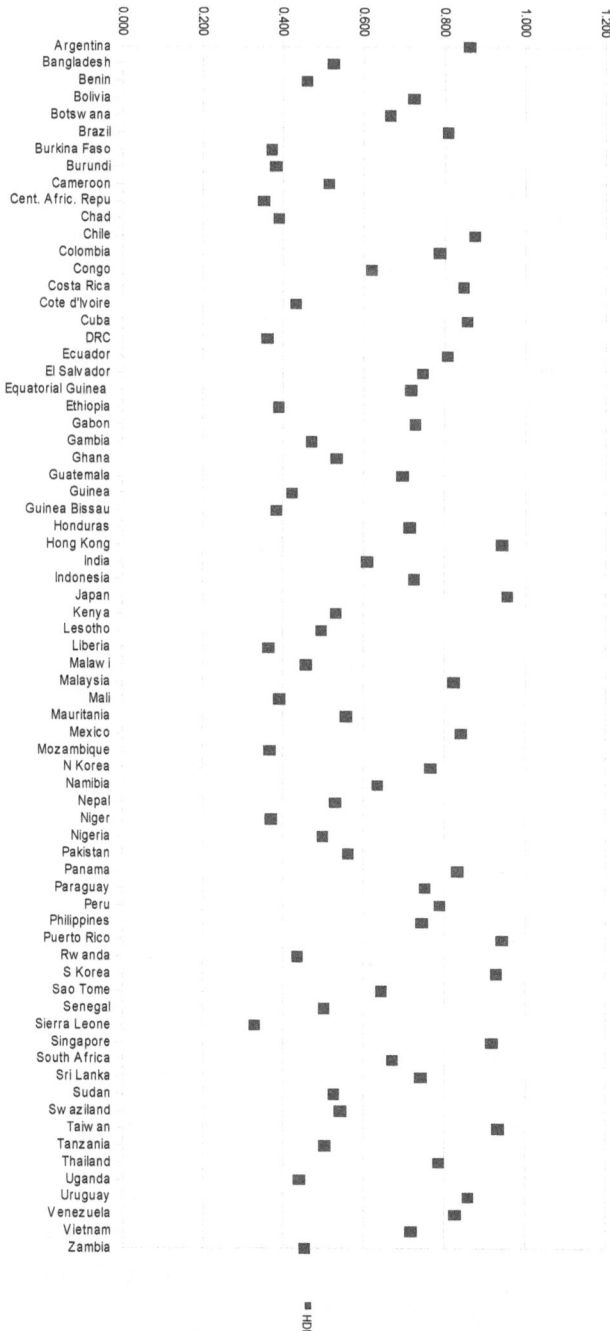

HDI for 71 Asian, African and South American countries grouped according to the language of education

Chart 2

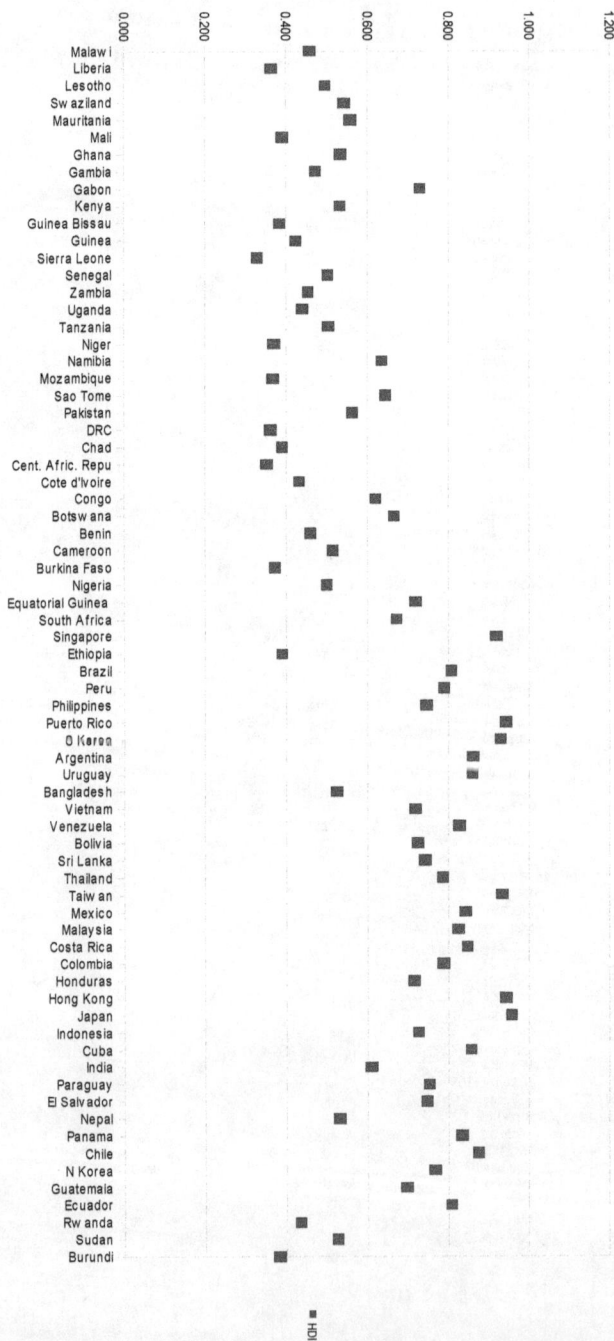

The charts show a graphical representation of the values of the Human Development Index (HDI) for 71 countries. In Chart 1, the countries are arranged from [top] to [bottom] in alphabetical order, based on the assumption that the names of the countries do not have any effect in the HDI values. Hence, the dots appear to be randomly distributed. This is the point of view from which people usually see HDI distribution of groups of countries.

In Chart 2, however, the countries are arranged according to the language of education. Users of a foreign language in education on the [top] and users the mother tongue in education on the [bottom] of the chart. As can be observed, this arrangement reveals that countries in which education is delivered in the mother tongue have consistently higher values of the HDI than those in which education is delivered in a foreign language. The mean of the HDI for countries in which education in delivered in the mother tongue is 0.75, with a standard deviation of 0.15, while the mean of the HDI for countries in which education in delivered in a foreign language is 0.45 with a standard deviation of 0.11.

Only three countries in which the mother tongue is the language of education feature HDI values lower than 0.6. These are Ethiopia, Nepal and Burma. Singapore is the only country in which a foreign language produced an HDI higher than 0.8. The three countries on the [bottom] of Chart 2; Burundi, Sudan and Rwanda, could not be correctly categorised due to lack of the necessary information to determine the language of education in these countries as at the time of this preliminary report.

The summary of the observations in this study is that there exists a statistically significant difference (at 0.05 significance level) in the HDI for countries in which education is delivered in the mother tongue and those in which education is delivered in a foreign language. It is also observed that the difference is such that the HDI is generally higher for countries that conduct education in their mother tongues.

The HDI is a normalised aggregate of a vector of development indicators such as life expectancy, literacy, education, standard of living and per capita gross domestic product. So, the results of our study suggests that by and large, those who learn in their mother tongues live longer, are more literate, have better education, have higher standards of living and higher per capita gross domestic product. Also, in general, these countries have achieved industrialisation.

We note however, that correlation does not necessarily imply causality, but, can this correlation between language and development be explained?

In explaining the rapid growth of the High Performance Asian Economies (HPAE), the World Bank Policy Research Report; The East Asian Miracle: Economic Growth and Public Policy (1993) makes it crystal clear that there is a no model that may be called the Asian model, as each of the HPAE of Japan, Korea, Hong Kong, Taiwan, Singapore, Indonesia, Malaysia and Thailand all used different and changing sets of policies to achieve rapid growth. Hence, the commonality in their rapid growth is not attributable to a commonality in their development models. The report notes however that the accumulation of production assets is key to economic growth, and that all the HPAE accumulated both physical and human capital more rapidly than other economies. This accumulation in physical and human capital, the report notes, accounts for a large portion of their superior performance. It notes furthermore, that the quality of education to both boys and girls of school age was consistently higher than in economies of similar levels of income. One other point that the report notes is that the HPAE put a premium on primary education.

The World Bank Policy Research Report however, did not make the connection that all the HPAEs (apart from Singapore) conduct their primary education in their various mother tongues. Such a socio-cultural development factor might have been considered to fall outside the scope of a study essentially in economic development. We note, however, that the HPAEs, having opted to educate their citizenry in their various mother tongues accumulate human capital more rapidly that countries that educate their citizens in foreign languages, including those with similar levels of income. This implies, first and foremost, that productive education leading to development of essential human capital can take place in various mother tongues. Secondly, and more importantly, it implies that the use of the mother tongue in education leads to a more rapid accumulation of human capital. Certainly, at this level, we can better explain and understand causality even if we still cannot establish it.

Language is an instrument of thought, hence it has inputs into the perceptual and cognitive make-up of a person. It is a system of symbols that describes reality in a given culture. If a reality does not exist in a culture the local language is not likely to accommodate it. To the Yoruba for example, hail, frost, snow and ice are all *yìnyín* whereas to the Inuits in the far north of Canada, there must be distinction between the snow that can be molded into building blocks for the construction of human shelter and the ice that has to be bored into in order to fish. Hence, a language that is developed to describe the realities of a given culture may not be necessarily adequate in describing the realities of another culture. Given the vast differences between English culture and the cultures of each of Nigeria's various ethnic nationalities, it would be unreasonable to expect the English language to describe the realities of these cultures efficiently.

If a nation teaches its young people science in a foreign language, the chances of developing scientific theories that account for phenomena that are more easily observable in such a nation are remote and the scientific world is the worse for it. Worse still, if a nation breeds its technologists in a foreign language, every technological wonder will be attributed to a more intelligent foreigner. That is why most Nigerians [upon experiencing] a technological wonder will involuntarily exclaim, *Oyinbo!* The simple implication of attributing any technological wonder to the "superior" intelligence of foreigners is that the observer's critical intellect is not engaged by such an observation. Hence, explanation is not attempted and the observer settles for mystification. This has been largely true of the Nigerian scientists and technologists that I have worked with and also interviewed for employment over the past thirty years.

Another problem of teaching science and technology in a foreign language is that the foreign language becomes an artificial filter (or more accurately, a barrier) for science and technology students. That is, only those that master the foreign language become eligible to be educated. This is rather exclusionary. Worse still, because language is a fundamental mechanism of thought, even those that master the foreign language and therefore qualify for education and are educated in the foreign language are constrained to understand through various cognitive proxies, thereby making their cognitive processes more demanding of processing and storage resources.

Also, because the resources for teaching a foreign language to all and sundry are usually inadequate, some key aspects of technology inevitably have to be taught in local languages. In Nigeria for example, artisans on various apprenticeship schemes usually learn their trades in their mother tongues while technologists that are educated in tertiary institutions are taught the relevant theories in English. Because the technologists that theorise and design on one hand and the artisans that build and maintain on the other hand study in different languages, a communication gap manifests between technologists and artisans. This results in a gulf between theory and practice and a major disconnection between the processes of education for knowledge and that of training for skills. Hence, when a professor of automobile engineering takes his/her car to be fixed at a mechanic workshop, even if he/she has contributions to make in the diagnostic process, he/she hardly has the language to communicate this idea to the artisan, yet they are both of the same ethnic and linguistic nationality and are both bona fide members of the same professional clan.

Technology is fundamentally built on an active interplay between theory and practice in which theory informs practice and experience in practice demands explanations from theory. Any society in which a communication gulf exists between theory and practice cannot be productive in its engagement of technology.

Furthermore, because artisans are trained in our local languages which describe our material and non-material realities more efficiently than any foreign language, they have cognitive advantage over those of us that are educated in a foreign language and are therefore forced to understand through various cognitive proxies. Even though artificial social fiats place us above them in society, we do and they do know too that we all depend on them to keep the wheels of technology turning in our society. They know that they are more productive than us in making technology work in the nation; hence, they engage us with cynicism while we engage them with a superiority complex.

As a nation, we ought to pause and inquire from historians if there is any account in history of a nation that became great using a foreign language. If there is, let's find out how they did it and consider if their approach is relevant in our situation. If there isn't, we should ask ourselves if we are trying to score a first or are we just being foolhardy. If we are trying to score a first, then we are not trying hard enough, because firsts are not made of our type of feeble efforts. If we are being foolhardy, then we should stop and start being reasonable.

These arguments are by no means novel. They are based on ideas that have been tested in various parts of the world as well as here in Nigeria and they have been found to be sound. For example, Fasokun (2000) reports that between 1970 and 1979, the Institute of Education of the University of Ife (now Obafemi Awolowo University) embarked on the "Six Year Primary Project (SYPP)," an experiment designed to test the assumption that a child would benefit cognitively, socially, culturally, and linguistically through the use of his/her mother-tongue as the language of instruction throughout primary school. An experimental class of primary school children was taught Social and Cultural Studies, Science, Mathematics, Yoruba Language and Literature, all in the Yoruba language. English was taught to them as a second language. A control class was taught the same subjects in English, and Yoruba was taught as another language. There were regular intakes into Primary 1 of both classes each year from 1970 to 1975.

Following are the key results of the experimental project:

- A total of 183 textbooks for the various subjects were produced in Yoruba as a result of the project;
- Students in the experimental class performed significantly better in all school subjects than those in the control class in the same external examination taken by all primary school children in the state;
- 10% of the experimental class dropped out of school, while 30% of the control class dropped out of school within the six year period. The national dropout rate was between 40% and 60% around the same period;
- 100% of the first group of the experimental class passed the First School-Leaving Certificate Examination while a sizable number of

the control class failed;
- While in Secondary School, students of the experimental class were found to be at an advantage academically over their counterparts in most subjects, especially in Yoruba, English Language and Mathematics;
- Out of the 820 pupils that enrolled in Primary 1 by 1973, more than 300 had graduated from Nigerian universities by 1987;
- Spurred by the success of the project, various scholars, groups and institutions produced orthographies for over twenty-five Nigerian languages that remained unwritten till then.

Given such scientific evidence, on what authority then do we base our present approach, and why have we not responded to this scientific evidence? Needless to say that the philistinism of Nigeria's successive military governments around the period of the experiment was so deep that they could not see the point, even with the lead investigator of the SYPP as the Minister for Education.

Indigenising HLT

We have tried to establish that productive learning is based on the use of a language that codifies local realities most productively and that the present rate of information and knowledge production in the information age demands the use of technologies in their management. It stands to reason therefore that if we want to remain relevant in the information age, we need to develop language technologies that address our languages so as to acquire the tools to manage information and knowledge within the contexts of our local languages.

Since humans started making tools according to the oldowan tradition over 2 million years ago, one central philosophy of tool-making has been specificity. That is, each tool is made for a specific function. In the mid-20th century however, the British mathematician Alan Turing designed a theoretical "universal machine" which could be programmed to duplicate the function of any other existing machine. The Turing machine (as it is now more formally called) is the pre-cursor to the digital computer. Hence, the digital computer is fundamentally different from all other tools ever made by humans in that it is the first and still is the only tool whose use is decided by the user rather than the maker. For all other tools, the use to which they are to be put is decided by their makers.

There are two important consequences of this change in tooling philosophy:

1. The computer is widely adaptable to any conceivable use;
2. We need to communicate with computers to tell them what use they are to be put.

First, the wide adaptability of the computer has important implications for the development and deployment of technology in the developing world. One of the core issues of the development discourse that started in the mid-20th century is that of technology and the developing world. As development theory moved between top-down and bottom-up models, so also did the technology discourse move between such top-down ideas of technology transfer from the advanced world to the developing world and bottom-up ideas such as intermediate and appropriate technology.

The British economist E. F. Schumacher in his popular (1973) book *Small is Beautiful* argued for Intermediate Technology, "something between the sickle and the combine harvester," which relies on local skills and resources, that fits economically and culturally into the local situation and does not harm the environment. Intermediate Technology by design is suitable to the needs and resources of the particular group of people that develop and use it.

Opponents of the Intermediate Technology approach argued that Schumacher's idea will further widen the technology gap between the advanced and the developing countries of the world by dissuading the developing world from aspiring towards advanced technologies. Reacting to this argument, the Intermediate Technology movement re-presented their argument within the context of appropriate rather than intermediate technology. This they did in order to bring more attention to the appropriateness rather than the low level of the technologies they propose. Unfortunately, the stigma of crude and low level technology continues to trail the best of the intentions of the intermediate/appropriate technology movement.

But the wide adaptability of the computer provides a necessary reinvigoration for the appropriate technology philosophy while at the same time it addresses the fears of its opponents. By design, the digital computer presents a general-purpose hardware that can be adapted to any use. With availability of the necessary software, the same computer that is applied in everyday mundane tasks such as word processing can be deployed in cutting edge advance technology, just by changing the software. Hence, computer technology is not necessarily intermediate technology even though it can be successfully deployed towards intermediate technology needs. Not only is it appropriate, it can also be appropriated into any technology need situation, be it low, intermediate or high technology. To a user, computer technology therefore is neither low nor intermediate technology and it is not necessarily high technology, but rather, it is Appropriable Technology.

The fact that computer technology can be appropriated to any desired use makes it possible for people in diverse circumstances to fashion appropriate solutions to specific problems using the computer. It therefore places a responsibility on people in peculiar situations to develop appropriate solutions to their unique problems by developing the appropriate computer software. This is of great importance to the developing world, and the community of Nigerian intellectuals should seize this opportunity to deploy computer technology in various ways as productivity enhancement for our national development efforts.

If we understand the full implications of a general-purpose hardware that can be made to do whatever the human mind can imagine, we would ensure that every young Nigerian who enrolls for tertiary education can write computer programmes by the time they graduate. Even though the computer has greatly enhanced efficiency at work and even at play, the great advantage of computing does not lie in word processors, spreadsheets and databases, as important they are. The great advantage of computing lies in the capacity to use the computer to realise whatever the human mind can conceive. To this end, I would like to charge all Nigerian universities that have programmes in computer science and linguistics to use the combined forces of these two important departments to produce computer keyboards that can be used to type efficiently in all Nigerian languages spoken within the larger communities that host such institutions. Universities without programmes in computer science or linguistics should use their departments of physics, mathematics, or any of the engineering departments on one hand and their language-related departments on the other hand to produce these computer keyboards. This is a simple responsibility that the intellectual community owes the public. It is one of the reasons these tertiary institutions exist.

Considering the second implication of a general-purpose hardware, the need to communicate with machines raises a language question, that is, what language should be employed in communicating with computers? Until now, the most popular method human-to-computer communication has been the use formal languages which are specially designed for use with computers. These include various levels of computer programming languages through which instructions are programmed into computers. So far, these formal languages have worked relatively well but they are understood only by computer specialists who have had to spend appreciable time learning them. As the demand for the use of computers rises and the computer permeates deeper into many more areas of ordinary human life, it will become more and more necessary to enlarge the group of humans that can give instructions to computers. We would need to empower a much wider group of humans than just computer specialists to be able to give instructions to computers in natural human languages rather than formal languages that are understood only by specially trained computer "geeks."

According to Rosenfeld (2000), "the computer age will truly arrive when computers learn to communicate with us humans on our own terms." So, what does it mean for the computer to communicate with us Nigerians on our own terms? Would it be enough for the computer to be able to take instructions in English?

Technology is a key input into development processes. We recall that development is about creating a better world for all citizens based on advances in skills, knowledge and capability (Iwayemi, 2001). In Nigeria, like most other parts of the developing world, we have had to obtain the advances in skills, knowledge and capability that we required for our national development from foreign sources. So far, we have been able to identify and purchase the technologies that some of our development processes require. Where we have not been able to identify them, those who are eager to sell them to us have been quick to point out these needs and sometimes, our mere wants. However, as we move further into the information age, we are going find it more and more difficult to import the technologies that fit our needs. Tapscott (1996) points out that mass customisation is a principal feature of the digital economy. The one-size-fits-all mass production philosophy is giving way to mass customisation. Hence, we need to develop home-grown technology as well as adapt existing technologies to our own needs by exploiting scientific principles for the solutions of problem that are peculiar to us. This is the essence of indigenising technology; making technology fit into and specifically address our cultural realities.

So far, we have been able to import the technologies we require because the problems that these technologies address are universal problems. For example, the problem of transportation is to a large extent a universal problem; people everywhere in the world need to move and move things from one place to another. Despite minor peculiarities such as terrain as well as tropical humidity and temperature, we have been able to address our transportation problems by importing motor vehicles. This is so because there is no peculiar German way of starting a Mercedes Benz, there is no peculiar French way of depressing the accelerator pedal of a Peugeot and no peculiar Swedish way of changing the gear in a Volvo. We can therefore afford to buy these foreign transportation technologies and use them with little or no modifications.

With language technology however, the situation is totally different. Language technologies are built specifically for specific languages and so they cannot be picked off-the-shelf. For example, until recently, speech technologies for most European languages treated tone and intonation as unimportant features of speech that may be overlooked and so these technologies did not regard pitch information. Most African languages however are tone languages and a language technology that disregards pitch information will not work for such languages. In Yoruba for example, any speech technology that does not distinguish between ọwọ́, ọwọ̀, ọ̀wọ́ and ọ̀wọ̀ holds great potentials for causing confusion as ọwọ́ means hand, ọwọ̀ means broom, ọ̀wọ́ means group or detachment while ọ̀wọ̀ means honour and also is the name of a Yoruba town.

This places a responsibility on the speakers of a language to develop the technologies that are appropriate for their languages, taking due cognizance of the peculiarities of such languages. It is not reasonable, practical, or responsible to expect others to do it. So far, we have been able to depend on others to develop technologies that we import because the challenges that these technologies address are common to most of humanity and the use to which the tools that address these problems is to be put has already been decided by the makers of such tools. Language technologies however present levels of peculiarities that do not allow for whole-sale importation of technology, hence we need to address our language technology challenges ourselves.

Considering the present states of our various local languages, we need to, first and foremost, reinvigorate and valorise our local languages by using then in all domains of our national life. The growing trend in which the Nigerian elite and even the barely literate among us now speak English to their children in preference to their various mother tongues is in error and it cannot yield any positive results. This has been variously demonstrated in the arguments presented above. The development of language technology may not yield much result if the language in question is not used by the people to whom it has been entrusted by providence.

Developing HLT capacity

In building the necessary capacities to address our language technology challenges ourselves, the first step is to remove the artificial boundaries that we have constructed around academic disciplines. At its core, language technology requires knowledge of linguistics, psychology, engineering, and computer science. Unfortunately, our general perception is that some of these departments are disparate and unconnected. Any university in which computer science students from the faculty of science find it inconvenient to take courses in linguistics in the faculty of arts or psychology in the faculty of social sciences cannot breed language technologists. Universities that find it strange to award a degree of MA in language technology in a faculty of arts may find it difficult to develop a programme in language technology. If departments of computer science, electrical engineering and linguistics do not work closely together, programmes in computational linguistics will either be impossible or may be run with a lot of inefficiencies emanating from unnecessary duplication and redundancies in faculty. Hence, we need to reevaluate the disciplinary boundaries that we have so far used to organise knowledge and learning.

According to Hennessy (2002), "large-scale complex problems cannot be addressed with knowledge and expertise from only one single discipline. The sheer scale and complexity of these problems require a multidisciplinary approach. It is the only truly effective way to make substantial progress towards their solutions." Definitely, HLT presents a large-scale complex problem that cannot be addressed with knowledge and expertise from only one single discipline. To cultivate language technology, we need to develop a multidisciplinary attitude to knowledge. We can start with cross-disciplinary study groups that address interdisciplinary problems, with the ultimate objective of growing a valid multidisciplinary program.

On this score, I must congratulate the University of Ibadan for the establishment of the Africa Regional Centre for Information Science (ARCIS). It is a proactive development and a manifestation of strategic thinking. I count myself privileged to have been associated with ARCIS from its inception in 1990 and I sure am the better for having maintained my association with ARCIS up to the present moment. ARCIS provided for me the appropriate intellectual melting pot in which my quest for investigating the Yoruba language as an information system was fulfilled. I had long taken a decision not to undertake such a fundamental research into the Yoruba language in a foreign university, but getting the right environment here in Nigeria proved rather challenging. It was most welcoming therefore that ARCIS, by virtue of its inter-disciplinary outlook was able to assemble a team of supervisors consisting of Prof. Mula Tiamiyu, of ARCIS, himself coming from a background in Economics, Prof. S. O. Oyetade of the Department of Linguistics and African Languages, and Dr. Amahia from the Department of Statistics. Working under the supervision of these intellectuals of distinction was such a most rewarding experience.

In ARCIS, I have also had the rare privilege of teaching Artificial Intelligence, Information Networking and Telecommunications to a mixed bag of graduates of economics, linguistics, psychology, religious studies, medicine and many other disciplines that many still regard as unrelated. This has generally tasked me to dig deep into the inner recesses of my knowledge-base to produce illustrations that explain abstract notions in everyday language without mystifying them in the language of complicated mathematics, even when they are best expressed in such a language. This has been sometimes frustrating, but in general it has been very rewarding. On many occasions, such adventures have helped me to gain even much deeper understanding of the underlying theories and have served to further illuminate my own understanding of these subjects.

Rewarding as this experience has been however, it has also drawn my attention to an unfortunate trend. I am usually excited whenever I am allocated linguistics graduates for project supervision at ARCIS. I always see such as opportunities to get these students to view language as an information system and thereby undertake quantitative and computational exploration of some of the linguistics theories that have been developed around our local languages. I hold the belief that employing information communication theory to interrogate these linguistics theories will reveal interesting information about the workings of the human mind and provide basis for important multidisciplinary study of our languages. The unfortunate trend, however, is that most of these students would wish to move as far away as possible from linguistic theories. It seems that they applied to ARCIS as a means of concealing their linguistics past. They have their eyes set on the banking and the petroleum industries and they see information technology as the passport. For them therefore, exploring linguistics theory is the last thing they expected to be made to do in ARCIS. One student once tried to persuade me to take the word Yoruba off the project title: the reason being that the appearance of this word in the project title will draw attention to the linguistics past that the 18 month sojourn in ARCIS was supposed to veil.

Of course, I can understand the economic logic of this position, but I can also see through its simplistic bottom-line philosophy. I find it quite bewildering because it suggests the existence of an endemic tendency to stroll away from some of the important solutions to our national problems.

Strategies for Addressing Local Needs in a Globalised World

As part of a global community of intellectuals, Nigerian intellectuals have a duty to contribute to the global knowledge production endeavor; however, we need to be strategic about developing and deploying our intellectual resources. Because these resources are scarce, the strategic approach is to develop and deploy them in ways that direct optimal quantities and qualities towards our peculiar problems, problems for which we do not expect the intellectual resources of other regions of the world to be ordinarily deployed. We must develop policy interventions that will encourage our brightest and our best to devote their intellectual careers to addressing problems that are peculiar to our cultural realities. *Ilé lati í kó ẹ̀ṣọ́ ròde:* Charity begins at home.

For Africa and the developing world as a whole, HLT is a logical inroad (or should I say a back door) into high technology. It is cutting-edge technology that is directly relevant to the African situation. Because language is the chief manifestation of human intelligence, HLT is one of the ways in which some of the new and powerful techniques recently developed within such relatively young subjects as Cognitive Science, Artificial Intelligence and Data Mining can become immediately useful within the African experience.

HLT is one of the few crossroads where advanced technology and the African situation meet. The *orita* where ambrosia offered to the deity of probability is also consumed by daring children who pick pennies from eerie preparations placed at road junctions and even the dogs dare to feed.

As the human race moves further into the knowledge age, the need to communicate through and with machines will continue to increase. As Nigerian parents and their children increase their exchange of text messages and e-mails as normal means of communication, inter-generational communication will increasingly get facilitated by machines. Those of our languages that such machines cannot cope with will become increasingly endangered if parents cannot use then to communicate with their children on account of the deficiencies of these machines. The loss of these languages implies a loss of the elements of knowledge uniquely codified within their structures and vocabularies, and in turn, a loss of the livelihoods built around the cultures they support.

The true value of our physical environment is embedded in the value bestowed on it by the way we describe and therefore use the fauna and the flora as well as the non-living materials that it consists of. Language holds the key as the necessary software component of the hardware we describe as our physical environment, the vital non-material complement of an essentially material world. Hence, preservation of our physical environment may not yield much profit if the languages through which it is described and understood are not also preserved. HLT holds a key to the preservation of these languages in the knowledge age.

Acknowledgments

In concluding, I must, once again, acknowledge the vision of the founders of Africa Regional Center for Information Science (ARCIS) and give special thanks to those that drew me into the ARCIS family, thereby providing me with a much needed new lease of life and an escape route out of the monotony of consulting engineering. I wish to thank the staff and students of ARCIS (both past and present), particularly the present Director, Prof. Fabian Ehikamenor for providing such a stimulating intellectual environment within which I have been able to exercise some of my intellectual quests and particularly, for offering the platform on which I stand to speak today.

I must also mention the staff and students of the Department of Linguistics and African Languages and their various associates, who have supported me in my foray into one of the most intriguing creations of the human mind; language. How I wished I started the foray much earlier. I would like to encourage young Nigerian scientists and technologists to take keen interest in our languages. I can assure you that **language is a very rewarding engineering subject.**

I have also enjoyed the support of some fine statisticians within the university community, and I wish to acknowledge and thank them too. My engagement with the University of Ibadan has been in a rather uncommon way which has given me equally uncommon access to its resources. I continue to marvel at the vastness of the untapped potentials within our academic communities.

The board of Alt-i, chaired by the distinguished Prof. Akinwumi Isola, and ably supported by Prof. Francis Egbokhare and Prof. Omotayo Fakinlede have been very supportive and their integrity as individuals have opened even tightly locked doors for us at Alt-i. The young and not too young people who constitute the full time and volunteers staff at Alt-i and our sister organisations; Tiwa Systems and CEDAR have also been sacrificial in many ways. I thank you all.

Pioneering anything of worth is never an easy endeavor. So, I must also acknowledge the strong support of my family who has long accepted its lot in harbouring a bohemian as a family member. My late father who kept the pressure high until I finally succumbed to undertaking a doctoral programme; my 85-year-old mother, from whom I still borrow money when we run out fuel for the generator in the office; my wife Inyang, who though far away is always there for me; my children, Emem, Edidiong and Imoh, who always find it difficult to explain to their friends what their father does for a living; and my sisters and brothers, Ade, Sade, Gbenro, Funso, and Akin who I can always count on.

Finally, I wish to acknowledge with great thanks the support of the organisations that have provided the grants with which we fund our work at Alt-i. Tiwa Systems Ltd., Bait al Hikma of South Africa, the Open Society Initiative for West Africa (OSIWA) in Senegal and the International Development Research Centre of Canada thorough the AnLoc Project. But for the financial support of these organisations, I might not have found out the information that I shared with you today and the exhibition at the entrance could not have been organised.

Despite the clearly external coloration of our funding sources, we have not totally lost hope that we will one day be able to acknowledge corporate Nigeria or one of the various levels of Nigerian governments for their support. This lingering hope is not borne out of any indicative signs; it is just a manifestation of faith that moves mountains.

I thank you very much.

Notes

[1] "Pure water" is sterilised water sold in small sachets of polythene in Nigeria. A ready antidote to dehydration in the tropical heat of West Africa, it is relatively cheap and commonly sold on the streets. Hence, it symbolises access to an essential commodity or facility. The term is usually employed to describe a modest success.

[2] Data obtained from *CIA World Factbook* and *Encarta Encyclopedia*.

References

Bamgbose, Ayo. (2005). "Language and Good Governance." Nigerian Academy of Letters (NAL) 2005 Convocation Lecture. University of Lagos.

Bird, S., et al. (2009). *Natural Language Processing with Python: Analyzing Text with the Natural Language Toolkit*. Sebastopol, CA.

Cole, R. A. (1997). *Survey of the State of the Art in Human Language Technology*. New York: Cambridge University Press.

Dale, R. (2000). "An Introduction to Language Technology." Course material for M.Sc. in Speech and Language Processing. Macquarie University, Australia.

Fasokun, T. O. (2000). "Aliu Babatunde Fafunwa," in *Prospects· The Quarterly Review of Comparative Education*. Paris, UNESCO: International Bureau of Education. Retrieved from <http://www.ibe .unesco.org/fileadmin/user_upload/archive/publications/ThinkersPdf/faf unwae.pdf>. Accessed 08 February 2009.

Hennessy, J. (2002). President's State of the University speech at Stanford University. Stanford, CA. April, 2002.

Iwayemi, A. (2002). "Nigeria's Fractured Development: The Energy Connection." Inaugural Lecture, University of Ibadan.

Omamoh, P. (2003). "Of Linguistics, Knowledge and Service to the Nation." Inaugural Lecture, University of Ibadan.

Tapscott, D. (1996). *The Digital Economy: Promise and Peril in the Age of Networked Intelligence*. New York: McGraw-Hill.

Rosenfeld, R. (2000). "Two Decades of Statistical Language Modeling: Where Do We Go From Here?" *Proceedings of the IEEE* 88(8): 1270–1278.

Schumacher, E. F. (1973). *Small is Beautiful: A Study of Economics as if People Mattered*. London: Blond and Briggs.

World Bank. (1993). *The East Asian Miracle: Economic Growth and Public Policy*. World Bank Policy Research Report. Oxford: Oxford University Press.

When the Vehicle for a Long Journey is Abandoned: The Case for Indigenous Language in Early Childhood Education in Nigeria

Ishola Akindele Salami

Introduction

One can describe education in several ways. While some see education as a process of acquiring knowledge and skills, others see it as a process of transmitting the cultural heritage of a society from one generation to the next. Among sociologists, education is widely understood to mean a process of initiating children into the society (Osokoya, 2011). If we are to accept the sociologists' definition of education, it would stand to reason that the function of school is to ensure that every young citizen is integrated into the society (Odejobi, 2014) This might be the reason why Ashiru in "Decolonizing the Curriculum" submits that functional and qualitative education can only play its critical role if the philosophy, content, process, and methods are entrenched within the social, cultural, spiritual, and environmental milieu of the immediate society. Therefore, early childhood education (ECE) in any society should help the child communicate in the language of the immediate community (LIC), taking into consideration the culture, history, values, knowledge and expectations of the people in the immediate community (Salami, 2014a). Such an approach to ECE is considered to be effective in transmitting the ways of life of the immediate society to the younger generations. This is what may be termed *the continuity functions of ECE*.

For ECE to be considered effective and functional, it must enhance or positively impact all of the developmental domains (social, emotional, physical and intellectual) of the child. This must be professionally handled such that in the teaching-learning process one domain is not emphasised or given priority over another. Salami in "University to Community Pilot

Preschool Programme" (2014b) opined that children exposed to well-implemented ECE enjoy solid foundation of holistic development in terms of social, emotional, physical, creative and intellectual exposure. This submission is also in line with Oduolowu's finding in *Contemporary Issues in Early Childhood Education* (2011) that the product of a good ECE programme is children who develop holistically. "Holistic" is the operative word, because a child cannot be said to be holistically developed if he/she cannot demonstrate the socially acceptable practices of the immediate community or if he/she has no knowledge of the culture, history, values, epistemological beliefs and general ways of life of the people in his/her immediate community. How holistically developed is a child whose character and ways of life are at variance with those of his/her immediate community?

There seems to be a gap between the products—in terms of the totality of learning outcomes—of the current ECE practices and societies in Africa, as a whole, and in Yoruba society in Nigeria, specifically. What can one make of the following situations: a Yoruba child who has received a rigorous primary school education but still stands upright while greeting his/her parents instead of prostrating himself/herself to the ground; or the young man who prefers dressing in a three-piece suit to wearing an *agbada*; or the child who disrespects his/her elders by the manner of his/her communication? What is one to make of the child who eats with utensils in the name of keeping "table manners?" What are we to do about the graduate who possesses no knowledge of the history of the various Yoruba sub-ethnic groups in Nigeria and is ignorant about the names of rulers of various regions and who dismisses Yoruba language and the culture as "local" and "very weak?" What can be said of the Yoruba child who has little or no understanding regarding the use of Yoruba proverbs (*owe*) and witty sayings? Sadly, such children are becoming the norm in the Yoruba world.

Much of the indigenous knowledge and many of the cultural skills of Yoruba people are either going into extinction or are being eroded. Some of the arts and cultural cornerstones that are in jeopardy include *igba finfin* (calabash decoration) of the Oyo people, *ma 'koko* (pot making), the use of the talking drum and various indigenous songs and dancing steps, *eewo omode* (forbidden) as means of training children, the production of *aso-oke* and *adire* (kinds of cloth), *ekun 'yawo* (a kind of wedding song), *oriki idile ati oriki-orile* (family and clan praise-names), the use of herbs and vegetables for healing and protection, to mention but a few. Because Yoruba arts, cultural, spirituality, and philosophy are inextricably tied to Yoruba language, important questions come to mind: How does the erosion or extinction of these cultural practices enhance "development?" Is "education" without cultural grounding complete? If Nigeria's concepts of "development" and "education" are actually English, what does that portend for the future of Nigerian society? What is responsible for the gradual extinction of Yoruba culture in the name of "educating" our children?

This paper takes a closer look at the benefits of using the language of the immediate environment in early childhood education, especially in preschool and lower primary classes, with special emphasis on Yoruba children and language. This paper examines why a foreign language should not be used as the language of instruction in preschool and lower primary classes, and it also details the diverse benefits of adopting LIC in ECE.

Nigeria's National Policy on Education

There is a policy on language of instruction in both preschool and primary education in Nigeria which is explicitly documented in the National Policy on Education (NPE) and the latest version of this policy is the 6th edition published in the year 2013. Section 2, Subsection A, number 16, item j of this document clearly states that instructors should *ensure that the medium of instruction is principally the mother-tongue or the language of the immediate community (LIC)* (20, emphasis added).

Also, while addressing primary education in Section 2, subsection C, Number 20 (Primary Classes 4-6) part, item 9 b and c states that:

(b) The medium of instruction in the Primary School shall be the language of immediate environment for the first three years in monolingual communities. During this period, English shall be taught as a subject.

(c) From the fourth year, English shall progressively be used as a medium of instruction and the language of immediate environment and French and Arabic shall be taught as subjects (24).

With these governmental pronouncements, one would imagine that Nigerian children are instructed in indigenous Nigerian languages during early childhood, but the opposite is the case. The only implemented language of instruction in the Nigerian educational system from preschool to the post-secondary education is British English (Salami and Nweke, 2015). As a matter of fact, as recently as 2015, almost all private preschool and lower primary sections and most of their public school counterparts across the Yoruba speaking states in Nigeria do not teach Yoruba language at all.

An examination of Nigeria's stated policies reveals ambiguities that may have led to English being Nigeria's primary or sole, in some cases, language of instruction. English is Nigeria's national language, and it is routinely spoken in communities and homes, indeed, some families only speak to their children in English. Because the NPE does not explicitly state that instruction should principally be in an African language, families and educators who use English as their language of instruction could assert that they are, in fact, adhering to policy. There is also ambiguity embedded in the word "principally" which leaves ample room for educators to use whatever language they choose. The phrase "in monolingual communities" is also vague. Very few communities in Africa, let alone in Nigeria, which boasts hundreds of languages including at least two forms English, standard and pidgin, are "monolingual." It was discovered that the phrase "in monolingual communities" was not in the earlier editions of the NPE but appears for the first time in the 6th edition. This might be as a result of the fact that some parts of the country are trying to justify teaching Nigerian children in a foreign language.

Two reasons are usually put forward to support the use of English language in ECE: (1) that Nigeria is a multilingual nation which has no common language and (2) that there is no orthography of the Nigerian languages and text materials are not available in the languages. However, in the article "African-Language Literature: Tragedy and Hope," P. K. Daniel attributes this linguistic dilemma found in the whole Africa to the conquest and subjugation of African nations by European powers and the subsequent forcing of European languages on dominated African populations.

The Importance of Using LIC in ECE

Because of the significance of language development to every child in the first eight years of life and the importance of language development to the whole of society, Nigerians cannot afford to exclude the languages of their immediate communities from the education of their children. Excluding LIC impedes child learners and it also leads to the extinction of languages, as is happening right now.

In addition to standard Yoruba which is spoken throughout south-western Nigeria, there are many other dialects of Yoruba language such as *Egun, Egba, Ijebu, Yoruba-Oyo, Ikale, Ondo, Ekiti, Owo, Akoko, Ijesha, Igbomina, Igbira, Ibarapa* among others. The best way to protect these languages from extinction and to support the rich cultures of these Yoruba sub-groups is to inject these dialects of Yoruba into the early education structure in the communities.

There are numerous examples of communities and nations that have successfully developed ECE curricula in LIC. In China, the language of the immediate community is used in many primary schools as the language of instruction while Mandarin, the national language, is used at the secondary level and the LIC may be taught as a subject. This situation is observable in the Dai community in Dehong (Zhou, 2004). It should also be noted that China has 293 languages but Mandarin Chinese is the official national language.

One of the most effective models for teaching early childhood education in the language of the immediate community in the world today is the Reggio Emilia approach which was pioneered by psychologist Loris Malaguzzi. The Reggio Emilia approach finds that children can also use the abundant elements in their environments to present their thoughts, and that, through painting, sculpting, farming, etc., children are gifted with fluency in "a hundred languages" (Salami, 2011). Nigerians can also learn from educational developments in the United States of America. In America, it is estimated that 381 languages are spoken; of these, 154 are indigenous to the Native Americans (Ryan, 2013). Lately, some Native Americans have established ECE centres in which Native American languages are the languages of instruction and American English is taught as a subject. An example of such a community is the Cherokee community. This movement started when it was realised that about 52 languages that were formerly spoken in America are now in extinct as a result of their non-use at any level of education (Ryan, 2013).

What the foregoing examples reveal is that teaching early childhood education in the language of the immediate community can be easily and effectively implemented in diverse cultures and languages. Teaching ECE in LIC is also practical and logical. The principle of developmentally appropriate practices (DAP) in ECE, asserts that in the first eight years, children's education should be structured around their immediate environment. Not only should the medium of instruction be the language of the immediate environment, but children should also be educated about the cultural significance and syntactic and grammatical rules of that language.

There is sufficient evidence in the literature that children are capable of learning up to four languages successfully. Many children simultaneously learn LIC along with both foreign languages and lingua franca. The problem that Nigeria and many African countries are facing is that, due to the long-lasting racial and psychological impact of colonization, many citizens, including educators and education administrators, argue the African languages are sub-standard in comparison to the colonizer's language. African languages are dismissed as "vernacular" or "local." The indoctrination is so thorough that in some Yoruba communities children are taught that speaking Yoruba language is not acceptable at all and that to be successful one must master English. Such communities are many in Lagos State, where one may find thousands of Yoruba children who know no Yoruba at all. The result is that most of the children raised in present-day Yoruba communities are unable to speak correctly the LIC. The situation is now negating a Yoruba adage that says *omo ajanaku kii yara, omo eya ba bi eya nii jo*, which can be translated to mean "A baby elephant can never be a dwarf, (and) the baby of a rat will surely look like a rat"): Yoruba children no longer resemble, culturally or linguistically, their Yoruba forebears.

The gap being created between Yoruba children and the Yoruba cultural practices on account of the adopting alien languages and ECE practices is getting wider by the day despite the past efforts of scholars and the government to reverse the trend. A. B. Fafunwa's *Education in Mother Tongue: The Ife Primary Education Research Project* (2015) confirms that using Yoruba as the language of instruction helps Yoruba children to learn all school subjects, including English Language, better. This is probably what informed the National Policy on Education that is yet to be implemented.

The Consequences of Abandoning LIC in ECE

Teaching young children demands a lot of thoughtfulness and creativity on the part of the teacher. Information must be delivered in an appropriate manner with interesting child-centred activities and resources. The interaction between the teacher and the children being taught must be rooted in mutual understanding, and the teacher must be able to present information clearly enough for the children to understand. Because many African educators are forced to abandon their native languages for a foreign language that they may not have fully mastered, many teachers may find it difficult or impossible to present some information. Because of their lack of fluency in English, many Nigerian preschools teachers are forced to rely on direct instruction as their sole method of teaching.

Learning itself is a challenging task but when the teacher and the learner are both struggling with an alien language, the tasks of learning and educating are made even more difficult.

Incomplete and Incorrect Linguistic Skills

Because of the belief that English is a superior language, the majority of Nigerian school children are learning in stilted linguistic environments in which both students and teachers have difficulty expressing themselves in English. One can find students and teachers struggling to compose their thoughts or expressing their thoughts incompletely. The following expressions are common among preschool children in Nigeria; they reveal the difficulties that occur when English language is transliterated as opposed to being mastered.

Table 1: Samples of English Language Transliterations in Yorubaland

What is meant	What is being said
He/She (An elder) is calling you.	They are calling you.
Open the door.	Open the door down.
I warned you not to do it.	Se bi, I told you not to do it.

These examples, which can be found throughout the nation, clearly reveal the extent to which language development of Yoruba children is seriously being affected by the language of instruction. Yoruba children routinely emerge from primary school with incomplete or incorrect English skills, zero knowledge of their Yoruba dialects, and below average skills in general Yoruba language.

Child Learners are Unable to Express Their Thoughts

A good ECE is expected facilitate the full expression of thoughts in child learners. However, in societies where children are not fluent in their mother tongues or the language of instruction, there is more difficulty in evaluating what the child really understands or knows and what the child is not fully comprehending. The primary way to access the thoughts of children is through speaking. When children cannot express their thoughts fully, the instructor can misinterpret what the children are saying: this hinders learning and development. Another common and worrisome situation that besets Yoruba children is when a child has a brilliant idea but cannot communicate it in the English language. While the child could express the idea in Yoruba language, Yoruba is not allowed in classroom because it is regarded as a "vernacular." Many brilliant children have been misjudged to be average or poor learners because of this linguistic divide.

Foreign Language Instruction Impedes the Teaching of Yoruba Moral and Social Values

A Yoruba adage has it that *kekere ni imole tii komo e laso*: "Muslims begin to teach religion to their children at younger age." The morals and values of Yoruba culture are supposed to be inculcated in children quite early in life. But adherence to a foreign national language impedes this. In Nigeria, British culture is given priority in the education and socialization of children. This situation has had adverse effects on the behaviour of many contemporary Yoruba children, especially in regards to the culture of showing respect.

The culture of respect in Yoruba language is such that the way you say something to your peer/age mate is different from the way you say it to elders. Consider the following:

a. *Ka a aro* (Good morning)—to an age mate.
b. *E ka a aro* (Good morning, in the plural form)—to an elder.
c. *Ki lo wi?* (What did you say?)—to an age mate.
d. *Ki le wi?* (What did you say? In the plural form)—to an elder.

"E" is translated as "you, an elder or a group"; whereas "o" is translated as "you, a peer." English language pronouns do not reflect respect and there is no way English can be used to present respect in Yoruba that will not lead to verbosity or confusion.

Yoruba songs and rhymes for children are not only for the development of language but are also a means of inculcating acceptable Yoruba behaviour, values, morals, and norms. This might be the reason Akintunde (2007) submits that Yoruba folktales (Alo apagbe/onitan) are important elements in the education of the child. Consider the following Yoruba songs and rhymes and the possible translations as presented in Table 2:

Table 2: Yoruba Songs and Rhymes Used in Children's Education

GENRE	YORUBA	TRANSLATION
Song	*Ojo n'ro* *Sere ninu ile* *Ma wo'nu ojo* *Ki aso re* *Ma ba a tutu* *Ki o tutu* *Ma ba a mu e o*	It is raining Play indoors Do cavort in the rain So that your clothes Do not get soaked So that you do not Get wet and cold
Rhyme	*Ja itana to n'tan* *To tutu* *To si dara* *Ma duro dojo ola* *Akoko sure tete*	Get materials to make fire fast That is cool And that is good Do not wait till tomorrow Time is quickly running out
Song	*Ki ni n'o f'ole se laye ti mo wa? (repeat twice)* *Aye ti mo wa kaka ki n'jale* *Kaka ki n'jale* *ma kuku deru* *Ki ni n'o f'ole se laye ti mo wa?*	Why should I be a thief in this life? *(repeat twice)* Instead of stealing in my life Instead of stealing I will become a slave Why should I be a thief in this life?

These traditional and educational songs and rhymes and many more have been abandoned in preschools and primary schools in Yorubaland for English songs and rhymes such as these:

1. *London bridge is falling down*
    Falling down, falling down,
    London bridge is falling down,
    My fair lady
    . . . .

2. *Pussy cat, pussy cat*
    Where have you been?
    I have been to London.
    London for what?
    London to see the Queen
    . . . .

These songs have no educational value and serve no purpose other than mindless entertainment and the inculcation of English culture.

Foreign Language Instruction for Children Leads to the Cultural Hybridization of Yoruba Children

Cultural hybridization is a significant problem that occurs when Yoruba children adopt English language and culture because Yoruba language and culture have not been taught or have been eroded and undermined. Individuals who are "culture hybrids" cannot be referred to as truly Yoruba, and they cannot be considered truly English: They are neither Yoruba nor English. They can perhaps be described as *hybridized Yoruba people.* Ashiru in "Decolonizing the Curriculum" (2014) quotes J. A. I. Bewaji who describes these hybridized subjects as

> a coterie of artificial, mentally emasculated and culturally denuded persons and leadership including a literate but culturally uneducated masses of graduates who fail to understand themselves, their societies, their world and the universe properly (Ashiru 146).

Foreign Language Instruction Speeds Loss of Dialects, Cultural Practices, and Values

Yoruba is a language that boasts many dialects which are spoken in different geographical regions. These dialects have such distinct vocabularies, grammars, and idioms that they are not mutually intelligible. For instance, *Oyo* people may not understand the dialects of *Owo, Ikale, Akoko* and *Ondo* people. My personal experience during interactions with university students is that majority of people age 30 years and below from communities like *Egba, Ijebu, Ikale, Ondo, Owo, Akoko, Ijesa, Igbomina, Egun,* and others with distinctive dialects are not able to speak their indigenous languages and do not understand the indigenous vocabularies of their dialects. If this observation is scientifically proven to be right, the implication is that very soon these dialects will go into extinction. This problem is not limited to just language; it embraces the whole gamut of cultural practices associated with different Yoruba communities. For instance, *ekun iyawo* (a song rendered during wedding ceremonies) is gradually going into extinction. So also is *opo sisu* (a traditional practice whereby a widow is made to marry a surviving brother of her deceased husband in order to keep the family line going), *ila kiko* (facial scarification or tribal marks), *alarina* (the use of a go-between during courtship) and many other cultural practices and values such as remaining a virgin (for young women) before wedding, maintaining a close relationship with relatives, living within one's income, showing respect to the source of one's wealth are no longer considered relevant or acceptable.

Foreign Language Instruction Reduces Pride and Patriotism

Nigeria is faced with the challenge of instilling patriotism in citizens who are longing to join a mass exodus to Europe, America, Asia and other parts of the world. Among the citizens who remain at home, many who enjoy success follow the custom of showing off their wealth by acquiring foreign/imported goods rather than products that are locally produced. Yoruba youths are also caught up in this malaise. Although Nigerian governments at various levels have been responding to this problem, they have generally neglected the root cause of the problem, which is the defective education to which the youths are exposed in childhood. This education presents indigenous Nigerian languages and cultures as inferior, substandard, "local," and less acceptable than those of the western world. This is a form of learned self-hatred and it manifests in different ways. For example, some Nigerians are convinced that a three-piece suit is a better form of dress than *buba ati sooro/buba ati 'ro* (Yoruba traditional dress for male and female respectively); rather than eating food with the washed bare right hand, individuals use cutlery; and students are trained to valorize non-Yoruba heroes such as Mahatma Gandi, J. F. Kennedy, the Queen of England, Barack Obama, and so on to the neglect of Yoruba heroes such as Obafemi Awolowo, Moremi, Ajayi Crowther, Ooni of Ife, M. K. O Abiola, Wole Soyinka, Fela Anikulapo Kuti, and others.

These and many more are the consequences of abandoning Yoruba language for English in educating Yoruba children. What I consider to be the ultimate consequence is the extinction of the Yoruba race. If a race or a people are about to go into extinction, the first thing they will lose is their language. But if ECE in Nigeria in general and Yorubaland in particular is made context-appropriate by adopting LIC as the language of instruction, all the negative consequences discussed can be reversed. What is more, there will be benefits.

The Benefits of Using LIC in ECE

Adoption of LIC in ECE Will Boost Cultural and Economic Development

For meaningful and lasting social development, teaching and learning must be rooted in the indigenous language of the learning community. C. Ake in *Democracy and Development in Africa* (1999) describes societal development as the process through which people create and recreate themselves and their life circumstances to realize higher levels of civilization in accordance with their own choices and values. Bewaji in "Africa: Neither East nor West but Within" submits that meaningful and sustainable development can only be achieved in Africa by looking within the African world and not by turning to the eastern or western world. From these we can infer that African societies must be grounded in African values, norms, languages, and cultural practices, and African people must consistently recreate and sustain the elements that contribute to their development. The meaningful and sustainable development of a given society cannot be based on the values, norms, and culture of an alien society. African ethnic groups who are adopting their colonizer's values, culture, and language can never hope to better their colonizers in the culture, language, and social systems that the colonizers' devised to oppress and control them. Africans who adopt the language and culture of their colonizers will always signify cultural, linguistic, and social inferiority, even in their own communities.

There is no reason for Africans to be locked in oppressive systems designed to perpetuate inferiority when they can excel in their indigenous languages, cultures, arts, and sciences. If the State Universal Basic Education Boards in all the Yoruba speaking states resolved to make Yoruba the language of instruction in preschool and primary school, utilization and respect for Yoruba language and its dialects would be revived both at school and at home. If this were achieved, then the long term benefits would include development that would positively impact all facets of life, including health, music and arts, clothing, sport and games, food, pedagogy, medicine, science, and technology.

Among some Nigerians, the use of herbs and leaves to heal ailments is considered to be fetish superstition, but drugs imported from western/eastern countries that are produced from leaves and herbs are welcomed. In certain circles, *ekun iyawo, awurebe, ewi, ijala* and other kinds of indigenous music are considered "common" or "bush," but western blues, country, and rock and roll music are welcomed. *Aso etu, alaari, sananyan, adire* and many other kinds of African cloth are considered outmoded by many young Yoruba people, but designer suits and dresses are welcomed. When Yoruba students and their teachers and children and their parents understand the richness, depth, and significance of Yoruba language, they will also develop deeper respect and appreciation for other aspects of Yoruba culture. The benefits of teaching and speaking Yoruba and other indigenous African languages in Africa will also provide a jolt to local and national economies, as citizens will seek out and support their indigenous musicians, physicians, and artisans.

Incorporation of LIC Will Support the Inculcation of Morals and Values

Yoruba language and culture are so seamlessly intertwined that it is only when Yoruba language is used as the language of instruction to educate Yoruba children that the totality of Yoruba culture can be inculcated. The correlation between Yoruba culture and character is such that when an individual is fully educated in Yoruba language, culture, and ontology, that individual demonstrates acceptable behaviour in the society at large. Individuals who are outstanding products of Yoruba holistic education are referred to as *omoluabi,* meaning someone with admirable character. The goal of Yoruba education is to develop *omoluabi* in all citizens and not to emphasize the development of intellectual capacity alone, as done in the British educational system.

The process of developing and sustaining *omoluabi* in Yoruba culture and society is cyclic and continuous because education and the inculcation of essential values and morals does not end at a certain age or with certain accomplishments. Because human growth and experiences are ongoing and because external influences are ever-changing and abundant, Yoruba ontology and such tools as *owe* (proverbs) and *itan* (historical and fictional lessons) are always prepared to offer guidance, correction, education, warnings, and expulsions, as necessary. In "The African Writer's Tongue," I. Akinwumi (2015) presents several examples of how Yoruba people cleanse society of bad leadership and antisocial behaviour using language and culture. This is not to say that by teaching ECE in LIC there will be no malefactors; however, with the proper inculcation of values and morals, the number of miscreants will be reduced and when found, they will be condemned in the society using traditional cultural norms and values.

History offers many examples of Yoruba leaders whose actions were detrimental to their citizens: Oba Awole of the old Oyo Empire, Basorun Gaa of the old Oyo Empire, Oba Adeyemi, the Alaafin of Oyo and his contemporary in Egba land—Alake of Egba—who reigned in the 1950s, Efunsetan Aniwura the Iyalode Ibadan, and many others. All these leaders experienced the force of the unwritten constitution of checks and balances of Yoruba traditional society. The effectiveness of the traditional Yoruba judiciary may have prompted Bewaji (2015) to argue that African societies have human and natural resources to ensure that human habitation in the communities is of the highest conceivable standard if properly harnessed and managed. In "From Indoctrination to Formative and Transformative Education as a Cultured Approach for Addressing Extremism and Terrorism in Africa," C. Majawa (2015) proposes that it may be possible to slay the hydra of extremism and terrorism in Africa by revisiting, transforming, and empowering educational curricula with integrated traditional moral values. The inculcation of the right Yoruba values into children, which will guide their behaviours up to their last day on earth, can only be achieved by delivering ECE in Yoruba language.

Conclusion

Yoruba and its numerous dialects are spoken by millions of people in more than six states in Nigeria. Yoruba language contains the cultural and traditional practices of this ethnic group. Colonization and neocolonization have resulted in the abandonment of Yoruba language in the formal education of Yoruba children, despite the Nigerian national policy on education. The effects of adopting a foreign language as the language of instruction in ECE are overwhelmingly negative. If Yoruba educators, leaders, parents, and scholars do not work together to implement the teaching of Yoruba and other African languages in ECE, the result will be a case of abandoning the only vehicle appropriate for the long journey of comprehensive linguistic, social, educational, and cultural development.

Recommendations

The major recommendation of this paper is that the language policy on preschool and lower primary education as detailed in the National Policy on Education (2013) be rewritten to remove all ambiguity and to mandate the use of indigenous African languages, such as Yoruba, as the languages of instruction in ECE, from preschool to primary three, with English being taught as a subject. Further, this policy should be enforced and implemented to the letter. In order to achieve this, the following should be considered:

❖ All State Ministries of Education in general and State Universal Basic Education Boards (SUBEB) in all Yoruba speaking states in Nigeria need to work together with experts in ECE to redefine the implementation of ECE in each of the states. As emphasized in this paper, ECE should be both community based and should be guided by the National and State standards and conditions.

❖ There is the need for government sponsored research projects on curriculum design and development, text material production in various dialects in Yorubaland, and implementation strategies for ECE so as to inject the culture, norms, values and beliefs of every community into their respective ECE. The participants in such research projects must be experts in Yoruba early childhood education and not political appointees.

❖ Secondary schools should make courses in Yoruba language, including, but not limited to, grammar, syntax, vocabulary, idioms, sentence and paragraph construction, and orthography, compulsory to ensure that knowledge and study of the language is sustained.

❖ Universities should offer teacher education courses and degrees in Yoruba language and its dialects, where appropriate, and Yoruba early childhood education to ensure instructors are available and properly trained.

While adherence to the national policy may be met with resistance, especially by parents who have been indoctrinated to believe that the English language and British culture are superior or essential for success, once the policy is implemented and mechanisms for its maintenance and support are in place, the benefits of using the language of the immediate environment as the language of instruction will evident in Yoruba culture, economies, societies, and, perhaps most important, in the holistic development of Yoruba children and the Yoruba people.

References

Ake, C. (1999). *Democracy and Development in Africa.* Ibadan: Spectrum Books.

Akintunde, A. (2007). "Oral literature, aesthetic transfer and social vision in two Yoruba video films." *Research in African Literature* 38:3. 122–135. Retrieved from <http://www.jstor.org/stable/20109500>. Accessed 01 July 2015.

Akinwumi, I. (1992). "The African Writer's Tongue." *Research in African Literature* 23:1. 17–26. Retrieved from <http://www.jstor.org/stable/2819946>. Accessed July 2015.

Ashiru, D. (2014). "Decolonizing the Curriculum: The Education System and the Imperatives of Development in Nigeria." A paper delivered at the 2014 Academic Staff Union of Universities (ASUU) Education Summit held in Abuja from 27th to 31st October 2014.

Archibong, E. I. (2015). "Science and African Cultural Ontology." Presented at the Second International Interdisciplinary Conference. Kisii University, Kenya, 2015.

Bewaji, J. A. I. (2015). "Africa: Neither East nor West but Within." Presented at the Second International Interdisciplinary Conference. Kisii University, Kenya, 2015.

Daniel, P. K. (1992). "African-Language Literature: Tragedy and Hope." *Research in African Literature* 23:1. 17–26. Retrieved from <http://www .jstor.org/stable/2819945>. Accessed July 2015.

Fafunwa, A. B. (1989). *Education in Mother Tongue: The Ife Primary Education Research Project (1970–1978).* Ibadan: University Press Limited Ibadan. 1989. Retrieved from <http://books.google.com.ng /books/.../Education_in_Mother_Tongue.html>. Accessed August 2015.

Kebeya, H. and Osoro, R. (2015). "Rethinking the Official Language Policy: The Case of East Africa and South East Asia." Presented at the Second International Interdisciplinary Conference. Kisii University, Kenya, 2015.

Mandillah, L. K. L. (2015). "Foreign Language in Kenya: Double Edge Swords to Development." Presented at the Second International Interdisciplinary Conference. Kisii University, Kenya, 2015.

Majawa, C. (2015). "From Indoctrination to Formative and Transformative Education as a Cultured Approach for Addressing Extremism and Terrorism in Africa." Presented at the Second International Interdisciplinary Conference. Kisii University, Kenya, 2015.

Odejobi, T. (2014). "Culture and Indigenous Knowledge Content in Liberating Education." Presented at Academic Staff Union of Universities (ASUU) Education Summit held in Abuja from 27th to 31st October 2014.

Oduolowu, E. (2011). *Contemporary Issues in Early Childhood Education.* Ibadan: Franco-Ola.

Osokoya, I. O. (2010). *History and Policy of Nigeria Education in World Perspective.* Ibadan: Laurel Education.

Ryan, C. *Language Use in the United States 2011.* American Community Survey Reports (2013). Retrieved from <https://www.census.gov/prod /2013pubs/acs-22.pdf>. Accessed June 2015.

Salami, I. A. (2011). "Quality Control and Leadership in Nigerian Educational System: Nigeria Early Childhood Care and Education Compared with Reggio Emilia." In *Contemporary Issues in Education, Health and Sport: The Way Forward. A Book in Honour of Prof. Ajala (rtd).* Ogundele B.O., Moronkola O.A., and Babalola J.F., eds. Ibadan: University of Ibadan Press. 157–169.

Salami, I. A. (2014a). "Attempt at Reforming Education and the Challenge of National Liberation in Nigeria: The Place of Early Childhood Education. Ppresented at ASUU, NAAT, NASU and SSANU in coll-aboration with Federal and State Ministries of Education National Education Summit. Abuja, Nigeria. October 2014.

Salami, I. A. (2014b). "University to Community Pilot Preschool Programme: The Effects on Learning Environment, Teachers Attitude and Whole Child Development." Presented at the 1st International Conference on Childhood Education. Department of Early Childhood and Primary Education. Kwara State University. Malete, Nigeria. September 2014.

Salami, I. A. and Nweke G. C. (2015). "A Comparative Analysis of Physical Environment, Instructional Method and Language for Pupils with Special Needs among African, Eastern And Western Countries." Presented at the Second International Interdisciplinary Conference. Kisii University, Kenya, 2015.

Zhou, M. (2004). "Minority Language Policy in China" Equality in Theory and Inequality in practice." In *Language policy in the People's Republic of China: Theory and Practice Since 1949.* Zhou M. and Sun H., eds. Boston: Kluwer Academic Publisher.

Narrating Nigeria: The Evolution of a Story

Oyinlola Longe

Call:	Omode meta nsere
Response:	*Ere ooo! Ere ayo!*
	Okan ni ohun o wekun
	Ere ooo! Ere ayo!
5	Okan ni ohun o tarun
	Ere ooo! Ere ayo
	Okan ni ohun o gun ope
	Ere ooo! Ere ayo
	Owekun Owekun Owekun
10	*Ere ooo! Ere ayo*
	Otarun Otarun Otarun
	Ere ooo! Ere ayo
	Ogunope Ogunope Ogunope
	Ere ooo! Ere ayo

The foregoing is the song from *Omode Meta Nsere*, a popular folktale among the Yoruba speaking people of Nigeria. Because of its catchy song and the important lessons it imparts, *Omode Meta Nsere* has developed a life beyond the traditional storytelling venue.

The traditional story focuses on three children who live in a peaceful village and love to play together. One child is a good swimmer; one is a good archer; and the third a good climber. One day, while at play as usual, the good swimmer boasted, "I will swim across the sea." The good climber responded, "I will climb the tallest palm tree in the forest without the aid of a belt." The good archer bragged, "I will shoot an arrow far into the sky and it will not return." These feats had never been attempted by anyone in the community, young or old.

As the three children were entertaining themselves with their fantasies, a tale bearing busybody who was passing by eavesdropped on the three children. The talebearer went to the King at the palace and told him that the children were idling and boasting of things they could not possibly achieve. The King summoned the three children and, in hopes of teaching them not to waste their time boasting idly, the king commanded the children to perform the feats they had bragged about. The community gathered to watch the children attempt to do what was impossible, but each child performed the task they boasted about expertly. The king rewarded the children for their efforts, the community cheered them, and everyone jeered the talebearer who went to hide in shame.

In Yoruba cosmology there is a belief in *anjonu*, a guardian angel. The children's *anjonu* knew that the children meant no harm and were only amusing themselves. Thus, the *anjonu* helped the children to accomplish their impossible tasks. This Yoruba folktale does not end with the formal moral; however, there are implied morals. One is that we must be mindful of what we say, for we do not know who might be listening. Another is that we should not wish one another ill because there are guardian angels who know the intent of the heart and who are supporting and defending their charges.

The talebearer plays a key role in this story because the busybody's eavesdropping and tattling in hopes of having the children punished force the children to exhibit a stunning mastery of their vocations. The talebearer's role holds a moral as well: There will always be somebody who is unhappy with you. There will always be someone against you, even if you are simply a child at play. However, the negative works of antagonists can have unintended positive consequences: The obstacles they create can become springboards to success.

In the traditional setting, the song quoted at the beginning of this chapter is sung when the children are performing their feats. The song is in a call and response pattern. The storyteller calls the first line while the listeners respond with the italicized line. It is significant that the song compares the children's boasts and feats to the game of Ayo. Ayo is a traditional Yoruba board game that involves boasting and sarcasm from the players and the spectators.[1] The song infers that the children's boasts are of the magnitude found among Ayo players. Bold bragging is only permitted during games of Ayo because players can back their boasts with performance. The song also implies that the three children are able to perform impossible feats as easily as expert Ayo players make their moves.

Omode Meta Nsere is embedded in the consciousness of millions of Nigerians; and, in addition to maintaining its traditional form, it has also taken on new life as *Everything It Takes*, a Nigerian television miniseries.[2]

The three protagonists of the drama are teenage female friends, Deola, Chinelo, and Boma, who are in their senior year in a boarding secondary school. Deola's aspiration is to become a television talk show host; Chinelo hopes to become a singer; while Boma's goal is to become an advertising executive.

Everything It Takes does not include a talebearer character as in *Omode Meta Nsere*. In the drama, the tattletale's facilitating actions take the form of obstacles that the young women must overcome to succeed. Deola's obstacle is her economic status. She is raised by a single parent who cannot pay for her to obtain the higher education and training necessary to become a television host. Chinelo faces opposition from her wealthy and dictatorial father who expects her to study to become a medical doctor. Boma's opposition comes in the form of her parents who want her to get married to a rich friend who has assisted them financially.

After secondary school, the three friends are separated for seven years. During a reunion, the audience witnesses the trajectories their lives took and the assistance they received from embodied *anjonu*. Deola's guardian angel takes the form of her manager at work who assigns her flexible hours so that she can work her way through night school. Deola obtains a communications degree and secures a job with a television station. Chinelo becomes a medical doctor, but a friend encourages her to secretly audition with a singing group. She does and is discovered at a talent show. Boma runs away from home to live with an aunt who houses her while she receives on-the-job training at an advertising agency.

Just as the three children demonstrate their skills in the folktale, the three friends in *Everything It Takes* reveal the experience they acquired during their seven years of separation. After Deola secures a job at a television station, her producer entrusts her with a live show to host for the first time, and she performs well. Chinelo finds herself thrust into the position of lead vocalist when the lead singer deserts the group. Chinelo's performance surpasses expectations, and she becomes the group's permanent lead singer. Boma rises to the top of her advertising agency when her proposal, out of all of the ideas presented for a prestigious client, is the one selected and successfully implemented.

The three friends reunite when Boma becomes the creative consultant for a talent show that Deola emcees and at which Chinelo is a contestant. They celebrate each other's successes and continue their friendship as women who have been tried, tested and proven successful. Similar to *Omode Meta Nsere's* song, the theme song for *Everything It Takes* celebrates three friends who are able to attain success on their own terms despite overwhelming odds:

> She hosts a TV show
> She's on the radio
> She sings the lead in her band
> ....

A creative hotshot
Solutions are always on hand
She is a champion
She gets the gold
She is a prima donna
The star of her show
She's not just a pretty face
She's got everything it takes

....
She's a winner
She's a sister

....
She's not just a pretty face
She's got everything it takes

The theme song also heralds the tenacity and persistence of the women with such lines as, "She works hard all day," "Drives a hard bargain," and "She's every woman." In addition to describing the characteristics of Boma, Chinelo, and Deola, the song is singing a message of empowerment to the show's Nigerian audience, especially its females.

In addition to injecting new depth and dimension into *Omode Meta Nsere*, *Everything It Takes* is also encoded with meaning particular to its country of origin. The three protagonists of *Everything It Takes* represent the three major ethnic groups of Nigeria, as their names signify. Deola is Yoruba; Chinelo is Igbo; and Boma is Hausa. Consequently, *Everything It Takes* champions both national unity and independent self-determination for the protagonists and for a country that has often found itself on the verge of disintegration.

Nigeria is located in West Africa and is bordered by Niger in the north, Benin in the west and Cameroon in the east. The most populous country in Africa, Nigeria presently has a population of about 160 million people boasting over 200 ethno-linguistic groups. However, because Nigeria was colonized by the British, English is the country's official language.[3]

The British created the country of Nigeria in 1914 in what is referred to as "the amalgamation of 1914." This amalgamation brought together 200 disparate ethno-linguistic groups. However, three main ethnic groups make up the majority of Nigeria's population: the Yoruba, the Hausa, and the Igbo. These names also signify the names of the languages spoken by these groups. Nigeria also has three main regions, northern, western, and eastern, where the Hausa, Yoruba, and Igbo predominate, respectively. These three regions are delineated by the Niger and Benue rivers.

Prior to colonization, relationships between the Yoruba, Igbo, Hausa, and other groups could range from cordial trading partners to warring adversaries and everything in between. Unlike the two analyzed stories, the British forced the people of these three regions to "play" together.

The amalgamation of 1914 benefitted the British. The forcing together of African peoples who were separated linguistically, culturally, and geographically created turmoil for the Africans: that is precisely what the English wanted. However, on October 1, 1960, when Nigeria became independent of colonial rule, its African leaders decided to remain amalgamated.

Since independence, the three regions have been "playing" together as one country determining their fate under self-rule. National and regional leaders have devised various schemes to facilitate the extraordinarily diverse country's unification and progress. Some ideas have worked and some have been discarded. Some ideas have led to strife, war, and conflicts. Unlike *Omode Meta Nsere* and *Everything It Takes*, Nigeria's story is still being narrated.

Just as *Omode Meta Nsere* and *Everything It Takes* have songs that sum up their trajectories, Nigeria has a song in form of its national anthem that discusses the importance of the decision of the country to remain unified, describes how to remain united, and elaborates on what the country hopes to achieve. The national anthem goes thus:

Arise, O compatriots
Nigeria's call obey
To serve our fatherland
With love and strength and faith
The labour of our heroes past
Shall never be in vain
To serve with heart and might
One nation bound in freedom
Peace and unity

Oh God of creation
Direct our noble cause
Guide our leaders right
Help our youth the truth to know
In love and honesty to grow
And living just and true
Great lofty heights attain
To build a nation where peace
And justice shall reign

The children of *Omode Meta Nsere* fantasize about doing the impossible, and when put to the test, they are able to fulfil their dreams. The protagonists of *Everything It Takes* have goals that appear unattainable when they are faced with obstacles, but they prevail. Nigeria, the country that is the source of these rich and educational works, is struggling against monumental and ever-shifting odds—from unchecked corruption to fuel shortages, from political unrest to religious strife, from gas shortages to a lack of electricity—to manifest its destiny as the "Giant of Africa." If the nation is able to apply the lessons of *Omode Meta Nsere* and *Everything It Takes*, Nigeria will be able to transform into a unified, self-sufficient, thriving African Giant.

Notes

[1] Odeleye A.O., *Ayo A Popular Yoruba Game* (Ibadan: Oxford University Press, 1977), 1.

[2] *Everything It Takes*, *Superstory* (Wale Adenuga Productions (WAP), 2007).

[3] Toyin Falola and Mathew M. Heaton, *A History of Nigeria* (New York: Cambridge University Press, 2008).

A Model for Success: The Importance of Traditional African-Centered Approaches in Educational Models

Ayoka Wiles

Healing comes when the individual remembers his or her identity,
the purpose chosen in the world of ancestral wisdom,
and reconnects with that world of Spirit.

~ Malidoma Patrice Some

Introduction

Incorporating or establishing an educational model based on an African centered approach is critical to the cultural identity development of young people of African descent. It also contributes to both the individual and collective consciousness and well-being of a community. Many communities of African descent (African-American, Latino, Caribbean, and African) are under-resourced, experience violence, and lack access to quality education, health care, and housing as well as opportunities for exposure to the arts and culture. These issues are often addressed using ineffective social service and youth development models that don't address the multilayered root causes of these issues. Many people of African descent have experienced levels of post-traumatic stress disorder, trauma, systematic and structural racism that create an emotional disposition and underlying consciousness of unworthiness, self-hate and/or unawareness of the self. In *Hope and Healing in Urban Education*, Shawn Ginwright finds that young people who are exposed to or who have continual violent experiences have stress, depression and other mental health issues that have a negative impact on academic achievement and healthy development.[1]

These issues have to be addressed in proper context and within a system that promotes healing, positive self-awareness, and self-actualization.

African-centered values promote a healthy sense of self, high levels of academic achievement, an ability to visualize a positive future, and self-confidence and self-worth among youth of African descent. What is more, the tenets of African culture build not only the esteem and psyche child but also those of the family and the greater community. African culture creates a sense of connectedness that establishes the basis for trust and promotes the bonding and familial connections that are vital to development. Educational models that are built with African-centered values and culture as the foundation of their pedagogy offer necessities that youths of African descent need to be holistically healthy and to thrive.

The Role of Traditional African Culture

The African worldview is vast and complex; however, there are four central themes, in particular, that are of significance to African-centered educational models:

1) Collective consciousness and social collectivism;
2) Connection with and reverence for the ancestors;
3) Connection with both God, or a higher force, and the divinity within oneself; and
4) Connection with and reverence for nature.

Constructing a pedagogy that is based on principles found in the African worldview ensures that specific core beliefs and values are instilled and embedded in the mental, social, and emotional development of young people of African descent. Such a pedagogy also contributes to the "well-being" and social, economic and political health of the community. As Ginwright argues in *Hope and Healing in Urban Education*, well-being is manifest through both external opportunities, such as access to jobs, good education, and quality health care, and our capacity to hope for a more equitable, inclusive, and fair society.[2]

Collective Consciousness and Collectivism

Central to the concept of collective consciousness is the concept of family. One's family may consist of biological relatives and/or chosen community members. The decisions of the community and individuals are made from the framework of a collective consciousness: community affairs are rooted in the collective consciousness. Where the basic philosophy of life is, "I am because we are," it is extremely important that the two components—"I am" and "We are"—be respected and balanced by all for the survival of all. In this worldview, the individual is very much at one with the community and autonomy is virtually out of the question.

Connection with and Reverence for the Ancestors

African philosophy and cosmology acknowledge that the ancestors play significant roles within their communities, and being connected to the stories, lessons, and histories of those who existed before provides human beings with "guideposts" and instructions on how to live and conduct one's self in society. In the words of a Kongo proverb, *"Kanda, (mbundania) bafwa ye bamoyo"*: "The community is the union of the ancestors and of living people. The community is an accumulation of the living unity of the physical and spiritual elements."[3]

In the African worldview, death, is not an ending, it is a transformation, a new beginning. In their role as guides of the living, the ancestors share their collective wisdom through inspiration and give us the necessary strength to succeed, to rear our children, and live ethically and authentically. We can at any time tap into the spiritual DNA passed down to us from our ancestors to resolve issues within our life.

Connection with a Higher Force (God) and the Divinity within Oneself

Because the traditional African ontology is holistic, community members are cognizant of their connections to nature, to the divinity within, and to others in society. Many African spiritual systems assert that God is a higher force or energy that is manifested through all things and that can create, guide, and protect infinitely. When an individual is able to connect with and access her or his inner divinity and unite with the divinity of all, individuals can better navigate life's obstacles and challenges and can live more fulfilling lives.

Connection with Nature

Central to the African worldview and cosmology is the recognition of and connection with the essence of nature, including the winds, trees, mountains, the sky, rivers and also the forces of peace, humility, and of motherhood. All stages of transformation are apparent nature. The divine is reflected in nature, and the divine is sacred and respected. Being at one with nature helps one to see all things as connected forces, one is also better able to understand that transformation and change occur continuously. By being in alignment and in harmony with nature, the world, and the universe, one develops a deep sense of respect and one learns how to live ethically and how to live in harmony with others.

Strong educational models based on the foundation of traditional African culture build within children a sense of self-worth and affirm for children that they are important and have meaningful contributions to make in this world. Community organizations, faith based and cultural institutions, and schools provide resources to foster a sense of collective hope, relevance and the inner resilience to build character and create a higher quality of life. It is within these institutions that youth develop a sense of connectedness, relevance, and efficacy, and they are better able to understand the purpose of their existence and see themselves as key contributors in the world.

Case Studies

While working with two African-centered organizations I researched the key tenets that are most instrumental in influencing communities of African descent. I gathered data from surveys, observations and individual interviews. The factors that had the strongest impact on youth of African descent were: 1) the creation of meaningful enrichment programs; 2) opportunities to obtain deep knowledge about African culture; and 3) strong family engagement and connections with caring adults. These findings underscore the critical importance of traditional African-centered education to youth of African descent. Cultural competency is essential to the identity-formation of youth of African descent and contributes, in the long term, to outcomes such as having a sense of belonging and self-worth, being driven to achieve excellence, having efficacy, and having a desire to contribute to one's community in a meaningful way.

Case Study: Ifetayo Cultural Arts Academy: A Rites of Passage Model in Brooklyn, New York

Ifetayo was founded in 1989 by Kwayera Archer-Cunningham, a seasoned professional dancer, educator and community builder. I had the pleasure of serving Ifetayo Cultural Arts Academy for 6 years as its first

Associate Director from 2002-2004 and then returning in 2011 as its Associate Executive Director.

For over 25 years Ifetayo Cultural Arts Academy has offered Rites of Passage, an after-school program serving youth between the ages of 8 and 21. The program provides educational enrichment and a nurturing community to build participants' intellectual and emotional skills. The comprehensive curriculum has been honed over time and incorporates intensive programming and coaching, which inculcate strong African values, cultural awareness/global community, and financial education and asset building. Ifetayo's unique youth development instruction engages youth and their families to not only reinforce cultural identity, but also to develop strong skills and competencies with respect to personal, emotional, social, academic, financial, and leadership development. The program also motivates participants to thrive and become self-sufficient members of the community. Through the lessons and activities structured in the Rites curricula, especially their study of the African Diaspora, youths develop a strong cultural identity and a global awareness. In addition, youths develop key skills in their chosen form of artistic expression, which encourages self-expression and the development of one's own voice.

Ifetayo also engages in a comprehensive system of assessment and evaluation, including employing an African-centered system called *Mbongi,* which is a Ki-Kongo term which means "a place of learning" and provides a system of governance for equitable and collective problem solving. This creates an opportunity for young people to share their experiences openly in a nonthreatening and nurturing environment.

Ifetayo Cultural Arts Academy examines and regularly evaluates the impact the Rites curriculum has on the youth and pays special attention to the youth's increased understanding and appreciation of their cultural identity. Ifetayo's teachers and guides gauged the progress of their work with the Obasi Survey,[4] which measures the youths' cultural identity, positive perspective, and personal power.

The Obasi Survey revealed that students demonstrated an increase in their understanding and appreciation of their cultural identity. In response to the Obasi Survey Question, *I was raised to maintain cultural practices that are consistent with people of African descent,* 62%–82% responded that they "strongly agree" and "agree."

To Obasi Survey Question: *I was raised to maintain cultural practices that are consistent with people of African descent,* 62%–82% students responded that they "strongly agree" or "agree." Additionally, we found the number of students in the 8–18 age range who maintain traditional African cultural practices was 71–85%, and this number is directly related to the number of students who demonstrated positive perspective and personal power.

74% of the students aged 8–18 stated that they developed a sense of purpose, strong cultural identity, and self-love. This was evidenced by Progress Note Questions, which asked the following, respectively:

- *How well does the student demonstrate self-respect and respect for others verbally and physically?* 70% of students demonstrated *"Excellent"* and *"Satisfactory"* rates.
- *How well does the student demonstrate a sense of self confidence and positive perception of their own abilities?* 73% of the students demonstrated *"Excellent"* and *"Satisfactory"* rates.
- *How well does the student demonstrate their own understanding of and connection with cultural traditions and African Diasporic perspectives as outlined in the curriculum?* 79% students demonstrated *"Excellent"* and *"Satisfactory"* rates.

The results of the survey were from students who had a combined participation in the program between 1 and 10 years. Of those students who had been in the program between 5–10 years their response rate is between 85%–90% to the above questions.

Case Study: Egbe Omo Orisa: A Model for Instilling Traditional African Values in Youth in Philadelphia, PA

Egbe Omo Orisa was created to nurture and educate young children of African descent in their growing identities as traditional Yoruba practitioners. The title of the organization means loosely "society of children of Orisa" and helps children to know their inner divinity as literal children of the Gods (deities). Egbe Omo Orisa strives to create a community of peers that is part of the larger Yoruba community locally, nationally, and globally. Egbe Omo Orisa endeavors to help children build the religious and cultural skills to become productive members of the Yoruba tradition.

In 2008, a group of concerned parents (Dr. Millicent Channell, Darcia Mobley, and me, Ayoka Wiles) in Philadelphia established a Yoruba children's program for children 3–13 years of age. Egbe Omo Orisa began as a cooperative effort primarily running on the energy and enthusiasm of parents and volunteers and grew to be sponsored by Always Orisa, a nonprofit organization founded and lead by Iyalorisa Gheri Garnett. Egbe Omo Orisa has the following objectives: 1) Educate students to become proficient in traditional Yoruba prayer and rituals; 2) Educate students to develop a working knowledge of Yoruba cosmology and of their role in community; and 3) Instill a sense of pride, excitement and social responsibility about being Yoruba and practitioners of Orisa tradition.

Egbe Omo Orisa offers a sequential cultural program for youth ages 3–13. The program is offered on weekends from September to June to provide youth the opportunity to learn about Yoruba culture, history, and language, as well as skills in art, dance, and music. In addition, as a result of participating in the program youth realize their own creative and leadership capacities and become a part of a supportive community. The program incorporates traditional African, especially Yoruba, values and principles as a foundation for building good character, cultural proficiency, self-sufficiency, a positive self-identity and a commitment to community service. The goal of Egbe Omo Orisa is to provide a meaningful, lasting Yoruba education to children and their families. Part of the core educational approaches and fundamentals to the program include:

1) *Emphasis on development of Iwa Pele (Gentle Character)*: The program and activities focus on high expectations, philosophy of excellence, leadership opportunities, discipline, structure, honesty, integrity and respect for oneself and others.

2) *Age Appropriateness*: Programs and activities are developmentally appropriate and include arts and crafts activities to Yoruba language study for ages 2–13.

3) *Youth and Family-Centered Involvement*: The program activities involve youths and their families. Families/Parents are the main teachers of the program, and they work to develop mutual trust and strong bonds with youths and their families. Learning and activities provide youths with an opportunity to engage and learn in an environment that is respectful, caring, and allows for growth.

4) *Strong Emphasis on African History and African Self-Identity*: All activities focus on teaching Yoruba and African history and teaching how they relate to each individual so that youths are confident and aware of their African identity.

5) *Sharing Goals, Assessment, and Reflections*: Program activities include assessment methods that are centered in traditional Yoruba values. Each session begins and ends with a circle of prayer, acknowledgment and affirmation. Youth acknowledge Olofi (The Creator), the ancestors, and their fellow brothers and sisters.

As a result of participating in Egbe Omo Orisa, youth are prepared to become strong leaders and advocates for their tradition and culture. They also become very driven and successful in their various learning environments as a result of the resilience, self-worth and pride that has been inculcated in them through traditional African educational models.

Additionally, they have built strong bonds with their peers, families, and communities.

Conclusion

In order for young people of African descent to develop social and emotional wellbeing, they must learn to navigate the structural, political and economic conditions of their communities. While their communities may lack economic wealth and the advantages money brings, youths can develop a strong senses of self through African-centered education, art, values, and culture. A curriculum that focuses on an African centered approach and pedagogy supports the emotional, cultural, mental and spiritual development and identity of youth of African descent. Once young people connect with and develop a strong cultural identity, they find themselves in places of empowerment and authenticity no matter where they live. Such empowerment creates a level of resistance to racial injustices and propels one to not only believe they deserve better and that their voice and presence matter in the world but also that they have a right to excellence in their education, assets, careers, family life and relationships. These young people understand that they are not defined by how the world may perceive them or by the oppressive systems that are designed to keep them oppressed; rather, they control and dictate their definitions of self, how they will be seen in the world, and how people will respond to them.

Notes

[1] Shawn Ginwright, *Hope and Healing in Urban Education* (New York: Routledge, 2015).

[2] Ginwright, *Hope and Healing in Urban Education.*

[3] Kimbwandende K. Fu-Kiau, *Tying the Spiritual Knot: African Cosmology of the Bantu-Kongo: Principles of Life and Living* (1980, Brooklyn: Athelia Henrietta Press, 2001), 105.

[4] Obasi Survey is a Measurement of Acculturation Strategies of People of African Descent (MASPAD) developed by Ezemenari Marquis Obasi, B.S., M.A. Ifetayo has permission to use the comprehensive survey which is a multidimensional instrument designed to assess acculturation strategies (i.e., Traditionalist, Integrationist, Assimilationist, and Marginalist) along

the dimension of beliefs and behaviors. The MASPAD is a strong predictor of dimensions of worldview and cultural values.

Works Cited

Fu-Kiau, Kimbwandende K. *Tying the Spiritual Knot: African Cosmology of the Bantu-Kongo: Principles of Life and Living.* 1980. Brooklyn: Athelia Henrietta Press, 2001.

Ginwright, Shawn. *Hope and Healing in Urban Education.* New York: Routledge, 2015.

PART FOUR

LIFE LINES FROM THE FRONT LINES

Interview with Mandingo

Jumbe Kweku Lumumba

JKL: [On today's program,] we have brother Mandingo, a Garveyite, coming out of England. Brother Mandingo, we want to introduce you as an advocate for reparations, for the crime of the *Maafa* (Disaster) of the African holocaust, and a comrade in the African liberation struggle. The listeners here would like to know what's going on in England. We know there was recently a reparations march, but we want some more details of that and how the movement is progressing in England.

M: Well, what happened is that African brothers and sisters decided, at a grassroots level, sometime ago, that we need to make a public stand where reparations are concerned. So, brothers and sisters, including myself, as a Pan-Africanist, meaning a Garveyite, we got together, both on an individual level and at an organizational level, and organized this reparations march that took place on Friday, the first of August, 2014. The first of August, being the commemoration of Emancipation Day in the Caribbean, when our African ancestors won their emancipation, their freedom from enslavement, and British colonialism in the Caribbean. So, the date for the march was significant in it taking place on the anniversary of Emancipation Day.

In all, we marched from Brixton, which is in the borough of Lambeth. We assembled at Windrush Square, which is opposite the town hall in Brixton, and we marched straight to Westminster, which houses the British houses of parliament, and also went to 10 Downing Street, where a petition demanding, not begging, demanding reparations was presented. It was a march of about 5,000 African adults and children that took place, and afterward, on our way returning, we finally met at the town hall in Brixton, where there was a meeting, and there were several speakers speaking about the issue of reparations, and I was one of the speakers.

JKL: So, what were some of the results of this reparations conference or march? We see that CARICOM (Caribbean Community)

has been coming together to push stronger and harder for reparations, from European countries.

M: Yes, well our difference, in terms of the CARICOM approach, is that the CARICOM approach has restricted itself to the Caribbean. Our approach is in the mode of Marcus Garvey; it's worldwide; it's global. We're talking about reparations for Africans, not just in the Caribbean, but reparations for Africans, at home and abroad.

JKL: So, a very Pan-African approach, absolutely?

M: Precisely because as the word *pan* means *all,* it's all-African. So, we are completely different from the CARICOM approach which is strictly being restricted to the Caribbean.

JKL: So, how is the European government receiving this march?

M: Well, first of all, when they heard about it, they thought that maybe just a few dozen people would turn out. They were quite astounded that the march was about 5,000 strong. The police here were caught off-guard because, if they had known that so many thousands would be involved . . . in other words, it goes to show that it's not everything that they can anticipate. And what is happening, as a result, there will be further plans to step up the demands for reparations.

One of the reasons that we use reparations is that it was a tool of mobilization. By doing the reparations, we were getting a lot of the African people who were not conscious, who were not aware of the issues involved, and things to be dealt with. So, the reparations march, the preparation for it, also helped to get our people, who were sleeping psychologically, to be awakened and to understand that they have to get involved, and take to their destiny into their own hands, in a collective way.

JKL: So, in anticipation of a higher police presence and a stronger political pushback, what is the next step for the reparations movement in Europe?

M: Well, certain steps that will be taken, for the future, will definitely not be aired on this radio station that I'm speaking on or any other radio station because, when one is engaged in liberation, one does not disclose all the cards in one's hand. But what can be assured with the mobilization that was achieved is that this will not only be maintained, but will also be strengthened, in preparation for other activities, from a Pan-African perspective.

JKL: What is the condition of the people who are now becoming more involved in this movement because, as you mentioned before, there were a lot of unconscious people, who are just waking up. So, what is their condition?

M: The immediate effect is that they want to get more and more involved, to help as much as they can to further our aims as a people. So, that means that different people have different skills, different abilities, and we will be utilizing the skills of our people toward our collective, toward our racial salvation.

JKL: It sounds like a comprehensive plan, but what is. . .

M: Well it has to be comprehensive because, as I said, it's not a CARICOM approach; we are dealing with a Pan-African approach.

JKL: Now, how did the EU (European Union) and African Leadership Summit, which happened this year, and also the relations between the continent of Africa and the countries in the EU, how did that affect the reparations movement in Europe?

M: Well, first of all, you used the term *African leaders*. I don't see those people as African leaders; I see the vast majority of them as African misleaders, who are in the employ of European imperialists in Europe and in the US. We have Obama, who is simply the front-face for the European imperialist camp.

JKL: In other words, a neo-colonialist.

M: Of course! And [. . .] the very fact that President Mugabe wasn't invited neither to Brussels, in Europe, nor to this Obama meeting, just goes to show that the so-called summits were not about any meeting of equals. It was about people from Africa, not leaders, people from Africa coming to take instructions, in Brussels and Washington, from their European bosses. Because, if President Mugabe, who is in the vein of Marcus Garvey, in terms of the recovery of our lands (Africa for the Africans, at home and abroad), if he had been to Brussels, Belgium, and if he had been to Washington, there with Obama, he would have told them precisely what time of day and what time of night it was, but they didn't want to hear what he had to stay because they know where he stands. They only wanted people there who take instructions and carry out their instructions. If those people had any integrity, what they would have done is they would have said that we are for African unity, and you cannot seek to have a meeting of so-called African leaders, and you're going to select and decide who should come to the meeting as African leaders.

JKL: So, has the grassroots movement in Europe been engaging any of these leaders, or just forgoing that altogether, in favor of the grassroots approach with movements on the continent?

M: No. They have had to be dealing with things at a grassroots level because the very fact that these people do not represent the interest of the people, it is impossible to be working with people who do not represent your interest.

JKL: What ultimately, do the African people in Europe see as their interest because, as we see more of these summits happening in different parts of the world, we see different interests being put

forward? We see American interests, as we saw in the summit with the USA and the African misleaders, as you say. Or it's the EU with the African misleaders. What is the interest of African people?

M: The interest of African people simply lies in the fact that these misleaders must be replaced as soon as possible. The only way in which the Africans at home and abroad will improve, will be liberated, is when we replace and get rid of these misleaders. They are the ones who the European imperialists use to maintain their control to practice their neocolonial designs, through AFRICOM (United States Africa Command) and so-called trading agreements. I mean, of course they use the World Bank and the International Monetary Fund, but these are economic and trade institutions that are designed to keep African people in subjugation at home and abroad.

JKL: With the growth of some of these institutions that you mentioned, like AFRICOM, the World Bank, the IMF (International Monetary Fund), it seems that African people and the African interests you expressed have very little safeguards against new leadership becoming puppets or neocolonial tools in the pockets of European imperialists. So, is creating safeguards part of the reparations movement and African liberation?

M: There have to be safeguards. There have to be measures put in place, that we don't replace one set of puppets with another set of puppets because it is the people, from generation to generation, who are feeling the brutality or what is going on, with respect to our people, as Africans at home and abroad. We are not after exchanging faces; we are after people who genuinely represent the interest of the African majority, at home and abroad. As constituted, in fact for hundreds of years, it is always a very tiny African minority, in collusion with the foreign imperialists, who have kept down, exploited and brutalized, and enslaved African people, for their own interests.

JKL: That being said, you mentioned President Robert Mugabe as one of the leaders, who identifies as connected with the African interest—

M: I said President Mugabe; you notice I didn't use that first European name?

JKL: Aha, yes, I did.

M: Yes, keep it African.

JKL: Well, President Mugabe then. Are there any other leaders that the reparations movement in England identifies as people or groups, who are working in the interest of African people?

M: Well, there is the brother Malema, in South Africa, Azania, who has come under a lot of pressure because he has echoed the cry of Africa for the Africans, the land question in South Africa. And in the recent elections there, he scored some good points; the signs were encouraging there to show that what the ANC (African National Congress), with Mandela as a front, was a betrayal of the interests of the African people because what happened with the ANC, in their selling out of African independence, is that they completely ignored, in fact, they are totally against the idea of land, in South Africa, for Africans.

In South Africa, a vast majority of the land, about 88%, is still owned by the Europeans, in South Africa. So, nothing has changed, except that you have people like Cyril Ramaphosa, Mandela, and others who have benefitted, since the so-called fall of apartheid, while the condition of the vast majority of Africans in South Africa is still bad, and in some cases is worse. What they have done, what Mandela pushed, on behalf of the European imperialist, is that we should fight for a one-man one-woman vote. What ZANU-PF (Zimbabwe African National Union Patriotic Front) and President Mugabe have said in Zimbabwe, our people did not fight for the right to vote; we fought to recover our land. He or she, who owns and controls the land, controls the country; this is what Marcus Garvey correctly taught, and this is what Malcolm X, whose parents were Garveyites, taught because revolution is based on land. He or she who controls land also controls power.

JKL: Yes, so let's sit in South Africa for a moment. You mentioned two names that are connected with the ANC—Malema and Ramaphosa.

M: Formerly, because as you know Malema brought up the whole issue about the land question. . .

JKL: Right, and now he's with the EFF (Economic Freedom Fighters)...

M: Well Ramaphosa [. . .] was with the exploitative firm that was responsible for the massacre at Maracana. So, they're on opposite sides of the fence.

JKL: And that's what I want to kind of analyze. How should we look at that leadership shifting from a revolutionary perspective because, on the one hand we can see, coming out of the ANC, Malema moving forward with the more revolutionary and Garveyite. . . ?

M: Well we need to push in that direction because the other direction is the maintenance of European dominance and hegemony over African people in South Africa.

JKL: And it could be represented by Ramaposa, after that massacre of miners in 2012, where 34 of them died.

M: Well, even before the miners, about 34 in one day, this selling out thing, as I was telling you, began when the ANC departed from the program of action in the 1950s and came about with a so-called freedom charter that said that South Africa belongs to all who live in it, meaning both those who came and stole the land of the African, and the African themselves, which is totally irreconcilable. You cannot have a situation where those who stole our land, and are still in the position of our land, you're saying that they have the right to our country. And we have a situation in South Africa, as I said, where almost 90% of the land is still owned and controlled by the Europeans, and this is why there is still so much suffering in South Africa; the racist minority still owns and controls the land, despite the façade of an African government. It's a mirage.

JKL: We also want to touch on this international approach because what we're dealing with in the United States right now, in Ferguson, Missouri, with the police brutality...

M: The murder! Yes. Another Trayvon Martin. Another many, many because we have known, over the years, that thousands of Africans, males and females, young and old, have been butchered in cold blood by the racist police in the US. So, what has happened to our young brother, to our young son, 18 year old Michael Brown, in Ferguson, Missouri, is nothing new. This is just one of the latest episodes in the vicious genocidal attacks against African people.

JKL: One of the Pan-Africanist perspectives on this is that a weak Africa leaves all Africans around the world vulnerable.

M: This is precisely why Marcus Garvey said that we must have, as a base, a continental African government, with one president, one army, one navy, and one air force. So that such a continental African superpower would command the respect of other races, and would lend protection to Africans at home and abroad. If we had such a power—as Marcus Garvey clearly outlined in his black-print, all we need to do is implement it—if we had such an African superpower, the kind of things that are happening to African people; the Maracana massacre, the cold-blooded slaughter of Michael Brown, etcetera, etcetera, these things would not have occurred because we would have had a powerful superpower government that would protect African people at home and abroad.

For example, whenever things happen to someone who is an American citizen, or a French citizen, or a British citizen, people otherwise know that their governments will come to protect their interests and to protect them. We, as Africans, we have to build such a continental superpower to protect our people at home and abroad, and to enable our people to live in peace and prosperity. Let us not forget that Africa, the second largest continent, is the richest continent on the planet; but, because of European and Arab imperialism, for centuries upon centuries, Africans have the lowest living standards and suffer all kinds of calamities as a result of us, as African people, not owning and controlling our continent, from North to South.

JKL: Now, the continent, as you mention this continental government, it was on the verge in 2007, but that's pretty much fallen apart since then, so how do we move forward with that kind of plan?

M: We move forward with, by wherever we are as Africans—and again, Marcus Garvey's black-print fully shows how this is done—we deal with our interests at a community level, at a national level, and at an international level. So, we interlock and communicate, and we work together; there is no other way. You notice what our enemies do? They are always having summits, they are always having meetings, and they are always communicating. This is not rocket science; we simply have to do the same to ensure our interests. They are doing what they're doing for their own interests; we, as Africans, have to do what we have to do, for our own interests. As Marcus Garvey said, this is all about self-reliance; we cannot depend on non-Africans, nor should we expect non-Africans to see about our African interests. Only someone who is a lunatic, only someone who is mad is going to depend on non-Africans to solve the problems of African people. The problems of African people can and will be solved only by African people.

JKL: I don't want to end this interview without giving resources, so let's shift back to England. What kinds of organizations are available for people who are interested in becoming involved in this kind of activity in England? And, if you know of more that operate internationally, give us some plugs for those.

M: As I have said, struggles take in covert and overt ways. There are certain things I will not mention publically, but what I can say is that people can get in touch, as a first step, people can get online to www.ipetitions.com/petition/rastafari-movement-uk. When one gets contact, that's a step onto other things, but at this time I will not be individualizing individuals and organizations because we're all in a public space, and we know that the enemy is always listening and monitoring, so we do not disclose certain things publically.

JKL: Well, thank you, brother Mandingo, for your time and your service. Thank you for coming onto the show today and updating us on the situation in England, and the Pan-African movement throughout the world.

M: Thank you very much, my brother, and I end with the words of Marcus Garvey: *One God, one aim, and one destiny.* And let us remember that this coming Sunday is the 127th anniversary of the birth of Marcus Mosiah Garvey, the greatest Pan-Africanist leader this world has ever known, who founded the UNIA-ACL (Universal Negro Improvement Association and African Communities League) on the 20th of July, 1914, at 32 Charles Street, Kingston, Jamaica. And one of the founding members was Amy Ashwood, who was later to become his first wife, Amy Ashwood Garvey; and incidentally, she is my mother's mother's cousin. And Marcus Garvey's son, Marcus Garvey, Jr., taught me physics at school, Kingston Technical High School, in Jamaica, and he and I worked as Pan-Africanists from the 1960s coming straight through. One God, one aim, one destiny; Up you mighty race; we must accomplish that which we will.

JKL: Thank you again, brother. We'll keep the African pride alive.

Interview with Kambale Musavuli

Jumbe Kweku Lumumba

JKL: Right now, family, I'd like to introduce our guest. Brother Kambale Musavuli is a native of the Democratic Republic of the Congo, and one of the leading political and cultural Congolese voices. He is a human rights advocate, student coordinator, and national spokesperson for the Friends of the Congo. Brother Kambale is an educator who mobilizes individuals and communities to work with the Congolese civil society and strives to end the country's conflict, control its enormous mineral wealth, and build lasting peace and stability in the heart of Africa. Also, Brother Musavuli lectures on conflict minerals, peace and security, use of social media and advocacy, building of international social movements, the role of youth in Africa, corporate social responsibility, and gender-based violence and its connection to resource exploitation and poverty. Brother Kambale, welcome to *What Good is a Song? The Friday Night Drum.*

KM: Congo week, Congo month, Congo 365. Thank you so much for having me on the show.

JKL: Yes. Thank you for your time and your availability. One thing I wanted you to highlight for the family: we're asking people to call-in to donate to the radio station; so I wanted to start with that piece—how cell phones relate to the crisis in the Congo.

KM: Absolutely. And thank you for segueing into the use of electronic devices. Our cellphones: all of us may have one with us on a daily basis, but we never ask: *How did we make that phone? Who built that phone? What manufacturer built that phone?* Well the connection that you hold to that phone is the Congo. In order for you to have a cellphone by function, it needs to have a key mineral, and that mineral is called coltan. Congo holds anywhere from 64 to 80 percent of the world reserve of coltan, and this key mineral has been at the center of the conflict in the Congo. Congo is blessed with so many different minerals, from gold to diamonds, but coltan is special to electronic devices; your cellphone, your laptop, your DVD player, your VCR, your microwave, and even your car.

So what does it do actually, this mineral? Coltan absorbs the heat of your phone and it helps in conducting electricity on the motherboard; it holds high electric charge on your phone, so that your battery will last longer. People don't even know that, but in the conflict in the Congo that I mentioned, you know it has been central to the battle on the ground; over six million black people have died due to that conflict. We don't hear it in the media; we don't hear it in the news. When you listen to CNN, you don't hear anything. What we're hearing right now are Hillary Clinton's emails, but no one is talking about how Bill Clinton, her husband, when he was in power, he supported the invasion of the Congo that unleashed the death of millions.

So it's great to educate the listeners and the world community to know, when we hold our cellphones, we need to remember the people who have died in the Congo; and, most of all, half of them were children under the age of five.

JKL: Brother Kambale, I wanted to go back to that conflict, that war, because, as you've said, the media, by in large, has not reported on it at all. And many of our listeners, and the general population, may be unaware of the war that's going on and the extent of the damage that's been done in the Congo. So, even yourself, can we start with the fact that you are here, in the United States, as a result of the war? Can you put a timeframe on that and paint a picture for us?

KM: Yes, definitely. Since 1996, there has been a war in the Congo, and as I mentioned, it has taken the lives of millions. Two years after the war [began], my family was able to get out of the country, so I came to the United States as a refugee. If there was no war in my home, no war in the Congo, I would not be in the United States; I would be in my home probably going to college, getting my law degree, and living with my people to help my country become a better place. Unfortunately, as that war started, many people fled, and many people died. But that war was a war of aggression, from two of the United States' staunchest allies: Rwanda and Uganda.

Some people know of Rwanda from the history of genocide happening in Rwanda in 1994, but what people do not know is what happened to the country after the genocide. The government that took power in Rwanda, after the genocide in 1994, became an ally of the United States, and that government, including the government of Uganda, invaded the Congo in 1996 and, in 1998, it has unleashed the death that we see in the Congo today. Now why would they invade the Congo, and what's the interest of one of Congo's neighbors, our African brothers across the border, to come invade another country?

Rwanda and Uganda are United States' allies on the *War on Terror*, but what does that actually mean? So we have African soldiers, from Uganda who are stationed in Iraq, in Afghanistan; we have them also in Somalia, we have them in Mali, we even have them in Haiti. But people don't ask how they end up in these countries. So, US military planes have been moving these African [soldiers] to many different places, mainly to serve US interest abroad. How many people, even during the presidential debate in the US, will say that we have African soldiers fighting in Iraq? None have said that; Americans don't even know that. But because of them being allies to the US, what they have done is cause havoc on the African continent and no one, even at the level of the United Nations, has held them accountable.

But there are things that are happening. While I'm talking, this desolation and what these nations are doing, the people of those countries are rising up. So, on the African continent right now, we have a lot of youth movements taking place. Now speaking about Rwanda and Uganda, if I look at what's happening in Burundi, for example, the youth of the country stood up to challenge the elite of the country. In Rwanda, it's very hard because, if you speak up, very easily you can disappear, you can be dead; in Uganda the same thing is happening. In Senegal, we saw the youth rising up and transforming the nation. When the president, who wanted to stay beyond his term limit was actually kicked out—in Burkina Faso that happened. And even in Congo today, this entire year we've seen youth uprising. But what is that movement doing? We have a youth movement developing on the African continent, where young Africans are saying *no*, and challenging the local elite and their foreign corporate backers from the West. And I'm seeing that same movement happening right now in the United States, with the *Black Lives Matter* movement.

JKL: Now, do you see a coincidence in that? You have this youth movement transforming the landscape of Africa . . . you have this youth movement, African young men and women, transforming the discussion and political landscape of the United States and Africa, simultaneously.

KM: It's not a coincidence; history repeats itself. The same thing happened in the 1960s. We had a young man in Harlem, New York, who was saying, if you can understand what's happening in Mississippi and Alabama, you can understand what's happening in the Congo—that was Malcolm X. Malcolm X, in Harlem, understood that. As he mobilized the African peoples in America, he always made it a mission to connect the struggle. As black consciousness rose in the '60s, black leaders were assassinated, sidelined, or given and offered jobs; look at Jesse Jackson today. And they forgot the struggle.

And we are repeating history, as black youth rise up in the United States and black youth are rising up on the African continent, it is essential to share stories, share experiences, and connect. What would it do to US foreign policy, if every African nation today said they will close every American embassy, until black people are treated as human beings in the United States? That would transform so many things, but the challenge that the African youth have right now is that many of the leaders they have now have been installed by the West. So that is why it's critical to have the synergy, that as we are successful on the African continent, as we are successful in the Congo, that as the people in the Congo are free, I believe Africa will be free. And as Africa is free, African peoples around the world will be free and liberated, and we can go and be in our home with our brothers and sisters, to transform the African continent.

JKL: Now, as we come to a close in this discussion, I wanted to go into something that is in the strain of sharing our stories—that component of black consciousness. You mentioned Malcolm X, someone who, as a youth, didn't live in that spirit. However, once he got it, he transformed himself and an entire environment, an entire country, and in many ways, he transformed the world. Now, your story is similar, in that, when you came to the US, there was a transformation that happened with you, in regard to black consciousness. Can you tell the listeners about that?

KM: Definitely. I was educated in Garveyism, specifically because I was blessed to attend North Carolina A & T University, which is a historically black college and university in North Carolina. When I came, I had my African name, but I also had my colonial name; it was a Belgian name because Congo was colonized by the Belgians. Being right on campus, I met this young man by the name of Amari. That young man walked on campus with a red, black, and green flag—the liberation flag. And I wondered, as a young African who just arrived as a refugee: *what was that flag?* And he approached me and asked my name. I told him my Belgian name, and he looked at me and told me that can't be my name, and asked me for my African name. And I was shocked, that right here, in the United States, a black youth was challenging the notion of my own identity. So, I shared with him that my name is Kambale. So he asked why I don't ask people to call me Kambale because that is a beautiful name.

That was the beginning of a personal journey that I'm still on today, of understanding what it means to be black, what it means to be African. But it took just one youth, on my college campus, to open my eyes, and for me to understand that, on both sides of the Atlantic, we have been bamboozled. We have taken something that is not ours; we have forgotten [ourselves]. Imagine today, what if when the white community closed their eyes, they envisioned God to be black? What would the world be like today? That's what has happened to us. We have even forgotten our identity. When we close our eyes and we're thinking about God, *Mungu*, as we say in Swahili, *Nzambe* as we say in Lingala, we have the skin tone of that God, of that power that we seek. What if that image were a black person? That's the journey I'm on, in educating people to remember their roots.

As I was helped by one of my great friends, brother Amari, I hope many people listening to this show can also start that journey of finding out why the African continent, why even the Congo has not been at peace for many centuries. And when we discover that and understand the struggle of that land, then we'll understand why a young man in Harlem, like Malcolm X, also said if you can understand what's happening in Mississippi and Alabama, you can understand what's happening in the Congo. And I will sum it up for you—if you can understand Ferguson and Baltimore, you can understand what's happening in the Congo today.

JKL: Yes. And thank you very much. I know in the true revolutionary spirit, you are on the move and have engagements coming up right after this discussion. So, I won't hold you any longer, but I do want to thank you for spending this time with us to shed some light on a place that has been blocked out of our minds for so long. Let us remember ourselves, and thank you, brother Kambale, for helping us put those pieces back together.

Kambale Musavuli can be contacted at www.friendsofthecongo.org.

Interview with Kuma N'dumbe III

Jumbe Kweku Lumumba

JKL: I'd like to introduce a special guest to the *Friday Night Drum*, a great Pan-Africanist, His Royal Highness, Prince Kuma N'dumbe III, of Bonabéri, Cameroon. He is briefly sojourning in Atlanta, Georgia, where we was invited to be honored with the 2014 A.D. King Award for Leadership and Social Empowerment. An activist, playwright, and university lecturer, author of several publications, and a visionary for Africa, Prince N'dumbe has received several awards for his works, which have mostly attracted the scorn of western colonialists for contradicting their story. His royal lineage and strategic geographic positioning of his origins at the mouth or the River Wouri, in Cameroon, which was, and still is the gateway to that part of central Africa, put him at a pole position to tell the African story. Welcome to the *Friday Night Drum*, Your Highness.

KN: Thank you so much, and thank you for inviting me.

JKL: Yes. It's a pleasure to have you, it's an honor. I just want to begin by welcoming you to the *Drum* and welcoming you to Atlanta, Georgia. How has your stay been?

KN: Well, I think that it's highly interesting. First of all, I thank the A.D. King Foundation for awarding me with this leadership award in social empowerment. When I came here, I asked him, I'm living in Douala, Bonabéri, in Cameroon, how do you know me, and then you invite me here to give me an award? They just start laughing. And then they told me, today the world has no boundaries anymore. So, even when you are doing something in Cameroon, the world is watching you, and if you are doing something that is good for humankind, please do it again. So, that day, November 15th up to now, I'm meeting a lot of interesting and marvelous people. It brings me in a kind of synergy, and that's great. When I'm back home, I will tell them what I've seen here and I will tell them which kind of opportunities I found here, so that we can work together. And we are not working together for ourselves, but for what the actual world needs; you here in the United States, other countries, and we, in Africa. If we have the opportunity to connect and reconnect, and build a new world, then it is great.

JKL: And talking about building a new world, reconnecting, I'm an African in the Diaspora, someone who was born in the Diaspora. . .

KN: Yes and your name is Lumumba! Your name is Lumumba! You see, 1968, I wrote a play entitled *Lumumba II.* I did it in the German language because I was living in the German area at that time, and you, as a US citizen, you took the decision to be named Lumumba; it means that you want to be reconnected. And, I'm not from Congo, I'm from Cameroon, and I was a young man at that time, when I wrote the play—it means, reconnection. That's the message of Africa today, the reconnection.

You know Africa is the origin of mankind, but in the last 600 years it was terrible what happened to Africa, and to Africans, but now we are coming again with a new vision, with a new message. That's the reason why it's so necessary that we, at home, we want all our children in the United States, in Brazil, in Europe, to come together, so that we can give this new message to the world because the world is getting crazy, really crazy, and we need something new. We are not saying we, Africans, should unite to conquer the other one, that's not our message. Our message is the message of reconciliation with the universe, the reconciliation with this earth because the world is getting crazy; we are destroying everything because we think that by destroying others, we will survive; that's not okay.

That's the reason why the Africans, who are the origin of all mankind, we are coming now to give a new message to the world—please, we need peace, we need wisdom, we need togetherness, and you should run away from this system that says *I am the most important, I want everything for me and nothing for the other*; you have to get away from that because you are destroying everything—you are not only destroying yourself, but you are destroying the world. The voices of Africa today, we are more than one billion, and we are young; the population in Africa today is a young one with new and very strong ideas. It is crazy that when people think about Africa they think on Ebola and all this rubbish, but we are coming with a new message, with a new hope for the world, and that's what we want to give people everywhere. Listen, if you do not reconcile yourself with yourself and the universe, you are lost . . . that's the message of Africa today.

JKL: You mentioned youth and how young Africa is, in light of this message. I believe you were maybe 15, when Cameroon became independent. . .

KN: Yeah, that's true.

JKL: Tell us about that experience, as a young man, in a country that is just realizing its independence. What was that like? What was the atmosphere like?

KN: Oh yes, I wrote a book, but because I'm in a French-speaking world, coming from Douala, it entitled it, *Cinquante Ans Déjà! Quand Cessera Enfin Votre Indépendance-là?* (*Fifty Years Already! When Will Your Independence Cease?*), because this independence is not an independence. What I saw at that time is we had a lot of problems in Cameroon. We had two groups—the group who took over the independence because the French obliged, I mean they chose the people and gave them the power, and those who really wanted the independence were martyred and so on, it was crazy what we saw as young men. I remember that we were singing, the day of independence, wow, this is the day of independence, now we are getting out of barbarism; we are getting out of the wilderness and we are coming to the new sun. Can you imagine that in the national anthem that you say that you are getting out of your barbarism?!

That's the kind of independence we got at that time, and when you are formed in this kind of context, it is very, very difficult to get free. That's the reason why I say that Africa is young today; these young Africans don't know what colonialism is because they were not there, so they are free in mind. We have to give them fundamental elements, so they can grow to real Africans because you cannot be an African, when you are living in Africa and you went to school and the university, but everything that you had in your hand, the books, are written by the white man, no, you are not a real African. So, that's one thing I say to these youth, you have to go back to your roots, even when you are in Africa, you are obliged to do research. What is the legacy, even the scientific legacy of your people, and you have to go through it.

It is not enough that you are a doctor, professor, and so on, and you don't know anything really about you, about your legacy. You cannot live in Senegal as a professor, or in Gabon, as a professor, and you have only US or British or French signs in your mind, no, it can't work because you will destroy the African youth, you will destroy them. If you want to build them really, okay, you went to this French or British school, but go back to the roots. If you are an economist, go back to the research and ask yourself how the economy was functioning before the white man came. What did our ancestors bring or write? If you can't answer these questions, you are not an African scientist. You see? When we are teaching law at a university in Gabon or Nigeria, and you can't say anything about how the African community was ruled by the law, and you only are able to say how the law functions in France or the United States, and you want to apply it in an African country, that's the wrong way. So, we, as professors, we have to go back to research, if we want to give, to this African youth, fundamental ground to stand.

JKL: And mentioning going back, you are part of the lineage of a precolonial leadership. So, tell us a little about that lineage and how we can connect, even though we may be distanced geographically, tell us how we can connect to that which continues to exist, even in an African world which is wrought by Eurocentric hegemony. How do you function in a world, where there is so much loss of African consciousness, even on the continent?

KN: Yes. My responsibility, as a prince, is to build a kind of linkage between the legacy of our culture, our history, and the modern achievements. This link is very important because, as a prince, from the beginning, you go through this legacy, you are obliged to; there is no way out. You are obliged to go from step to step. So, in my case, I am a university professor, so I went through all these modern European theories and so on. Well, and then I tell myself, if I want my people to be successful, it is extremely important that they know, not only what the modern world is bringing in, but what we had, and that's the reason that I came to the resolution that I have to build up this AfricAvenir International Foundation, to do this work because I know the university will not do that, and only traditional structures cannot do that.

You need this linkage to build a kind of synergy between the heritage and the scientific achievements in the modern world. If we are successful in doing this, in giving to this young generation both possibilities . . . for example, take medical plants, in Cameroon we have a lot of medical plants. Three quarter[s] of medical plants, you can find them in Cameroon, but when you are studying pharmacy, you don't know anything about it, and that's wrong. That is now our responsibility as kings and university professors, to bring a kind of awareness; telling the university you are doing wrong, if you don't go to the medical plants of Cameroon, if you don't bring these medical plants to the university, you are doing wrong because, otherwise, if you have medical doctors, every time they write prescriptions, you are going to import drugs from Europe and the US. That's crazy! You don't need to import drugs! God has given you all the medical plants, so use these medical plants for your people. To be able to do that you have to bring a scientific legacy, into the university, and teach it so that the students can discover what they have in their environment and use it for the people. The colonial mentality is that you should learn what is taught in Berlin, in New York, in Paris, and bring it to Africa. No, you can, but you first have to have your own ground. When you have your own ground, and you are sure of this ground, then you can add experiences from all over the world.

JKL: So, you mentioned your foundation, AfricAvenir International Foundation, and what does that mean for the world today? You started in 1985, correct?

KN: Right. 1985. It started in Douala, Cameroon.

JKL: What is this foundation?

KN: The foundation has to build this linkage between the African legacy because it is a tremendous one, when you discover it, and so, we bring what belongs to this legacy together—the scientific and cultural legacy—we bring it together in the foundation, so you can have access to it. You know children from the university, in Douala, and Buea, and Yaoundé, they are so astonished; they say what we find here, we don't find in our university library. You'll find a lot of African authors, Cameroonian authors, and different scientific achievements, but you don't find it in our libraries, at the university, because the university libraries have a lot of donations coming from outside. With these donations, the books are not research results of Africans, but when they come to AfricAvenir, they find this; they find it, and then they can work with it.

We need a kind of rebirth. We need a kind of renaissance, cultural renaissance; in music; in theater; in performing arts, and so on. So, the language is central. You don't speak your language and you are a doctor? You are a doctor in mathematics or literature, and you are unable to speak your own language? What is that?! Which kind of doctor are you? And then I say no, you are not a doctor, you are illiterate. Yes! You cannot say that I am a doctor in this or that, and you can only speak French or English. What about your language? Because the message, the vision is in your head, and if you have only the language of the colonial master, then you have only the vision and the thought of the colonial master; no, it can't work. So, in this cultural work, African languages are central.

So, for example, in 1997 we had two months of competition between sixteen schools, and the competition was in the Cameroonian languages, not in French, not in English, and every child had to make the competition in his own language. We have so many languages in Cameroon, and it was exciting. That's the way, that's the way. You cannot say you have a master's, you are a doctor, you do it in French, you do it in German, you do it in English, and you cannot speak with your *Douala* language, you cannot speak your *Wuté* language, you cannot write in your *Fulfulbe* language. No.

JKL: That's an interesting dilemma we have as African people. Our official languages are often the languages of those who colonize us, and even if we do commerce or have conversations in our indigenous languages, we do international business and education in the language of our colonizers. So, in talking about an African renaissance, let's talk about the entire continent, and the African Union moving toward a

unified Africa. How does the African continent and the governing structures deal with that language barrier?

KN: Yes, well listen, Europeans are, most of the time, unilingual; they are speaking in one language. Africans are multilingual; that's our culture. We have a culture of multilingualism, but when the colonial master came in, they wanted to make us unilingual. That's the destruction of black culture; that's the destruction of black civilization, as Chancellor Williams said. No! We are rich because we are able to speak so many languages. When you go to Cameroon, I don't know if I know somebody who is able to speak only one language, but when you go to Europe, most of them speak only one language. A Cameroonian, a Nigerian, a Congolese, we are multilingual. So, the issue is not to say we, in Africa, are supposed to have one language for the whole continent. Please, don't forget that the continent is a huge continent; in this, you can bring in North and South America, plus Europe, plus Asia, plus India. So, you cannot say, if you want to be united, you have to use only one language. Take Switzerland, they are multilingual officially; they have German, French, *Rumantsch*. So, why do you want a whole continent to have only one language?

I know that the African Union has decided that Swahili should be learned by everybody, so we can have a kind of language of communication, but the African culture is not a unilingual culture; we are multilingual. Even if you don't speak French or English, you are speaking two or three African languages because that's our way of communicating. I think that we should cultivate it because when you speak your mother tongue, it is possible for you to speak other languages. I speak my Douala language very good, I dream in my Douala language, I write in my Douala language, and I was capable of writing 14 books in the German language, and more than 40 books in the French language. That's not a problem, and I think that's the way; we need our language because the key of the world is in the language. The key of the vision, how you understand the world, is in your language. Losing your language is losing the key for the world.

JKL: So, once someone has lost their language, like so many of those who are taken from the continent in the slave trades, how does one reconnect? We may not even know what region we came from, and it's difficult to find out what languages our forefathers and foremothers spoke. So what do we do?

KN: I think that the first thing is to reconnect. Please, come to us, you are so welcome. And then we will find solutions. In this case, some with the DNA test can say I'm from Tanzania or I'm from Cameroon because, in Cameroon for example, we have received groups from the United States because of these DNA tests. They can come back, but even when they come back to Cameroon, we have so many languages. When you come you can say I am Bamileke, I am Tikar, alright, but please, learn one African language because you will see the difference.

You know, when I speak French or German, it is so different. When I come back to my Douala language, it is a world, a quite different world. When you don't have access to a language, you don't have access to the world. You cannot come to Africa for reconnection and you have only the English language. When we have, for example, our purification rituals, our reconnection rituals, how can you do that in French? How can you do that in English? You are reconnecting somebody with whom? With their ancestors? They don't speak French. They don't speak English. And I remember when, two years ago, a group came to Cameroon, I brought them to Bimbia, and then I brought them to the water for this purification ritual. I mean, it was not possible for me to think or to speak in French or English; I did it from my memory. And I can tell you that what happened, the visions were there, what happened was tremendous. You could see the answer of the ancestors on the body of our African Americans. If I had spoken French or English, or German, no, it would have been useless. That's the reason why I think a language is a key, so in this process of reconnection, please learn one or two or three languages. But start with one, and learn it well, and use it.

JKL: So, Your Highness, in closing, I'd like to read something, I think you'll recognize it.

"Today is my birthday. I'm 24 and I'd like to know what I think of my life, that is, what I want to do with my life. Yet, up to now, I can't give my life another direction as the one leading to total liberation of African people; to the respect of the black man's dignity, and to a personal contribution to humanity throughout this whole process. But since this is a belief I've been having since first grade of primary school, that is, since 13 years now, it seems to have some weight. But what's important, for me, is to wait; wait until I have achieved this goal. Then I will say, Kuma N'dumbe III, you're a serious man, go on, I trust you. But not before. And I ask myself, if I will ever get there. I don't just have to get there, but I have to surpass this stage and go further.

When I speak of the liberation of Africa and the black man, it all includes love, art, religion, etc. One thing becomes clear: my life only makes sense, in the total liberation of Africa. I don't know if I could express what I feel, but, nevertheless, this primary formulation will improve from day to day, and only reach its final expression, after my death. What I ask myself is to fulfill this task. I'm between the past and the future, so my position doesn't depend on me. It's therefore important to do one's little work, in the present, which will be history tomorrow. Since there is a definite issue about Africa's unification, (I assume that the total unification of Africa presumes its unification) and about the disdain of some races for mine, this specific situation offers me a solid basis for work. It's therefore a plausible basis."

That was you at 24 years old.

KN: Yes. I wrote this . . . it was the first of November, 1968. It was my birthday, and I wanted to know what I want to do with my life. Today I am 70 . . . and I am impressed that you are reading this . . . that you know this . . . wow . . .

JKL: So, what would the 24-year-old, who was writing this on his birthday, think of the 70 year old man I am conversing with now?

KN: I think I can say that it was a grace that my ancestors were surrounding me because I was in France, at the university, at that time; I was not in Africa. I was in France, in Lyon, and I wrote this and it means that I was not alone. It means that my fathers and mothers told me what to do. And I think that I accepted it; I said alright, I will do that. Now that I am 70 years old, I can say yes, I did it, thanks to God and thanks to my ancestors because you cannot do it without them . . . impossible.

JKL: Yes, a real exercise in reconnecting.

KN: Yeah.

Prince Kuma N'dumbe III can be contacted at www.africavenir.org.

Interview with Hilary La Force

Jumbe Kweku Lumumba

JKL: I'm here with Mr. Hilary La Force, Executive Director of the Folk Research Centre in St. Lucia, in the Caribbean. I'd just like to thank you for the opportunity to have a discussion about St. Lucian history, culture, and the local milieu. I'd like to start by asking you to tell us about the Folk Research Centre (FRC).

HL: The FRC was established in 1973, 42 years ago. It began with a group of students from St. Mary's College, who, along with their teacher, sought to explore the culture of St. Lucia by doing research. As such, they called themselves *The Studies and Action Group*. These youngsters went around speaking to various persons about St. Lucia's culture, as it relates to music, dance, food, and everything that is St. Lucian. They were joined by some other youngsters after this and, here, the Folk Research Centre was born. At the time they didn't have resources, so they used to use a room in one of the Catholic Church buildings. And that went on for a while, until they got their permanent home at this location called Monte Pleasant, which is French for *pleasant hill*. And the building was bought, with a loan from the bank, by the Folk Research Centre.

The major objective of the FRC is to promote research of St. Lucia's culture, and to basically promote St. Lucia's cultural heritage. We have been doing that, initially, by doing research on almost every aspect of St. Lucian culture and, to an extent, its politics and history. We have a very comprehensive library with lots of information, as part of the documentation center, where we have an audio-visual library with well over 2,000 hours of material that is collected via video and interviews with various people. It contains lots of music; all the indigenous music of St. Lucia, and dance.

Now, as you realize, St. Lucia was one of those countries where the slave trade began. So, most of our African people got to St. Lucia through the slave trade. So, we are basically children of those persons who came in as slaves. Invariably, part of the culture was affected. You've probably heard about calypso singing in these islands. Calypso actually began with the slaves, who, after a hard day's work, would relate the stories to their friends, either orally or through song. Then, they came from Africa with the drum, so the drum is one of our favorite instruments which we inherited from our African ancestors.

It has been said that we are basically *creole* people, meaning that once you are born in the country and your parents are from somewhere outside of that country, you are called creole. Although, in some instances, people argue that you are creole because your parents were slaves, we've tried to refine it and say, once you are born in St. Lucia or born into a country of foreign ancestors, you are creole. So, it would not be only black people who are creole. There are Indian people in St. Lucia, their parents came from India, and so we call them creole. There are Chinese, who came from China and children were born in this country, so they're also creole. Similarly, there are also Syrians who came here through buying and selling, and have children born here, so we call them creole. So, it's a potpourri of creole persons in our country, quite a wide variety, but dominated by black people.

JKL: Now, the creole designation, for those who are born here from various ancestries, does that relate to the language of St. Lucia as well, or is that something separate?

HL: It is something separate. Of course, by virtue of being colonized by the British, our official language is English. However, we do have the *Kwéyòl* language, which is a mixture of some of the African languages and the French. It's about 80% the French language, and that is being spoken in countries where the French had established themselves. So, within the Caribbean, there's a Martinique, Guadeloupe, Dominica, St. Lucia, and Haiti. To a lesser extent, it was in Trinidad and Tobago and Grenada, but they've almost lost the Kwéyòl language. But the language continues to be spoken widely in the countries I mentioned before, as well as French Guyana, in the South American mainland. So there is something common, with that language, in that it's spoken mainly by black people because of the fact that our ancestors were Africans, and some of the languages that they spoke became a mixture of the French and that language.

Now we, at the Folk Research Centre, are basically promoting that language and that it is considered part of our ancestry. In the past, and up to a point today, if you spoke/speak that language, you were considered illiterate—someone who didn't go to school and not properly educated, therefore, that was their means of communication. Be that as it may, it's part of our culture; it's part of what we knew, what we learnt. So, in effect, we call it our national language, but the official language is English. At the FRC, as part of the promotion and development of Kwéyòl, we have several organizations who try to put together the orthography, the writing system.

We had institutions like the University of the West Indies, based in Barbados, and we had organizations in Martinique and Guadeloupe. In St. Lucia we had *Mouvman Kwéyòl* (Movement for the Creole Language) which came together. There is also a movement in Dominica, and we all met at various stages and put together that orthography. We've had so far two dictionaries; one done by a St. Lucian gentleman, in 1992, and, more recently, one produced by the Ministry of Education in St. Lucia. But we, at the FRC, also teach people the language.

There several persons who can speak the language, but they seem illiterate (meaning they can't read and write it), so we teach them. Those persons can learn within four one-hour sessions; that is how simple this language can be. But persons who cannot speak the language at all, and would like to speak and write the language, we are able to teach them in three months. So that is basically the core of our activity—the promotion and teaching of the Kwéyòl language.

But, in addition to this, we have the Harold Simmons Folk Academy. Harold Simmons was the mentor at the FRC, one of the first persons who began doing research in St. Lucia's culture. So, we have him as our mentor and we named that academy after him, and as part of the curriculum of that academy is the Kwéyòl language, and we do all the various dances in St. Lucia. There are dances where persons dance to a violin and what is called a folk band, and there is something called *kwadril*, the square dance. As part of this folk music, we also play something called *lakonmèt, schottische, kwibich,* and there are several other pieces. We, at the Folk Academy, teach those dances, as well as the music that goes along with those dances. In addition to this, we also teach people how to drum, do African drumming, and there's drumming that was developed locally. There is drumming that came from Africa, called *tumba,* which we continue to teach people. Also, the dance that goes with drumming; there is *kont* and *sulu,* among others. There is also dancing which we have developed, particularly in St. Lucia, which is from American music, country and western.

JKL: Yeah! That's something that struck me as kind of peculiar, actually. How did country and western music become so popular in St. Lucia?

HL: Ah yes. Many years ago, in the days when AM (Amplitude Modulation) and the shortwave radio bands were very popular, our farmers, who left very early in the morning to work on their farms, would have those radios and pick up those American stations, especially from the South, that played country and western. And so they developed a liking for it. In those early days you had Hank Locklin and George Jones, and our people developed a liking for it by hearing it on the radio. Eventually the workers, some who were farmers, left the country and migrated to the United States to be part of a farm labor program, where they got to harvest cane, harvest apples, and harvest oranges. And while there, they also bought the records of these musicians they were hearing, and brought it back to St. Lucia.

They actually developed a dancing style to it which is unique to St. Lucia, so much so, that some time ago we brought in a country and western singer from the UK, and he was amazed to see people dance to his music . . . he had never seen it before. Now, it's become so popular that it is actually part of St. Lucia's dance culture, and it's the most popular dance in the country. Almost every weekend, there are various dancehalls playing country and western music. So, it's one of those cultural forms that was developed by St. Lucia.

JKL: Now, is that generating any native St. Lucian artists who sing country and western music?

HL: Yes, there have been some. In fact, some have even gone to Nashville, Tennessee! That is rather unfortunate because it is, as people in America call it, redneck music. So, it's still very strange to see a black person singing it . . . in fact, I'll give you a story. There was this St. Lucian, who was in Louisiana, and he was speeding, and the cops pulled him over. The cop asked him why he was in such a hurry. The man told him he was just coming from work and was a bit tired, so he wanted to get home quickly to get a rest. So, the cop was about to charge him, but then he heard he was playing country and western, and found that rather strange. Then he asked him where he comes from, and the man said he was from St. Lucia. The cop then told him next time he better be careful and slow down. So, the cop gave him a break, the fact that he played country and western music is what saved him.

But back to the Harold Simmons Folk Academy, we do cooking, we teach indigenous cooking. We have our famous bread fruit and salt fish or green fig and salt fish, we have a *bouyon*, and we also do what we call bake and float made with flour (the Jamaicans call it fried dumplings). There is a difference though, you may have seen it; the float is the light one and the bake is the heavy one. Some people don't know how to do it, unfortunately, so we teach people how to do this. And we also get involved in what we call non-traditional medicine; we have a doctor who comes in here to teach it because of the various herbs that are around that can be used for various ailments. We try to encourage persons to continue growing these plants around their yards which can keep the doctor away.

But then, we have our flagship project that is called Creole Heritage Month, held in October. This arose out of the declaration of International Creole Day which is normally done on the 28th of October. Now all Francophone countries that speak the Kwéyòl language celebrate that day. So countries that are part of the Caribbean, and you have places like the Seychelles, and you have places in the United States, like Louisiana, that do celebrate that day. But, in St. Lucia, we have expanded it to an entire month, and within that month, we do a number of activities that involves the Kwéyòl language, which involves our culture.

Lawenn Kwéyòl, which means *Queen of Creole,* and we sometimes do a king of Creole, but it's mainly a queen, for grownups, 50 years and over, and we do one for secondary school youngsters. We also have storytelling evenings, where people tell stories in the Kwéyòl, in fact, if you understand the Kwéyòl language, and someone were to read for you a story in English, that very same story sounds much better in Kwéyòl; it's more dramatic. Even in French, the story would not sound as good as it does in Kwéyòl. Leading to the big day, we do Kwéyòl music, poetry in the Kwéyòl language, and the big day itself, the last Sunday closest to the 28th of October, we have this big island-wide celebration.

Of course, we, at the Folk Research Centre, actually began this celebration and are the ones in charge of it. So, we designate four communities throughout St. Lucia, preferably in the North, South, East, and West, to host the events. At that event, the first thing that hits you is a crowd of people of all walks of life, across boundaries and religions; the people are dressed in the *madras,* the creole-wear, invariably buying creole foods and drinks, there is entertainment of local creole music, and as part of that celebration, the particular community displays their creole technologies. For example, they would show you how they used to saw boards years ago, with the primitive saw (we call it primitive, but that's what they used in those days). Today, you have a chainsaw, but in those days you had a very big saw controlled by three people, on a log (one person above and two below the log), and while that was being done, somebody was on the drum, and the drum beating controls the rhythm of the sawing.

JKL: That seems very African.

HL: Yes, exactly. Now around that kind of activity is what we call a *koudmen.* Now *koudmen,* in French, is *coup de main;* in Kwéyòl we say *koudmen,* meaning *helping* or *volunteerism.* Unfortunately, that aspect of our culture is, more or less, diminishing, but years ago, that's what it was. *Koudmen* was very prevalent among our people, everybody helped each other, there was one homogenous society; there was no difference in economic status, and therefore everybody helped each.

JKL: So, in your opinion, what is the reason for that drastic shift?

HL: It was because of economic reasons. The persons were able to work and fund their own activities, and, therefore, they will not rely on people to come together to help them. Whereas, you have a more homogenous society, the persons being poor and prepared to assist each other, it continues to a certain extent, but not at the rate it used to be, where almost everything one did was done on that basis. Persons were mainly farmers, and would do a particular activity where everyone came to assist in one day;

they left your place, they went to another farmer, and that's how it was done. Whether planting, harvesting, or cleaning the area, that was how it was done. Even building a home, you get the materials, and everybody came together and built a home for you, usually in one day. All you had to supply was food, and even then, some people brought food to assist in the amount that's required, as well as some strong drink which would get the thing going; and it's usually rum.

So, that *koudmen* spirit, which the FRC has been promoting, is something that needs some more...we are still pushing the idea. So, this major flagship project of ours, Creole Heritage Month, ends up in what we call *Jounen Kwéyòl* (International Creole Day). In Kwéyòl, we say *jounen*, meaning *the day*, and *jounen Kweyol*, meaning *the day of Kwéyòl*. That's, in a nutshell, what we do at the FRC. As a matter of fact, as part of our contribution to Carnival, we produce a calypso magazine called *Lucian Kaiso*. In there we have lots of information on the calypsonians, and that is also used as reference material, for persons who want to educate themselves, as well as do research.

JKL: Now, we've talked a lot about the history of St. Lucia. February 22, 1979 was not that long ago. I've made note that many of the citizens of St. Lucia were born before that.

HL: Yes, I was one of those, who were born before.

JKL: So, how was that transition from being a colony of Great Britain to becoming independent, in 1979?

HL: OK. At the time, we weren't properly educated about independence, unfortunately. There was not sufficient education about the benefits of independence for our country, and more...I would say unfortunate again, there was some discussion along political lines, where the party that was against it found their supporters, and at the same time, those who were proposing it found their supporters. So, it became a political issue. But before full independence, we had what was called statehood. This meant the country would have its own flag, and it was more like semi-independence; in other words, England would allow you to have your own government, what you call internal self-government, but any foreign issues and defense was handled by UK government. That was conferred on us in 1967. At that time, we had our national flag and we had our national anthem, but up came independence in 1979, then we had full independence where we were able to see about our own affairs, foreign affairs, have our own national symbols, coat of arms, and any other symbols like any other country. We had, at this time, a prime minister, whereas, under the internal self-government, we had a premier. Before that, when we were a colony, we had a chief minister, then we had a premier, then we became independent and now have a prime minister.

Now, the question was what was the feeling? Again, not understanding the whole ramifications and benefits of independence, I was one of those who were supporting the side that was not for it. But in hindsight, I thought we were being fooled, and that the politicians at the time were purely doing it because they thought it had to be under their party, rather than the other party. So, in some instances, I boycotted the celebrations. That was rather stupid. One can see today, the progress we've made as independent, versus when we were not is, a huge difference. Of course, when we became independent we were able to establish diplomatic relations with other countries and receive aid, whereas, under the British government, we couldn't have done that. So, going forward, we look and realize there was a need to become independent and do our own thing, but, at the same time, it is always a challenge for a country like St. Lucia, small population, small size country. Up to this point, we have just about 165,000 people; as much as one of the small villages in one of the African countries. In fact recently, I was hearing Mugabe was celebrating is it his 90th birthday?

JKL: Actually, his 92nd.

HL: Yes. And they said a small town was celebrating along with him, and they had over 200,000 people. Much more than the population of our St. Lucia! There are advantages and disadvantages to that, but I think there are more disadvantages because when you're small, you have a very small market. If we are going to produce anything substantial, it must be in the overseas market; you cannot sell locally because the market is too small. If, we had a bigger population, we probably could grow even faster.

JKL: Well, where does CARICOM (Caribbean Community) fit into that economic piece, for St. Lucia?

HL. CARICOM is a question of the countries doing certain things together, but it still has not helped us to propel to the kind of development we would like. And even apart from CARICOM there is the OECS (Organization of Eastern Caribbean States); we have done things, we have a currency union called the EC dollar, and it's one of the strongest currencies in the Caribbean, by virtue of that collaboration that we have. We also buy drugs . . . and I mean pharmaceuticals; once you mention drugs people are thinking marijuana or cocaine! We buy as a unit, so, therefore, it becomes cheaper for us. We share embassies, in some instances, and we also have various policies which assist us in being more efficient, but there is still need for more.

I was one of those, many years ago, that was promoting the aspect of OECS political union. Now there is a loose union among us that is not bearing on each country; they may agree on something, but when they get back home, they say *okay, let's forget about that*. This happens all the time, even in CARICOM. But, if you have a political union, you have one head of these countries, you have a bigger population, therefore, you have a bigger market, and then there would be less inefficiency around. Currently, within the OECS, there are seven prime ministers, with less than half a million people. In the UK, you have over 60 million people, with one prime minister, and, to make it somewhat more dramatic, in India there are 1.2 billion with one prime minister. And you have seven prime ministers among these little islands. So, obviously, you have a big civil service, a lot of inefficiencies, and you can see there are challenges ahead.

There is every reason for these countries to come together in a political union; it may not happen today, I may not see it, but going forward, we will be forced to do this. I remember, when I was promoting this, I was saying look at the United States, there are fifty states and St. Lucia can fit into one state so many times, yet there are together to form this powerful nation, why can't we in this Caribbean? And you hear arguments like, oh well, the United States is one contiguous land space, but here we have water. I said there is nothing wrong with this; look at the Philippines, there are many more islands. But there is something that is very difficult for some people to understand—we fought for independence, and now we're saying let go of this and become part of a grouping; that was one of the problems.

JKL: Interesting to see that there, because we've got the same kind of thing going on all over the world. In Africa, you have the kind of push to get a political union. You've got the economic sectors kind of like you do in the Caribbean, but there is this push to form the African Union into a political union. . .

HL: Exactly, a political union.

JKL: So, where do you feel like the Caribbean fits in, and the rest of the Diaspora? There are so many Africans, as we've mentioned before, who have been taken away from Africa and have formed their lives and had children, and have become part of the world that we know in the Diaspora. So, if that happens, do you see the Caribbean Community joining in with an African Union government, in the same way that a couple of the countries in the Caribbean have become member states?

HL: What I can say is that I would hope so, but based on what has been happening, with what I've seen, it could be a bit of a difficult sell. We tend to be a bit more individualistic, and that's our problem today. I was mentioning a while ago that we lack this *koudmen* spirit because everybody thinks that they have their own load and I don't have any need for you, I can do my own thing. But, as you begin to promote that kind of attitude, you institute failure at some point. So, there is a need for people to start thinking of alliances. I've said to people look, England and France fought many, many wars, but when they were threatened by Germany, they came together in an alliance. OK? Because when you get together, you get stronger. But it appears this proverb of *unity means strength* doesn't seem to work with some people; individualism is stronger, as far as they are concerned. And that is our problem; we have to begin to change that thinking. Our youth must be able to gravitate to that kind of thinking that says we've got to get together.

JKL: Thank you very much, Mr. La Force, we will stay in touch and stay family.

HL: Oh, I hope so. You are most welcome, again.

Hilary La Force can be contacted at www.stluciafolk.org.

I Am African: African Face, American Voice[1]

Chinwe Ezinna Oriji

I am African.
African is what you see, until you approach me.
You realize my voice isn't what you expected, and quickly I get rejected.
I am African.
I fight to prove who I am, but it's never enough when the accent still stands.
What do you want me to do, change my voice to prove my point?
No, I am African!
I will not conform so I can fulfill your social norm.
Your boundaries were made until you met me.
I showed you being African goes beyond,
Yes, overseas.
Really, I am African.
Here, I have an objective and that's to change your perspective.
To create a new direction, something like a reflection
So you can see that there is more to Africa than its natural boundaries.
Then you will see that I am African.
History shows forced displacement or "volunteer" migration dispersed the
people of Africa.
But you say I'm not African?
My final plea is to tell you I am African not because I was born in Africa
but because Africa was born in me.
Yes, I am African.

Note

[1] This poem arose from my constant questioning of my African identity
while in Cape Town, South Africa. April 2012.

Me[1]

Chinwe Ezinna Oriji

I embody this person that I'll never be.
Chinwe Ezinna Oriji.
That's what they named me.
A name that I wear proudly, but it doesn't proudly wear me.
Constantly striving to be *Chinwe Ezinna Oriji*
But as I get older, the ambition of becoming my name seems to leave me.
The stronger my grip the further it slips.
Yearning for it but nothing seems to stick.
Hearing it ring in the tones where it belongs pulls me closer to home
but as I say it aloud I'm reminded that my name has the wrong home.
It's embodied in the wrong bones.
Take thee from me.
Place them where they are supposed to be.
Because I can never be
Chinwe Ezinna Oriji

Or at least that's what I used to believe.

Note

[1] This poem represents the different experiences, including inadequacy, detachment, and irresolution, that occur when one is raised in the diaspora. The inability of one to relate to one's name reflects one's lack of understanding of the language, history, politics, and cultural mores of one's country of ancestry. It is in this interstice that the diasporic subject must find peace. March 2015.

In Their Own Words:
Children of Nigerian Immigrants in the U.S.

Chinwe Ezinna Oriji

If I could choose to be anything or anyone else,
I would choose to be me.
Exactly as I am, with no discrepancies.
With no deviations from what You've made me to be.

I'd choose the same colored eyes, the same exact skin.
I'd choose the same smile, and the same heart within.
I'd choose the same life, with every bump in its road.
I'd choose the same path, regardless of where it goes.

If you gave me a choice to be someone else.
Lord, I would undeniably choose myself.
I would choose all my flaws and I'd choose all my strengths.
I would choose all of my many mistakes.

If you gave me a chance to do it all again.
I'd pick the same family and all of the same friends.
I'd pick every fight, and every acquaintance made.
I'd pick every laugh and any joy you sent my way.

If you gave me the chance to change it all.
I'd pick the same heartaches and every brick wall.
I'd pick the same road that led me to you.
Your acceptance of me makes me accept me too.[1]

~ *Chinaza Okonkwo*

INTRODUCTION

Aside from a few studies, the lives of children of Nigerian immigrants have not received much attention in mainstream academic discourse. Few studies profile the lives of the children of Nigerian immigrants or examine how they deal with such issues as race, gender, ethnicity, and identity in the United States. Few studies compare and contrast the experiences of contemporary Nigerian immigrants to their forebears.[2] The objective of this chapter is to fill a gap in the scholarship by allowing the reader to listen to the often unheard voices of the children of Nigerian immigrants.

Nigeria is a populous and diverse country, and the children of Nigerian immigrants often have diverse backgrounds. Some of the interlocutors I interviewed for this study are grandchildren of Nigerian-Biafran war survivors, and all are first generation U.S.-raised racialized individuals. They are navigating a plethora of experiences that will provide unique insight on the immigrant experience through the lens of diaspora-raised children. These young peoples' narratives are essential to understanding the duality of being and knowing that informs the knowledge of black American as well as of Nigerian American experiences. Their historical memory and life experiences produce multiple perspectives that cannot be relayed in one single narrative.

This chapter will profile the lives of four children of Nigerian immigrants. Each of the interlocutors is of the middle-class, and they all hail from two parent homes. There are similarities in the young peoples' understanding of their identities and relationships with other communities. They all also evince respect for education, hard work, and the strict nature of upbringings which diverges from the stereotypes regarding members of the historical African diaspora.

The interviews presented are oral history accounts that aim to reveal multiple voices of this generation. These interviews are taken from a larger project[3] that analyzed the racialized ethnic identities and notions of belonging of children of Nigerian immigrants. The lives of these four interlocutors where chosen due to varying perspective in their understanding of the immigrant experience. I've taken a verbatim approach in presenting the interviews and avoided adding my interpretations until the end of the presentation of all interviews to refrain from obscuring their accounts. Displaying the narratives through the voices of the narrators also allows for the reader to gain a broader understanding of the fluid nature of racial and ethnic identities through their lived experiences in difference spaces.

In addition, the main influence for recording and presenting full-length narratives of second generation Nigerian-Americans through their voices is to prevent what Chimamanda Ngozie Adichie terms "the danger of the single story."[4] To explain this concept, Adichie shares a personal experience with her roommate in college that occurred when she arrived to the U.S. from Nigeria:

> She [my roommate] had felt sorry for me even before she saw me. Her default position toward me, as an African, was a kind of patronizing, well-meaning pity. My roommate had a single story of Africa: a single story of catastrophe. In this single story there was no possibility of Africans being similar to her in any way, no possibility of feelings more complex than pity, no possibility of a connection as human equals.[5]

As Adichie explains, many times people are given a single story about a specific community or individual through outside viewers. This is detrimental because this single story shapes one's perception and results in stereotypes and a one-sided reality. The single story limits the individual's ability to perceive the projected group in other ways. This single story can also be seen in the way that some people define blackness in the U.S. as those who share a history of enslavement in the U.S. The single story limits a broader understanding of how racial structures effect populations differently, and it ignores the varying dynamics that enrich and diversify the meaning of being Black.

Nigerian immigrants tell their stories with their own words and through their own mouths. This approach to research helps humanize the voices and experiences of those within this generation. It also allows the readers to become active in the production of knowledge through identifying patterns in these experiences before the final analysis.[6]

The narratives of Nigerian immigrants are more than fodder for analysis; these are stories that are lived daily. Their interpretations of their development of self are raw and authentic. These accounts are full of victories, pain, pride, humor, memories of war and trauma, and consciousness of blackness in the U.S. It is in this context that I present the voices of four children of Nigerian immigrants.[7]

* * *

God Answers Prayers

[I am][8] *Chi Chi . . . Chinazaekpere Okonkwo.*[9] *Chinazaekpere means God answers prayers. [I was born in] Aba Nigeria. I came here when I was three. I'm* **Nigerian American**.

Racial/Ethnic Identity

I am very much a Nigerian woman, though, I would say I am American too because I've lived here for so long. So, I guess the proper ethnic identity would be Nigerian-American, but definitely Nigerian first because that's where I was born. I was raised in a Nigerian household so even though I was in America, when I came home my mom would speak to me in Igbo, we would eat Nigerian food, I went to a Nigerian church, and all of our friends were Nigerian. So, it was kind of like a little Nigeria in America. So I definitely relate to the immigrant experience because I mean I am an immigrant. It's not like I was born here.

Nigerian–Biafran War

[In Nigeria, during the Nigerian–Biafran war] they took my father's house. I think my mom said they left every Igbo man with like 20 naira[10] or something crazy like that. Essentially, what you had was Igbos fleeing towns because these towns would be bombed and food production was stopped in any kind of Igbo towns. People were starving to death and getting blown to bits. It was crazy. It was kind of like, I don't want to say a genocide because it wasn't really a genocide, but I mean if you talk to any Biafra war survivor who had to struggle, it was an Igbo.

My mom was a survivor of the war. During the war they would run. They ran from their city to their village because that's what most Igbo Nigerians did at the time to flee the bombs and all that stuff. They would go to their village because you can't really track that down and bomb it. As they were running away to the village, my grandfather got lost in the forest somehow and the opposing side found him. I think they were military men from the Hausa and Yoruba side that found him and found out he was an Igbo. They were going to kill him and he was begging like, "Please don't kill me, please don't kill me. I have my two kids." The guy said back, "Okay I'm going to shoot in the air" just so his head officer can hear. So, he shot it in the air and told my grandfather to go home, but this was the middle of the bush and my grandfather had no idea where he was. For three months, he was just wandering the bush and my mom said she thought he had died because they were all trying to get to this village together and he got lost. They had a funeral for him essentially and she said three months later this sickly man is wandering into their village and they are all wondering who it is. They realized it was her father but he was so out of it and she said the day he came back she dropped her bucket and ran to her father. It was hard. The war really messed people up. So, I know a lot about it. It affects my own life honestly. My mom would of died, but she didn't.

Childhood

My mom separated from my dad in Nigeria. . . . We were leaving the situation in Nigeria for a better life here. In Nigeria, things had gotten really bad and we weren't being taken care of and the money situation wasn't looking good. So, we came here because it was a better option for my mom.

My mom was very good at raising us in suburbia. She did not want us to live in urban areas, and that was good. It was good that we lived in the suburbs, but in kindergarten to 8th grade we lived in a city suburb. . . . I lived in a very diverse area but very segregated and we lived on the Black, immigrant side and there was a very white affluent side. It was very black and white. So that's how I grew up and it also played a role in [me having difficulty] fitting in.

The very first time we came to America it was really hard. The first town we lived in, we were the only Africans in that town, I'm one hundred percent convinced of it, and everyone else was white. I remember my brothers would get beat up all the time because they just came from Africa. They had these thick accents in an all-white town. They drew a lot of attention. My family struggled, you know we lived in a two-bedroom apartment and there was five kids. I shared a room with my sister. We shared a crib and I was like 3, she was 2. My other siblings slept in the room with my mom. It was really hard and we didn't have a lot. We would get clothes and underwear from people, like we didn't have anything. And then slowly my mom had to work her way up, and eventually we bought a house and things got better. . . . We started getting Christmas gifts and having birthday parties and all that stuff.

Maplewood was where I feel like most of my childhood happened. I made most of my friends there. It was more diverse and I remember most of the neighborhood kids would play outside all the time and we played with white kids, Haitian kids, Hispanic kids, all of us, because we lived in that side of town. So, the memories of my childhood were good because it was mixed.

The Nigerian household is like, kids are seen but they are not heard. . . . As a child you don't really have a say in much. Your parents run your life. They tell you what to wear, where to go, what to study. Everything is kind of set up for you and it's really important to respect and obey your parents. Anything that goes against their rules is not good. Your job is to obey your parents and honor them. And by honoring them, it means you just listen to what they say and you don't really have an opinion, for lack of . . . better words.

Growing up as a kid, I remember if anyone came to my house, an older person, I would just do what my mom told me to do. I didn't really talk. I would just watch them eat and ask, "Oh uncle, auntie do you need me to clear your plate?" kind of thing. If they asked me questions it would be very short one-word answers because I am not going to sit there and start having a conversation with them. That was definitely one part of it, and discipline was also part of it. We got spanked. We didn't have time-outs or anything like that. If you did something wrong you get spanked, and I remember my mom saying things like don't do this or don't do that but certain things are just expected. My mom wouldn't even have to say it; you just knew you had to get good grades. When you got into high school, you know how some people say, "My parents have the birds and bees talk with me," that doesn't happen in a Nigerian household. You just know you're not doing that until you're married and that's just what it is. There is no ifs, ands, or buts. They don't even have to talk to you about it. Discipline wasn't always spoken. Sometimes it was just expected that you knew what to do and when to do it.

The middle school that I went to in Maplewood was in the affluent side of town. So, there is this really nice village named Maplewood Village. There is all these really nice coffee shops and pizzerias and a movie theater . . . and it was right by the middle school. So, every day after school all the kids would go and buy bagels and pizza and go to the movies. I would always be like, "Oh, mom, all my friends want me to go to Maplewood Village; can I go with them?" Her answer would be, "No you can't go with them. You have to come right home. Why are you gallivanting?" (laughs). I'd just say okay and every time [I'd] tell my friends . . . "I can't go with you guys. . . . I can't go to your Bat Mitzvah because my mom won't let me." . . . [But] they just didn't understand. They would say things like, "You never go out. You're always home. I don't understand." So, that was a big thing, not being able to go out because my mom was so scared that something would happen or that I would lose my mind and become a bad kid or something, so she just never let us go out. That was always hard and I think that is common with a lot of Nigerian kids.

The reason my mom was afraid to move to Maplewood was because she didn't want my sisters and I to identify with African American culture because she knew it was so close to Newark and Irvington. So, it made her kind of scared and she was like, "I know Newton is bad because there was only white people, but I'm scared to move to Maplewood because I don't want my kids to identify with African American culture." I know my mom has this idea of African American culture. She doesn't respect that culture. She thinks it's very bad. She will say things like, "African Americans are this way or they don't do this." She just has a very negative view of them, so she didn't want us to identify with them. She'd always make it clear, saying things like, "Make sure you guys don't go out to that part of town." If our friends were Black she'd say things like, "I don't like you hanging out with that girl. She's not good company." If anything ever happened or any of my siblings ever did anything wrong it was because we were hanging out with that "akata" girl: that word is a derogatory way of saying African American.[11] I feel like my mom would prefer me having white friends instead of having any African American friends.

My mom spoke Igbo to all of my siblings up until we came to America and . . . was even trying to speak it to us as [children] when I came here, but one day my sister was in class and was mixing up words. The word "efe" means shirt and my sister would say, "Teacher, I got my efe dirty," and the teacher would be like, "What's efe?" The teacher had to call my mom and said, "listen I can't understand her (my sister), you need to stop speaking Igbo to her." So after the teacher told her that, she kind of just stopped speaking Igbo to us. Before it was just only Igbo, but with us being in ESL, and she wanted us to do well with English so she stopped and the repercussion of that is I can understand Igbo but I can't speak it. So, it's sad.

[Being Nigerian-American] has definitely not always been my childhood identity. As a child you kind of don't want to be seen as "the African." Especially because I grew up here it was easy to pass because I lost my accent and I don't really even look African; so I could kind of pass as American. . . . If someone asked me, "Oh what are you?" I would say, "Oh, I am American. I am from New Jersey." I wouldn't go in detail and say, "I am from Nigeria I was born in Africa," because that just had a negative connotation. Like, "Oh, you're from Africa? You live with monkeys." You know no one wants to be identified with that. So as a child, I wasn't trying to be an African.

Because I was so light skinned, when I was growing up it was hard to fit in certain circles. Like, I was definitely Nigerian, and when you go to school if you're Nigerian you're brown skin and most of your friends are Black. But, I was Nigerian and light skinned, so it was very hard for me to kind of find a group and stick with one because, even if I said I was Nigerian, and me, I was very shy so, I feel like people would look at me and they wouldn't know where to place me. I had a hard time fitting in because of my skin color. Like, I knew I was Black; it's just that I didn't look it quite so. So, I would have a difficulty figuring out if I should hang out with the white kids or should I hang out with the black kids. In my school, not to generalize, but we had levels and for some reason all the Black kids would be put in the lower levels, and I wasn't trying to do that. I was trying to do well, so all my classes would be the high levels and all the kids in those levels would be white, so I didn't know where I fit in. Who should I hang out with? That really affected figuring out my identity.

As I got older, I started to see the value in [being Nigerian], especially when I started going to my church and getting more involved and seeing that people were actually interested in that part of who I was. I thought it gave me some kind of uniqueness, something cool, and something exotic. I started appreciating it more especially when I started talking to my mom and she would tell us my family's history and all the things that we passed through. It became a thing of pride to be Nigerian . . . I know that I have to be more upfront about my identity, more so than other people, because again of how I look . . . I try really hard to let people know that I'm African by saying it. I might not have the clothes and the hair but I definitely verbalize it.

Home

When I went home to Nigeria, it was home, but it wasn't really home because [America] is where I'm living. This is where I have my home. Home is New Jersey. Home is the United States. This is where my family is and my friends are. But my mom's definition of home is more tied to her heritage and ancestry so when she defines home, she defines it as Nigeria because to her, ancestry and heritage is also part of your home.

Nigeria

I remember landing [in Nigeria], the smell and the sound, it's almost like I had been here before. It was familiar to me, but it didn't really resonate until I was actually there. It was really nice to just be there and to be in that environment. Honestly though, I have to say that it was really crazy there too. Honestly, the Nigeria we left isn't the Nigeria that it is now. It's chaotic. There is no rule or order. It is kind of like anarchy. It was fun, but it was scary. I remember we got off the plane and this lady gets punched in her face because some guy wanted her luggage trolley and she wouldn't give it to him. He punches her in the face and she was bleeding all over the place. It was just like, this is a great welcome . . . .

Everyone knew we were American and when you go to the village it's even worse because they're all Nigerian, really Nigerian. You don't find any Americans there. It was interesting. Then we went to the market and everyone wants you to buy from them because they know you are American; they can smell it on you . . . I am going to go back only because it is where I'm from. I want to keep that legacy or that part of me alive. I'll go and hopefully it will get better.

Career Goals

For . . . my career . . . I decided to do social work because it's a really meaningful career field and my focus is working with students, specifically minority students. I was an immigrant from Nigeria, I know the struggle that happens when you come here, you know? You don't have any family, you don't have any friends, you're kinda just doing this thing on your own, and I know that if there were nonprofits or agencies that addressed that issue, especially in the African community, I don't know if there are any nonprofits that address African immigrants, that's something that I'm interested in. So, I am getting my master's in social work, with a focus on nonprofit and public management, because I want either to start a nonprofit or, right now, I'm seeking to work in higher education with students, but my focus is minority students and students of that background, who maybe are first generation and second generation immigrants of African or other ethnic groups.

I think now, especially as a graduate student, as someone who is trying to pursue a greater level of education, like get my doctorate and all that, it's hard not to be very aware of the fact that you are a minority or you're Nigerian. It always comes up on my resume, Chinaza, you know. Who is that girl? In academia when you are always around the majority, you are always the minority. You're forced to think more about the fact that you are Nigerian. It stands out more now that I'm in the "real world" trying to get a job because now it's like the higher you move up, the less minorities you see.

Marriage and Children

I do see myself marrying an African or someone of African descent [but not Nigerian]. He can be Black or Caribbean. I can even see myself

marrying someone that isn't Black, but my preference would be African. . . .
I see myself having the typical white wedding, but I do see the traditional
dress coming on during the reception. . . . [My children will have] English
first names but Igbo middle names . . . I want them to know where they are
from. Personally, I think that if you think about culture here in America and
you think about race, when someone says they are white they say my
parents are Irish or Italian. I don't want 100 years from now children to just
say I'm Black but not know. I think taking them back home will really give
them the opportunity because again like I'm Black, but I'm not African
American. The history of slavery is not something that I can identify with. I
know where I'm from in Africa and I want my kids and great grandkids 100
years from now to still know that their heritage is Nigerian, even if it's gets
mixed. That's important to me.

* * *

God's Friend

*[I am] Edwin Ikenna Aufuru.[12] Ikenna means God's friend. . . . According to
when you are filling out paperwork . . . I usually say [I am]* **Black**. *African
American is what I would say [because] usually that is the only option on
the paper. If I could choose I would say* **African: Nigerian**. *But . . . I say*
Black *because that is the option on the paper. I don't want to be the
different guy who puts "Other:* **Nigerian**. *"*

Childhood

Growing up in a Nigerian home you are embedded with Nigerian
morals and qualities. . . . You . . . rarely really indulge in regular African
American culture. You rarely know what it feels like to be a regular Black
kid. A regular Black kid gets to do things that a regular Nigerian kid just
won't do. They get away with a lot of stuff that a lot of Nigerian parents
won't tolerate.

Back in school [my parents] wouldn't settle for B's and C's; it's just
A's. That is how Nigerians operate. "You got a B. Now I have to call all
twenty-seven of your aunts and uncles and tell them of it." . . . I feel like . . .
African Americans make everything they do an accomplishment. I feel as
though . . . a Nigerian household or any of these ethnic backgrounds . . .
make these expectations, not accomplishments. That's pretty much the
difference. Everything is like, "I have a job, and I don't have a kid, and I'm

going to county college": Okay, cool. They want to be praised for that. Whereas [in a] Nigerian household or Caribbean household . . . it's not an accomplishment, it's an expectation. We expect you to go to school. We expect you to handle your responsibilities and be the best that you can be. You don't need to be rewarded for those kinds of things. My mom was like, "When you graduate college nobody is going to congratulate you because you got a bachelor's degree. There is more to accomplish." That's the kind of mindset that me and my peers that are Nigerian were brought up [with] . . . it's not an accomplishment but an expectation.

[As a child] I always tried to run towards [being] Black . . . because growing up Nigerians . . . Africans and . . . Haitians . . . just weren't accepted. We were different. There was always a stereotype that we lived in huts and we eat lions. . . . Sometimes we felt inferior. I remember in 2000 the biggest thing was Spanish so you needed to be Spanish . . . I had Black kids with the nappiest hair looking so far in their family tree to find the littlest bit of Spanish in them. "Oh, grandma made empanadas last night. I'm Spanish." . . . That's just how it was . . . . I used to see this kid who came from Africa, and he came and started school and he had a little accent and he was bullied. I used to see a lot of bullying and name-calling and he was just constantly tormented every day. You see that stuff and you are almost scared to embrace that . . . . When you are in elementary school and you are growing up you would be lucky to find another person that is Nigerian in your class. It's maybe 2 or 3 in your entire school. It's a handful . . . [but,] I'm telling you if one strand of your hair was curly they would say they were Spanish. That's just how it was. This is real.

I think [a Nigerian event] was the only time as a kid you felt proud to be African because you saw a lot of people like yourself. The food was great and you are just running around with all of these kids and you remember falling asleep on the table and the music just all in your ear. The ride back you're asleep and your dad will tell you to go to sleep and you're going upstairs. It's just those things you can't take away from my memory. I will miss those things. It's nice to see aunts and uncles and everyone is happy and the little traditions, money spraying[13] and all this other stuff . . . you are proud of [being Nigerian] at that moment. Then you go back to school and it's like, "You know, I am actually Spanish."

Parents

My dad came in the 70's. He was here and lived in New York and went to Seton Hall in Jersey City. . . . My dad went home and married my mother in 1990 and then my mother came here a couple months before I was born. .

. . They are two hardworking people. I feel as though their knowledge and wisdom always keeps me two steps ahead of the game. I come from a well-educated background. . . . My mother has lived the craziest life. She came from nothing, and she came into this country and you just saw this evolution of working hard. . . . To see where she is at now is just a proud thing to see. I remember she used to work so many jobs and not be home at night so it was just pretty much me and my father. I would actually say my grandmother raised me because she was around all the time. She used to come in from Nigeria and stay two years at a time and take care of us. They work very hard and expect a lot out of me. . . . They require respect, and you respect your elders. . . . I have a big happy loving family that is demanding. . . . I look at my mother and I see everything she has been through and has overcome, and she is my biggest role model. She instilled in me that hard work. You can't watch her do her deskwork and not be inspired.

There are so many days I've stayed at Essex County, and she was the chairperson for the nursing department when I was going to school there. I used to just come in on my lunch break and I used to just see her work so hard. I used to just buy her lunch because . . . if I don't buy her lunch, she won't eat. . . . To see her finally get her Ph.D. and being one of the 5 people up there accepting the degree was big to me. To see a metamorphosis of someone who used to work two jobs to get an offer for a six-figure job, it was a proud moment.

That is like my rib. That woman! I'm telling you. It's just different. A lot of men are just close to their mothers. Me and my mother are just on a different level. There are just so many things we have been through together. I feel as though every time she's hurt, I feel some way. I have always stood up for her. . . . I have always protected her and she has always had my back. I feel as though sometimes one of the reasons she strives to be the best and go the extra mile is because growing up we didn't have it like that and she didn't have it like that growing up. She just goes over and beyond to make sure that we don't want. That woman is a soldier. The kind of things she has been through—to bury her brother, her sister, and her father, and then to deal with the kinds of things she's dealt with in this country. She is a fighter. . . . My mother will call me for the biggest things in the house and everything goes on. It's because I've been with her so long. She'll call me her Struggle Child. I remember she told me when she first came to this country she . . . didn't have a job. My dad was working and we were living in East Orange in a dangerous area at that time so when she finally started working, then you just saw little things happening. It was like "let me get you these pair of sneakers and you and your friends could look nice together." That woman has always been a lifesaver to me, and that is just my heart. There is nothing I wouldn't do for that lady. She's always been my biggest support and my biggest critic, that's one thing I respect about her. . . . She worked hard. She did what she had to do. She took care of her family. That is what it's all about.

Nigeria

I went one time . . . I went to Nigeria at 11 or 12 and it was one of the best times of my life. I think it actually helped a lot in my maturation process in terms of when I came back to the states, I kissed the floor. I had a lot more appreciation for the things that I do have like running water, the lights always being on, your T.V. being on . . . . The village is not like how it's depicted in movies and stuff. They make it look like it's a jungle, but it's a town where everyone knows each other. . . . There is no worries. You are just out there having a ball, running around, you don't even have time to think. It was so much fun, and it's one of those places where I can see why the day Nigerians retire they go back home, because it's no worries. . . . I have to go again for my grandmother. I talked to her not too long ago. She said she wants me to come. . . . If I was established I could probably live there for a year or a couple months, maybe six. I don't think I could see myself spending the rest of my life there, that's just a "no."

If I was able to speak [Igbo] I think I would feel a lot more at home at Nigerian events with older adults. . . . I mean I understand but it's just different. You are accepted, but you are not accepted, not within family, but you look at other people outside of your family [and] it is different. They look at you like, "Can you speak Igbo?" They just give you a stiff look when you say you can't. You are probably one of them, like African American: Akata.

College

I didn't actually become very proud of my culture and really willing to accept and be happy with it until . . . probably my freshman year in college . . . You had so many people that thought the same [as] you . . . and were brought up in the same mentality. The same kind of traditions and together we outshined a lot of people. . . . When you get to the college level when you look at academic performance and now it's even spilling over into sports excellence, you are seeing a lot of African people doing well. You can actually grab onto the fact that there is a Nigerian dude who just got picked tenth in the draft or my African friend just got picked for the NFL or this new actor that every chick is on now, he's Nigerian. You can say I'm proud now. . . . My freshman year at Essex County College I was actually the Vice President of the African Association and the next year I was the president. I was so happy to see Nigerians with the same mentality that were just proud of their culture. I never really witness that growing up.

My circle of friends are Nigerians. I feel good about it. These are the best set of friends I have actually ever had. They are all driven and doing something. They are all up my alley in terms of their drive and their focus on what they want to do. It's the same thing that my parents preached and what their parents preached as well, so we are all heading in the right direction. I feel as though that is why they are my best set of friends. One of my closest friends is Black, but we are all together.

It's nice to see so many people with the same pride and to be proud of your culture makes me happy because I know what I went through as a youngster, being African. Me and my friends joke about it all the time. Now every Black person wants to date an African. I'm like, "Woah. We've been around for a while now. You are now just seeing that we have some type of value. We want to go somewhere and want to do something." On top of that, now we've caught up with fashion and stuff. We are pretty much like African Americans 2.0. That's what we are now.

We look like these African Americans. We're looking better than some of them. We're going places, and on top of that, we have respect and morals. Not to say that African Americans don't have morals, but if I had to bank on who was better raised, I feel as though it would be Africans. I don't like to say stuff like that but that is just me. I'm just confident in how we were raised because we were taught to respect elders, have respect for one another, care and share with another. There is no way I could sit in my house and eat and my brother says he hasn't eaten. That's just how we were. That's how I was raised. . . . The way we were raised was more superior, not to say that we are more superior than them. But the way we were raised, the overall experience in the household is better. How many times are you going to find a Nigerian [household] without both parents there? That's very important for kids. There is a lot African Americans who are successful with just one single parent in the home, but I think it's great to have both, to have a father and mother both working together to build a child. Like the saying goes, it takes a village to raise a child. When you have so many people in your corner you have the sense that you just can't fail. Regardless of what you do, you are going to have that support behind you.

Marriage

Because of how I know Nigerian people to be, it's almost subconscious that you feel you need to marry a Nigerian, somebody that is actually similar to you. [But] I feel as though stuff like that, race, doesn't really matter, and my dad and my mother back me with that and say that it doesn't really matter who it is as long as that person really loves you. I have uncles that have married Indian people, and I have had uncles that have married Black women so it doesn't matter in my family. As long as a person is brought up the right way . . . then it's fine. I'm happy that our family is moving in the right direction. . . . Too many times people are stuck in tradition and sometimes that is not always the best thing. Times are always changing.

My dad had a lot of [previous] wives, and they were all African American. He had two and I actually have a stepsister now who is an African American.[14] My mom always says to me, joking, but I still feel in the back of her mind there is some type of hate towards it. She'll say, "Don't go out here and mess with these Black Americans. You think that's where it's at?" She always tells me when it comes to marriage that "I don't care who it is as long and the person loves you." That is the kind of growth I see in her. If it was her stone cold traditional personality she would say, no one should come home unless she knows how to cook jollof rice. That's the kind of change she has made.

Future Children

I have been imbedded with Nigerian traditions so I feel as though it's only right that I give them Nigerian names. I don't think I would give them Nigerian first names but I would definitely have to give them Nigerian middle names. I think that helps a lot with jobs and moving forward. . . . Some of these employers just don't want to see thirteen letter first or last names and that's just how it is. Racism and discrimination is still embedded in institutions in our country. Regardless if you have that 3.5 [gpa], no one wants to see extensively long names. That goes for Black people too. No one wants to see Kazeem something or any other crazy African American names they give their children now.

[I want to take my children back to Nigeria] so that they can see that they have it pretty good here and see that this is the land of opportunity. I have my faults with America but with any good thing you have your faults. You have to take the good with the bad, but I feel this country always has opportunities for you to grow and do things. There is people that have gone from poor one day to rich the next day. That is just opportunities and I don't think those opportunities reside in Africa. I want them to see that [Nigeria] is life and this is how people are living. You are more willing to help others. Now I'm all about community service whatever community service I can do I try to do because I have seen that early in the game. When all you see is good things you forget the people who are going through things; so whatever little things I can do I try to do.

True Nigerian

I think that the big thing is just representing the culture to the fullest in the right way. We get bad connotations for this 419[15] nonsense and that we do all these stupid schemes and we are uncivilized. . . . But I think to be a true Nigerian is to do the country proud by doing things the right way . . . take advantage of the opportunities here . . . go back and give back to Nigeria. Guess what? Without those traditions and laws do you think you would be half the person you are? I feel as though when you do something [give] back to your homeland and do what you have to do there. I embrace the culture and love the culture. . . . I feel like I am a true Nigerian in that sense because I embody those traditions that I was brought up in. If I was raised in a Nigerian home doing everything that African Americans are doing, I don't think I would be saying I am a true African man.

* * *

Glorious King

[I am] James Obaniyi.[16] I've been told by my dad [that my last name] means glorious king because his great grandfather was a chief in a village.
Chinwe: If someone were to ask you what is your cultural/ethnic identity, what would you tell them?
*James: **Black.***
*Chinwe: Why would you say **Black**?*
*James: Because I'm **Black**.*

Childhood

I was raised in the New Jersey suburbs because my parents did not want to live in the city. They didn't want to raise children there. They didn't like the environment. . . . Where I was raised was predominantly Black. I would say school was mostly Spanish and Black. . . . It was a happy childhood. [I don't remember going through any challenges as a child of immigrants] . . . [and I don't really think about my ethnic identity.]

[My parents] didn't want to teach my brother anything Nigerian-related because that would mean he had to learn the language and because he had mental disabilities they didn't want to switch between English and Yoruba. We never really got to experience the culture because of that, not at home anyway. . . . I talk to them now and they say they regret it and that they should have done it anyway because it's an important part of the culture to have. [I didn't feel culturally different from my peers because most of them were children of immigrants but] I did notice that a lot of kids don't have both parents. I didn't really start to notice that until high school, and the ones who did have both parents didn't value education as much as my parents did and still do. I think that really affected me because I value education a lot now.

My dad didn't really want [to go to Nigerian events]. My mom used to be invited to parties when we were children but she didn't want that to interfere with her raising us, so she cut that out and we didn't really go to Nigerian parties.

Parents

I don't [know when my parents came to America]. I never really asked them. My dad was raised in a city area [in Nigeria], and I think my mom was too. My mom was raised more in a suburban area in Nigeria [and] they both went to college.

Nigeria

[I've never been back to Nigeria.] I would like to go because I just want to see how my parents and relatives lived. I want to know what it's like. I've talked to my parents about it and they always tell me once you go, you see everything here, the opportunity in America so much differently because there is so many people living there that don't have the opportunity we have here. I would like to not take the opportunities I have here for granted. I think seeing a place that obviously isn't would be a good experience. . . . [But I wouldn't live there for an extended period of time because] my home is here. . . . [America is] where I was born and raised and where the people I care about are. I just don't see any other place as home. . . . I was never in contact with most of my family in Nigeria to begin with so I don't really see a reason to. . . .

Language

[I want to learn the language, but I don't intend to.] [I think knowing the language would impact my identity]. Knowing a different language is a connection to your culture. Knowing a different language and being able to speak it fluently and having people you can speak it fluently with changes how you view yourself and the connections you have with other people. It would ultimately affect the culture that you associate yourself with. I think knowing Yoruba would change how I feel about my culture with respect to my parents, family, and most of the people I know.

Future Children

I'll probably give my children Yoruba middle names because Yoruba names are so cute. They always have some special meanings that are so deep. [Also,] if I go [to Nigeria] in the near future I would probably [take my children in the future] just so they don't take the opportunity in American for granted and experience the culture. [But] If I don't go [first], I probably wouldn't [take them].

* * *

God Loves Me

My name is Adefemi Jones.[17] [My name] means God loves me or The Crown loves me.
*I am **Nigerian American**.*
*I was born in **Nigeria**. My whole family is from **Nigeria**. I identify with the **Nigerian** culture. I am also **American** because I live here and I am a citizen here.*

Childhood

Before I used to be a little bit embarrassed of [being Nigerian]. I used to shy away from my Nigerian heritage, but when I came to college and I was surrounded by my other African peers who had so much pride in their culture, it brought it out of me as well. [I shied away from it] because my classmates didn't understand it. They made fun of me a lot about it. I actually didn't really understand it, so because they were embarrassed of it, I was embarrassed of it too. I shied away from it and kept it hidden.

Some of the stuff I went through as a child was pretty grueling because people don't understand the culture. They just see what they see on T.V. that represents African and that's what they think. I had a best friend who legit asked me, "Do you guys wear leaves and run around naked!" I was like, "No!" Those were the sorts of questions I grew up being asked. People would make jokes like saying your family hunts stuff with spears—little things like that. That is one of the reasons I rejected my Nigerian heritage before college.

I had such a strong upbringing. My parents were so strong in everything, in the sense of learning our culture. The crazy thing is wherever we go now and my friends and family hear me and my siblings speaking Yoruba, which is our [language], to our parents, they tell my mom, "Wow, you did very well." Me and my sibling are thinking it shouldn't be a big deal that you speak your language, but a lot of kids don't know their language. When we were at home we always spoke it so at home I never felt that I had to reject my heritage—ever. At [high] school I would reject it because I felt it was a way to protect myself. As opposed to over here at school [college] I will speak it in front of all my friends, and I won't be nervous to speak Yoruba in front of a white person, a Spanish person because I'm very comfortable with it. As opposed to high school, if my mom came around and was speaking to me in Yoruba, I would answer in English because I was embarrassed I was speaking Yoruba.

Growing up . . . home was hard because my parents were strong in our upbringing, so they never wanted us to blend into the American culture like some of our other family and lose ourselves. My parents always made sure that we weren't really able to hang out with our friends. We weren't really allowed to go over our friends' houses. No sleep overs, none of that. It was really frustrating not being able to do that and that's another thing that I would get made fun of a lot about. It was always like you are locked down at home. One of the big jokes would be, "Oh, Femi is in his cage this weekend." It became like a joke because they knew my parents would always say no. I wasn't able to do anything. My parents really had a lot of discipline and they basically wanted me to go through college and that was it. No socializing, none of that. Because I was the only guy out of my three siblings, I kind of was able to fight for more things. My parents would say no to sports or something and I would still go and do it. I kind of felt they were giving me a little more leeway than my siblings. That was a little bit more encouraging, but that didn't start happening until like sophomore to senior year in high school. The main thing I remember growing up in a Nigerian home precollege was just a lot of discipline.

Perceptions

[My parents] basically had a negative view of the American culture. They definitely didn't like the American music. Rap music, they definitely didn't like that. They didn't want us to ever act like that, especially under their roof. The same way that my non-African friends at school viewed Africans was the same way my parents viewed Americans. It was like living in the middle of two worlds. The people on both sides judged the other side by what they saw on T.V. and that was one of the most frustrating things.

Nigerian Functions

As a child I had no choice, but as I grew up I barely went to any Nigerian functions ever. Starting around high school I stopped going. I was so bitter in high school of how my parents used to raise us I guess I didn't want to have anything to do with it so I kind of shunned it. It's crazy now that college and post-college, those are the best parties. It's crazy: now everything is reversed: Now I want to go. I remember for my cousin's wedding, a cousin I was very close to, her wedding was last year, and I just had a blast. I was in the wedding and everything and it was just amazing. That was the first time I actually realized that I love the Nigerian culture. Let me rewind it a little bit more, my sister's engagement party, two years ago, I was 21 years old and that's when I started saying, "Wow my culture is really really beautiful." That's when I really became obsessed with it and started asking my parents more questions.

True Nigerian

[A true Nigerian] is someone who loves their culture. I don't think that you eat more Nigerian food, or you speak more Nigerian, or you dress more Nigerian that you are more Nigerian than someone else. I just think that it has to deal with how much do you actually appreciate and love your culture. Do you actually take time out to understand why they do certain things in your culture or do you just accept things the way they are? Do you ask question[s of] your parents, for example, where is this side of the family from or why do you do this? I feel that's what makes an individual a true Nigerian.

Friends

My best friend is Ghanaian. I surround myself more with African people because I just love my culture and the African culture so much. It is so beautiful and so unique. I don't go out and say, "Oh you're African, be my friend." It just naturally happens. I just get more attracted to those groups of people.

Marriage

I'm still sort of struggling with this is the type of person I want to marry and the type of family I want to marry into. I constantly keep going back and forth. Honestly, my parents said they want me to marry a Nigerian, but it's whatever you decided at the end as long as she's a Christian. That is all they really care about in the end. That was the big thing, but I'm still struggling with it. I still go back and forth. Just a couple of months ago I was thinking I don't care who I marry, now I don't know if I'll marry a Nigerian person. I just don't know what I want because I realize it causes a block, maybe, in the family or the relationship sometimes when both sides of the family speak two different languages or they have totally two different ways of doing things. That is the thing that is stressing me out. At my wedding is my wife's side of the family going to understand that we have to do this and that? We have to spray ourselves with dollar bills? These are the things that are getting to me. What if they aren't accepting of that? But at the same time, I have met people who aren't African who would love stuff like that so it gives me hope but at the same time it keeps making me go back and forth about what kind of family I would want to marry into.

The person I marry, I know for sure that, in order for them to marry me, if they aren't Nigerian, they have to want to know about it because I am going to want to know about their culture. It's only fair. My fear is that, like, I may start pushing it aside again. I feel like I may start becoming a sell-out or something. I don't know. It's crazy. These are the things I think about.

Home

Home is where the heart is: period. Honestly, if I die I think I would want to be buried back in Nigeria because that's like my homeland. That is like the country that made me and made who I am. It defines everything about me. When I think of home I think of Nigeria and the Yorubaland. I think about that and that is where my heart truly is because at the end I want to do something in Nigeria. Even though I don't want to live there for an extended period of time, I definitely want to do something like make my part of the country or like the whole country a little bit better.

Genealogy

I found out at my cousin's wedding, there is this thing called Oríkì,[18] where you basically start gassing somebody up and start telling them their genealogy and about the people who came before them. My aunt always says one phrase that always starts it off. She always says, "You are the child of a warrior. You are the child of a tiger." I always hear that. Finally, I asked about it when we were coming back from the wedding. My cousin said the reason she says that is because the first king of our tribe, in order for him to become king he had to kill a tiger. I'm like wow! I came from people who are hardcore. I was told that is the main trademark of our family. As I sat back and starting realizing that all the people in my family, especially from my mom's side, are like straight up warriors. The women . . . I was raised by some of the strongest women I have ever met in my life. I was raised by all women. Growing up, I used to think it was my weakness that I was raised by too many women, but these women are so strong.

When you read the Bible you will see they go through genealogies and they name all the males and everything. It is the same thing as ours. They basically go through it. My dad explained that "the person that you and your friends understand you as is just the tip of the iceberg of who you really are until you really understand all the people who came before you. All the people who came before you and made you who you are today." I've been told not a lot of cultures are like that. Not a lot of cultures can dig deep into their genealogy. . . . It's pretty cool.

* * *

CONCLUSION: EXISTING BETWEEN HEGEMONIC
TROPES OF BLACKNESS

The same way that my non-African friends at school viewed Africans was the same way my parents viewed Americans. It was like living in the middle of two worlds. The people on both sides judge the other side by what they saw on T.V. and that was one of the most frustrating things.

~ Adefemi Jones

Adefemi Jones' emphasis on the difficulties of living among varying tropes of Blackness, Africanness or African Americanness, is a powerful signifier of this generation's existence. They are constantly negotiating between racialized ethnic identities and using memories to solidify their existence, and, in some cases, to survive. How this negotiation is managed depends on the individual. Some people, like James Obaniyi, find it necessary to reduce the Nigerian side's level of negotiation to the point of mostly silence. Chinaza Okonkwo's mother's memories of war indelibly texture her daughter's existence. Her family's narrative of the near-death of her grandfather is a recollection that will reverberate with the millions of Igbo families who lost their love ones in the Nigeria-Biafra war.

The presence of the contemporary Nigerian Diaspora in the U.S. relates directly to the colonial construction of the nation known as Nigeria. When the British colonizers created the nation-state of Nigeria, they combined a region of distinct and diverse people and strategically pit these different ethnic groups against each other. The calculated forcing together of so many opposites led to the secession of Biafra and Nigeria's brutal war to force the Biafrans to maintain a fictional unity of the colonizer's benefit and design.

Many Nigerians migrated because of the brutality of the war and in search of an autonomy denied them in Nigeria. But Nigeria is more than a nation: it has become a way of life and a touchstone, for not only the migrants but also for their American born offspring. In many ways, Nigerians reconstructed their nation, to their needs, in the Diaspora. As Chinaza reveals, through language, food, church, Nigerian events and her social networks, she and her family have "little Nigeria in America."

Despite their efforts, my informants' existences in the U.S. are ridden with negative tropes of Blackness. For Ikenna, Chinaza, and Femi, negative depictions of Africa in the minds of others results in interpersonal violence through bullying and exclusion. Accent, name, and phenotype become markers of otherness within both predominately white and minority communities. Insinuations that Africans live with monkeys and kill lions are used by outsiders to dehumanize African heritage and to create feelings of inferiority. Such abuse caused the majority of my interlocutors to at times reject their African heritage as a form of protection. Protection for Chinaza comes in the form of "passing" as "American." Passing reduces the number of attacks to which she was subjected and made social navigation easier.

Children of the Diaspora must also confront and navigate stereotypes and tropes that relate to African American identity. Chinaza's mother worried about her children's ability to progress in America given the nation's tense racial politics, and she strove to find ways to help her children be more successful and acceptable in a predominately white community. In addition to being conflicted because of the violence and isolation that her children experienced from whites, Chinaza's mother also used myths and stereotypes about African Americans and African American culture to reify and reinforce her belief in African American amorality. Her mother's framework reveals a limited understanding of the systemic racism that deprives Black communities of resources and that employs racist policing policies in lower-income predominately minority communities. Chinaza's mother evidently concluded that her children should stay away from spaces racialized as "Black" out of fear of her children's safety.

Ikenna's racialized existence leads him to compare himself to others who look like him, which are other Black people. Therefore, his comparisons exist within a framework of undifferentiated Blackness that is reinforced by both dominant and marginalized groups with no regard to one's mode of entrance in the country or one's economic, educational, and social capital. In such instances, Nigerian immigrant families are quicker to compare themselves to historically Black populations than to Black or non-Black immigrant families. This segment of the diaspora may lack the language to describe their experience which causes them to use terms historically recognized in this country to describe the self and stake a claim to their existence. Terms of like "African American 2.0" should be understood as operating in a dominant narrative that inaccurately homogenizes Blackness in order to silence structural differences within groups racialized as Black. Therefore, Ikenna is using the language most recognized in dominant discourse due to lack of alternative descriptors.

Tropes of Africanness and African Americanness are all created by the dominant culture to detract from the structural violence caused by colonization and enslavement. In various communities, the detraction of Blackness means rejecting Africanness, separating from African Americanness, or claiming non-Black ancestry.

Over time, children of Nigerian immigrants profiled here were able to accept and find pride in their Blackness when they were able to find others like them in the public sphere, such as friends or Nigerians in popular media that were proud of their heritage, that coincided with the validation that they were usually receiving in the private sphere of their homes. Where there is a continuation of validation in both public and private spheres, individuals like Ikenna, Chinaza, and Femi are able to claim their heritage—an ancestry that they were once ashamed of. They also used agency to define their own Nigeria where language or location of upbringing were no longer limiting factors of belonging. Instead, their commitment to their history, culture, and development of their community were used to assert their claim to Nigeria.

Studying the contemporary Nigeria Diaspora is necessary because these narratives help reveal that this diaspora is a result of racialized colonial and neocolonial marginalization; however, African immigrants do not experience the same structural narrative as historical African Americans. Although similar in many ways, there is a stark difference based on racial history, capital and social perceptions that must be recognized.

Structural racism in the U.S., in its current manifestation through racist policies of racial segregation, police brutality, and incarceration, targets lower income predominantly African American communities. This is not to suggest that members of the Nigerian Diaspora do not experience structural racism, as various studies show that Africans and Black immigrants do.[19] However due to their differences, Nigerian immigrants will operate in U.S. racial structures differently than lower income African Americans and other racialized black communities who are regarded as having less human capital. Most Nigerians do not live in these highly targeted lower income areas, so they will experience different kinds of racism due to their black middle class positionality. Ultimately, without recognizing the diversity in their structural existence, a comparison of the two groups can be problematic as it ultimately leads to privileging one group over the other.

Notes

[1] Chinaza's poem was written before this project. Chinaza gave me this poem when I asked if she had a poem about self, identity, or culture. This reveals that Chinaza had been reflecting on the topics of self and identity prior to our interview.

[2] See Oluwakemi Balogun, "No Necessary Tradeoff: Context, Life Course, and Social Networks in the Identity Formation of Second-Generation Nigerians in the USA," *Ethnicities* 11:4 (2011): 436–466; Janet T. Awokoya, "Identity Constructions and Negotiation Among First and Second Generation Nigerians: The Impact of Family, School, and Peer

Contexts," *Harvard Educational Review*, 2(82) (2012): 255–281; Onoso Imoagene, "Being British vs Being American: Identification among Second-generation Adults of Nigerian Descent in the US and UK," *Ethnic and Racial Studies*, 35:12 (2012): 2153–2173.

[3] My research on the Nigerian Diaspora began in New Jersey in 2012.

[4] Chimamanda Ngozi Adichie, "Chimamanda Adichie: The Danger of a Single Story," TED Conversations, July 2009 <http://www.ted.com/talks/chimamanda_adichie_the_danger_of_a_single_story.html>. Accessed 14 April 2015.

[5] Adichie, "Chimamanda Adichie: The Danger of a Single Story."

[6] This approach can be a model for professors to use in the classroom to help students take part in understanding, analyzing, interpreting and developing theories from qualitative data that is led by the lived experiences of the interlocutors within research.

[7] Full permission was given to present full names and images from my interlocutors.

[8] Since the narratives were based on certain questions their answers were not always in sentence form so brackets [ ] are used in order to properly put answers in sentence form.

[9] At the time of this interview, Chinaza was 23 years old. She was a first year graduate student in the social work program.

[10] In this era, twenty naira would have be about five dollars, U.S.

[11] [Editor's note: As I discuss in this book's introduction, akátá is used largely by Igbo people to denigrate African Americans. It is both telling and sad to note that not only did racist oppressive Caucasians view *all* Africans as akátá, but also that throughout Francophone West Africa, Igbo immigrants are stereotyped as being far worse than akátá. . . Such inter-African stereotyping and dehumanizing, which is becoming pandemic in the African world as groups compete for dwindling capitalist Caucasian/Asian controlled resources, is often rooted in jealousy.

The akátá-issue is analyzed on numerous internet sites, and this reveals how often this slur is being hurled at individuals. It also reveals the level of tension, lack of communication, and depth and breadth of the cultural divide left for us to bridge. It is significant that Nnedi Okorafor, who is a Nigerian-American Igbo writer, named her acclaimed young people's novel series *Akata Witch*. Her work attacks both the hatred that some Igbo have projected onto some African Americans and the hatred that some members of the Igbo community have for other Igbo people.]

[12] Ikenna was born in New Jersey. At the time of this interview, he was 22-year-old senior in college. His major was Criminal Justice and he planned to go to law school.

[13] Ikenna is referring to a period at a Nigerian event when the host takes to the dance floor and guests place money on the host to show their appreciation. Money may also be placed on performers during special dance ceremonies and on individual guests who are dancing, but all money goes to the host of the party. Versions of money spraying can also be found in countries such as Hungary in which guest pin their money to the bride's dress or within her shoe to offset the new couple's expenses. [Editor's note: Similar customs can be found throughout the African world especially among African Americans who have globalized the concept and call it "making it rain," as John Funmi Feyide mentions in his article. . .] John Funmi Feyide, "The Art of Money Spraying," *Afro Style Mag* (2010) <http://afrostylemag.com/cover3/articles/The_Art_of_Money_Spraying.php.>. Accessed 14 April 2015.

[14] Ikenna's father was married to African-American women in the 1970s. After his two marriages ended, Ikenna's father returned to Nigeria and married Ikenna's mother, and she moved to America with him in 1990.

[15] 419, pronounced as three numbers, four-one-nine, is a type of scam associated with Nigerians in which people use the internet, mail, and fax to run confidence schemes. The number gets its name from a section of Nigeria's penal code which deals with fraud.

[16] James was born in New Jersey. At the time of this interview, he was a 19-year-old sophomore in college. His major was Biomedical Engineering and, he hoped to pursue a medical degree.

[17] Adefemi was 22 years old at the time of the interview. He worked at a medical school preparatory program. He was a Pre-Physical Therapy and Public Policy major as an undergraduate.

[18] Oríkì is a Yoruba cultural production for various forms of praise. In this particular instance, Femi is referring to how a family is praised through a recital of achievements of their ancestors.

[19] See Nii-Amoo F. Dodoo and Baffour K. Takyi, "Africans in America: Black and White Earning Difference among American Africans," *Ethnic and Racial Studies* 25 (2002): 913–941; Vilna Bashi, "Globalized Anti-Blackness: Transnationalizing Western immigration law, policy, and practice," *Ethnic and Racial Studies* 27(4) (2004): 584–606; and Jemima Pierre, "Black Immigrants in the United States and the 'Cultural Narratives' of Ethnicity," *Identities: Global Studies in Culture and Power* 11 (2004): 141–170.

Obtaining the American Dream: Sometimes an Impossible Feat for African Immigrants

Jacqueline Bediako

Introduction

According to a Pew Research Center analysis of U.S. Census Bureau data, much of the recent growth in the black immigrant population has been driven by African immigration. Every African immigrant has his or her own unique story. Some immigrants are escaping persecution, poverty, and war; others may be focused on the quest for academic achievement and economic stability and upward mobility. This study will examine the diverse and complex experiences of African immigrants by exploring some of their successes as well as the difficulties they face.

This study also takes a close look at the lives of the children of African immigrants who are sometimes referred to as first-generation African Americans. Many African immigrant families are grounded by morals and values of which academic excellence is central. Many children of African immigrants have been featured in American media because of their academic accomplishments. However, some of the children of African immigrants are presented with constraints that prevent them from accessing opportunities for personal growth. Indeed, even with a good education, social constraints can make the attainment of the American dream difficult for both adults and children.

African Communities Together (ACT) is an organization of African immigrants based in New York City that is fighting for civil rights, opportunity, and better lives for their families in the U.S. and in Africa. Amaha Kassa is the founder and Executive Director of ACT. The present analysis will examine various definitions of the American dream, as well as the conditions that may prevent the children of African immigrants from progressing through the necessary steps to success. This analysis will refer to testimonials provided by members of ACT[1] and media reports to examine the unique and varied experiences of African immigrants. The Black Lives Matter movement and its relevance to African immigrants will be explored, and constraints precipitated by immigration laws will be delineated. Finally, possible solutions to the challenges faced by African immigrants and their children will be presented.

American Dreams and Realities

In his book *The Epic of America*, which was written in 1931, James Truslow Adams states that the American dream is

> that dream of a land in which life should be better and richer and fuller for everyone, with opportunity for each according to ability or achievement. It is a difficult dream for the European upper classes to interpret adequately, and too many of us ourselves have grown weary and mistrustful of it. It is not a dream of motor cars and high wages merely, but a dream of social order in which each man and each woman shall be able to attain to the fullest stature of which they are innately capable, and be recognized by others for what they are, regardless of the fortuitous circumstances of birth or position. (405)

For African immigrants, the American dream is a complex notion, realized through an understanding that those who come to America—and many have unique explanations of why they made the move—often come with a preconceived notion about what life in America will be like. Many accept that obtaining the American Dream will be a difficult feat, but some hope that the journey to America and the struggle to survive there will result in long-term benefits such as: a stable job, educational opportunities for themselves or their loved ones, opportunities to accumulate assets, and, quite simply, a better life.

To refer to a significant aspect of Adams' quote, it should be noted that the American dream for many immigrants "is not a dream of motor cars and high wages merely," but instead means being safe and protected, especially if the move was ignited by a need to escape war, poverty, or natural disaster. Under these circumstances, the American dream isn't necessarily something tangible, but a quest for a peaceful state of mind and a life lived without fear. This alternative definition of the American dream, which is rooted in the quest for emancipation, is and more firmly associated with an ideal than it is linked to material objects. Consequently, the immigrants' backstories will logically impact the immigrant's version and vision of the American Dream. With a deeper analysis of the immigrants' backstories, the American dream is revealed to have elements in common with American indigenes while also maintaining a degree of subjectivity, which is heavily defined by personal experience, self-concept, and values.

An article written by Teresa Wiltz and published by *The Pew Charitable Trusts* on May 14, 2015 sheds further light on the American dream for African immigrants. The article explores the case of Nasser Diallo, whose experience corresponds to that of many African immigrants. Diallo, 33, is from Guinea, West Africa and holds a law degree. Diallo worked as a political journalist for a radio station back home. Back in 2009, when Diallo discovered that the military government was hunting him, he escaped to Paris and later travelled to the U.S., where he was granted political asylum. Without access to his academic transcripts, Diallo could not find gainful employment commensurate with his experience. As a result of his successful bid to flee persecution, Diallo became one of many African immigrants who are highly educated and yet underemployed.

For many African immigrants, obtaining the American dream is limited by the degree to which their plights generate sympathy and activism, their ability to translate and transfer their educational and employment history credentials, and their ability to use their existing skills or develop the necessary skill to succeed in their new societies.

Given the impediments they face, some African immigrants delay their actualization of the American dream. These immigrants accept that they may never experience their subjective definition of the American dream in their lifetime, so they lay the foundation for their children to benefit from their sacrifice. From this perspective it becomes clear that many African immigrants possess a state of mind that acknowledges that "at the present moment things might be bad, but in the future things will be better, and my children will live a better life." These thought processes are fueled by important character traits such as determination, optimism, and resilience. Such traits are paramount to the survival of African immigrants who recognize that the impoverished nature of their current circumstance is quite possibly temporary, and their future or the future of their children can still include opportunities for prosperity and enrichment. The acceptance that the future will be better if one can just endure the harsh realities of the present, demonstrates African immigrants' strength of character and ability to endure aversive conditions. Further, it is the same kind of optimism and resilience, which enabled enslaved Africans to summon the strength to endure unimaginable tragedies.

Examples of the resilient and tenacious African spirit abound. An article written by Alexia Fernandez Campbell titled "Africans Sacrifice for Their American Dream in Oil Boomtown" published by the *National Journal* on August 12, 2015, tells of the story of 27-year-old Dassyn Bakaruga who moved to Williston, North Dakota in July 2015 looking for work. Bakaruga is a refugee from eastern Congo where war has been responsible for the deaths of millions of people over the past few decades. Bakaruga moved to the United States in 2001 and graduated high school before working in various restaurant jobs.

In July 2015, Bakaruga caught a bus from Louisville, Kentucky to Williston after hearing that people were making "crazy money." When Bakaruga heard that the Walmart in Williston was paying $17 an hour, he decided to leave town. At the time, Bakaruga's girlfriend was three months pregnant and he needed a reliable income to support his family. However, by the time Bakaruga arrived, there were fewer jobs in what seemed to be a dwindling oil boomtown. The article reported that since Bakaruga's arrival in Williston, he never made more than $10 an hour and has slept in cars and motel stairways. Most people could not imagine living in a car, but for many African immigrants, initial living conditions are similar to Bakaruga's. Indeed, Bakaruga is among many Africans who are moving to northwestern North Dakota for work—the number of Africans living in the state increased by 82 percent between 2009 and 2013.

Other Africans in Williston helped Bakaruga feel supported; Bakaruga became friends with a group of brothers from the Congo who were also seeking employment. After obtaining free meals and using computers at the Salvation Army, two of the brothers were able to secure $16-an-hour construction jobs.

The poverty and difficulty experienced by Bakaruga—who one day hopes to secure a $17-an-hour job—makes it seem as if the American dream is distant reality.

Indeed, Bakaruga has only been able to secure work through Craigslist helping people move furniture. Nevertheless, Bakaruga remains positive about being able to find suitable employment and has no plans to move back to Kentucky. He stated, "I still feel the air of opportunity. I feel like something is going to give."

Many African immigrants believe that the key to a better life depends upon personal empowerment and development through education. For Bakaruga, employment as opposed to education has been the focus of his efforts. Bakaruga's determination may translate into improved educational opportunities for his child. Indeed, a belief in liberation through education unifies many in the African immigrant community. This belief in the value of education contributes to the success of some African children, whose parents encourage them to improve their lives through education. Given the adherence to values rooted in education, it isn't surprising that there have been numerous media reports of the academic achievements of children of African immigrants. The next section of this essay will explore some of the success stories associated with the children of African immigrants.

Success Stories: Walking the Path to the American Dream

In May 2014 Kwasi Enin, a New York high school student was accepted to eight Ivy League schools including Columbia, Harvard, Cornell, Brown, and Yale. Enin's parents emigrated from Ghana in the 1980s. After a visit to the campus, Enin opted to pursue higher education at Yale. An article written by Edgar Sandoval and Dareh Gregorian published in the *New York Daily News* on April 30, 2015, quoted Enin as saying: "I met geniuses from all over the world. And everyone was so friendly and inviting."

His father, Ebenezer expressed pride in Enin's achievement. However, Ebenezer expected his daughter Adwoa to do even better. According to an article written by Maya Rhodan published in *Time* on April 30, 2014, Ebenezer told his daughter, in a manner that is typical of Ghanaian parents with high expectations for their children, "If there was another Ivy built, you will be the first person to be accepted at nine Ivys."

The media isn't short of success stories regarding the children of African immigrants or first-generation African Americans. According to an article written by Katie Lobosco published by *CNN Money* on May 10, 2015, another New York high school student Harold Ekeh was accepted to 13 top U.S. schools (all of the schools he applied to) including: Princeton, MIT, Cornell, Dartmouth, and Columbia. Ekeh moved to New York from Nigeria at the age of eight.

Ekeh told *The New York Post* in an article written by Taylor Vecsey and Natalie O'Neill on April 5, 2015: "My parents left comfortable lives in Nigeria for their kids to have opportunities. So I take advantage of every single opportunity that has been afforded to me."

It seems Ekeh's story evokes the level of sacrifice demonstrated by many African parents who hope to secure a better future for their children. Importantly, Ekeh lived up to his parents' dream, not only achieving academic success, but also developing into a well-rounded and exceptional young man. Among other activities, Ekeh spent his free time focused on biochemistry experiments. As a consequence of his grandmother's diagnosis with Alzheimer's, Ekeh became motivated to find a cure for this degenerative disease of the brain. Like Enin, Ekeh opted to pursue further study at Yale. In a statement published by *CNN Money*, Ekeh stated that "ultimately, through my experiences with Yale University, I realized that Yale would truly become my home away from home for the next four years."

The humility and foresight exhibited by these successful children of immigrants are telling and they highlight the significance and impact of an upbringing rooted in good values, hard work, determination, and academic achievement.

According to an article written by Daniella Silva published by *NBC News* on April 9, 2015, Munira Khalif, the daughter of Somali immigrants and a senior at Mounds Park Academy in St. Paul, Minnesota was accepted to all eight Ivy League Schools in addition to several other prestigious schools. The eight Ivy League Schools included Yale, Harvard, Dartmouth, Brown, Columbia, Cornell, Princeton, and the University of Pennsylvania. Khalif was also accepted to the University of Minnesota, Stanford, and Georgetown. Khalif expressed the same feelings of humility exhibited by Enin and Ekeh. When speaking of her achievements to *NBC News* Khalif stated that: "I'm humbled to even be able to have these choices because I know that that's not the case for everyone." According to an article written by Peter Jacobs published by *Business Insider*, on May 7, 2015, Khalif opted to attend Harvard.

C. Charles Anyiam, who is Nigerian, published an article in *The Premium Times* on August 27, 2015 where he provided an explanation as to why these success stories may occur:

> Other factors that play into the equation that is producing such prodigious results include the average immigrant survivalist mind-set that compels them to be doubly better than the competitor to survive. Some of the parents I also talked to were vicariously living out their dreams through their children.

For these families, educational success becomes necessary to survival and influences the formation of parents' belief systems.

Anyiam highlights that the children of African immigrants have succeeded in securing careers in college and professional sports, and the successes of these children are associated with the field of sports, law, medicine, engineering, IT, academia and media. Indeed, Anyiam highlights the success of his own children:

> In my own household, I am proud to say that we are not without a record to brag about. One of the daughters, Ikechi is a freshman at UCLA with an exceptional GPA average carried over from High

School while the other daughter, Chidera is headed to San Diego State University in the fall.

There are many inspiring stories of African intellectual accomplishments. An article written by Charles Honey published by *School News Network* on May 22, 2015, tells the story of a Somali family who escaped war in Africa to find peace within a caring community located in Cedar Springs, Minnesota. This family, including husband Maxamed Ceymoy, wife, Maryan Jibriil, and their six children—arrived in America in 2010. Maxamed and Maryan's children's successes include attending college, securing placement with the military, and becoming Teen Bible Challenge champions.

Like so many other African immigrants, Maxamed evinces high respect for education. In his words: "When you become educated, you read. When you read, you know. When you know, you act."

For some, the American dream is about securing assets and the consequential emotional and physical sense of stability that may come from their acquisition. In the case of Maxamed and Maryam, establishing a secure home for their family was paramount. With the help from an affordable-housing nonprofit organization, Inner City Christian Federation, Maxamed and Maryam were approved to build a new house. Although Maxamed and Maryam's story is one with a happy ending, not every story ends in a positive way.

Obstacles to the American Dream

Because they face significant obstacles to success, the lives of African immigrants may also take negative turns. Through the discussion of the experiences of Maxamed and Maryam's family we understand that their move towards securing aspects of the American dream was not only about their intrinsic values and determination, but access to the relevant social supports, which contributed to their successes. Such supports included, but were not limited to, the presence of a caring community and creative educators who worked at Cedar Springs Public Schools.

As a consequence of being immersed in their community, some children of African immigrants adopt values that conflict with traditional African beliefs. This conflict can create disconnects between the children and their parents. In some instances, familial disconnects can lead to misfortune, failure, and tragedy.

Tragic Endings

In April 2015, 17-year-old Hakeem Kuta—who was born in Ghana and moved to the U.S. with his parents and younger sister between 2011 and 2012—died from the injuries he incurred from a 60-foot plunge while attempting to flee from police on a rooftop.

According to an article written by Michael Schwirtz, published in *The New York Times* on April 4, 2015, reports from police imply that Kuta and a younger teen were with a group of youths smoking marijuana in the lobby of a building. After running to the roof, everyone in the group except Kuta and a 14-year-old were able to escape the police. According to officials, Kuta tried to step over a short wall at the edge of the building, but instead he stumbled. The 14-year-old grabbed Kuta by his vest, preventing him from falling. An article written by Tanisha Morris et. al., and published by the *New York Daily News* on April 4, 2015, reports that Officer Edmundo Rivera attempted to grab the 14-year-old boy. Unfortunately, the 14-year-old then lost his grip on Kuta, who fell 60 feet to the alley below. The Police Department reported that the officers acted appropriately, but many wonder why the teens were chased to the roof.

The New York Times reports that after Kuta fell, the officers raced from the roof to deliver first aid. Officer Maria Imburgia applied chest compressions until paramedics were on the scene. Although Kuta was hospitalized and placed on life support, his injuries were too devastating for him to survive.

Kuta's relatives, led by his father, deny that he was part of a group smoking pot. Kuta's father's denial of his son's involvement in drugs evokes a larger problem in which some African immigrants fail to acknowledge the social landscape that may influence their children's choices, and the reality that some of these choices might be bad. Further, depending on the choices these first-generation African Americans make, the consequences can be positive, but in some instances the consequences can be tragic as was the case for Hakeem Kuta.

Another tragedy is that of 21-year-old Matthew Ajibade who was a student at Savannah Technical College. According to an article written by Nick Chiles, published by *Atlanta Blackstar* on January 8, 2015, Ajibade, who was born in Lagos, Nigeria possessed a level of creativity that led him to engage in various pursuits including designing t-shirts and fashion photography. Like many immigrants, Ajibade was intent on making a better life for himself as reported by an article written by Max Blau, published by *The Guardian* on June 8, 2015: "He wanted the best of everything," said his friend Jo Jo Jones. "He wanted to be really successful. He wanted to be really rich. He wanted the American dream."

According to *Atlanta Blackstar*, Ajibade who also had bipolar disorder, was found dead in a Georgia jail cell after police arrested him for resisting arrest and domestic battery. According to police reports, when they came upon Ajibade and his girlfriend on New Year's Day on a Savannah street, blood ran from her nose and her face was bruised. It is thought that Ajibade was in the middle of a manic bipolar disorder episode. However, rather than taking Ajibade to the hospital, the police bought him to Chatham County Jail.

According to an article written by The Associated Press and published in the *New York Daily News* on June 25, 2015, Ajibade died in an isolation cell, he was found dead on January 1, 2015 strapped to a restraining chair. A death certificate released by Ajibade's family demonstrated that the coroner had ruled his death a homicide caused by blunt-force trauma. The Chatham County coroner, Dr. Bill Wessinger, stated that Ajibade suffered several blows to his upper body and head. A health care worker, Gregory Brown and two former jail employees, Jason Kenny and Maxine Evans, were indicted by a grand jury for Ajibade's death.

An article written by The Associated Press, published by *The Guardian* on October 16, 2015 reported that Brown, Kenny, and Evans were acquitted on involuntary manslaughter charges, but convicted on lesser charges. Evans was found guilty of public record's fraud and lying to a grand jury, and Kenny was found guilty of cruelty to an inmate. In addition, Brown was found guilty of making false statements to law enforcement. Ajibade's senseless death remains a tragic loss for his family.

African Immigrants, Police Officers, and Human Rights

At a membership meeting of African Communities Together, members shared their charged experiences as African immigrants interacting with American law officers. Like similar conversations among African Americans, much of the discussion focused on mitigating or managing the risks of interacting with police. One member of ACT stated that: "We need to educate our people in terms of understanding police. We need to know how to behave when seeing an officer, when they stop you, and what is expected of you. When we don't know the protocol we can lose our lives."

Another member stated that: "We have a different culture: In Senegal and Côte d'Ivoire, if the police stop you, you run. But here (in America) you can't run."

Unfortunately, police working in various African countries are often associated with corruption. *Human Rights Watch* reported that Liberian police have extorted goods from street vendors who sell items such as toiletries, clothes and fish. Liberian police have also been involved in gaining money via extortion from crime victims at various stages of investigations.

As reported in *The Economist*, a survey conducted by Transparency International, a Berlin-based anti-corruption watchdog, found that over half of South Africa's motorists claimed that traffic police had asked them for a bribe in the previous 12 months. According to human rights organizations, police corruption leads to negative experiences for Africans. Further, when police fail to follow explicit moral codes, negative encounters with African police can be made to disappear with a bribe. Due to the fact that bribery isn't a means to escape punishment in the West, many Africans lose more freedom than they gain when they immigrate to the US. Further, the idea that one can be profiled and interrogated—as is the case for Black people in America—is extraordinarily slim to nonexistent in Africa.

Interactions with American police can be complicated and unpredictable; they also often prove fatal, especially when the individual facing criminalization is dealing with a serious mental illness, as was the case with Matthew Ajibade.

Members of ACT were perplexed by the behavior of the police, especially when they behaved in ways that were morally indefensible. Many within the African community view the killing of Eric Garner—an unarmed black man who was choked to death by police officers after allegedly selling loose cigarettes—as abhorrent. One member of ACT said: "Look what they did to Eric Garner; you can't do that in Britain or Ghana."

Many ACT members are familiar with the British system, which is focused on verbal negotiation to de-escalate potentially threatening situations. In the U. K. for example, police officers do not carry firearms. Although the police in the U. K. have faced criticism for exhibiting institutional racism, Africans recognize the difference in the British approach to law enforcement compared to the American approach, the latter being far more violent.

Various examples demonstrate the profoundly inhumane and brutal nature of the American approach to policing. On multiple occasions when black men and women are unarmed, their interactions with police have ended in their deaths.

In November 2015, a dashcam video was released showing a police officer, Jason Van Dyke shooting and killing 17-year old Laquan McDonald. Although McDonald had a knife in his hand, he was walking away from officers when he was shot. In seconds, McDonald was shot 16 times by Van Dyke. Cases in which Black men are subject to unnecessary violence are extensive; the case of Amadou Diallo is yet another case of an unarmed black man losing his life because of police violence. According to an article written by Michael Cooper, published in *The New York Times,* Diallo was an unarmed West African immigrant who was killed by four New York City police officers in 1999.

Diallo—who was unarmed and had no criminal record—was shot at 41 times in the doorway of his Bronx apartment building by four police officers: Kenneth Boss, 27, Sean Carroll, 35, Edward McMellon, 26, and Richard Murphy, 26. The officers said they initially approached Diallo, because they mistook him for a man wanted in connection with a rape case. The officers stated that when he took out his wallet to show identification, they mistook his wallet for a gun.

At the time of his death there was considerable confusion about why Diallo was shot at 41 times. His friend Demba Sanyang, 39, mentioned in *The New York Times* that: "We have a very undemocratic society back home, and then we come here. We don't expect to be killed by law enforcement officers."

An article written by Jane Fritsch and published by *The New York Times* on February 26, 2000 reports that following Diallo's death, the four officers were charged with second-degree murder, but in a trial that proved to be controversial, all of the officers were acquitted.

Diallo was originally from Guinea, and had been living in America for over 2 years; he was a hardworking man and a devout Muslim who did not drink or smoke. Diallo sold items such as socks, videos, and gloves on 14th Street in Manhattan. According to an article written by Alexandra Starr, published by *PRI's The World* on February 5, 2014, his mother, Kadi Diallo discussed her son's professional aspirations: Diallo's dream was to go to school to become a computer programmer. Like so many African immigrants, Diallo saw the value in pursuing education and was saving money in the hopes of building knowledge in his area of interest. Diallo wanted to experience the American dream, but sadly his life was cut short.

The brutality of Diallo's murder and the officers' subsequent acquittal were both rooted in racism. Racism is the irrational hatred of one person by another because of race. Hatred arises from false beliefs, which suggest that one race is superior to another. Racism includes an assumption that one person is less than human because of language, customs, skin color, place of birth, and any other feature that demonstrates the basic nature of that person. Racism was an influential factor in the formation of laws, nations, wars, and slavery, and is a dangerous social construct that has been responsible for injustice and violence on a global scale.

Prejudice and racism are concepts that are closely linked. If racism exists, prejudice exists in the same space. Prejudice can be understood as a bias, which results in the favoring of one group over another. For example, critics of the booming Californian technology industry—an industry that seems to favor white scientists and engineers over black scientists and engineers—has been heavily criticized for prejudice and discriminatory hiring practices against black people.

American society has allowed for the creation of a system that favors white life over black life. Consequently, Civil Rights movements have emerged which emphasize the relevance of black life and black liberation. One movement, the Black Lives Matter movement, arose out of this need to recognize the value of black life and its equality with white life. The senseless killing of Amadou Diallo demonstrated a blatant disregard for black life. The next section will examine racism in greater depth and the impact of racism on African immigrants' ability to obtain the American dream.

Racism

Racist laws and practices decreed enslaved people to be less than human. This labeling of Africans as subhuman promulgated racist stereotypes about black people, and categorized them as inferior to white people. The labeling of Africans as subhuman, or the dehumanization of Africans, was used to justify their enslavement. By creating a divide between human attributes and black people, an environment was created in which the abuse and murder of black people was accepted. With dehumanization in effect, the oppression of black people becomes normal, and society fails to challenge or question obvious evils.

Members of ACT recognize that in some situations black people "are not seen as human," and, therefore, they are aware of the reality of dehumanization and the negative implications of this for black immigrants.

Dehumanization also involves an acceptance of an imagined concept of black people rooted in misguided notions of animality and raw sexuality, which in turn leads to the rejection of the value of the well-being of black people. Consequently, the dehumanization of black people creates an existence for black people heavily immersed in poverty and oppression.

Further, dehumanization not only leads to suffering for the victims, but also reveals the lack of compassion among members of society who have become automatons in a system of paternalism and blindly accept the oppression of members assigned to "racialized" categories.

The Black Lives Matter movement—which was cofounded by Alicia Garza, Patrisse Cullors, and Opal Tometi—arose in 2012 after the murder of 17-year-old Trayvon Martin, and the subsequent failure of a Florida jury to hold the murderer, George Zimmerman, accountable for the crime. Martin's death, and dehumanization and defamation that followed, sparked dialogue and protest on a national level.

The Black Lives Matter movement is intent on rebuilding the black liberation movement; a movement that advocates for black immigrant rights as well as the "500,000 Black people in the US who are undocumented immigrants and relegated to the shadows." The Black Lives Matter movement is in alignment with many of the goals of ACT, which is committed to supporting Africans in their fight for civil rights, opportunity, and a better life for their families in the U.S. and Africa. At the heart of these shared goals, is the need to provide black immigrants with a voice on issues that directly affect their lives.

The Black Lives Matter movement is also defined by several guiding principles including Black Globalism: "We see ourselves as part of the global black family and we are aware of the different ways we are impacted or privileged as black folk who exist in different parts of the world."

The movement recognizes that contextual factors influence the black experience, and envisions a world in which black people are united at an international level by placing them within the arms of a "global black family." In addition, the movement intends to go "beyond extrajudicial killings of Black people by police and vigilantes," by affirming that all Black Lives Matter "regardless of immigration status or location."

Marybeth Onyeukwu wrote an article published by *Truthout* on July 22, 2015 that demonstrates how black immigrant movements are related to the Black Lives matter movement: "Black immigrants continue to experience racial profiling by the police, compounded criminal charges and discriminatory sentencing, increasing their chances of later being detained and deported."

Onyeukwu's article reveals the racist tactics embedded in policing in America and the influence of these tactics on the black immigrant experience. For African immigrants, "discriminatory sentencing" negatively impacts their freedom to live, work, and build wealth in America—without these freedoms, personal and professional success becomes impossible.

African Americans and African immigrants are faced with the daily fear of racial profiling and victimization as highlighted by one ACT member who laments, "We must understand that sometimes we can die just walking to work. That sometimes we can be victims simply because we are black. We have seen this time and time again with the killing of black men by police."

Because of their ethnicity, African immigrants in America find that, as do indigenous African Americans, they must confront and strategize to survive the everyday horrors of violent American racism and negation of basic human rights. The UN Deputy High Commissioner for Human Rights, Flavia Pansieri addressed the struggle of all Africans in America in 2014:

> Whether as descendants of the victims of the transatlantic slave trade or as more recent migrants, studies and findings by international and national bodies demonstrate that people of African descent still have limited access to quality education, health services, housing and social security. In many cases, their situation remains largely invisible, and insufficient recognition and respect has been given to the efforts of people of African descent to seek redress for their present condition. They all too often experience discrimination in their access to justice, and face alarmingly high rates of police violence, together with racial profiling.

It is significant that Pansieri acknowledges that for many immigrants and other groups, "their situation remains largely invisible." Indeed, when one is compelled to hide due to their immigration status, integrated members of society are unlikely to notice their existence. Pansieri's research also draws attention to the groups of people whose lives, struggles, and deaths have been ignored because of their ethnicity.

Racism is the chief impediment to Africans obtaining the American dream. The idea of the American dream was introduced in the 1930s, a period in which African Americans endured poverty, racism, and barriers to building wealth—the American dream became a realistic goal for some members of the white population, but not the Black population. Some African Americans created wealth in America, but when it came to securing wealth for themselves and their families for generations to come, they were prevented from doing so because of racism.

One member of ACT stressed that the quest for equal opportunity is hard work for African immigrants because, "Being black and African we have to work 10 times harder because we are learning a new system and the color of our skin is another issue."

Members of ACT are deeply aware of the existing stereotypes, which affect the daily experience of black people in America. These stereotypes may assert that black people are "violent," "dangerous," "stupid," "lacking self-control," or "lazy."

These stereotypes not only represent fallacies, but they also confirm the irrational nature of racism. However, these stereotypes are enduring and have given birth to institutions built on racism—the criminal justice system being one such institution. An added problem is that members of the stereotyped group are placed in a position where they feel compelled to challenge stereotypes by attempting to be exceptional or perfect. However, when racism predisposes individuals to be labelled as criminals— irrespective of facts that prove otherwise—the illusion of the effectiveness of respectability politics is exposed. When racism is allowed to flourish, judgment about a person's character is rooted in false beliefs about their race. Consequently, dressing in a respectable way, speaking in an appropriate manner, and behaving in a way that labels an individual as a model of rectitude will not save that individual from the deprecating effects of racism.

Rather than lamenting a socially-imposed status, Africans in America are working to undo the damage caused by centuries of racist propaganda. A member of ACT encouraged working with other forward-thinking movements:

> People look at black men and they are afraid. We need to change that. There is no reason for police to look at us as if they are scared. We need to partner with African American movements which aim to challenge racist stereotypes about black men being dangerous or a threat.

The African immigrant is not only placed in the tricky position of trying to navigate new waters and assimilate into a novel culture, but the immigrant must also grapple with the opaque tapestry of violence and oppression inflicted upon them just for being members of the "black" category. The threat of this violence leaves the African immigrant—who is adjusting to his or her new surroundings—fearful or anxious. This debilitating anxiety is maintained by the discovery that within a Western democracy the perpetrators of violence are the very people assigned to protect the community.

With the increased use of social media, the evidence of this violence is documented in real time. In March 2015, 39-year-old Charley Leundeu Keunang, an unarmed homeless man originally from Cameroon was shot dead by Los Angeles police on skid row. According to an article by Lindsey Bever, published by *The Washington Post* on March 4, 2015, Keunang was known on the streets as "Africa," and his death prompted protests outside of the LAPD headquarters with many lying on the ground holding signs that read "#BlackLivesMatter."

When we consider cases such as the murder of Keunang, it seems inevitable that members of ACT would question the professionalism and objectives of the police. One member inquired, "What is the role of police officers? Are police officers trained to kill or what? Why not shoot them in the leg?"

The police routinely use nonlethal methods first to subdue assailants—when the assailants are white, again demonstrating whom the American dream is intended to benefit. An article I wrote, which was published by *Atlanta Blackstar* on December 27, 2015 revealed that a white man, 57-year-old Robert Lewis Dear—who engaged in anti-abortion terrorism, which resulted in the murder of three people—survived an arrest after police SWAT teams crashed armored vehicles into the lobby of the clinic that Dear attacked. Events would have ended differently had Dear been a black man.

For many black men, criminalization and victimization are inescapable. The wrongful imprisonment of Abreham Zemedagegehu, an Ethiopian immigrant who spent six weeks behind bars in an Arlington County, VA., jail, reveals the role of the criminal justice system in the oppression of African immigrants. As reported by Patricia Sullivan of *The Washington Post*, Zemedagegehu, who is deaf revealed that "he missed two or three meals a week," due to the fact that he could not hear announcements informing inmates that it was time to eat. The humiliation and neglect that Zemedagegehu experienced while locked inside the prison-industrial-complex ignites pressing questions about the need for criminal justice reform.

While locked in a criminal justice system that is rife with racism and oppressive social control, Zemedagegehu was treated inhumanely. The systematic dehumanization and criminalization of black people must be rejected in every segment of society, otherwise cases like Zemedagegehu's will continue to occur. Consequently, a rejection of dehumanization in favor of equal access to basic rights for black people is a crucial next step in the journey towards the American dream.

The Black Lives Movement and allied movements are crucial at this time because there is pressing need for access to Civil Rights in black communities. For black people, Civil Rights abuses happen frequently in areas including, but not limited to, criminal justice, employment, education, healthcare, and housing. Given the examples of police brutality, murder, and wrongful imprisonment discussed thus far, one wonders whether abolition of the current criminal justice system as opposed to reform will be necessary for black liberation.

Unity, Equality, and Education

Pan-Africanism—a doctrine that states that people of African descent around the world must form a union—is needed to begin the process of eradicating racism. Pan-Africanism proposes that members of the African diaspora should form political alliances, which in turn will drive social and economic growth. Through Pan-Africanism, power is proliferated by the merging of African Americans and black immigrants, who combine resources and use this renewed strength to dismantle systems of white supremacy. Members of this alliance must be equipped with the knowledge and expertise to demand basic human and civil rights. Therefore, education is of paramount importance to African immigrants and African Americans alike.

Here, education is not only about amassing credentials but also about creating an inquisitive and critical mind that seeks to challenge the oppression imposed by structural racism. Africans who were enslaved were restricted from intellectual development, and denied the right to a basic education. Therefore, education not only becomes a means to further oneself professionally and personally, but also a way of accessing valuable and deserved rights as a citizen. The obtainment of education becomes a form of radical resistance to oppression. Therefore education, by any means necessary, is a goal for those seeking liberation and freedom.

The struggle for education also involves trying to maneuver through the web of indoctrination and racist teachings that assert that Western education is the only acceptable standard. Consequently, blacks in America must obtain a "private" education that is personally, politically, and culturally liberating, as well as a "public" education with credentials recognized by potential employers and school admissions officers that attest to one's ability to succeed in the western educational system. Given the dual tracks they must master, for black people, liberation through education is also a struggle.

Lost Credentials

My mother married an educated man who gained a scholarship to study to be a pilot in the U.K. In Ghana, my mother was a qualified teacher, and she was fluent in five languages including English. However, when she arrived in the U.K. in the 60s, she discovered that if she wanted to continue working as a teacher, she would have to go back to school and retrain. Because she did not have the financial means to undertake retraining, my mother, a highly educated and competent woman, opted to become a housewife.

Many African immigrants are highly qualified, but they are unable to secure employment due to challenges associated with the transfer of their credentials to other countries' systems. These credentialing issues are also grounded in racism and the belief that an African education must be substandard—if it is real at all.

The inability to practice one's chosen profession presents one with serious economic constraints. Indeed, many African immigrants, including members of ACT, are forced to accept jobs beneath their qualifications to survive. The inability to work in the profession for which one is qualified also impacts self-esteem, mental health, and level of social acceptance.

As a British citizen, the transfer of my undergraduate degree to its U.S. equivalent was relatively easy. I sent my transcripts and degree certificate to World Education Services (WES), a non-profit organization that offers credential evaluation services. I was confident that my degree would be accepted. Not once did I consider the possibility of having to redo my undergraduate degree. Holders of degrees from African universities can also have their degrees evaluated and judged equivalent to U.S. or U.K. degrees.[2] However, many Africans are not informed that such credential evaluation services exist, so they end up unnecessarily duplicating degrees. Some immigrants may fall victim to scams. According to Jeff Gross, director of the New Americans Integration Institute at the Massachusetts Immigrant and Refugee Advocacy Coalition (MIRA), "Many immigrants pay hundreds of dollars to a service to validate their educational credentials. Some services are 'rip-offs,' others are legitimate."

The problem regarding credentials is widespread. Research published by *The Pew Charitable Trusts* reveals that although there are some support services for immigrants, "Many African immigrants face obstacles, including obtaining licenses that states require to work in educational, medical, and other professions."

An article written by Teresa Wiltz published on May 14, 2015 by *The Pew Charitable Trusts* demonstrates the degree to which some African immigrants are under employed. The article describes the shift in employment status as such: "At home (in Africa), they were doctors, lawyers, accountants or professors. Here (in America), they are cab drivers, parking lot attendants, cashiers or nannies."

We can return to the case of 33-year old Nasser Diallo, who possessed a law degree and worked for a radio station as a political journalist in Guinea, West Africa. When in 2009 the police sought Diallo to question him about his activism, Diallo fled first to France and then to the United States where he was granted political asylum. The boon of asylum was accompanied with a serious setback: Diallo had to flee Guinea without his academic transcripts, and he had no way to obtain his transcripts because of his political situation. Without an academic record, Diallo was unable to find work that matched his experience. Diallo came to bleak realization, "I had to make a very, very tough choice to go back to school and restart from scratch."

Diallo's story is comparable to that of immigrants who arrive in America and experience a step backwards in regards to career progression. According to social scientists, the pressure for black immigrants to secure employment shortly after arrival in the U.S. frequently means they will accept work beneath their skill level. Indeed, Diallo's uncle told him, "You don't have to aim high." Diallo's uncle encouraged Diallo to give up hopes for professional glory and drive a cab instead.

Wiltz also reports on 55-year-old Haddi—the owner of Fatima's African Hair Braiding and Boutique, in Harlem. Back home in The Gambia, West Africa Haddi had a college degree and a stable job in a bank. In 1989, Haddi settled in America to be closer to her husband who was studying in New York. Haddi was told by some (many of whom came from families of immigrants) "to go back to Africa." But Haddi was keen to work to obtain the American dream. Haddi began working on an assembly line. As time progressed, she also worked in a hair-braiding salon on the weekends; eventually, she was able to open her own hair-braiding salon. Haddi's work ethic, optimism, and resilience resulted in her becoming an independent business owner.

The efforts of both Haddi and her husband resulted in their two children attending college preparatory school and then college. Haddi is motivated by a desire to provide her children with better opportunities than even she had. Haddi says, "Yes, I went to college. But I want more for them. All parents want more for their children."

Again we see that education is a valued outcome. Africans and African Americans alike view education as a means to liberation. Haddi's husband—who came to America to study—is similar to other Africans who seize the chance to study in the West. Once Africans secure educational opportunities in the West, some decide to stay and build a life instead of returning home. Many, like my mother and Haddi, believe that staying will be beneficial to their children's future.

For African immigrants, a life in the West involves a continued connection with the family back home. Phone calls and discussions over the internet help maintain and strengthen bonds. Sometimes the realities of life in the West are not fully and accurately shared. The family back home in Africa may assume that relatives in America or Europe are earning a sufficient income. Immigrants may feel that they have to pretend that they are living stable lives, and they may at times send money back home as a symbol of this newfound stability. In these cases, Africans living in the West are placed in position of conflict: they wish to maintain their pride and dignity, and so they portray themselves as successful when in fact they are struggling to make ends meet, or even worse, living in extreme poverty. Given these difficult circumstances—in which transcending the confines of poverty and oppression become almost impossible due to racism—it seems illogical for these Africans to stay in America.

There are complex reasons why some choose to stay in America rather return to Africa, but some common themes prevail. For example, once the move is made, returning to Africa isn't a simple act of retracing one's steps. Pride may make it difficult to return to Africa without having achieved the "American dream" or something concrete to "show" as recognition of the effort expended. Some may choose to stay and persevere.

What might constitute a small amount of money in the West, may possess high purchasing power in Africa due to the differences in the strength of the currency in Europe and America, compared to African countries. Consequently, while residing in the West, Africans may send money back home to build a business or invest in property. Others may send money back home to support relatives. Some Africans have dreams about retiring back home and spending their final days in a house that is fully paid for. Unfortunately, for those who work long hours doing laborious tasks— while being exposed to financial worries, racism, poverty, and stress—such dreams may never materialize.

Despite challenges, African immigration to the U.S. seems to be on the rise. An article written by Monica Anderson on April 9, 2015 published by *The Pew Research Center* highlights the increase in immigration. Between 2000 and 2013, the number of black immigrants living in America has increased by 137%, from 574,000 to 1.4 million. Currently, Africans comprise 36% of the total foreign-born black population; this is an increase from 24% in 2000 and just 7% in 1980.

For some African immigrants, residing in America is based on a desire to fulfill personal needs or the desires of their immediate family. Rather than return to their native countries and share their new skills with the local community, these immigrants adopt an individualistic mindset, defined by a focus on personal gain. This focus on personal gain may arise in tandem with a concern for the acquisition of material goods: nice houses, flashy cars, and expensive clothes. This individualistic mindset, along with an acceptance of materialism, prevents many from focusing on collectivist African values centered on giving back to the wider community and extended family.

It is important to note that there are many Africans who "give back" and, after enjoying success in the West, use their skills to help grow economies in Africa. According to an article written by Michael Floreak published by *The Boston Globe* on March 1, 2016 Senegalese chef and restaurateur, Pierre Thiam has used food to form ties with his current home of New York City and his West African roots. Thiam, who owns restaurants in New York, also opened a restaurant called Nok by Alara on Victoria Island in Lagos, Nigeria. Thaim came to America as a student back in the 1980s, and now lives in Brooklyn with his wife and three children.

Makinde Adeagbo was born in Nigeria and raised in Louisville, Kentucky. According to an article written by Ricky Riley and published by *Atlanta Blackstar* on March 2, 2016, Adeagbo, who studied software engineering at MIT, founded a non-profit organization, /dev/color [*sic*], which helps black engineers advance in their current companies, assume leadership roles, and develop the skills and strategies needed to be successful in the growing technology industry. Although Adeagbo did not return to Nigeria, his company focuses on empowering people of African descent currently residing in America.

While there are uplifting stories of immigrant success, many black immigrants do not experience financial stability as a consequence of living in the West. Many, like Haddi and Diallo, make significant sacrifices. An important question remains: Why would anyone relocate to a foreign country in the prime of his or her life to endure under-employment and even unemployment because of a belief that the future will be better? From the stories discussed so far, the reasons are complex and unique. Essentially, what connects these stories of immigration—while also connecting African immigrants to African Americans—is the ability to endure sacrifice and pain. This resilience allows black people to continue to pursue hopes and dreams despite the presence of racism, discrimination, and hardship. It is this strength of character, laudable determination, and optimism that fuel the movement towards obtaining the American dream.

A thriving family, material wealth, and a well-paying career is at the heart of the American dream—a dream that portrays America as the "land of opportunity" or a place where "anyone can make it." In conceptualizing the American dream in relation to African immigrants, one questions if, in the face of structural racism, the American dream is a dream that can be realized by all or just those with white skin. As I have grappled with this question, my own version of the "American dream" has dramatically changed. Instead of wishing to build a life in America, I hope that one day I can enjoy my own "Ghanaian dream" with a beautiful house and family in Accra, Ghana. Interestingly, the movement of my family would end up being circular: My mother moved from Ghana to the U.K., I moved from the U.K. to America, and I hope that one day I will return to Ghana.

When I arrived in America, I knew that my time here would not be easy. I did not expect that success and increased wealth would be an inevitable consequence. For some black immigrants, initial elevated expectations about freedom to achieve success may create false beliefs;

these false beliefs are often quickly destroyed upon arrival in America. The "America" that Africans learn about while residing in their native countries may not correspond with reality. Africans may assume that employment opportunities are greater in the West. However, they may not be fully attuned to the ways in which racism, and not just the availability of jobs, impacts their career prospects. Indeed, members of ACT stated that in Africa they never experienced racism due to the racial homogeneity of cities and towns in which they inhabited. In America, where racism has become a social construct designed to maintain both inequality and social control, Africans and African Americans are equally vulnerable to racism and discrimination. Africans are placed in the same racial category as African Americans. For some Africans—who view themselves as different or indeed superior to African Americans—this categorization can challenge their reasoning about their identity.

As a corollary of racism, Africans are placed in a position of inferiority because of the color of their skin. For Africans and African Americans alike, the subjective experience of racism can be shattering and emotionally traumatizing; this experience not only causes one to alter expectations, but it creates anger and frustration. To make matters worse, outrage at the presence of racism must be repressed if one is to survive and secure any type of employment. Survival, then, is not only about accepting positions that do not match one's level of education, but also remaining silent when exposed to racism.

Some immigrants may leave Africa to join family already in the West, as demonstrated by Haddi's case. Prior to arrival, these immigrants may have an understanding of obstacles they might face through discussions with family members already residing in the West. Some African immigrants may assume that keeping the family together, as opposed to living on a different continent, is worth the sacrifice and hardship.

African immigrants who are underemployed can find it difficult to earn a living wage; consequently, they must work multiple jobs to survive. For these individuals, an examination of the future may be short in its scope. Success may be defined as the ability to survive until the next paycheck. This is also an existence that results in "brain waste" because people are not being intellectually challenged in a way that matches their potential and fosters personal growth. Juggling two or three low-wage jobs is not a dream but an American nightmare that many black people are living. However, the nature of black people is to persist when times are hard. Black people are resilient, and history tells us that we are able to emerge victorious from difficult and even horrific experiences.

Legal Constraints and the Undocumented Student

My mother came to the U.K. and was intent on ensuring that her children—all five of us—received an education. Due to my mother's efforts, I have continued to value education long into adulthood—even as I write this essay, I am pursuing studies beyond my master's degree.

Many young African Americans and children of immigrants are seeking empowerment and liberation through education. However, when students are undocumented, the barriers to education can become insurmountable. Consequently, the DREAM act is important legislation for African immigrants.

The DREAM Act would extend eligibility for State financial aid to undocumented college students. This is important because the rising cost of tuition fees is proving to be too expensive for many undocumented students who are forced to work multiple jobs just to make ends meet.

In May 2015, dozens of ACT members and black immigrants rallied as part of Black Communities for the DREAM (BC4D). ACT members initiated the BC4D rally to advocate for financial aid for undocumented students living in New York and pursuing higher education. One member of ACT spoke to the crowd emphasizing that "being an undocumented student is added on to the stress of how to pay for future semesters."

Because undocumented students aren't eligible for financial aid, they must find ways to pay for tuition and other fees associated with obtaining a university education. Many students work part and full-time jobs to pay for their education. Under these circumstances, the possibility of graduation for the undocumented student seems like a distant dream, and for many, enjoying the personal and professional development opportunities associated with education is an impossible feat.

Many undocumented students are keen to support their families and give back to parents and guardians who have sacrificed to establish a life in America, and yet they are prevented from doing so because tuition fees are far beyond what they can reasonably afford. For some African immigrants, preoccupation with materialism can cloud judgment and prevent thoughtful spending. A motivation to appear to be "doing well" in America can become a quest to maintain a facade, and this may result in money being diverted from important investments, such as books. Although many students are keen to gain knowledge and skills to help them create a foundation for a better future, preoccupation with materialism can challenge students' commitment to hard work and education. To ensure African children "remain on the right track," African parents will need to challenge materialistic values and monitor their childrens' progress at school.

Language Access

The African immigrant diaspora in the U.S. is doubling in size every decade. Over 130,000 Africans live in New York alone, significantly more than the number of New York's Haitians (94,000), Indians (76,000), Russians (76,000), or Koreans (73,000). However, New York's seemingly progressive language access policies, including Local Law 73 and Executive Order 120, generally fail to reach African immigrants.

Local Law 73, also known as the "Equal Access to Human Services Law," is a city law that strengthens language access services for those who are limited English speakers. This law supports those seeking important health and human services. Local Law 73 places language access requirements on the Administration for Children's Services (ACS), the Department of Health and Mental Hygiene (DOHMH), Human Resources Administration (HRA) and the Department of Homeless Services (DHS).

Executive Order 120 mandates that all city agencies that deliver direct public services create a language access implementation plan to add meaningful language access to their services. The citywide priority languages are Spanish, Chinese, Russian, Korean, Italian, and Haitian Creole.

While French is a primary language for many West Africans, it is not among the six "priority languages" identified by city and state language access policies. Without French being included as a "priority language," many African immigrants will miss opportunities as consequence of broken or insufficient communication lines. These missed opportunities become barriers to the attainment of the American dream.

In the US, immigrants have a Constitutional right to receive equal access to essential services regardless of English language proficiency. This is protected by, among others, Title VI of the Civil Rights Act. There is no question that African immigrants have language access rights, only whether African immigrants will be able to enforce them to the extent that other immigrant groups have.

Although many African immigrants are highly entrepreneurial, the NYC Immigrant Business Initiative initially targeted only Haitian, Korean, Chinese, Russian, and Spanish-speaking immigrants, and has no specific strategy for serving African immigrant business owners. In addition, when New York City launched its municipal identification card in early 2015, the application form was translated into 29 language—but not French. Sustained advocacy by ACT secured a commitment to translate the application, but this was a small first step. Beyond French, widely spoken West African languages such as Fulani, Kru, and Bambara, are virtually non-existent among city and state agency staff and translation services.

This problem arises because city and state agencies rely on Census questions that ask only what language respondents speak at home—failing to reflect the reality that many French-speaking West Africans also speak a native African language, but are used to using French for official business and inter-group communications.

Furthermore, even if Africans speak many different languages at home, and provide details of this on the Census, this information would only trigger translation services if large numbers of Africans speak the same language at home. The issue here is that Africans are not receiving services in either French or an African language.

In addition, the problem is also due to a failure of advocacy. For example, New York City's policy explicitly authorizes agencies to consider factors beyond the number of speakers citywide when determining priority languages, including proportion of speakers among the service population, how frequently speakers come in contact with an agency, and how important the service is to the population. Despite this latitude, only the New York City Department of Education designates French as a priority service language. ACT is in the process of creating an African language cooperative. ACT is also campaigning to have the York high school equivalency exam to be administered in French. Until 2014, both Spanish and French speakers could take the GED in their native languages However, when New York adopted a new test, the TASK, it dropped the French language option. As mentioned earlier, education is a key African value and a tool for achieving success. The campaign for language access in the realm of education, as well as other areas, is crucial to the success and wellbeing of African immigrants living in New York and the rest of the country.

ACT is working hard to ensure equitable language access, but the problem is not just linguistic but also cultural. Even when Africans are fluent in English, agencies are often ignorant of African cultural, religious, and gender dynamics that affect service delivery. For example, in some homes, African women's entrepreneurship can create tensions with male partners who adhere to rigid patriarchal beliefs. These family dynamics have to be carefully managed by service providers. For another example, many West Africans are Muslim and may be reluctant to take out business loans due to Islamic prohibitions against usury. Service providers working with Muslims would need to be able to offer alternative methods of funding and wealth creation.

Ignorance about the vastness of Africa and broad generalizations and racist stereotypes about Africans, such as the myth that Africans harbor and carry disease, are profoundly detrimental to African populations in America. At the height of the Ebola outbreak, the stigma around Africans having Ebola went far beyond affected nations. In an interview with *PRI's The*

World, the Executive Director of ACT, Amaha Kassa spoke about two children in the Bronx who were assaulted by their classmates who yelled "Ebola" at them. An article written by Amanda Terkel published by *Huffpost Politics* on November 10, 2014 also referred to a two children who moved to New Jersey from Rwanda, but were prevented from attending school as a consequence of paranoia from the community.

ACT created a hotline to help African immigrants fight Ebola-related stigma; Africans from around the country called the hotline to report the harassment they had experienced, such as insults and jokes. The stigma not only affected African immigrants, but also those traveling to the continent. In addition, people who were travelling to the US from Ebola-free countries were forced to isolate themselves. Further, the Ebola stigma led to significant risks because people were scared to seek routine medical treatment for illnesses like asthma or the flu due to fears that they would be profiled or quarantined.

Possible Solutions to Challenges

The challenges faced by African immigrants are complicated and, therefore, solutions will need to be extensive and systematic.

1. Explicitly Teach Social Rules Especially Those Associated with Police Interactions

For many African immigrants, success, as defined by the attainment of the American dream, depends on the degree to which they can assimilate by understanding and incorporating existing American social norms. These norms may be implicit, making them difficult to understand and adopt. Such norms may relate to details about how to dress, speak, and engage with others in both social and professional situations. Therefore, it is important for African immigrants to be educated about the intricate rules which define social interactions and precipitate success in their new environment. African Americans can play a pivotal role in the creation of educational programs aimed at teaching black immigrants. These educational programs could be devised after research is conducted to examine the circumstances under which African immigrants have difficulty with social rules. Identifying implicit social rules and strategies for teaching such rules is not an easy endeavor, but it is a first step in promoting integration and social acceptance for members of the African immigrant community.

The act of teaching African immigrants social rules does not eliminate the threat of racism. Lessons about social rules must become part of a comprehensive system of education, which places the realities of violent racism at the forefront of black immigrants' consciousness. Through the delivery of this education, an empowering and revolutionary bond can be formed between African immigrants and black immigrants—a bond that is necessary in the current climate, where the combined efforts of black immigrants and African Americans can drive the liberation of black people.

Many African immigrants speak English among other languages, and yet the *way* they speak English can be a source of discrimination. The inherent bias against those who speak English with an African accent synthesizes barriers to integration, which often translates into limited access to employment. My mother, who was fluent in five languages including English, faced discrimination in the U.K. not only for being black, but for speaking English with a Ghanaian accent.

Africans in America face discrimination on many fronts. Discrimination can translate into the inability to obtain safe housing, a job in one's field, or affordable housing. For black people in America, interactions with police and law enforcement can be deadly. We only need to look to the deaths of Oscar Grant, Trayvon Martin, Michael Brown, Matthew Ajibade, Charley Leundeu Keunang, and countless others for proof.

Due to the omnipresent threat of police brutality and extrajudicial killings, African immigrants must be familiar with social rules about how to interact with police. One ACT member, James, shared his view of how to interact with police: "If they say stop you must stop. Don't do anything suspicious. If they say squat, don't reach for your phone, because they might think it's a gun. Always follow what law enforcement asks you to do."

James recalled an incident during which police stopped him while he was on the way to church. James intended to reach for his Bible to illustrate to the officer that he was on his way to church, but his friend who was also in the car told James to stop as the police may believe that he's reaching for gun. Since that experience, James places his hands on the steering wheel whenever he is stopped by police.

In order to survive, black immigrants must understand the rules associated with the unique topography of police interactions. To elaborate on James' assertions, there are rules immigrants must learn that pertain to how to act when one is stopped by an officer. When one is stopped by police, one must: keep one's license and registration in one's hands and place one's hands on the steering wheel when the officer approaches the window; always keep one's hands in full view of the officer at all times; request permission if the retrieval of an object is necessary; and use formal labels when speaking to officers such as, "Sir" and "Ma'am." When stopped by police, one must maintain a level of respect so as to put the officer at ease, and to deescalate the situation; one must also refrain from providing information beyond what is demanded, and refuse to consent to any search. In addition, one must abstain from contradicting or arguing with the officer, and maintain body language that is passive and non-threatening. The goal of any police interaction is to ensure one survives in order to live to file grievance and/or sue, if necessary. Significantly, each rule is nuanced and dependent upon multiple contextual factors which dictate how and when each rule can be applied. Consequently, the teaching of these rules must come with an awareness of the unpredictable nature of police officers, and the subsequent extraneous variables that confound police interactions, for example the mood or temperament of the officer.

Teaching rules about how to cope with police interactions only puts a band-aid on a deep wound. Nevertheless, education about police interactions becomes necessary for the black immigrant and his or her family.

2. *Support Children with Identity Formation*

Education is not confined to Western academic, social rules, or police interactions. Education should also be about the examination of the self. Self-examination should be an unfiltered analysis of the social, political, and cultural values that help synthesize one's African identity. Self-examination should be a process of confidence building and self-actualization. In essence, the examination of the self should lead to identity formation.

The children of African immigrants, by virtue of circumstance, are required to develop an understanding of their American identity while acknowledging their African heritage. For some parents, this can create tension as children (and parents) may be keen to embrace American ideals which may directly oppose African values.

A member of ACT named Cassandra discussed her response to her son's decision to embrace a way of dressing that is associated with "street styles" adopted by some young African American men. Cassandra stated that when her little boy started first grade he came home with his pants hanging very low beneath his waist, when she saw him dressed this way, a way that she viewed to be inappropriate, she slapped him as a means to discipline him and bring an end to his waywardness. While this approach to discipline could be considered child abuse by many U.S. agencies, and immigrants should be made aware of this, since Cassandra's use of this disciplinary action, she recalls that her little boy tells his friends that, "I need to cover my body," and refrains from wearing sagging pants.

Of course, supporting children with identity formation is more complicated than introducing disciplinary measures to scare them into following parental requests.

Identity formation should serve to embrace the aspects of African culture that will build resourceful, thoughtful, and successful individuals. Defined values, such as respect for elders, listening and learning before you talk, self-control, and speaking in a respectful manner, are all values that would translate into success for an individual trying to navigate the American world.

Identify formation is a complex multifaceted process. Consequently, children should be encouraged to embrace positive American ideals that would function in their favor, and reject those aspects that would be detrimental to their success. In this way, children will be helped to create a nuanced definition of the self that is an amalgamation of their African and American identities.

It is very important that the identity formation of African children be rooted in their African culture. Children should never be made to feel ashamed of their African heritage, language, ancestry, and culture. One way to assist children in embracing their African identity is to teach children their native language. My mother made the conscious decision not to teach me Twi (my native language) because she felt this would affect my fluency in English. Unfortunately, my mother was wrong. There are many advantages to being bilingual including having an understanding of your identity and heritage. I do not fault my mother for her decision. Similar to the desires of many immigrants, my mother wanted the best for her child; she wanted me to become an integrated and successful member of society, and she believed that she could do this by ensuring I spoke English fluently from a young age.

My mother did everything in her power to assist with my assimilation and integration with British culture in the hope that this would forge a better future for me. Although my mother chose not to teach me Twi, she made sure I respected the customs and rituals associated with my culture. Consequently, I was able to assume a Ghanaian identity while growing up in inner city London. For some parents, including parents like Cassandra, frustration emerges when their children adopt American customs while failing to develop a level of cultural appreciation for their African heritage. Indeed, many parents experience alienation from their children because of a perception that African parents cannot adopt foreign cultural values. Cassandra highlights this alienation: "My children look at me as if I'm an immigrant."

Cassandra's statement highlights the disconnect that often forms between children's identities and their parents' identities. A young volunteer with ACT further delineated this disconnect by stating that, "My parents are from Senegal, but I'm from here (America)."

Parents have a major role to play in their children's identity formation; they will need to understand that their children can become "Americanized" or develop an American identity. Likewise parents who wish to maintain their cultural appreciation will need to be open to forging a connection with American culture. Therefore, parental support should hinge on the formation of their children's complex identity, which merges their American identity with their African heritage.

Challenges associated with integration with the foreign culture are further heightened when immigrants are not as skilled as the indigenous population. However, the research demonstrates that African immigrants are usually highly skilled, but the barriers to success are caused by difficulties with the transfer of the credentials. The next section of this essay examines the ways in which streamlining the process of transferring credentials is significant to the empowerment of black immigrants.

3. *Streamline the Process of Accrediting and Transferring Credentials*

Another way to address the obstacles faced by African immigrants is to streamline the process of credential evaluation. According to *The Pew Charitable Trusts,* some states have already begun to streamline the process. The state of Michigan worked in collaboration with *Upwardly Global*, an employment advocacy agency for immigrants, to create clear-cut licensing guides for 20 professions. In 2014, Michigan passed a Barber Bill which allows barbers who can demonstrate they possess necessary training and experience to significantly lower the number of instructional hours necessary to obtain a license. In the past, barbers were required to complete 2000 hours of training to obtain a license.

African-style hair braiders have sued in 12 states arguing that restrictive licensing laws inhibit their ability and constitutional right to earn a living. An article written by Jenni Bergal published by *The Pew Charitable Trusts* in April 2014, states that Nivea Earl was excited to open Twistykinks hair braiding salon in Jacksonville, Arkansas. However, Earl was forced to run her business through word of mouth because Arkansas licensing laws require Earl to obtain a cosmetology license to braid hair. Further, the attainment of a cosmetology license is challenging because it requires passing two exams, 1,500 hours of training, and paying thousands of dollars to attend a cosmetology school that would not be equipped to teach hair braiding—a skill she already possessed.

In an article published by *The Pew Charitable Trusts,* Earl highlighted the discrimination inherent in strict licensing laws: "I don't think we should have to be held to the same standards and guidelines as cosmetologists and barbers. Hair braiding does not involve chemicals or cutting or dying the hair. We don't even shampoo it."

For African immigrants who wish to transfer credentials, there are number of credential evaluation agencies, including Academic Evaluation Services, Inc.; International Evaluation Service Center for Applied Research, Evaluation, and Education, Inc. (IESCAREE); Educational Perspectives; International Education Research Foundation (IERF); and World Education Services (WES). Specific disciplines, universities, and regions may rely on specific credentialing agencies.

The challenges facing African immigrants, including credential evaluation and strict licensing laws, demonstrates significant obstacles to the American dream. Such challenges hinder self-improvement and liberation through education, and result in restricted access to economic independence.

4. *Build Alliances*

Overcoming obstacles to the American dream will involve aligning with other progressive movements, organizations, and individuals who are intent on improving living conditions for African immigrants.

Building alliances may involve organizing and attending public rallies and working to introduce laws that will allow undocumented students to secure financial aid. Through the formation of alliances, a powerful collective can be formed that can challenge oppressive social and economic policies. There is power in numbers, and a united immigrant community will increase the likelihood of establishing economic freedom.

ACT is committed to building alliances with other organizations serving the African immigrant community. In October 2015, ACT joined forces with the African Services Committee to host a free clinic providing information to immigrants about becoming a U.S. citizen.

As mentioned earlier in this essay, the Black Lives Matter movement is intent on rebuilding the black liberation movement, and it advocates for justice and freedom for all black lives. The concerns of the movement extend to various areas including in the fact that "500,000 Black people in the US are undocumented immigrants and relegated to the shadows." Black Lives Matter is cognizant of the challenges facing African immigrants, and it encourages African immigrants to join the progressive political action and activists of the Black Lives Matter movement.

Conclusion

James Truslow Adams describes the American dream as "a dream of social order in which each man and each woman shall be able to attain to the fullest stature of which they are innately capable" (405).

This chapter reveals the ways in which African immigrants and their children are able to attain the American dream through education, hard work, and perseverance. This chapter also explores how immigrants are prevented from reaching their potential because of specific social, cultural, psychological, and economic barriers. Such barriers are erected as a consequence of police brutality, racism, difficulties associated with transfer of credentials, denied access to financial aid for undocumented students, and the failure of language access policies to consider the needs of African immigrants. These barriers also prevent immigrants from utilizing their skills and qualifications and contributing their full spectrum of talents to America. Progressive organizations like ACT are fighting to remove barriers to success and ensure equal opportunity for all.

The construction of this analysis was dependent on the insight and testimony of members of ACT. ACT members not only shared their experiences and highlighted the challenges they face as immigrants in America, but they were also instrumental in suggesting strategies to overcome obstacles. In sharing their experiences and insight, ACT members revealed their possession of such traits as resilience, foresight, optimism, and determination—the very traits that helped to nurture children such as Kwasi Enin, Harold Ekeh, and Munira Khalif to success. These youths, who likely have bright and satisfying futures ahead of them, should be commended for their successes. They confirm that the potential of African immigrants is unlimited.

With the removal of unnecessary barriers and with increased social supports, African immigrants and their children will have everything they need to make their American dreams realities.

Notes

[1] To protect privacy and confidentiality, the names of ACT members quoted in this essay have been changed.

[2] [Editor's note: I earned my Ph.D. at Obafemi Awolowo University (Great Ife!). The first university at which I was employed in the United States underwent accreditation during my employment. As part of the university's accreditation process, every professor who earned a degree from any foreign institution had to submit to the International Education and Research Foundation (IERF) all documents pertaining to their degree, including transcripts, theses, dissertations, as necessary, for equivalency evaluation. I submitted my materials along with other employees Mali, France, Russia, etc. After a few weeks, IERF sent me a certificate stating that my Ph.D. was the equivalent of a Ph.D. earned at any accredited institution in the United States of America.

When I applied for other jobs, I would simply include my equivalency certificate with my transcripts. I never had an issue at all landing any job, and I have worked at universities all over America. I encourage all Africans to take the initiative to have equivalency reports done independently when applying for admission to school and for jobs. This could save tens of thousands of dollars in tuition and years of wasted time.]

Works Cited

Adams, James Truslow. *The Epic of America*. Second edition. New York: Greenwood Press, 1931.

Anderson, Monica. "A Rising Share of the U.S. Black Population Is Foreign Born." *The Pew Research Center*. 09 April 2015. <http://www.pewsocial trends.org/2015/04/09/a-rising-share-of-the-u-s-black-population-is -foreign-born/>. Accessed 13 March 2016.

Anyiam, C. Charles. "Nigeria: African Immigrant's Children Beat All Odds to Excel in America." *Premium Times*. 27 August 2015. <http://allafrica. com/stories/201508271499.html>. Accessed 13 March 2016.

Bediako, Jacqueline. "How White Privilege Allows White Men to Survive Police Encounters." *Atlanta Blackstar*. 27 December 2015. <http:// atlantablackstar.com/2015/12/27/white-privilege-allows-white-men- survive-police-encounters/>. Accessed 13 March 2016.

Black Lives Matter. "About the #BlackLivesMatter Network." 18 October, 2015. <http://blacklivesmatter.com/about>. Accessed 13 March 2016.

Black Lives Matter. "We Affirm that All Black Lives Matter." 18 October 2015. <http://blacklivesmatter.com/guiding-principles/>. Accessed 13 March 2016.

Bergal, Jenni. "A License to Braid Hair? Critics Say State Licensing Rules Have Gone Too Far." *The Pew Charitable Trusts*. 30 January 2015. <http://www.pewtrusts.org/en/research-and-analysis/blogs/stateline/2015/1/30/a-license-to-braid-hair-critics-say-state-licensing-rules-have-gone-too-far>. Accessed 13 March 2016.

Bever, Lindsey. "The homeless man killed by Los Angeles police and why we still don't know his real name." *The Washington Post*, 04 March 2015. <http://www.washingtonpost.com/news/morning-mix/wp/2015/03/04/the-troubled-past-and-stolen-identity-of-the-homeless-man-killed-by-los-angeles-police/>. Accessed 13 March 2016.

Blau, Max. "Family of Georgia man who died in custody: 'We want to know why.'" *The Guardian*. 08 June 2015. <http://www.theguardian.com/us-news/2015/jun/08/georgia-matthew-ajibade-family-died-in-custody>. Accessed 13 March 2016.

Campbell, Alexia Fernandez. "Africans Sacrifice for Their American Dream in an Oil Boomtown." *National Journal*. 12 August 2015. <http://www.nationaljournal.com/next-america/population-2043/africans-sacrifice-their-american-dream-oil-boomtown?mref=landing-list-bottom_3>. Accessed 13 March 2016.

Chiles, Nick. "The Family of Matthew Ajibade, a 22-Year-Old Savannah College Student, Wants to Know How He Died in a Georgia Jail Cell." *Atlanta Blackstar*. 08 January 2015. <http://atlantablackstar.com/2015/01/08/family-matthew-ajibade-22-year-old-savannah-college-student-want-know-died-georgia-jail-cell/>. Accessed 13 March 2016.

Copper, Michael. "Officers in Bronx Fire 41 Shots, and an Unarmed Man Is Killed." *The New York Times*. 05 February 1999. <http://www.nytimes.com/1999/02/05/nyregion/officers-in-bronx-fire-41-shots-and-an-unarmed-man-is-killed.html>. Accessed 13 March 2016.

Crossan, Andrea. "A new hotline fights Ebola-related stigma against African immigrants." *PRI's The World*. 12 November 2014. <http://www.pri.org/stories/2014-11-12/new-hotline-fights-ebola-related-stigma-against-african-immigrants>. Accessed 13 March 2016.

Dash, Wayne. "The killing of Laquan McDonald: The dashcam video vs. police accounts." *CNN*. 19 December 2015. <http://www.cnn.com/2015/12/17/us/laquan-mcdonald-video-records-comparison/>. Accessed 13 March 2016.

Floreak, Michael. "The surprising Senegalese origins of many American foods." *The Boston Globe*. 01 March 2016. <http://www.bostonglobe.com/lifestyle/food-dining/2016/02/29/the-surprising-senegalese-origins-

many-american-foods/dE7WJIDHn2ZcMUHTQzJtEI/story.html?event
=event25>. Accessed 13 March 2016.

Fritsch, Jane. "The Diallo Verdict: The Overview; 4 Officers in Diallo Shooting Are Acquitted of All Charges." *The New York Times*. 26 February 2000 <http://www.nytimes.com/2000/02/26/nyregion/diallo-verdict-overview-4-officers-diallo-shooting-are-acquitted-all-charges.html ?pagewanted=1>. Accessed 13 March 2016.

"Georgia jail employees indicted in college student Matthew Ajibade's New Year's Day death, strapped to a chair." *New York Daily News*. 25 June 2015 <http://www.nydailynews.com/news/crime/georgia-jail-employees-indicted-college-student-death-article-1.2270482>. Accessed 13 March 2016.

"Georgia sheriff's deputies acquitted of manslaughter in Matthew Ajibade death." *The Guardian*. 16 October 2015. <http://www.theguardian.com/us-news/2015/oct/16/georgia-sheriffs-deputies-acquitted-of-man slaughter-in-stun-gun-jail-death>. Accessed 13 March 2016.

"Grand jury indicts three people in death of college student in Georgia jail." *The Guardian*. 24 June 2015 <http://www.theguardian.com/us-news/2015/jun/24/grand-jury-indicts-three-people-in-death-of-college-student-in-georgia-jail>. Accessed 13 March 2016.

Honey, Charles. "Fleeing from Civil War in Africa, Family Finds Peace and Caring Community in Cedar Springs." *School News Network*. 22 May 2015 <http://www.schoolnewsnetwork.org/index.php/2014-15/fleeing-civil-war-africa-family-finds-peace-and-caring-community-cedar-springs/>. Accessed 13 March 2016.

Human Rights Watch. "Liberia: Police Corruption Harms Rights, Progress." 22 August 2013 <https://www.hrw.org/news/2013/08/22/liberia-police-corruption-harms-rights-progress>. Accessed 13 March 2016.

Jacobs, Peter. "These students got into all 8 Ivy League schools—here's where they're actually going." *Business Insider*. 07 May 2015 <http://www.businessinsider.com/where-students-who-got-into-all-8-ivy-league-schools-are-going-to-college-2015-4>. Accessed 13 March 2016.

Limited English Proficiency: A Federal Interagency Website. "Frequently Asked Questions." 19 March 2016 <http://www.lep.gov/faqs/faqs.html#OneQ2>. Accessed 13 March 2016.

Lobosco, Katie. "Teen accepted by all 8 Ivy League schools chooses Yale." *CNN Money*. 10 May 2015. <http://money.cnn.com/2015/05/08/pf/college/accepted-all-ivy-league-schools-yale/>. Accessed 13 March 2016.

Morris, Tanisha, Barry Paddock, Keldy Ortiz, and Larry Mcshane. "Bronx teen who fell 60 feet off rooftop while fleeing police dies." *New York Daily News.* 04 April 2015 <http://www.nydailynews.com/new-york/bronx-teen-fell-60-feet-rooftop-dies-saturday-article-1.2173465>. Accessed 13 March 2016.

NYC Mayor's Office of Immigrant Affairs. "Executive Orders and Local Laws." 13 March 2016 <http://www.nyc.gov/html/imm/html/eoll/eoll.shtml>. Accessed 13 March 2016.

Onyeukwu, Marybeth. "Black Immigrants" Lives Matter: Disrupting the Dialogue on Immigrant Detention." *Truthout.* 22 July 2015. <http://www.truth-out.org/opinion/item/32007-black-immigrants-lives-matter-disrupting-the-dialogue-on-immigrant-detention>. Accessed 13 March 2016.

Rhodan, Maya. "Long Island Teen Accepted to 8 Ivy League Colleges Chooses Yale." *Time.* 30 April 2014 <http://time.com/83203/kwasi-enin-ivy-league-yale/>. Accessed 13 March 2016.

Riley, Ricky. "Nigerian Entrepreneur's Startup Invests in the Next Generation of Black Engineers, Receives Funding from Top Incubator." *Atlanta Blackstar.* 02 March 2016 <http://atlantablackstar.com/2016/03/02/nigerian-entrepreneurs-startup-invests-in-the-next-generation-of-black-engineers-receives-funding-from-top-incubator/>. Accessed 13 March 2016.

Sandoval, Edgar and Dareh Gregorian. "Long Island wunderkind reveals he's going to Yale after being accepted to all eight Ivy League schools." *New York Daily News.* 30 April 2014 <http://www.nydailynews.com/new-york/wunderkind-kwasi-enin-yale-article-1.1774361>. Accessed 13 March 2016.

Schwirtz, Michael. "Bronx Teenager Who Fell From Roof While Fleeing the Police Dies." *The New York Times.* 04 April 2015 <http://www.nytimes.com/2015/04/05/nyregion/bronx-teenager-who-fell-from-roof-while-fleeing-the-police-dies.html?_r=1>. Accessed 13 March 2016.

Silva, Daniella. "Minnesota Teen Accepted to All Eight Ivy League Schools." *NBC News.* 09 April 2015 <http://www.nbcnews.com/news/us-news/minnesota-teen-munira-khalif-accepted-all-eight-ivy-league-schools-n338661>. Accessed 13 March 2016.

Starr, Alexandra. "How the legacy of Amadou Diallo lives on in New York's immigrant community." *PRI's The World.* 05 February 2014 <http://www.pri.org/stories/2014-02-05/how-legacy-amadou-diallo-lives-new-yorks-immigrant-community>. Accessed 13 March 2016.

Sullivan, Patricia. "Deaf man says jailers held him incommunicado for six weeks." *The Washington Post*. 19 March 2015 <https://www.washington post.com/local/deaf-man-says-he-was-held-incommunicado-for-six-weeks/2015/03/19/5b798c44-ce5a-11e4-a2a7-517a3a70506_story.html>. Accessed 13 March 2016.

Terkel, Amanda. "Hotline Launches to Help African Immigrants Facing Ebola Stigma." *Huffpost Politics*. 10 November 2014 <http://www. huffingtonpost.com/2014/11/10/ebola-stigma-hotline-african-communities-together_n_6133452.html>. Accessed 13 March 2016.

"South Africa's Police: Something Very Rotten." *The Economist*. 23 June 2012 <http://www.economist.com/node/21557385>. Accessed 13 March 2016.

Vecsey, Taylor and Natalie O'Neill. "Meet the student accepted into all eight Ivy League schools." *New York Post*. 05 April 2015 <http://nypost .com/2015/04/05/meet-the-student-accepted-into-all-eight-ivy-league -schools/>. Accessed 13 March 2016.

Vernon, Patrick. "Black Lives Matter: International Decade for People of African Descent." *Media Diversified*. 15 January 2015 <http://media diversified.org/2015/01/15/black-lives-matter-international-decade-for-people-of-african-descent/>. Accessed 13 March 2016.

Wiltz, Teresa. "Growing African Immigrant Population Is Highly Educated, Underemployed." *The Pew Charitable Trusts*. 14 May 2015 <http://www .pewtrusts.org/en/research-and-analysis/blogs/stateline/2015/5/14/ growing-african-immigrant-population-is-highly-educated-underemployed>. Accessed 13 March 2016.

PART FIVE

GENDER, POWER, AND INFINITE PROMISE

The Quiet Scream Within: Perspectives on Culture, Violence, and Transformation within Afrikan Masculinities

Baba A. O. Buntu

I am a Black man
An Afrikan man
In time of war
Present me with harmony but
Speak not to me of peace
Until victory is ours
Present me with unconditional love
that I might present us with unconditional liberation

~ George Edward Tait

Introduction

The family, as a social institution, is generally seen as the foundation in Afrikan cultures. It represents the cornerstone of social, political, and economic development and a platform for learning and prosperity. A brutal history of invasions, oppression, and colonialism has, to a large extent, destroyed some of the cultural foundations that inform the Afrikan institution of family. In addition, as the Afrikan family strives to keep up with "modernity"—a hegemonic experience that for all intents and purposes easily translates into "Westernization"—traditional values are further exchanged for new, and often alienating, principles of livelihood. Faced with expectations to "modernize," the foundation of indigenous knowledge has suffered erosion, and this erosion promotes social disintegration within communities and families. The challenges that families are facing are evident in many parts of the Pan-Afrikan world.

This chapter will examine how changes within the Afrikan family have impacted on the role of men and the understanding of Afrikan masculinities. The man is traditionally seen as the head of the household, a title that indicates the ability to provide fair and just leadership that empowers each and every family member. However, a number of obstacles have caused instability and have deteriorated the role of the Afrikan man within the Afrikan family. Escalating divorce rates; domestic violence; the alarming increase of pedophilia, sexual abuse, and rape; absent fathers, and the now universal stereotype of the Afrikan man as a violent criminal all reveal the degree to which the Afrikan family and the Afrikan man are imperiled.

The objective of this study is to understand the impact of Western domination on Afrikan masculinity and to develop recommendations that can help Afrikan men liberate themselves from the psychological shackles of an alien culture. The goal is to help Afrikan men to position themselves as relevant resourceful forces of transformation and empowerment.

(MIS)UNDERSTANDING AFRIKAN MASCULINITY

What is Masculinity?

Masculinity has been defined as a set of behaviors that most men are encouraged to perform. Gilmore (1990) studied masculinity cross-culturally and found it to be an achieved status which almost universally includes toughness, aggressiveness, stoicism and sexuality. Scholars discuss masculinity as a collective gender identity, one that is fluid and socially constructed, rather than a natural attribute (Courtenay, 2000).

Multiple masculinities exist in all societies, reflecting factors like race, class, age, religious affiliation and geographic location (Morrell, 2001). But, even if a pluralistic nature of masculinities has been identified, not all masculinities are equal. Instead, cultural groups construct ideal notions of masculinity that may be enforced. This hegemonic masculinity (Ratele, 2008) is the ideal that men measure themselves against and are measured against by others.

Habermas (1976) and Connell (1995) have traced the notion of hegemonic masculinities to the emphasis on power in capitalist cultures. As Connell points out, however, to identify hegemonic masculinity solely with physical aggression would be a misrepresentation, as the hegemonic idea also embodies the power of reason and claims to represent the interest of the whole society (Connell, 1995).

The study of masculinity has largely been a Western-dominated analysis of how white men in Europe and North America negotiate an identity in relation to expectations, positions, and roles. The collective experience of Afrikan men is quite different to men of European descent. Both the historical injustices of enslavement and colonialism meted out against Afrika, current global racism and neo-colonial power imbalances have marginalised Afrikan men, both in their own perception and in the eyes of the rest of the world.

Morrell (2001) has described the construction of masculinities in Afrika as both a local and a global process. Globalisation reshapes the arena in which notions of masculinity are expressed, necessitating an in-depth examination of transformations that are occurring in particular contexts. In times of change, Morrell finds men demonstrate reactive, accommodating, or progressive responses.

Interestingly, the study of masculinity in Afrika has been overwhelmingly represented by female researchers who are not of Afrikan descent. Perhaps in response—or in opposition—to the adaptation of Western-based feminist scholarship and interventions throughout the Afrikan continent, a shift is occurring in masculinity studies. Increasingly, the studies of gender—male and female—are favoring a more self-reflective, forward looking approach to that of an anthropological investigation of "subjects" by external researcher. Additionally, the fact that more Afrikan scholars and activists have moved away from Western-based feminism and have embraced Afrikan-centred womanism has inspired more scholars and activists to undertake an Afrikan-centered analysis of Afrikan masculinities.

THE STRUGGLES OF AFRIKAN MEN

The Afrikan Family

The institution of family is generally seen as the foundation in Afrikan cultures (Mbiti 1989). Family in this context includes many sub-institutions, such as extended family structures, polygamous marriages, and the inclusion of the spiritual realms of the not-yet-born and the deceased (ancestors).

Political unrest and socio-economic challenges have forced many Afrikans in rural areas to leave their families in pursuit of opportunities in urban city-centres. These migrations have strongly impacted family structures. Throughout many parts of the Afrikan continent, the deterioration of the Afrikan family is evident in escalating divorce rates, domestic violence, alarming statistics on sexual abuse and rape, and the rise of single-parented households. As observed by Burrell (2010), a growing tendency to stereotypically label Afrikan men as violent, criminal, lazy, and unreliable has emerged. Of the many studies that describe increasing incidents of violence among Afrikan men, few explain the root causes of these phenomena, and few seek to understand the impact that escalating violence has on modern Afrikan family structures. In short; there are many analyses of Afrikan men behaving badly, but few studies seek to develop guidelines for transformative Afrikan masculinities.

Afrikan History—The Missing Pages

The text books on Afrikan history in most learning institutions reflect a Eurocentric perspective and essentially constitute the history of the European presence in Afrika. Impressive volumes of academic Afrikan scholarship, including studies of Afrikan history, have been in existence for centuries but are largely excluded from mainstream educational institutions. These works are of great importance as they document the monumental impact of Afrikans on world history. The work of Cheikh Anta Diop, Yosef ben-Jochannan, Theophile Obenga and many others, sheds light on the many Afrikan civilizations that flourished for thousands of years throughout the Afrikan continent; Ta-Seti, Kemet (Egypt), Kush, Axum, Nubia, Songhay, Ghana, Mali, Oyo, Benin, Congo, Carthage, the Swahili coast states and Great Zimbabwe.[1] According to Robin Walker, there is ample evidence that Afrikan civilization dates back a good 10,000 years (Walker, 2006). Despite disagreements between some scholars about research details, it is increasingly accepted that Afrika played a significant part in contributing to other world civilizations and laid a strong foundation for developments within sciences and philosophy.[2]

A saying asserts that "the darkest aspect of Afrika is our ignorance about it." The miseducation about Afrika has devastating effects on both non-Afrikan and Afrikan peoples. Professor Amos N. Wilson has described many Afrikans as suffering from a form of collective amnesia and not remembering history, not remembering culture, not remembering sense of self:

> Amnesia means an undiscovered self, an emptiness, a self incapable of self-understanding its own motivations, a self incapable of self-direction and self-determination, a reactionary self, a self that does not understand others or the world in which it exists—a fatalistic

externalized self. To rediscover one's history is not only an act of self-discovery; it is an act of self-creation—a resurrection from the dead, a tearing away of the veil, a revelation of the mystery. (Wilson 2002:52)

The loss of history is also loss of culture. Chinweizu has described culture as an immune system with an inherent defence mechanism against external destructive forces (Chinweizu, 2005). Referring to how Afrikans have been so gravely dislocated from their cultural ethos, Chinweizu talks about the "niggerized consciousness" of Afrikan people. With the use of this term he is implying that the Afrikan has internalised a misconstrued understanding of self, which impacts all social behavior he/she engages in. Embedded within this analogy is a strong notion that perpetuated oppressive behavior (ex. enslavement), in the case of Afrikans, has led to self-alienation and, on a deeper level, acceptance of its "truth" (i.e. performing the role of the enslaved). This not only poses a serious limitation on the Afrikan personality and purpose, but also separates the Afrikan from his/her potential to assert power. The Afrikan becomes inherently powerless because he/she believes being oppressed is his/her final destination; this is a notion which the Afrikan must vehemently debunk and liberate himself/herself from.

Why Are Afrikan Men Angry?

Many Afrikan men seem to have a deep-seated rage which sometimes manifests in violence and can be seen as a multi-layered response to hundreds of years of oppression. Bell hooks asserts that Black men are often "stuck in the place of rage. And it is the breeding ground for the acts of violence large and small that ultimately do black men in" (hooks 2004:60).

Amos Wilson has described the existential outlook of many Afrikan men as that of "a frustrated man . . . an angry male; an enraged man, whether or not the anger and rage are consciously acknowledged" (Wilson, 1990:117). The frustration and aggression born of being Black in an anti-Black world can lead to a deep sense of fear-based rage and a disposition to act out in hate against the oppressor or oneself (Cress Welsing, 1991). Joy Degruy Leary (2006), in her book *Post Traumatic Slave Syndrome*, examines how injustices meted out against Afrikans over many generations during enslavement and colonialism manifest as a legacy of reproduced social ills.

Psychiatrists, Price M. Cobbs and William H. Grierson, in their classic study *Black Rage* (1968) write that Black rage is a "healthy cultural paranoia" developed by Black men as a coping mechanism to deal with constant racial stress. This may be a more meaningful approach when trying to understand Black men and anger than the labelling of Black men as stuck in the past, emotional, or self-pitying.

Tom Burrell (2010) believes that a theory of Black inferiority has been advanced, to the extent of having become a "brand," through a history laden with racism and color-consciousness. By ascribing to stereotypes of Black behaviour and a multitude of dysfunctional social institutions, in which violence and disintegration form the basis of Black people's self-image, a cycle of hatred against self and others has become a norm. Additionally, as observed by Ratele (2008), constant exclusion from the institutions and life processes that, in modern culture, define manhood (i.e. employment, material wealth and power to influence society), breeds a traumatic experience of powerlessness.

Rage: Rooted In Violence, Manifested In Violence

It is in the expressions of rage that the unhealthy nature of some Black men's choices are demonstrated. Behaviors of violence, abuse, suicide, and drug abuse do little more than channel aggression. The end result of each action rarely changes the power structure it is done in opposition to. Invariably, the person will end up being more of a victim of his own actions than a conqueror. Yet, these behaviors continue to be manifestations of inner traumas. Bell hooks (2004) describes a situation where Black men are driven to enact "rituals of blood" to desperately achieve patriarchal manhood through violence to dominate and control:

> If black males are socialized from birth to embrace the notion that their manhood will be determined by whether or not they can dominate and control others and yet the political system they live within (imperialist white-supremacist capitalist patriarchy) prevents most of them from having access to socially acceptable positions of power and dominance, then they will claim their patriarchal manhood, through socially unacceptable channels (hooks 2004:57–58).

Political changes in the post-enslavement scenarios of Afrika have also shifted the cultural assumptions around family and community. Eurocentric dogmas of hegemonic and oppressive masculinities have been enforced to such an extent that they are almost seen to be inherent in Afrikan social organisation. In many parts of the continent one can find proverbs, allegories and symbolic language that justify, and even promote, violence. Young Afrikan men today, heirs to Pan-Afrikan liberation thoughts of the 1960s, but also prisoners of a globalised world in which Afrika has been placed on the bottom, now ask themselves "What is Afrikan manhood"? And the answer is not necessarily provided by fathers, uncles, and community leaders anymore. Increasingly, the commercial idolisation of Black hyper-masculinity has taken precedence in defining manliness. The iconography of Black men in music videos, magazines, TV shows and within the music industry objectifies the ideal Black man in the images of thugs, scheming tricksters, and womanisers with few responsibilities other than to party all night long.

A destructive myth has been reinforced through popular culture, especially commercialized music and media: It is the myth of the Black brute who only has money and sex on his mind and could care less about honor, traditions, and planning for the future. This myth becomes a model for young men who are in need of identities that can respond to their sense of powerlessness and represent clear alternatives to their own fathers' failures. When such a one-dimensional and racist stereotype is linked to popularity and influence, it can be mistaken by some youths as a liberated ground-breaking depiction of masculinity.

As Westernization has become the sole reference point for modernity, Afrikan knowledge and spirituality appear backward and irrelevant. In a worldview ruled by extreme materialism, cultural traditions seem redundant. As spirituality is associated with submission, collectivism and selflessness—the opposite of idealised masculinity—it also represents a non-desirable direction for young Afrikan men who want to feel powerful.

Violence is often discussed in terms of the acts of destruction it results in. However, there is a pressing need to understand what violence is a response to. In the Afrikan experience, violent behavior has become an expression of complex conflicts stemming from multiple sources, including a long history of repeated layers of domination, conquest and societal upheaval, racism, stereotypical imagery, and continuous derogatory stereotyping of Afrikan males. Systematic violence creates a minefield of disconnections. Loss of cultural identity leaves the Afrikan man trapped in a position of not fully knowing who he is, while, at the same time, he is being bombarded by stereotypes and assumptions about who he is: such conflicts can result in deep-seated anger. With few constructive ways for Afrikan men to analyze and release their rage, a cycle of negative patterns may develop. While we do a great job of criticizing and discussing such cycles, we have rarely devised ways to break these destructive cycles.

AFRIKAN MASCULINITY—AFRIKAN APPROACHES

Men, Masculinity, and Violence in Afrika

The strict social education of boys and young men in traditional Afrika did not allow the murder or rape of human beings (Black, 1997). Boys were raised to be respectful and productive husbands and family heads. In her critique of Western definitions of the role of gender in Afrika, Ifi Amadiume sees the Afrikan, pre-colonial, traditional society as organised through matriarchy with a moral system that was based on "peace and cooperation, and [that] forbade human bloodshed, [and] imposed a check on excessive and destructive masculinism" (Amadiume, 1997:122).

However, modernization has caused a paradigm shift that directly affects contemporary definitions of masculinity. Barker and Ricardo (2005) find that in southern Afrika, masculinity exhibits certain recurring beliefs and behaviors. They found that masculinity:

- has, traditionally, a place of priority;
- depends, often, on an older man who holds more power who decides when a young man is able to achieve socially recognised manhood;
- is expressed through initiation practices, rites of passage, often including male circumcision, holds an important place in the socialisation of boys to men;
- for many young men, manifests itself in violence and coercion (threats, force);
- is sometimes related to sexual "conquest" and the perceived right to violate and/or dominate women;
- is responsive to the multitude of social changes, urbanization, and political upheaval, including civil unrest and lack of national-level social institutions.

To a certain degree, notions of masculinity are linked to expressions of violence. Baker and Ricardo found the following correlations in many young Afrikan men's experiences:

- An increasing number of young men have been combatants in armed conflicts, to such an extent that participation in conflict has become an important part of socialization;
- The extreme nature and magnitude of some conflicts has made brutal violence a learned behavior, reinforced by social structures in the community and in the family;
- Traumatic after-effects experienced by men who have witnessed, participated or otherwise been affected by violent situation, further cements violent associations with manhood;
- There appears to be a link between violence and masculinity in criminal activities, gang-activity and ethnic-related violence;
- Unemployment and systemic poverty in many regions force men who are expected to provide and sustain families to engage in criminal activities where violence may play an integral part.

Masculinities develop and change with cultural fluidity and are not static. It is obvious that multiple sources of historical and political oppression have caused much anxiety, confusion and misdirection for Afrikan men. Consequently, it is important to challenge current understandings of Afrikan masculinity, to create awareness about the causes of violence, and to formulate recommendations and solutions that are practical, useful, and rooted in Afrikan indigenous knowledge systems.

Culture as Guideline for Thought and Behavior

Afrikan indigenous traditional knowledge systems are rich and can play a vital role in helping individuals and communities to curb violence, promote healing, and guide the development of relevant masculinities.

An example of an Afrikan institution that has traditionally given voice to what men go through, what they must face, and how they should carry themselves is the rites of passage ceremony or initiation ritual practiced across the continent. The objective of this ritual is to guide and educate young men to become responsible and useful men in the broader community. If we examine the principles these initiations have been founded upon, we realise that they articulate positions we easily can revive and adapt in response to modern challenges.

Rites of Passage—Principles to Shape Afrikan Masculinity

The male initiation ritual encompasses a number of principles of strong educational value and assists young men in their self-development and socialization process. The following is an outline of some key principles in Afrikan Rites of Passage.[3]

1. Separating the child from the community and routines of daily life
Separation allows the participant to focus fully on the ritual experience and the knowledge being conveyed. Aspects of the initiation require each individual to spend time alone, which allows for reflection and self-knowledge. Other aspects are group-based, teaching the initiate about the importance of collaboration and communality.

2. Observing nature
Traditionally, Afrikan schools were built on observing nature. Cycles of growth and development are based on universal principles of life. These principles, which also guide agricultural processes from planting to harvesting, provide males with vital tools of development, such as putting ideas into practice, fomenting stability within the family, and understanding inter-dependency.

3. A social process based on age
Traditional education in Afrika is a social process as opposed to the Western educational emphasis on individualism. Children are expected to master requirements from beginning to end as a group. There are no gifted, average, and impaired groupings; there is communal education and advancement.

4. Rejection of childhood
Completing the Rites of Passage ritual helps to separate manhood from boyhood. In both symbolic and practical ways, the initiate is assisted in parting with the immaturity of a boy and embracing a new position, that of a responsible man.

5. Listening to the Elders
In Afrikan traditional education, the most significant part is conducted by the Elders. Wisdom is more than information. The initiate is taught to seek and respect the experience possessed by Elders and gets insight into the sacrifices and achievements of those who have lived longer than him. This is a valuable contribution to the participant's problem solving and decision making skills.

6. Cleansing rituals

An important part of the Afrikan sacral world is marking transitional journeys (for example from boyhood to manhood) with cleansing rituals. On a spiritual level, elements like water, fire, clay and masks can assist in protecting the individual from harm and warding off negative emotions and harmful spirits.

7. Tests of character

Being confronted by adversity in life, Afrikan men are expected to demonstrate courage, confidence, bravery, strength and endurance. In the initiation space, participants take part in exercises and activities that help them to shed fear, irresponsibility and cowardice. Life is seen as a journey of challenges, and a strong character is essential in order to be a productive man.

8. Use of special language

As part of the initiation process, a new vocabulary is created. Particular words, sayings, songs, wearing of cloths, use of natural elements, use of objects from the animal kingdom, dance and food all form part of a symbolic language helping to make the process memorable and also mark the journey from old to new identity (boy to man).

9. Use of a special name

Special names are used which are symbolic of certain characteristics. Symbols or names that have special meaning to the initiation process are also chosen.

10. Symbolic resurrection

Upon successful completion of the rites, the participant is no longer the child who began the ceremony. The boy has "died" and given way to a man who is better equipped to maneuver through the adult world. The last part of the initiation takes place when the entire community gathers to celebrate the arrival of the new men. This becomes, at once, a validation and public officiation. An announcement of the responsibilities men are expected to carry.

THE QUIET SCREAM WITHIN

The title of this article alludes to some of the conflicts that impact Afrikan masculinities: the expectation of being a provider and protector in a disempowering world, the burden of discredited history, the loss of knowledge of self, marginalisation in the global space, exclusion from economic power, unresolved anger, self-hate, and the many effects these conditions have on Afrikan men and their families. Struggling to find effective ways to understand, overcome, and dismantle their challenges, Afrikan men find it difficult to develop a solution-oriented discourse. Faced with intimidating expectations and being over-determined and, at the same time, undermined, many men chose to "keep things inside." Because of this, there is a lot to read in between the lines, for Afrikan men may articulate many unspoken experiences in their silences. Complex textured realizations are hidden behind walls of muteness and there are myriads of undisclosed intense narratives masked as unbothered faces.

The quiet scream within, the agonized silence of Afrikan men indicates a problem that should concern all of society. When some Afrikan men are confronted with problematic issues, they seem to adopt a militant we-cannot-talk-about-this stance: Neglect and denial appear easier and more acceptable than solving problems. This might stem from perceived—and experienced—sanctions against what we could call expressions of vulnerability. The muted Afrikan man may find himself spinning in a mental whirlpool of doubt, confusion, revelation, and resignation. The following is a hypothetical illustration of a silenced voice speaking truthfully:

Since society has a strict expectation as to how I should assert and demonstrate my Afrikan masculinity, and since I continuously experience failure as I try living up to these expectations, I have become insecure about, and even doubtful of, my own masculinity. I look at the men who have been in my life since childhood, and I can find few whole, empowering, caring role-models among them. I know that there is more to masculinity than the simplified notions of manhood our society offers, but I don't know how to find alternatives or if I am ready for what I will find. Trapped within the skin of non-being and descending from a continent that appears void of power, my energy is divided between managing my anger on the inside and emulating authentic strength on the outside.

Because I struggle to identify a relevant model of "real Afrikan masculinity" I teach myself coping mechanisms and adopt internal and external behaviors which, at the very least, enable me to act out a convincing masculinity for the society in which I live. My sense of masculinity will grow proportionately with the feedback I get as to how convincing my acting is. Should I fail to convince, I am acutely aware that my masculinity—and, with it, the whole purpose for my existence as a man—will be questioned, ridiculed, doubted, or destroyed. But if I express my vulnerabilities, I will make a complete fool out of myself and announce to the world that I am unable to assemble the very basis of my identity as an Afrikan man, a mission the world around me already doubts that I can successfully complete.

This is one example of a quiet scream. Frantz Fanon articulates another one in *Black Skin, White Masks*: "I came into this world anxious to uncover the meaning of things, my soul desirous to be at the origin of the world, and here I am an object among other objects."[4] If this illustrates painful truths unspoken by many Afrikan men, we can only begin to imagine how such an existence compromises human potential, for there is a price to be paid when pain is bottled up. The pressure that is never given an outlet will eventually start to harm its host; and, as we know, hurt people hurt people. Pain multiplies and can become vicious cycles of violations against self and everyone within reach. A channel—sufficiently broad, safe, and impactful—must be developed to give voice to this quiet scream—not only for the scream to be heard, but also to make it inspire effective solutions.

Notes

[1] The history of ancient Afrikan civilizations is well documented in the works of Asante (1994), Walker (2006), Jackson (1995), Diop (1974, 1981, 1987), Houston (1985), Van Sertima (2004), Obenga (1992).
[2] See Asante and Mazama (2002), Rashidi (1995), Van Sertima (1976) and Davidson (1991).
[3] The principles listed here are adapted from Paul Hill, *Coming of Age* (Chicago: African American Images, 1992).
[4] Franz Fanon, *Black Skin, White Masks* (New York: Grove Press, 1967), 109.

Bibliography

Akbar, Na'im. (2003). *Papers in African Psychology*. Tallahassee, FL; Mind Productions and Associates, Inc.

Amadiume, Ifi. (1997). *Reinventing Africa: Matriarchy, Religion and Culture*. New York: Zed Books.

Ani, Marimba. (1994). *Yurugu: An African-Centered Critique of European Cultural Thought and Behavior*. Atlanta: Nkonimfo Publications.

Asante, Molefi K. and Ama Mazama, eds. (2002). *Egypt vs Greece and the American Academy: The Debate Over the Birth of Civilization*. Chicago: African American Images.

Asante, Molefi K. (1994). *Classical Africa*. Saddle Brook, NJ: The People's Publishing Group.

Asante, Molefi K. (1987). *The Afrocentric Idea*. Philadelphia: Temple University Press.

Asante, Molefi. K. (2003). *Afrocentricity: The Theory of Social Change*. Chicago: African American Images.

Barker, Gary and Christine Ricardo. (2005). "Young Men and the Construction of Masculinity in Sub-Saharan Africa: Implications for HIV/AIDS, Conflict, and Violence." *The World Bank Social Development Papers: Conflict and Reconstruction*. Paper No. 26.

Black, Daniel P. (1997). *Dismantling Black Manhood: An Historical and Literary Analysis of the Legacy of Slavery*. New York: Garland Publishing.

Brown, Jill, James Sorrell and Marcela Raffaelli. (2005). "An exploratory study of constructions of masculinity, sexuality and HIV/AIDS in Namibia, Southern Africa." *Culture, Health, and Sexuality* 7:6: 585–598.

Burrell, Tom. (2010). *Brainwashed: Challenging the Myth of Black Inferiority*. New York: SmileyBooks.

Chinweizu. (2005). "Ancestral Culture and Modern Survival: The Example of Meiji Japan." Retrieved from <http://www.worldafropedia.com/afropedia/Ancestral_Culture_and_Modern_Survival:_The_Example_of_Meiji_JaJapan>. Accessed 19 June 2016.

Connell, Raewyn. W (1995). *Masculinities*. Cambridge (UK): Polity.

Courtenay, Will. (2000). "Constructions of Masculinity and Their Influence on Men's Well Being: A Theory of Gender and Health." *Social Science and Medicine* 50: 1385–1401.

Cress Welsing, Frances. (1991). *The Isis Papers: The Keys to the Colors*. Washington, DC: C.W. Publishing.

Davidson, Basil. (1991). *Africa in History*. London: Phoenix Press.

Degruy Leary, Joy. (2006). *Post Traumatic Slave Syndrome: America's Legacy of Enduring Injury and Healing*. Milwaukee: Uptone Press.

Diop, Cheikh A. (1981). *Civilization or Barbarism: An Authentic Anthropology*. Brooklyn: Lawrence Hill Books.

Diop, Cheikh A. (1987). *Precolonial Black Africa*. Brooklyn: Lawrence Hill Books.

Diop, Cheikh A. (1974). *The African Origin of Civilization: Myth or Reality*. Brooklyn: Lawrence Hill Books.

Fanon, Frantz. (1967). *Black Skin, White Masks*. New York: Grove Press.

Gilmore, David D. (1990). *Manhood in the Making: Cultural Concepts of Masculinity.* New Haven, CT: Yale University Press.

Grier, William and Price Cobbs. (1968). *Black Rage.* New York: Basic Books.

Habermas, Jurgen. (1976). *Legitimation Crisis.* London: Heinemann.

Hill Jr., Paul. (1992). *Coming of Age.* Chicago: African American Images.

hooks, bell. (2004). *We Real Cool: Black Men and Masculinity.* London: Routledge.

Houston, Drusilla D. (1985). *Wonderful Ethiopians of the Cushite Empire.* Baltimore: Black Classic Press.

Jackson, John G. (1995). *Introduction to African Civilizations.* New York: Carol Publishing Group.

James, George G. M. (2005). *Stolen Legacy.* Dreweryville, VA: Khalifah's Booksellers.

Mbiti, John S. (1989). *African Religions and Philosophy.* London: Heinemann.

Morrell, Robert. (2001). "The Times of Change: Men and Masculinity in South Africa." In *Changing Men in Southern Africa*, edited by Robert Morrell. Pietermaritzburg: University of Natal Press. 3–37.

Mosha, R. Sambuli. (2000). *The Heartbeat of Indigenous Africa: A Study of the Chagga Educational System.* New York: Garland Publishing.

Obenga, Theophile. (1992). *Ancient Egypt and Black Africa: A Student's Handbook for the Study of Ancient Egypt in Philosophy, Linguistics and Gender Relations.* London: Karnak House.

Rashidi, Runoko, Ed. (1995). *African Presence in Early Asia.* London: Transaction Publishers.

Ratele, Kopano. (2008). "Analysing Males in Africa: Certain Useful Elements in Considering Ruling Masculinities." *African and Asian Studies* 7: 515–536.

Shefer, Tamara, Kopano Ratele, Anna Strebel, Nokuthula Shabalala, and Rosemarie B. Buikema. (2007). *From Boys to Men: Social Constructions of Masculinity in Contemporary Society.* Landsdowne: UCT Press.

Tait, George E. (1995). "I am A Black Man." In *Brotherman*, edited by Herb Boyd and Robert L. Allen. New York: Ballantine Books.

Van Sertima, Ivan. (2004). *Egypt Revisited.* London: Transaction Publishers.

Van Sertima, Ivan. (1976). *They Came Before Columbus: The African Presence in Ancient America.* New York: Random House.

Walker, Robin. (1994). *When We Ruled: The Ancient and Mediaeval History of Black Civilisations.* London: Every Generation Media.

Williams, Chancellor. (1987). *The Destruction of Black Civilization: Great Issues of a Race from 4500 B.C. to 2000 A.D.* Chicago: Third World Press.

Wilson, Amos. N. (1990). *Black-on-Black Violence: The Psychodynamics of Black Self-Annihilation in Service of White Domination.* Brooklyn: Afrikan World Infosystems.

Wilson, Amos. (2002). *Understanding Black Adolescent Male Violence: Its Remediation and Prevention.* Brooklyn: Afrikan World Infosystems.

Rising From Ashes:
About Black Men and Cheating

Baba A. O. Buntu

Introducing the Fear of Fears

> "I'm a queen,
> and I can't say I've run across a full-blown king"
>
> ~ *Lil' Kim/The Notorious K.I.M*

Frantz Fanon was painfully on point when articulating the Black man's psyche: "I move slowly in the world, accustomed to aspiring no longer to appear." That is what I do. I drag my feet to avoid disappointments or to avoid being caught off guard. I have grown used to not appearing, to not being expected to achieve excellence, to being misrepresented. I am not sure if I'm present in my own life, and I don't know if it makes any difference. I am a Black man. There is nothing I know better than being lied to, cheated on, stolen from, and castrated for standing up against injustice.

As Brothers begin to articulate the longing for purpose and to challenge the notions of what makes a strong Black man, a soul-search of unprecedented proportions takes place. We know too well that many of us have messed up. We know too well that some of us have forfeited new chances. But as some of us step into our warrior-hood, lower our guards, open our minds, and actually listen and speak with a voice we never knew we had, we need to know if our fears are worthy of acknowledgement.

The fear I carry is best described like this: If I were you, I probably would have cheated on me too. . .

Cheating: What Does It Mean?

Cheating has a thousand parents. Getting caught is an orphan. . .

~ Anonymous

"You must listen!" "I am the man of the house!" "Who do you think you are?" "Why don't you answer your phone when I call?" "All Black men are dogs." "All Black women are using men for material gains." "Who is the woman you were talking to outside the shop?" There is plenty of drama in Black lives with a disproportionate number of episodes revolving around where you were last night. Some Afrikan mothers tell their daughters: "If you are going to run away from every man who cheats on you, you will forever be running." Some Sisters say they no longer believe in marriage. Many Brothers say they are sick and tired of being tricked by conniving women.

Although dictionaries define fidelity as adherence to honesty and truth, fidelity is essentially about ownership. We engage in relationships where we take for granted that we own each other's freedom, loyalty, and behaviour. We have moved from sacred unions to investments in compatibility, physical attraction, and what the latest lifestyle magazine tells us is hot. Matrimony—which originally defined inheritance through maternal lineages has become a term for marriage that articulates men's control over property owned by women, including their bodies.

What Brothers Do

The more the Black male strives to stand,
the weaker the white male feels by comparison,
and the greater the white male's thrust
to effeminize the Black male in order to weaken
the Black male's psychological potential for
aggressive and assertive challenge,
forcing him to remain submissive to "The Man."

~ Dr. Frances Cress Welsing

As Black men, we carry big loads of insecurities. Behind our manly attributes is a sea of things we cannot figure out: all our psycho-emotional stuff, our self-doubt, our harsh self-criticism, our need to always compare and compete, our judgement that we might not really amount to much, and the list goes on. You might not see it—or at least we'd like to believe you can't—but our fears are there in abundance. They constitute psychological baggage that dates back to the first invasions of Afrika and the first generation of enslaved Afrikan men. The Black man has accumulated numerous wounds from constantly being attacked, judged and excluded. So severe are these wounds that it appears that a certain amount of brokenness is a part of Black manhood.

When we become possessive and jealous control-freaks, we are acting out a hopelessness that has been engraved in us for the last thousand years. If there is one thing we know as Black men, it is that we are not really powerful. We might try to get all kinds of material possessions to create an illusion of power, but we don't really own stuff. We don't produce things. We don't control wealth. We make vague contributions. And we consume. It is on the strength of our backs, through our sweat and by our blood that white power has been constituted and maintained. We are the underdogs: we are *under* the underdogs. So when we suspect that a Sister is looking for bedroom gratification somewhere else, we flip. It means the end of the world, the end of our manhood. First and foremost because it provocatively resonates with an unspeakable truth within us: We are replaceable.

Black men must perform, act, convince, compensate, and navigate. We are not real men until we can prove it. We need to convince the world around us that we are men so at least we can also start believing it. If I can make you submit to me, I will "see" my own power in how I make you relate to me. Our manhood is qualified by the extent to which we can copy European behavior—or at least what we perceive it to be—and disguise it with some touches of slick Blackness and a vague notion of Afrikan authenticity. Not having dealt with our traumatic past of continuous enslavement and otherness, we will go to any length to prove our manhood. Is it only now you understand what the saying "a man's gotta do what a man's gotta do" means? Does this saying even make sense? That is irrelevant. Don't ask too many questions while we do what we gotta do! The Black woman must know her place! I'm still looking for mine.

What Sisters are Not Supposed to Do

> Don't mean no harm, I just like what I see
> And it ain't my fault if he wants me
> Got what I wanted and the feeling was right
> So if that's your boyfriend
> He wasn't last night
>
> ~ Me'shell Ndege'Ocello

"I don't need a man; I can buy my own car." "If he doesn't give me what I want, I go and find it elsewhere." "I need a man who can satisfy me." Rough statements like these, uttered by bitter or selfish Sisters scare us senseless. We shiver behind our quiet don't-seem-to-care faces. We tremble hysterically under the condescending laughter. We manipulatively act out. Because let's face it: Sometimes we are scared of Sisters. There is nothing as frightening to a man as an independent woman. A woman who is fingersnapping with her hand firmly on her hip, announcing that she can buy her own car, can earn more than me, can buy a house and let me be her live-in boyfriend . . . until she finds another one, can dictate the rules, and yet, wants to be held like the white women she has seen on TV provokes something so deep in our Black-Man-soul that even we even get surprised by our reactions. But our fear is not really about attitude. It's about substance and purpose. The attributes we keep hunting for in our own lives.

Afrikan women are fascinating beyond words. Sisters have had to go through a lot of rubbish and every "ism" in the book. Yet, it seems as if nature has given the Black woman a box of tools to let her grow into her rightful being of power with ease: The mystic cycles of monthly ovulations; her inner sense of an earth-bound sensuality; her body which, once inseminated, turns into a perfect 9-months incubation laboratory to guide every human towards becoming a being; her breasts that carry life and the promise of a self-sufficient snackbar for her baby. Her physical shape and sinuous curves make a Brother's head spin, while she strolls down the street blissfully oblivious. The mysteries of womanhood include mother-daughter closeness, a flock of female relatives, and an intimate Sisterhood that we cannot match! Beyond our voice cracking, some pubes and face hair, a couple of balls, and our much-treasured penis, we don't have much of an earth connection. We don't get adopted into mystical unions. Our bonding is limited to a few taps on the shoulder, shouting our throats sore at soccer stadiums and a few words of encouragement from a drunk uncle. And it ends there. At least that's how it seems.

The Sisters seem to be so affirmed, so assured, so purpose-filled, so *destined*. Just like that! Whereas Sisters seem to follow a nature-inherited script, Brothers must repeatedly design and convince the world—and themselves—that they are men. They must invent, re-invent and maintain, by all means, a sense of masculinity in contrast to the horrible thought of being . . . well, not masculine. A straight Brother's existence is often justified by the extent to which he can convince the world that he is not a woman. And the best way to do that is to put everything womanish on the bottom of all value scales. And to let women know their place.

You see, Black women are out of control! They've taken women's liberation too far. They earn more; they expect more; they set standards. They put their feet down, their attitudes up, and you must talk to their hands. And they cheat! Even the sanctity of playing the field is no longer only a man's domain! Sisters see nothing wrong with committing the ultimate sin against a Brother who . . . well, actually . . . also cheats. But as we all know, men just *play* when they go outside, women are serious and actually *mean* it. Imagine! No wonder we need more space to complain about how hard it is to be a Black man these days.

Why would a Sister cheat? My very unscientific research is based on conversational empiricism carried out with ethnographic cheekiness on women around me. My informants have revealed that women cheat when there is an emotional detachment from the man. Sisters claim that when they no longer feel wanted, loved, and comforted it becomes easier to be wooed by someone else. I am not happy with the results of this study.

I say these Sisters are lying. Without getting into too much about Brothers' faults—I mean, let's **focus** here and not get distracted by emotions!—look at the devious pattern Sisters are following in their manipulation of Brothers. Who are really the victims of Sisters cheating? The very men they say they want!

Let us look at some of the characters Afrikan women collectively seem to have agreed will not be given the time of day. First, there is Mr. Nice. Sisters won't admit it, but they love to cheat on this "softie." The one who actually does what Sisters say they want. He communicates; he is in touch with his feelings; he is supportive; he stays. But Sisters have internalised the stereotypical image of Brothers as aggressive, hard, violent and in control so much that Mr. Nice comes across as a fraud. Or a trap. Or, perhaps, just too good to be true? In any case, he will soon find out he is replaceable.

Then there is the Abstainee. The Brother who dutifully waits until the wedding day. The Sister scratches her weave and suspiciously eyes him up and down, "You sure you into women?!" Oh, yes, Sisters, that is a very effective tactic. Question our sexual orientation and you will see Brothers who bend over backwards to convince you.

There is also the Boring Bloke who actually is only trying to be as chill as you say you like men to be. But, as it turns out, Sisters prefer spice more than chill. Then we have Mr. Exhausted who works extreme hours to provide Sisters with the finer things they desire. The problem is, they will say, he is away all the time. There is the Intellectual Conscious Brother who prefers thick books to shallow clubs in his quest to ensure that wisdom is the cornerstone of his life and relationships. Sisters are impressed with knowledge, but, "Come on, consciousness all the flipping time?"

There's the Dude Boy who earns less than you and tries hard to maintain his sense of self, but only comes across as a fumbling twat. "No prospects" is the condemnation from the Sister who initially had said she likes a simple man. Lastly, there is the Spiritual Philosopher who owns more incense than condoms and wants to expand the mind rather than hitting "that." "Kemet might be nice," the Sister says to herself, "but a girl's gotta her groove on." Kemet, apparently, does not score very high when groove factor is measured.

Women's liberation men's style: What men have done, Sisters now do better. Cheating has become a competition in who can hurt their partner more and an accepted form of self-liberation. Black women are breaking new ground. Escapades may or may not include White men, Arabs, Indians, Mexicans, other Sisters, or toys from shady shops. Astonishing. Horrendous. Flabbergasting. Black women have sunk to our level. Where does **that** leave the Black Man? What is behind all our madness?

The Internalization of Patricentrism

> The look that the native turns on the settler's town is a look of envy; it expresses his dreams of possession—all manner of possession: to sit at the settler's table, to sleep in the settler's bed, with his wife if possible. The colonised man is an envious man . . . . It is true, for there is no native who does not dream at least once a day of setting himself up in the settler's place.
>
> ~ Frantz Fanon

Trinidadian writer Corey Gilkes has done a thorough study of the roots of patricentric behaviour. By patricentric he means the ideas revolving around European-founded authoritarianism, individualism, possessiveness, aggressive militaristic pursuits, and fatalism. This war-based culture dictates that males are superior to women and must control them. What we have learnt to exclude from the narrative is the fact that prior to contemporary male chauvinism, many traditional Afrikan societies were matricentric. Sisters in ancient Afrikan societies were priests, magistrates, entrepreneurs, land owners, agriculturalists, and leaders. Socially and economically, women enjoyed as much autonomy as their male counterparts. In many Afrikan societies, women were the governors of production and livelihood. In others, they were the ones who ordained men into leadership positions and held them accountable should they not perform as expected. Women were holders of power.

Matricentric societies, as described by such Afrikan scholars as Cheikh Anta Diop, John Henrik Clarke, and Ifi Amadiume, functioned through a strong sense of honour, obligation and reciprocity, which is an indication that abuse was minimal. Systems were in place to resolve of conflicts, mediate divorce, and—probably—handle infidelity issues. According to Diop, European tribes, at the end of the last Ice Age found themselves caught between massive natural barriers, and they had to fight each other to secure access to scarce food. This gave rise to a fatalistic mindset and a thought process which dictated that everything in the natural world must be subdued and controlled for people to survive. Masculine warrior traditions rooted in violence emerged and shaped a manhood of brutality, as is evident in Roman, Jewish, Arab, and Christian traditions.

Individualistic behaviour, private possession, dictatorial rule, and cyclic warfare became the hallmarks of European societies. Within these cultures, women's roles were passive, weak and largely insignificant. Women became the subordinate property of men and had to be "trained," first by their fathers and male relatives and later by their husbands. Western patriarchy, then, is logically based on conflict, defining the one in opposition to the other and then using those differences to show which is better.

The Afrikan practice of matriarchy is not the opposite of European patriarchy. Afrikan culture did not teach superiority but balance and order, typified by pro-female, mother-focused societies. Evidence indicates that in matricentric societies marital unions were neither closed nor permanent. Also, they were not determined by sexual jealousy or a sense of ownership by either gender.

Let's be honest, ancient Afrikan unions are difficult to conceive of with our current mindsets. Fulfilling our needs has become a human rights issue and finding "the right one" has become a nightmarish competition in which men think they must charm women into submission. Clearly, we lost something. Not just lost: We completely erased it from our social memory. The philosophical foundation of a capitalistic economy supports your right to do what you want, when you want, as long as it is beneficial to you. When this philosophy is exported into sexual realms, a relationship also becomes an economy of supply and demand. If your partner cannot fully "supply," you have the right to take your "demand" somewhere else for fulfillment.

Negotiating a New Era: The Quest for Afrikan Loyalty

> What you know about hard?
> Can you assemble your heat in the dark?
> Take it apart and clean all the parts?
> Life is a journey, a course,
> like learning a martial art
> You can't have partial heart
> Gotta give it all
> If you drop your ball, dog, we all fall
> It ain't over 'til the problem solved
> Get your back up off the wall
>
> ~ "Walk Like a Warrior," dead prez

Our situation is grim. The institutions that are supposed to be our most effective means for reclaiming our dignified lives are often the ones filled with mistrust, suspicion and agony: Relationships. We can't wait to get into one. And, once we are in, we start contemplating how to get out.

Brothers talk about relationships too, especially the ones that are not working, and search for solutions. Enter the talk about polygamy as the **real** Afrikan social institution. Perhaps it is because many of us have not been in polygamous relationships that we just seem to think they work. Some of us are misled into thinking that polygamy is an institution to take care of infidelity. Instead of having mistresses outside, you can rotate between many in an agreed union. First of all, that is not the objective of a polygamous relationship. In most parts of the continent, polygamy was a well-guarded institution set up in response to situations where there were few men in relation to women. It had a societal function far beyond the members of the union. Second, do you really think polygamy is the end of cheating? I mean, really now?

Should we consider polygamy? Absolutely. We should examine every possible solution because the relationships we are practicing at the moment do not seem to empower us. But before we adopt any solution it may be a good idea to agree on what kind of **foundation** we want to build as Afrikan people. We need to determine how we can relate to each other with loyalty and genuine trust in all our relationships, not just the romantic ones. Secondly, we need to understand the **purpose** of our relationships. If we want to examine the practicality of polygamy, let's do that. But, let us also understand what it means to us in this era, not only what it meant in the past. We also need to ask ourselves if polygamy will make us a more powerful people, a more loyal people. Confused as we are, if we just jump into another social order uncritically, there is absolutely no guarantee that we will not mess that up too. I know Brothers who have a hard time just managing themselves and who find it tough to manage a relationship with **one** woman. I can only imagine the struggles they would encounter attempting to manage a union with two women—or more. . . .

But the issue doesn't even start with our relationships. It starts with our selves. Nigerian writer Chinweizu has stated that the single most important project for us as Afrikans is to build a Black superpower. Not unity. Not democracy. Not Ubuntu. Power must come first: a power that constitutes our political, economic, and social ethos. A superpower can only be a result of many, smaller powerful units that make a power-collective when combined. It is up to each and every one of us to build a foundation of loyalty with ourselves and each other, understand and fulfil our purpose. From there we can build powerful relationships, organisations, communities, businesses and nations rooted in an Afrikan agency.

We are so busy chasing romantic illusions, tracing compatibility diagrams, and researching techniques for earth-shattering orgasms that we lose ourselves. All we consume is based on a philosophy of individualistic pleasure. We keep feeding an animal inside that eventually takes us away from our sense of collectivism, responsibility, pride and honour. Sisters and Brothers, we need to treat each other honourably right now. We are tired of hurting. If we just could take time to sit at the feet of our Ancestors and learn a lesson or two, we would understand the cyclic movements of life energy. We would learn how we are interconnected. The ancient Order of Divine Law, expressed as Ma'at, would teach us truth, justice, righteousness, harmony, balance, reciprocity and order. We would understand the respect we command when the words we speak are truthful, when a promise is not a wish, but a will, when a union is not bondage but freedom to be.

Let us also take time to appreciate what actually works. We are so used to our own failure that we find it hard to believe we can rise. Let's applaud and learn from the many healthy Black unions that do exist, the great Afrikan families built on loyal commitment, sacrifice and balance, the Sisters who support their men without becoming shadows of them, the Brothers who empower their women without becoming doormats, the fearless couples who radiate Black pride and who share ancient wisdom without getting lost in it. We come from greatness and shall revive with greatness again.

Outro: The Warrior Man

> Afrikan women cannot afford to give up on Afrikan men.
> After all, their spiritual liberation is intertwined.
>
> ~ Mmatshilo Motsei

Dr. Na'im Akbar has stated that to fully take on the identity of an Afrikan Man is a declaration of war. It is a rebellious and empowering stance. We must confidently **be** self-determined Afrikan Men. We must debunk white supremacy without becoming contaminated by its venom. Mind you, when faced with a Black community that has internalized cardinal sin, a white Jesus, gender politics, market forces, and coleslaw, your biggest obstacle in declaring Afrikan manhood will probably not be white people. It will be your own Black people with PhDs: Pull Him Down.

Cheating is not our problem; it is just a symptom. As we tumble around as confused children of a soil we don't claim, let us stop for a minute to redefine our vision and mission. At what point do we stop being puppets in a game whose rules we don't fully comprehend? At what point will we have the courage to resurrect the Afrikan Warrior within? When will we dare to look our Ancestors in the eye and say "let Thy will be done"? Where is the line that we will not cross in becoming alien to ourselves? When will we lose our stubborn doubts and relearn Afrikan spiritual guidelines that will instill in us a quiet confidence? When will we respect ourselves and our partners enough to demand and accept, the love we deserve?

I lean back and look at my people: I love my people beyond sense. Even when they frustrate me beyond reason. I gaze at us and see the tremendous powers we have. We possess the mystical keys to ancient wisdom that we can use to unlock the doors of wholeness and healing in this confusing world. We have the means to restore ourselves and this incredible continent, and one day in a distant future we will laugh at the times when we allowed anyone, including ourselves, to use, abuse, and mistreat us. From ashes of chattel slavery, being sired out, rape, and racist breeding, we will rise to not only take ownership of ourselves, but to take responsibility for each other. We will reinstitute radical Ubuntu; we will bring humankind back into the centre of truthful and cyclical existence. We will rise from these ashes.

Rapping with the Gods:
Hip Hop as a Force of Divinity and Continuity from the Continent to the Cosmos

Teresa N. Washington

Most contemporary rap music exhibits no evidence of African continuity. References to sexual imbecility and abomination abound as is evidenced in lyrics that confess, "I got the dumb dick," and "My little sister's birthday / She'll remember me / For a gift I had ten of my boys take her virginity."[1] Emptyheaded odes to vanity prevail: "On my mama / On my hood / I look fly / I look good."[2] Also ubiquitous are advertisements for European fashion and beverage companies: "I like a lot of Prada, Alize, and vodka"; ". . . I look sick in my six with my Christian Lacroix"; and "Bury me inside the Gucci store."[3] One would be disinclined to associate most rappers with the sacred West African tradition of storing in the mind and sharing in song the history, culture, power, and promise of the people. However, the living libraries of West Africa did in fact give birth to rap music and hip hop culture.

The terms "rap" and "hip hop" originate in the Wolof language of West Africa. "Hep" or "hip" means to have knowledge or insight; "to open one's eyes, to be aware of what is going on."[4] One could surmise that hip hoppers are individuals with knowledge of important social, cultural, and political issues that they share with the masses through the verbal artistry of rap to inspire sociopolitical evolution. The African American phenomenon called rap also boasts a Wolof root, and its meaning is central to this study. In "The Sacred and the Feminine: An African Response to Clément and Kristeva," Molara Ogundipe reveals that in Wolof language and culture Raap are important and potent Gods "of the sea and waters" to whom particular hymns are sung.[5] Just as it takes true emcees years to master the art of rap, Ogundipe reveals that "[i]t takes eleven years of apprenticeship to learn all the hymns to be sung to a *Raap*."[6]

When one considers the two-month long journey that enslaved Africans made across the Atlantic Ocean—a body of water August Wilson called "the largest unmarked grave in the world"[7]—one could assert that the resilient Raap ensured African ancestors' survival and encouraged their progeny to rap and thereby communicate, document, and spread knowledge of ancient and modern struggles, trials, and triumphs. Furthermore, because of the religious terrorism and ethnic cleansing that Caucasian oppressors enacted, it was not safe to give effusive praise to African Gods; indeed, such reverence often resulted in death. So the Raap switched reels, so to speak, and became rapping Gods whose lyrics serve the divine purpose of creating more raps and more Raap.

In tracing the path and proliferation of Raap through the Middle Passage to African America, it becomes clear that not only did these Wolof Gods sail and survive the high seas of a man-made hell, but they were also reborn in both African American rap music and in African Americans themselves, most notably in the Five Percenters who exert a profound influence on the hip hop nation and rap music and who do, in fact, consider themselves to be Gods. Having withstood the horrors of slavery, sodomy, rape, lynch law, and Jim Crow, Raap were revivified in Gods of the grassroots who are truly at one with the people because they literally *are* the people. These Gods do not demand adoration, prayer, sacrifice, or obeisance; they do not revel in self-aggrandizement. These unassuming Deities take a page from the revolutionary manual of Kwame Ture, the call to African unity and Pan-Africanism of John Henrik Clarke, and the Africentric philosophy of Maulana Karenga. Rather than ascend to mystical and mythical heights, they commit "class suicide."[8] They submerge themselves in studios, gather in ciphers on street corners, pull the wisdom of the ancients from their souls, and drop science on platters to continue the work that is central to their existence, which is to use their divine creativity to create more Divinities.

The Rebirth of Raap in Rap

One of the most protracted myths about rap is that it started in New York in the 1970s. In actuality, rap—along with other musical genres, such as the blues, rock and roll, heavy metal, funk, and jazz—is an ancient African art form.[9] While one can find manifestations of indigenous rap throughout the Continent—from the Yoruba Odù Ifá (divination verses) to the recent example offered by Yoweri Museveni, the Head of State of

Uganda[10]—geographically, etymologically, rhythmically, and spiritually, Raap is the mother of rap. One of the most important aspects of both rap and Raap is their tie to the Divine. Raap, also pronounced Raab, means God, and some of the most important, profound, and provocative rap is spit by artists who are Five Percenters or Gods.

There are many analyses that discuss the origin of the Five Percent Nation and its vast cultural and musical influence, such as Wakeel Allah's *In the Name of Allah: A History of Clarence 13X and the Five Percenters*; Michael Muhammad Knight's *The Five Percenters: Islam, Hip-Hop, and the Gods of New York*; Ted Swedenburg's essay "Islam in the Mix: Lessons of the Five Percent"; Felicia Miyakawa's *Five Percenter Rap: God Hop's Music, Message, and Black Muslim Mission*; The RZA's *The Wu-Tang Manual* and *The Tao of Wu*, and *Manifestations of Masculine Magnificence: Divinity in Africana Life, Lyrics, and Literature* by the present author. With the exception of *Manifestations of Masculine Magnificence*, few studies contextualize the Five Percent Nation as part of a divine African continuum that is as old as time and as far-reaching as the cosmos. This omission is ironic because the Five Percent is an essential aspect of that divine continuum, and it may be the continuum's most dynamic and magnetic manifestation—the Gods certainly have the tightest theme songs.

In order to understand the impact that ancient Raap have on modern rappers and rap music, it is necessary to examine the rebirth of divinity in the Nation of Gods and Earths, also known as the Five Percent Nation, Five Percenters, and Nation of Gods.[11] The Nation of Gods has made monumental contributions to the proliferation of divinity across time, space, and musical genres. But it was not created in a vacuum; as part of the African continuum, the Nation owes its cosmological and ontological insights to a number of sources, including Wolof Raap and their divine orature; Pan-African organizations, philosophies, and philosophers such as Sun Ra, Rastafari, and the Moorish Science Temple; and such holy tomes as the Qur'an, the Yoruba Odù Ifá, and the Bible. The most significant influence on the Five Percent is the Nation of Islam whose philosophies comprise the core of the Five Percent ethos. It is interesting to note that Islam, the religion that threatened the veneration of Raap in Africa, ironically took a new form in African America that facilitated the proliferation of Gods of Rap.

W. D. Fard (also known as Wallace Fard Muhammad), the founder of the Nation of Islam, and Elijah Muhammad, the organization's legendary leader, taught their followers that Africana people are divine. In the speech titled "I Want to Teach You," Muhammad avers: *"Every righteous person is a god. We are all God. When we say 'Allah' we mean every righteous person. Allah teaches me that He is a man—not something that is other than* man. The Holy Qur'an refers to Him in such pronouns as 'He' and as 'We' and as 'Us.'"[12] Elijah Muhammad uses such Qur'anic surah as Al-Baqarah 49–58 to buttress his assertion that Allah is a divine collective that includes contemporary Africana people. He could also have quoted from the Bible's Genesis 1:26, Psalms 82:6, and John 10:34 to enlighten his congregation about their numinosity. However, Muhammad's revelation on divinity is arguably more empowering than the surahs and scriptures because it avers that, through the cultivation of righteousness, divinity can be developed and expanded infinitely. Consequently, God is not restricted to any particular culture, individual, or era: God is always present in the limitless potential of the Self.

Fard and Muhammad insisted that the only religion worthy of consideration is one rooted in fact as opposed to faith. They also stressed that the only Deity suitable for reverence is one whose existence is actual as opposed to mythical. Elijah Muhammad's 1961 "Atlanta Speech" emphasizes the connection between religious demystification and self-actualization:

> God is not a mystery today; He is not something invisible. He is not a spirit. He is not something other than flesh and blood; He is in the flesh and in the blood. God is a human being! God would have no joy or pleasure in humans (us) if He himself were something other than a human being. God would have no joy or pleasure in the material universe if He Himself were other than material. . . . There is no such thing as seeing God or the devil after you die. There is no such thing as a heaven up in the sky or a hell down in the ground. All of that is fantasy, false stories made up by your slave master to further enslave you. God is a man! The devil is a man! Heaven and hell are two conditions, and both are experienced in this life right here on this earth.[13]

Elijah Muhammad's dismissal of mythical heavens, hells, and devils and his assertions about the inherent divinity of Africana peoples extend beyond references in organized religious texts—they find their roots in the holistic spiritual systems of the Kemites (Ancient Egyptians), Kushites, Yoruba, Dogon, Mande, and other African ethnic groups. What is more, the contention that Africana peoples are divine is an ancient one, and evidence of humanodivinity can be found in sacred orature and ancient monuments and temples throughout Africa. Consequently, while Muhammad's and Fard's revelations may appear inconceivable to some, these men were actually reminding their followers of the ancient birthright and ontological reality of which slavery, racism, and natal alienation sought to rob them.

To elucidate the political, geopolitical, astronomical, and spiritual significance of Africana people, Fard and Muhammad crafted intricate scientific, historical, and philosophical lessons. Of those teachings, the most important to this study is "Lost-Found Muslim Lesson No. 2" which asserts that three types of people inhabit the world:

14. **Who [are] the 85%?**
ANS. The uncivilized people; poison animal eaters; slaves from mental death and power, people who do not know the Living God or their origin in this world, and they worship that they know not what --- who are easily led in the wrong direction, but hard to lead into the right direction.
15. **Who [are] the 10%?**
ANS. The rich; the slave-makers of the poor; who teach the poor lies --- to believe that the Almighty, True and Living God is a spook and cannot be seen by the physical eye.
Otherwise known as: The Blood-Suckers Of The Poor.
16. **Who [are] the 5% in the Poor Part of the Earth?**
ANS. They are the poor, righteous Teachers, who do not believe in the teachings of the 10%, and are all-wise; and know who the Living God is; and Teach that the Living God is the Son of man, the supreme being, the (black man) of Asia; and Teach Freedom, Justice and Equality to all the human family of the planet Earth.[14]

With "Lost-Found Muslim Lesson No. 2," Fard and Muhammad not only categorize humanity in a very simple yet insightful hierarchy, but they also offer a compelling redefinition and reconceptualization of God. Rather than an invisible individual sitting on high and being glorified while he haphazardly doles out blessings and curses, the " True and Living God" is actually a multitude of "poor righteous teachers" who, as a result of their enlightenment, are charged with battling ten percenters and also, and more importantly, enlightening and "civilizing" "eighty-fivers" and thereby creating even more Gods.

Similar to other religious organizations that make pronouncements on humanodivinity that range from veiled intimations and bold proclamations, the Nation of Islam placed the seed of divine realization and actualization in the fecund soil of humanity but dared it to grow. Of the Nation of Islam's tens of thousands of followers, few had the courage to proclaim their divinity outright because, ironically, they would have been deemed heretics and been ostracized. However, Clarence 13X (formerly Clarence Smith) carefully applied to his life the lessons taught by Fard and Muhammad, and in 1963, Clarence 13X proclaimed and renamed himself "Allah." To paraphrase Ntozake Shange, Allah "found God in [himself],"[15] and, rather than position himself as an overlord, he did something that is unimaginable and unpardonable in organized religions: He taught every Africana person he could reach that they too were Allah.

Referencing "Lost-Found Muslim Lesson No. 2," Allah, who also came to be known as Allah, the Father, acknowledged that there is a nation of Gods—five percent of the world—who only need knowledge of self to manifest their divinity. Allah expanded the catechisms of Fard and Muhammad to create relevant and all-embracing definitions of God that were designed to empower the Africana community in general and Africana men in particular. Furthermore, rather than bury it under rhetoric or in another language, Allah made recognition of inherent divinity as effortless as a greeting, "Peace, God," which is how members of the Nation of Gods greet one another. Thanks to the global influence of hip hop, this greeting has become so common that it has been truncated to "Peace, G," and, as a result, the "G" has been erroneously associated with "gangster." However, rather than a killer and destroyer, "G" signifies one who gives life and who builds—a God.

In addition to grouping human beings into three categories, "Lost-Found Muslim Lesson No. 2" states that it is the duty of those who are civilized to teach those who are uncivilized.[16] Allah, the Father, devised a systematic methodology for enlightenment. He supplemented knowledge and recognition of inherent divinity with the academic foundation supplied by W. D. Fard's Supreme Wisdom Lessons, which include Lost-Found Muslim Lesson No. 1, Lost-Found Muslim Lesson No. 2, Actual Facts, Solar Facts, and intricate existential problems, lessons, and riddles.[17] Allah's curriculum also includes the Supreme Alphabet and the Supreme Mathematics which reveal the "alphabetical computation of the mathematical evaluation" of existence by associating certain numbers and letters with specific concepts.[18] Armed with a holistic curriculum, Allah undertook his life's mission of introducing dislocated African Americans to the reality of their divinity.

Allah, the Father, was assassinated in 1969, and his murder remains unsolved.[19] However, his work was so successful that from his death a Nation of Gods was born, and the impact of these Divinities is most apparent in rap music and hip hop culture. Signature phrases from W. D. Fard, Elijah Muhammad, and Allah, the Father, such as "show and prove," "break it down," "right and exact," "word life," and "word" along with revelations from "Lost-Found Muslim Lesson No. 2" and the Supreme Mathematics and Alphabet, are part of the DNA of rap and, consequently, the global language and identity of hip hop.[20] Similar to the wide dissemination and misinterpretation of the meaning of "G," "Sun," which is a Five Percent term of respect and recognition for the Africana man, who is symbolized by the Sun because of his life-giving power,[21] became widely used and eventually confused with the biological affiliation "son." In Wu-Tang Clan's "Wu-Gambinos," Method Man makes it clear that a divine association is intended when he explains, "I call by brother Sun 'cause he shine like one."[22]

While the deeper meanings of "Sun," "word is life," and "right and exact" may elude the minds of many, for some these terms serve as symbols and signposts that reveal pathways to knowledge of self. With a powerful cocktail of banging beats, tight rhymes, and knowledge of the divine self, African American rappers rebirthed Raap, and thanks to their mastery of lyricism and symbolism, rapping Raap created lyrical labyrinths that their audiences could navigate to arrive at the doorway of their divinity. The RZA asserts that "[a]bout 80 percent of hip-hop comes from the Five Percent."[23] Taking seriously the duty of civilizing the uncivilized, and following the lead of the ancient Raap, Five Percenters found rap music to be the perfect vehicle for transmitting the wisdom, knowledge, and understanding necessary to facilitate the proliferation of Divinity.

Conversing With the Continent

For decades, members of both the Nation of Islam and the Nation of Gods described their ethnicity as "Asiatic," a term popularized by Noble Drew Ali, the founder of the Moorish Science Temple of America.[24] "Asiatic" was a comforting concept to individuals who had been taught to shun associations with Africa and to be ashamed of their African identity, culture, and origin. However, in the late eighties hip hop turned to its African geographical, intellectual, and genotypical roots and found there infinite sources of political empowerment, philosophical depth, and pride. One group of hip hop Gods who held up to African Americans a mirror that reflected their true identity and depth is X Clan.

Eschewing the dubious concept of "Asiatic," Brother J, the group's wordsmith, proclaims his ethnicity and power to be "African," in fact, "*very* African," and he invites listeners to "step in Brother's temple see what's happenin'."[25] X Clan knows that in order for Africana peoples to understand their divinity they need to know and embrace the many African Gods who brought them into existence and who are residing inside of them and awaiting actualization. Consequently, X Clan's songs repeatedly invoke such African Gods as Ptah, Ra, Atum, Amen, Ausar, and Aset; and the group's Òrìṣà, or select guiding God, is Èṣù Ẹlẹ́gbára, the Yoruba Trickster Deity. Henry Louis Gates, Jr. introduced the Western academic world to Ẹlẹ́gbára with his book *The Signifying Monkey*, but Ẹlẹ́gbára has long been one of Pan-Africa's most well-known, revered, and frequently invoked Gods, and his significance is highlighted by X Clan. In addition to invoking Ẹlẹ́gbára with samples of Haitian praisesongs and Brother J summoning the God outright—"Ẹlẹ́gbà! Meet me at the roads"[26]—Ẹlẹ́gbára is present in the very name and the genesis of the group. The "X" of X Clan is not a reference to an unknown African identity; it represents the home of Ẹlẹ́gbára, the God who resides at the literal and metaphysical crossroads of existence.[27]

Protected by the red, black, and green of African liberation and armed with the ankh, the Kemetic key of life and symbol of the mysteries of the universe, X Clan enlightens multitudes. Most significantly, they impart upon Blackness something deeper than mere beauty. By incorporating the tenets of the Five Percent with traditional African spiritual systems, science, and cosmology, X Clan makes it clear that the inherent divinity of Africana peoples is not an expression of neo-religious egomania but a reality that is as ancient as the African self. By embracing its African roots, X Clan does precisely what Allah, the Father, did with the teachings of Fard and Muhammad; the group builds upon and expands the lessons of its forerunners. Additionally, the charge that is arguably the most important to the Gods remains intact, for in the song "Grand Verbalizer, What Time Is It?" Brother J reveals that X Clan is ever-journeying "To the East" with the goal of "Teaching Gods to be / What it was, what it is, and again shall be."[28]

The members of X Clan are more than rappers; they are educators who, by "making God-music in sync with the universe,"[29] instruct their listeners about Pan-Africanism and African history, revolutionaries, ontology, and cosmology as well as the power of their numinosity. Taking a verse from X Clan's lyrical scriptures and highlighting the relationship between identity and divinity, hip hop duo dead prez marries geopolitical, personal, and artistic directives in the song "I'm A African." After making explicit both their ethnicity and identity—"I'm a African / Never was a African American"—and the fact that knowledge of self brings cultural and political awareness, dead prez inquires of its audience, "You a African? / Do you know what's happenin?"[30] With "I'm A African," dead prez, in its characteristically unadorned and intense style which is described as "natty dread lock / fuck-a-cop hip hop" as well as a "socialist movement" to which one can "bounce,"[31] offers a powerful example of the original purpose of hip hop—to educate, provoke, and elevate the community.

Understanding hegemony's pull on Africana youths and the oblivion that awaits those who have been boiled in the Great American Melting Pot, dead prez consistently educates its audience about identity politics. The aptly named M-1 of the hip hop duo conflates pride in his origin and identity with his spiritual-political imperative in the song "Psychology" as he proclaims, "Fuck what you heard, I'm from Africa / This ain't no act, it's mathematical."[32] M-1 does not embrace his African identity because it may increase his record sales: His ethnicity is an indisputable Supreme Mathematical fact that signifies his divinity. Not only is M-1's identity not alterable by time, circumstance, or dislocation, but it naturally endows him with political purpose that, far from a window-dressing for demagoguery, is "past the Black radical."[33] Emphasizing the shared sociopolitical goals of Africana freedom fighters and Gods, M-1's level of consciousness and dedication to the struggle are also evident in his name which is also his weapon of choice. He reveals that he chooses M-1 because it is a "practical" tool for his work, and utilitarianism is the cornerstone of revolutionary praxis.

Choosing the functional over the flashy is a recurrent theme of dead prez, and this philosophy extends to the group's critique of formal education and its hallowed halls. As former students of Florida A & M University, M-1 and stic.man of dead prez are aware of the fact that Western education is often anti-intellectual and routinely anti-African and is not designed to educate students about African history and contributions to world civilization, let alone reveal paths for self-actualization and manifestation of destiny. As the chorus of dead prez's "They Schools" confirms: "They schools ain't teaching us what we need to know to survive / They schools don't educate; all they teach the people is lies."[34] Rather than struggle to revise slave-making curricula, dead prez shares with its audience the revolutionary skills and the supreme mathematical understanding of the world that are mainstays of the syllabi of the Five Percent.

At first listen, one would be more inclined to associate dead prez with the Black Liberation Army than the Nation of Gods. But not only are the members of dead prez Gods whose tracks are God-produced and who deftly encode God-symbolism in their lyrics, but the group's messaging reveals the inherent interconnectedness and shared values of Africana movements that many have categorized as disparate.[35] While the necessities of physical and political combat are recurrent themes in dead prez's lyrics, the duo effectively uses its art as bullets and cudgels in the war for a complete liberation that is born of a true education.

Despite the ever-escalating cost of tuition, education is free. Public libraries, community wisdom keepers, ciphers, and consciousness-raising rap albums are some of the various educational outlets that are available to all.[36] Indeed, one can and should consider rap from Raap as course materials required for matriculation in the school of the Gods. The significance of education and elevation in rap is also apparent in Reflection Eternal's song "2000 Seasons" which is a dialogue between the group and Ayi Kwei Armah, the Ghanaian author of the historical novel *Two Thousand Seasons*.

Talib Kweli of Reflection Eternal frames his rap with Armah's wisdom as the song begins with Kweli reading from *Two Thousand Seasons'* prologue:

> For whom do we aspire to reflect our people's death? For whose entertainment shall we sing our agony? In what hopes? That the destroyers, aspiring to extinguish us, will suddenly suffer conciliatory remorse at the sight of their own fantastic success? The last imbecile to dream such dreams is dead, killed by the saviors of his dreams.[37]

Kweli makes it clear that his song "2000 Seasons," like its literary progenitor, will not be an exhibition of how to dance in one's chains or sing eloquently in a cage. "2000 Seasons" will promote honest self-evaluation and demand holistic evolution.

Kweli begins his rap, proper, by defining himself in veiled Five Percenter terminology: "I'm not a human being into no spiritual shit / Spiritual being manifested as a human, that's it."[38] Guided by his spiritual consciousness, Kweli informs members of his audience that the majority of them—85%, perhaps—are "volunteer slaves" in a nation that advertises itself as the leader of the free world.[39] Under the façade of blinding bling and abundant booty is the diseased, crippled, blighted reality that Africana people are stumbling and struggling in an annihilation campaign that is many millennia old. Kweli reveals that while the West's reign of terror is fomented by the manipulation of laws, "psychologies of war," and high technological means of destroying entire nations and ethnic groups, he places his confidence in "war tactics" like those of "Shaka Zulu" and in African science and technology.[40]

As evidence of the technological and architectural superiority of the African ancients and their creations, Kweli offers irrefutable proof: "The Leaning Tower of Pisa and the Pyramids of Giza? / No comparison."[41] Kweli reminds his audience of the permanence of the only one of the seven ancient wonders that is still in existence. Not only is the Great Pyramid the most perfectly constructed building in the world, but it is impervious to all threats including fortune-seeking thieves, 747s, earthquakes, tornadoes, *ad infinitum*. Most important, Kweli cues his listeners in to the fact that the pyramids are the product of African genius—his genius. This is important because so many Africana peoples believe the lie that they are "niggers" and the fabrication that Egypt is in Europe that they are not aware of their vast contributions to world history, architecture, and civilization.[42]

Armah's *Two Thousand Seasons* gives an unflinching account of the plight of African victims of the West and the brainwashed masses who believe the propaganda that America is "God's Own Country."[43] Some twenty-six years after *Two Thousand Seasons* was published, Kweli finds that the mirage-fronted quicksand about which Armah warned his audience continues to swallow Africana people whole. Kweli describes the West as undertaking a "genocide mission" that has left innumerable fathers "missing" and countless sisters "whoring."[44]

Throughout his lyrical quest to inform eighty-fivers about their ancient identity and their current misdirection, Kweli receives guidance from Armah. In *Two Thousand Seasons*, Armah describes the desert and its inhabitants as being synonymous with disease, death, and destruction. Kweli informs his audience that the Sahara's sands stretch across the sea to clog the brains and blind the eyes of America's hip hop nation. Kweli finds himself rapping against the grain to an audience that is blissfully blighted and blinded by the desert's neon mirage, an audience that is "stuck off in America freezing for like 2000 seasons."[45]

Kweli uses castigation as a tool to spark self-evaluation and liberation as he accuses members of his audience of "raping and crossbreeding," "deceiving and misleading," and "causing mass confusion, drug abusing."[46] Those who are not killed by their excesses find themselves "all caught up in institutions."[47] Many individuals are introduced to their divinity while they are incarcerated, so Kweli's reference to the prison industrial complex has powerful resonance: Even those who have completely defiled themselves and others can find a mirror that reflects their actual identity and their hidden divinity. No matter the level at which one currently subsists, Kweli reveals that the path out of Babylon's dystopic abyss is knowledge of self and recognition of one's divinity and its attendant responsibilities. Kweli closes "2000 Seasons" by informing his audience that his lyrics are not written to please the Artists and Repertoire executives of record companies or to fit a commercial formula. He uses his lyrics as literal "catch phrases" to capture, captivate, and initiate the transformation of as many people as possible.

As the Nation of Gods and the hip hop nation grew intellectually, references to the African and Divine blossomed; this is especially true of neo-soul artists who often meld poetry, rhythm and blues, and Five Percent philosophy into a heady blend. D'Angelo is one of the most well-known artists of this genre, and in *Voodoo*, his second album, there are both veiled and overt references to Five Percent wisdom. In the song "Devil's Pie," D'Angelo invokes "Lost-Found Muslim Lesson No. 2" and warns, "With eighty-five dumb and blind / There can be no compromise."[48] "Devil's Pie" is an appropriately titled complex account of a person who has knowledge of self but is caught between embracing the "devil's" temptations and the Gods' obligations. When D'Angelo admits in the song, "I myself feel the high of all that I despise," he is speaking as a victim of the snares of two thousand seasons of orchestrated destruction and depravity.

The Sahara's blinding sandstorm may cause him, and all of us, to drift, but it will not obliterate from his consciousness D'Angelo's knowledge of his origin, identity, and divinity. In the song "Africa" D'Angelo muses on the tragedy of being an African who is not only dislocated and "far from home" but who is also living in a land "meant for many men not my tone."[49] Although he is geographically separated from the continent where Voodoo, philosophy, culture, mathematics, and language were born, D'Angelo recognizes that within him are the tools for eternal healing, re-membering, and numinosity, and he proclaims, "Blood of God is my defense / Let it drop down to my seed."[50] The divine blood to which D'Angelo refers is his own. Within him are abundant life-giving and life-sustaining tools that comprise the foundation of his existence and that directly support the life of his "seed," the son to whom "Africa" is dedicated. With his divine and empowered blood, D'Angelo has the ability to protect his progeny "for all eternity."[51] Rather than seeking solace in a symbolic soaking in Jesus' blood, D'Angelo agrees with the Five Percenters that "knowledge and wisdom, understanding's what we need."[52]

In the song "Africa" D'Angelo reveals that his son, like D'Angelo himself, is on a curvilinear mission to heal, evolve, and elevate, and his duty is to prepare his son for the divine self-cognizance that will lead him to "remember what [he] already [knows]."[53] The pair is not only bound in their future development, but they share an ancient relationship that predates their terrestrial births. D'Angelo concludes "Africa" by telling his son, "You and my soul are one / Through all the time and history."[54] D'Angelo uses the song "Africa" to forge an eternal cosmic bond that re-members the Continent to himself and to his son, and he uses the power of song and encoding to educate his progeny about the daunting struggle, divine inheritance, and eternal obligations that await him. Numerous Africana worldviews hold that, while they are in the spiritual realm, children select the parents that they need or want to be born to.[55] Appreciative of his son's decision to spend his life with him, D'Angelo closes "Africa" by offering his thanks to his progeny.

Gods of Rap at War

While there are many moving Five Percent-oriented songs about love, exuberance, and grace—Erykah Badu's "Ye Yo," Lord Jamar's "The Sun," and Wu-Tang Clan's "Sunlight" are rich examples—the majority of the Gods' songs are replete with reminders that Africana people are at war.

When one contrasts Africans' historical accomplishments and their contributions to humanity and world civilization to their inglorious exile to foreign lands and the physical and mental slaveries to which they have been and continue to be subjected on the Continent and throughout the world, it is easy to understand the Gods' focus on battle.

Elijah Muhammad repeatedly stressed to his congregation the importance of preparing for Armageddon. He argued that rather than fighting for America in any of its cyclically fomented wars, "the American Negro should be saving his energy and ammunition for 'The Battle of Armageddon,' which will be waged in the wilderness of North America. This battle—and this is one of the central teachings of the Nation of Islam—will be for freedom, justice, and equality. It will be waged to success or under death."[56] Despite the numerous distractions in this era, the Gods stay on message, and while commercial entertainers are busy gyrating into oblivion, the Gods are oiling and loading lyrical and literal machine guns.

In Killarmy's song "Allah Sees Everything," Islord demands his audience wake up and realize, "We in the middle of a war zone, Black," and the battlefield was created and is dominated by the "Caucasian man."[57] Dismissing the Christian trinity as mere myth, Islord makes it clear that all the Africana man has is "one man," but that individual is the true and living God who is equipped with spiritual and material weaponry. Having initiated his listeners into themDivineselves, Islord leads them to war: "With your God U Now to god you right now / Cock back with off safety one in the head / Enough said."[58] Islord employs compelling plays on words to emphasize the Africana man's ultimate obligation. The phrase, "God U Now" is a Supreme Alphabetical representation for the word "gun."[59] Following his encoded call to arms, Islord uses elision to meld the words "guard" and "god" and verbalize and make active one of the most powerful nouns in the English language.[60] The phrase, "to god you right now," is a reiteration of the fact that salvation is the responsibility of the individual, and, as such, the powers of guarding and saving are intrinsic characteristics of every Warrior God.

African history is replete with Warrior Gods. Kemet's Ausar, the Lord of Perfect Blackness, and Ramses the Great enjoy eternal regard. The Kandake, or Divine Queen Rulers, of Kush overawed Alexander of Macedonia and stunned Augustus Caesar into submission.[61] Ògún, the Yoruba God of iron, technology, and weaponry, and Ṣàngó, the Yoruba God of divine retribution, are invoked on every continent. Ọya is the Yoruba God of transformation who is praised as "the wife who is fiercer than the husband" and the "woman who grows a beard on account of war."[62] Niger's Saraounia Aben Soro, the Queen Who Instills Fear in the Hearts of Her Enemies, confounded French colonizers.[63] The dislocated descendants of these and countless other African Warrior-Gods find themselves in foreign lands fighting wily foes.

Gil Scott-Heron reveals the nebulous nature of the war in his song "Winter in America." He describes a terrorized and demoralized country in which "[a]ll the healers done been killed or put in jail," but rather than rail against these injustices, the masses mill about befuddled and lost: "Ain't nobody fighting 'cause nobody knows what to save."[64] Winter provides the perfect symbol for the West's literal and figurative relationship with Africana peoples as even the climate is hostile to African existence. In Goodie Mob's song "Black Ice (Sky High)" Andre 3000 muses, "There's even lower levels you can go / Take Sun People put 'em in the land of snow,"[65] and provides a poignant reminder that the concept of the "African American" is a creation born largely of forced exile. One could effectively argue that African Americans are not and cannot be fully at home in America and that living in the West constitutes a perpetual assault against the nature, humanity, and divinity of Africana peoples.

Social psychologist Wade W. Nobles describes Africana peoples as being held hostage in America and asserts that if one calculates from the mid-1700s, when it is thought that enslaved Africans were first brought to America, to the mid-1990s when Nobles was writing, "African American families have been held hostage for more than 89,000 days."[66] Nobles offers not only a sobering tally but also a remarkably appropriate description of America's relationship to its Africana citizens. As disturbing as Nobles' assessment of this monumental tragedy is, the reality is more chilling. As William Loren Katz reveals in *Black Indians: A Hidden Heritage*, enslaved Africans first arrived in the United States of America in 1526 courtesy of an enslaver named Luis Vasquez de Ayllon.[67] With this information, the hostage crisis becomes one of 177,025 days and counting: The Battle of The American Winter has been lengthy indeed.

While some individuals are blissfully oblivious to the struggle and others are too dazed to stand and defend, some warriors have amassed *Silent Weapons for Quiet Wars*,[68] and this title of a Killarmy album serves as a code for the covert battle being fought against Western world domination, and it reassures listeners that African Gods are eternally equipped with weaponry that protects, educates, and elevates. In the song "Dangerous Mindz" from the Gravediggaz album *The Pick, the Sickle and the Shovel*, Too Poetic informs his audience that the oppressors who are not slain by an army of poor righteous teachers will be exterminated by the omniscient forces of justice and reciprocity: "[E]vil men will soon be on the receiving end of Universal Law."[69] Too Poetic enjoins his listeners to recognize their divinity and the responsibilities and accompany divinity and join him in battle: "I'm callin' on the meek and the poor / to fight back and never forfeit the day you have to go to war."[70]

In his verse on "Dangerous Mindz," The RZA invokes Nimrod to assist him in the annihilation of opponents: "[I] cause war like the grandson of Kush," and he celebrates success in battle with a ritual that revises pagan European practices: "I'm hangin' devils' heads on a evergreen bush."[71] The RZA traces his genealogy to Nimrod, who is described in the Bible as an African hunter, warrior, ruler, and master architect who is the progeny of Kush, the African empire-builder. In addition to having knowledge of his own ancestry and divinity, The RZA is aware that holidays like Easter and Christmas have little if any tie to the Christian religion; they are holdovers of pagan Caucasian rituals. Consequently, after invoking Nimrod to facilitate the destruction of ten percenters, The RZA takes the Christmas tree back to it pagan roots, so to speak, but with a twist: He decorates the tannenbaum with the heads of vanquished ten percenters.

The cultural awareness, lyrical élan, and political depth of the Gravediggaz's lyrics cannot be found in commercial rap. But it is interesting to note that the philosophies of the Gods can be found in various Africana cosmologies, worldviews, and artistic genres. A resounding example of shared philosophy and political directive surges in the reggae classic, "Get Up, Stand Up" by Bob Marley and Peter Tosh. The entire song constitutes an attack on the "heavenly father" myth and a demand for the listener to stop praying, fully self-actualize, and fight. In the second verse Marley chastises people who think a "Great God will come from the skies" to liberate and glorify humanity.[72] He urges his listeners to manifest their own divinity in their lifetimes. Peter Tosh is even more forthright when in the third verse he compares Christianity to a con game designed to obfuscate the fact that "Almighty God is a living man."[73] Not only does Tosh make it clear that he is not fooled, but his lyrics serve as a wake-up call to his audience who may have been lulled to sleep by the lies of ten percenters and by the mewling of eighty-fivers.

"Get Up, Stand Up" is one of the most popular and respected songs in the world, and it is a song fully in accord with Five Percent philosophy. Jah Rastafari is routinely described as being either a supernatural entity or Haile Selassie, but Mutabaruka, the renowned Jamaican poet, actor, activist, philosopher, and Rasta, reveals that those associations are erroneous and the result of christianized misinterpretations and political manipulation.[74] In an interview with Ian Boyne of "Religious HardTalk," Mutabaruka demystifies the concept of Jah and avers, "Man is really a divine being in earth. There is no entity outside of himself that is signaling him."[75] Mutabaruka goes on to assert that not only does religion prevent human beings from reaching their full potential as Divinities, but also that the world would be a better place without the Bible and religion "because the search for self does not lie in a supernatural connection with any being outside of yourself."[76]

The RZA echoes Mutabaruka's findings and argues that divisiveness and strife are inherent aspects of religion. Exhibiting his knowledge of etymology, The RZA reveals that the problem with religion originates in the word's root, as religion "basically means to rely on something. If you're relying on anything other than yourself you're always gonna have a problem."[77] To avoid being dependent on any person, place, or thing, Five Percenters stress the fact that they are not a religious organization but a way of life; that way of life is I.S.L.A.M., an acronym that can be translated through the Supreme Alphabet in a number of ways, including *I Self Lord Am Master*, *I Stimulate Life And Matter*, and *I Sincerely Love Allah's Mathematics*. In the organic holistic worldview of the Five Percent and Mutabaruka, the very concept of religion is antithetical and opposed to divinity.

One could glean from Mutabaruka's assertions that the most arduous and rewarding spiritual journey one will ever make will occur internally; for there, inside the infinitude of the Self, are the powers, weaponry, skills, intellect, and wisdom of the ages. Perhaps it is the case that with knowledge of one's identity and responsibilities as an Eternal Immortal, the wars in which one is engaged take on a different character. The chorus of Wu-Tang Clan's song "Impossible" celebrates the fact that the Gods will always be victorious: "You can never defeat the Gods / Impossible for you to defeat the Gods."[78] Given this, one could argue that the real Battle of Armageddon, the real jihad or struggle, has more to do with the Gods' personal and communal actualization than with physically destroying ten percenters.

Killarmy's apocalyptic charge "Wake Up" offers a stunning exposition of earthly and cosmic battles underscored with codes as dense and layered as Dark Star Sirius B and delivered with the intensity of an AK-47. But in his verse, Hell Razah lets his listeners pause and peer into the cosmos and the future. Hell Razah describes the Gods' unification as facilitating the ultimate revolution: "Soon as we unite the sky crack / A group of UFOs form the seven in the heavens."[79] The divine unification Hell Razah envisions is one that is intergalactic in scope but still undergirded by the principles of the Supreme Mathematics, as the seven that is formed in the cosmos is a reference to Gods uniting across time and space. Hell Razah reveals that the unity of the Gods will, in and of itself, be sufficient to render the devil irrelevant and signal his "death day." And devils will not die alone; eighty-fivers who refuse to manifest their divinity and wait in vain for an external savior will also be obliterated.[80]

Ninety-Three Million Miles Above—and Beyond

Whether they follow the way of life of the Nation of Gods, Rastafari, or traditional African spiritual systems, the wordsmiths that I discuss have deep knowledge of various philosophies, spiritual systems, organized religions, and sacred texts, especially the Bible. In addition to being familiar with the biblical confirmations of inherent divinity in Psalms 82:6 and John 10:34, the Gods understand the important roles of Africans in Christianity and the Africanity of Jesus Christ. The ubiquitous Caucasian depictions of Jesus may confuse many, but the Gods know that they share both physical and divine attributes with Yashua ben Yoseph.

With a lyrical tribute that marries his divinity to that of Jesus, The RZA in "Dangerous Mindz" reveals that his hair "grows in knotty spirals" and that his feet "resemble Christ's description from the Bible."[81] While The RZA confirms that he, too, can walk on water, his skills surpass those of Jesus. Not only is The RZA "immune to all physical torture" but because he is conversant with modern modes of mobility he can simply hop in his Porsche and drive away from his enemies.[82] The RZA's divinity will not make him assume the posture of an eternal lynching victim; it leads him to the storehouse of existence and moves him to embrace the power of divine creation literally. The RZA, like the African Gods who surround him, understands the power of the penis. Rather than become neutered by religion or raped by religious indoctrination, The RZA revels in the fact that his penis rises up every morning "like a Phoenix."[83] Unlike Christ, The RZA boasts a fully functioning phallus with which he can impart sensual bliss and sexual healing while releasing the sperm which galvanizes the souls of new Gods.

The Gravediggaz's song "Dangerous Mindz" is a study of cohesion. In his verse, Too Poetic reveals that his visage can be found "etched inside of pyramids,"[84] and this is a revelation that every person of African ancestry will have upon visiting the monuments of Kemet. In his attempt to give his audience more tools by which to comprehend his provenance and power, Too Poetic asserts that he is as "ancient as Amen."[85] Too Poetic is not referencing the borrowed closing for a prayer but the primeval source of All, the African God Amen, whose name means "The Hidden One."

As the seafaring Nubians and Kemites of 1600 BCE, Abubakari II and the Malian mariners of 1310 and 1311 CE, and the lyrics of the Gravediggaz and Talib Kweli make abundantly clear, Africana people are a global people. Furthermore, many Africana people understand the significance of being *cosmic* people. To risk stating the obvious, the Earth is in space, and it is part of a gargantuan galactic community. The cosmologies of the Dogon, Mande, BaKongo, Kemites, Kushites, Dagara, Yoruba, and Igbo, to name but a few African ethnic groups, offer ample evidence of a Pan-African knowledge of and relationship with the cosmos. Human beings' interconnectedness with not just the flora and fauna of the Earth but also with the stars, nebula, and galaxies of the universe is a recurrent theme in contemporary Africana life, literature, and lyrics.

In his autobiography *Of Water and the Spirit: Ritual, Magic, and Initiation in the Life of an African Shaman* Malidoma Somé describes the technologies of the West African Dagara people which include suspending the laws of gravity, entering the time-space continuum, sojourning in the spiritual realm, and traveling to and conversing with the stars to obtain detailed information about one's curvilinear existence. Certain Africans are endowed or entrusted, depending upon the manner of acquisition, with such abilities because of their cosmic origins, connections, and responsibilities. Somé elaborates on the purpose of African Divinities and divine technologies:

> I had heard that we usually come to Earth from other planets that are more evolved and less in need of mediation. Our errand on this planet is informed by a decision to partake in the building of the Earth's cosmic origin, and to promote awareness of our celestial identity to others who are less evolved. Our elders taught that some of the universe's inhabitants were as much in need of help as others had the need to help them. This Earth was one of many places where those who needed help could easily become recipients of it.[86]

Mirroring the efforts of Africana writers to re-member themselves to their divine progenitors, hip hop artists remind Earthlings that not only are we not alone, but also that we are not necessarily Earth-bound. When Andre 3000 raps, "Alien can blend right on in with your kin / Look again cuz I swear I spot one every now and then" and when R&B singer Kelis croons, "There is nothing special about me; I am just a little star / If it seems like I'm shining it's probably a reflection of something you already are," they are not speaking metaphorically.[87] Andre 3000 and Kelis are sharing their experiences as cosmic beings with complex earthly relationships, profound powers, and intergalactic responsibilities.

Another Raap of rap who understands his curvilinear and interstellar responsibilities and mobility is Rakim, whose full name is Rakim Allah. In "Guess Who's Back," Rakim uses the wisdom of the Supreme Mathematics to reveal that he is not only God, but he is God to the third power who was "born with three sevens in [his] head."[88] Rakim Allah's three government names—William Michael Griffin—all have seven letters. In the Supreme

Mathematics, the number seven relates to the letter G because it is the seventh letter of the alphabet, and G represents God. With three highly symbolic sevens signifying his identity, Rakim Allah cannot help but manifest his divinity. Furthermore, as the bearer of magnified and compounded numinosity, Rakim Allah has wisdom that "philosophers and anthropologists / astrologists, professors from your smartest colleges / with knowledge of scholarships" cannot comprehend.[89]

The meaning of Rakim Allah's divine name deepens the power of the three sevens endowed on him at birth. In an interview with Wakeel Allah, the author of *In the Name of Allah: A History of Clarence 13X and the Five Percenters*, Rakim states that the Arabic name "Rakim" means "Writer," which befits his occupation as a wordsmith; however, to him, "Rakim" is a compound construction of "Ra," the Kemetic God of the Sun, and "Kim," which signifies Kemet, the Land of the Blacks.[90] The name Allah, which many Five Percenters adopt, provides a clear confirmation of both the bearer's divinity and the divine potential of humanity as the first letters of the five major extremities—*A*rm, *L*eg, *L*eg, *A*rm, *H*ead—spell "Allah." With his identities signifying compounded astronomical and terrestrial divinity, Rakim Allah embraces his destiny as an immortal with eternal responsibilities.

Cognizant of his curvilinearity, Rakim Allah reveals that when his present life is over, he will be interred in Cairo with his notebook, as is befitting a "great God from Egypt."[91] Rakim's notebook is a powerful signifying force not only because it will be the foundation of the "next Bible,"[92] but also because that text solidifies Rakim's cosmic continuity. The Gods of Kemet were interred with scrolls and scriptures that are similar to the rhymes in Rakim's notebook. Caucasian Egyptologists termed these texts "books of the dead," and this mistranslation reveals the inability of Westerners to comprehend the principles of African divinity and immortality.[93] The dead have no need for books: The Kemites were interred with Books of the Coming Forth By Day.[94] These scrolls, incantations, and inscriptions ensure the immortality of the soul through time and space. With his notebook as his vehicle of celestial projection, Rakim Allah will enter the galactic womb, "align with the stars," and be eternally reborn so that he can continue disseminating soul-power as he "bless[es] the mic."[95]

Rakim's lyrical musings on his cyclic numinescence find a complement in Zora Neale Hurston's humble revelations on her immortality and numinosity. In a chapter titled "Religion," that is included in her autobiography, *Dust Tracks on a Road*, Hurston dismisses myths of heaven and death and finds strength in science:

Somebody else may have my rapturous glance at the archangels. The springing of the yellow line of morning out of the misty deep dawn is glory enough for me. I know that nothing is destructible; things merely change form. When the consciousness we know as life ceases, I know that I shall still be part and parcel of the world. I was a part before the sun rolled into shape and burst forth in the glory of change. I was, when the earth was hurled out from its fiery rim. I shall return with the earth to Father Sun, and still exist in substance when the sun has lost its fire, and disintegrated in infinity to perhaps become a part of the whirling rubble of space. Why fear? The stuff of my being is matter, ever changing, ever moving, but never lost; so what need of denominations and creeds to deny myself the comfort of all my fellow men? The wide belt of the universe has no need for finger-rings. I am one with the infinite and need no other assurance.[96]

In her meditation on the sublimity of existence, Hurston reveals herself to be the embodiment of Life. She has no fear of death because in the Africana worldview there is no death, and this fact is also articulated in Western science through two of its most elementary principles: the first law of thermodynamics and the law of conservation of mass. Relying, like the Five Percent, on "actual facts," science, and mathematics, Hurston is not moved by propagandized images of angels, and she eschews prayer because she is equipped with the skills to manifest her destiny—or, to be plain, she is the answer to her prayers. In full possession of what Toni Morrison refers to as "ancient properties,"[97] Hurston was enjoying her immortality long before her body took its last breath.

Jazz legend Sun Ra, whose broadsides and philosophies alternately inspired and were inspired by the Nation of Islam, understood all too well his astronomical nature.[98] Hurston, not unlike Sun Ra, anticipates a dazzling reunion with the Sun of her origins while respecting her infinite bond with the Earth. The Five Percent also revere their cosmic sources of self. In cognizance of their role in fomenting life, the Gods refer to themselves as Suns and Suns of Man.[99] In the song "The Sun," Lord Jamar sings a praisesong to his celestial self: "Just look at me shining as I rise in the East / I welcome you with the universal greeting of 'Peace.'"[100] Although he warns his audience, "Don't look directly at me / My light is too intense," if Lord Jamar's listeners have difficulty comprehending his relationship to the Sun and the Sun's relationship to the Earth, he spells it out—"G – O – D"— repeatedly in the song's chorus.[101]

While male Gods extol their solar supremacy, the Earth is the body often associated with women of the Nation because it rotates around the Sun in a manner that some Gods describe as subordinate. For example, in the Gravediggaz's song "The Night the Earth Cried," Gatekeeper juxtaposes his astronomical superiority to female inferiority when he chants, "I'm God: Control nine planets / Wisdom revolves around me; understanding / Science."[102] While female Five Percenters are honored as "Wisdoms" and as "Earths," some Gods feel the need to delimit the sphere of Wisdom's influence and to diminish Earth's revolutionary significance. However, without the Earth, life as we know it and the rays of the Sun are irrelevant. Furthermore, Woman is the architect of all human existence—including that of Man. In cognizance of the centrality of women to life and numinosity, many male and female Gods refuse to allow the disease of gender bias that has contaminated organized religions to infect their spheres.

Mary Ann Vieira, the female emcee of Digable Planets, adopts a powerful name to describe her divinity: As "Mecca" she is Islam's holiest city, and it is to her that Muslims orient themselves and prostrate in prayer. In Digable Planets' song "9th Wonder," Mecca reveals the astronomical complement to her terrestrial icon, and, in doing so, she shows and proves that her divinity is a supreme mathematical reality: "Now you see that I'm 68 inches above sea level / 93 million miles above these devils."[103] Mecca stands 5 feet 8 inches tall physically, but astronomically she is the Sun, which is 93 million miles from the Earth. Boasting in the core of her being innate life-giving powers that are as essential as those of the Sun, Mecca claims her rightful identity as a God whose brilliance is equal to, if not greater than, that of any male.

Erykah Badu's appeal for gender balance among the Gods in the song "On and On" is achieved with understated pronoun use as she croons: "If we were made in his image / Then call us by our names."[104] There is neither room nor need for gender oppression and hierarchies among the Divine, especially not when women are born, like Badu, with "three dollars and six dimes," which signifies 360 degrees, the sum total of all wisdom, knowledge, and understanding in the world, according to Five Percent philosophy.[105] The repository of women's amalgamated celestial and terrestrial power—the bank of her immeasurable riches—is also the source of all human existence—the womb.

In the song "Ye Yo" Badu elucidates the numinosity of the female anatomy and uses the dynamism of her divinity and humanity to inform Seven Sirius, her appropriately named Sun/son, that she alone has the power to provide him with eternal protection, perfection, and immortality: "The Sun's in the East and the moon reflects / Like the knowledge and wisdom I manifest."[106] With the compounded power of the Sun and Moon resonating in her being, the mother instructs her son: "If you want to go to heaven lay up on my breast / I'm Ye Yo, your Ye Yo."[107] Badu artfully interweaves celestial facts and Five Percent wisdom with neo-Yoruba linguistics for "Ye Yo" is a "Baduazation" of the Yoruba word "Yèyé," which means "Good Mother." With this song, Badu and Seven Sirius become both living manifestations of astronomical forces and the embodiments of divine knowledge and wisdom.

The Sun and the Earth are the celestial symbols most often heralded in Five Percenter lyrics, but the Gods' association with astronomy goes beyond our solar system and extends into infinite ellipse of the cosmos. In the song "Deep Space," Lord Jamar invites his listeners to join him on a trip to the "seventh dimension," the realm of the Gods, where he will ascend "like Christ on the third day."[108] Unlike Jesus, however, Lord Jamar will not disappear into the domain of an amorphous entity. Lord Jamar enters the seventh dimension to reconnect with his cosmic forebears so that he can share their celestial wisdom with his terrestrial audience.

Confessing that "the Milky Way can't satisfy [his] sweet tooth," Lord Jamar counts among his kin "a constellation of stars," and he mocks scientists who can only observe galaxies "from afar" on Earth.[109] Lord Jamar continues his role as intergalactic tour guide in "Deep Space" so that he can lead his audience to the threshold of a fundamental truth: "Let's take a trip through the galaxy / Mystery god is a fallacy."[110] Astronomers, satellites, and space probes have yet to find a gigantic Caucasian man with billowing hair scanning the cosmos and answering some prayers and ignoring others. Like Marley and Tosh before him, Lord Jamar encourages his audience to cease the search for a myth and embrace their actual and factual divinity as does he.

May Raap Bless You

Whether it is afforded respectful recognition or not, the Five Percent Nation is one of the world's most important artistic, spiritual, social, and political institutions. Unlike the Civil Rights and Black Power Movements, the revolution fomented by the Gods is a perpetual one. Rather than place all hope in a leader only to suffer discombobulation and disintegration when that leader is assassinated or expires, the Gods each constitute his own leader, her own God. What is more, the Gods' reciprocal obligation to civilize and enlighten others ensures the birth of new divine leaders— through wisdom if not the womb—everyday.

Lil Wayne, 2 Chainz, and Nikki Minaj may be some of the most recognizable names in hip hop—at the moment—but the Wolof Raap are reincarnated in artists like Killarmy, Mecca, The RZA, Sun Ra, Mutabaruka, and Erykah Badu. The reason that these artists and their songs do not often receive the recognition and rotation of others is because they stand in opposition to the commercialism, hyper-sexuality, racism, and dismemberment that the West glorifies. In a society that strives to convince its inhabitants to "forget where you came from and dance,"[111] the Gods create art that educates listeners about their true identity, their infinite powers, and their soul-deep responsibilities.

The Wolof Raap did indeed survive the horrors of the Middle Passage, and upon every shore that their waters caress, Gods of Rap spring forth. The ancient and sacred praisesongs of the Deities are reborn as underground hits that educate the masses, spark recognition of divine identity, and illuminate the path of evolution. The contemporary Gods, like their forebears, are courageous and formidable. They reveal biting and often frightening truths without fear of reprisals—for what would God fear? Undaunted, unashamed, and under-appreciated, Gods rise from the same waters that nurtured their ancestors and chant celestial promises to the unborn. Thanks to rapping Raap, the umbilical cord that connects Africana peoples with their inherent divinity pulsates with deific beats and throbs with numinous rhymes. Just listen.

Notes

[1] Level featuring Mz. Trill, "Dumb Dick," *Street Credit 2: Disorderly Conduct (The Mixtape),* (Easy Hustle Entertainment, 2010); and Eminem featuring Bizarre, "Amityville," *The Marshall Mathers LP* (Interscope, 2000).

[2] Chalie Boy, "I Look Good" (Dirty 3rd Records, 2009).

[3] Jay Z, "Can I Get A. . ." *Vol. 2 . . . Hard Knock Life* (Roc-a-Fella, 1998); Lil Kim, "Crush on You," *Explicit* (Big Beat/Wea, 1996); and 2 Chainz, "Birthday Song," *Based on a T.R.U. Story* (Island/Def Jam, 2012).

[4] Joseph Holloway and Winifred K. Vas, *The African Heritage of American English* (Bloomington: Indiana University Press, 1993), 142.

[5] Molara Ogundipe, "The Sacred and the Feminine: An African Response to Clément and Kristeva," in *The Sacred and the Feminine: Imagination and Sexual Difference*, edited by Griselda Pollock and Victoria Turvey-Sauron (New York: I. B. Tauris, 2008), 95.

[6] Ogundipe, "The Sacred and the Feminine," 96.

[7] August Wilson, "Preface," *King Hedley II* (New York: Theatre Communications Group, 2000), x.

[8] Maulana Karenga, "The African Intellectual and the Problem of Class Suicide: Ideological and Political Dimensions," in *African Culture: The*

Rhythms of Unity, edited by Molefi K. Asante and Kariamu W. Asante (Trenton: Africa World Press, 1985), 92–93.

[9] The blues was born in the same region of Africa as rap. For a resonant revelation of the African origins of the blues see *The Blues: Feel Like Going Home*, directed by Martin Scorsese (PBS, 2003). Also read Robert Farris Thompson's discussion in *Flash of the Spirit: African and Afro-American Art and Philosophy* (New York: Vintage, 1983), 104. For information on the development of rock and roll and heavy metal from the blues, see *"Can't You Hear the Wind Howl?" The Life and Music of Robert Johnson*, directed by Peter Meyer, narrated by Danny Glover (Winstar, 1998), and listen to Jimi Hendrix!

[10] In 2010 President Museveni dazzled his constituents and the world when he offered a freestyle rap to show that the genre has deep East African roots. For Museveni's original rap, see <http://www.youtube.com/watch?v=B3fSwwPArqo&NR=1> accessed 24 October 2012. For the remix, see <http:// www.youtube.com/watch?v=3Bj OHc_R0PA> accessed 24 October 2012.

[11] "Nation of Gods" is the phrase that I coined and prefer to use because it positions males and females equally as Gods—no sexist language, no hierarchy, just Gods. See Teresa N. Washington, *Manifestations of Masculine Magnificence: Divinity in Africana Life, Lyrics, and Literature* (Oya's Tornado, 2014), 127–128.

[12] Elijah Muhammad, "I Want To Teach You," *The Final Call Online*, 20 March 2014 <http://www.finalcall.com/columns/hem/teach_you.htm> accessed 10 August 2011. Capitalization is retained from the original.

[13] Quoted in Louis E. Lomax, *When the Word is Given. . .* (New York: Signet, 1963), 108–109.

[14] W. D. Fard and Elijah Muhammad, "Lost-Found Muslim Lesson No. 2," *The Nation of Islam*, 20 February 1934 <http://www.thenationofislam .org/muslimlessontwo.html> accessed 19 December 2007.

[15] Ntozake Shange, *for colored girls who have considered suicide/when the rainbow is enuf: a choreopoem*, in *Totem Voices: Plays from the Black World Repertory*, edited by Paul Carter Harrison (New York: Grove Press, 1989), 274.

[16] Fard and Muhammad, "Lost-Found Muslim Lesson No. 2."

[17] Master Fard Muhammad, *The Supreme Wisdom Lessons*, The Nation of Islam <http://www.thenationofislam.org/supremewisdom.html> accessed 30 October 2012. See also Wakeel Allah, *In the Name of Allah: A History of Clarence 13X and the Five Percenters* (Atlanta: A-Team Publishing, 2007), 152–154.

[18] Michael Muhammad Knight, *The Five Percenters: Islam, Hip Hop and the Gods of New York* (Oxford: Oneworld, 2007), 49–64.

[19] Allah, *In the Name of Allah*, 278–292.

[20] The RZA, *The Wu-Tang Manual* (New York: Penguin, 2005), 43 and Allah, *In the Name of Allah*, 315–317.

[21] Allah, *In the Name of Allah*, 141.

[22] Wu-Tang Clan, "Wu-Gambinos," *Wu-Chronicles* (Priority, 1999).

[23] The RZA, *The Wu-Tang Manual*, 43.

[24] "Moorish Science Temple of America, Inc." *Moorish Science Temple of America, Inc.* 30 August 2008 <http://www.moorishsciencetempleof americainc.com/MoorishHistory.html> accessed 6 May 2012.

[25] X Clan, "Grand Verbalizer, What Time Is It?" *To the East Blackwards* (4th and Broadway, 1990).

[26] X Clan, "Tribal Jam," *To the East Blackwards* (4th and Broadway, 1990).

[27] Davey D, "Interview with Brother J of X-Clan," *Davey D's Hip Hop Corner: Anti Thug* <http://www.daveyd.com/interviewbrotherj.html> accessed 10 August 2011.

[28] X Clan, "Grand Verbalizer, What Time Is It?"

[29] X Clan, "Tribal Jam."

[30] Dead Prez, "I'm A African," *Let's Get Free* (Relativity, 2000).

[31] Dead Prez, "I'm A African."

[32] Dead Prez, "Psychology," *Let's Get Free* (Relativity, 2000).

[33] Dead Prez, "Psychology."

[34] Dead Prez, "They Schools," *Let's Get Free* (Relativity, 2000).

[35] Mat Caputo, "dead prez: Let's Get Free 10th Anniversary Feature," *Hip Hop DX*, 30 July 2010 <http://www.hiphopdx.com/index/interviews/i d.1575/title.dead-prez-lets-get-free-10th-anniversary-feature> accessed 12 August 2011.

[36] Music can be heard for free from various internet sites like YouTube, which may also include videos. One can listen to and learn from the music while one saves the money to *purchase the music and support the artists*. It is also possible to buy individual songs for under a dollar and get one's divine artistic fix while respecting the vessel of artistry!

[37] Ayi Kwei Armah, *Two Thousand Seasons* (London: Heinemann, 1973), xiii.

[38] Reflection Eternal, "2000 Seasons," *Fortified Life/2000 Seasons* (Rawkus/UMGD, 2002).

[39] Reflection Eternal, "2000 Seasons."

[40] Reflection Eternal, "2000 Seasons."

[41] Reflection Eternal, "2000 Seasons."

[42] While shopping at a home improvement store 31 March 2010 I had a discussion with an African American woman about fifty years of age who revealed, "I've been to Egypt but not to Africa." Shocked that there were still people who did not know that Egypt is in Africa—including people who had visited the Continent—I launched into a mini history/geography lesson about not only where Egypt is but also about the Africans who created it and where they are now.

[43] While I was a doctoral student at Obafemi Awolowo University in Nigeria, a huge banner that was flown on the "white house" building that housed the electrical electronics department read, "AMERICA: God's Own Country."

[44] Reflection Eternal, "2000 Seasons."

[45] Reflection Eternal, "2000 Seasons."

[46] Reflection Eternal, "2000 Seasons."

[47] Reflection Eternal, "2000 Seasons."

[48] D'Angelo, "Devil's Pie," *Voodoo* (Virgin, 2000).

[49] D'Angelo, "Africa," *Voodoo* (Virgin, 2000).

[50] D'Angelo, "Africa."

[51] D'Angelo, "Africa."

[52] D'Angelo, "Africa."

[53] D'Angelo, "Africa."

[54] D'Angelo, "Africa."

[55] See Washington, *Manifestations of Masculine Magnificence*, 30.

[56] Lomax, *When the Word is Given*, 48.

[57] Killarmy, "Allah Sees Everything," *Dirty Weaponry* (Priority, 1998).

[58] Killarmy, "Allah Sees Everything."

[59] Knight, *The Five Percenters*, 150.

[60] See also Sun Ra, *The Wisdom of Sun Ra*, compiled by John Corbett (Chicago: White Walls, 2006), 125.

[61] Jeremiah Wright, *Africans Who Shaped Our Faith* (Chicago: Urban Ministries, 1995), 272.

[62] William Bascom, *Sixteen Cowries: Yoruba Divination from Africa to the New World* (Bloomington: Indiana University Press, 1981), 459; and John Mason, *Orin Òrìṣà: Songs for Selected Heads* (New York: Yoruba Theological Archministry, 1992), 314.

[63] Washington, *Our Mothers, Our Powers, Our Texts:* 58.

[64] Gil Scott-Heron and Brian Jackson, "Winter in America," *Winter in America* (1974; reissue, Tvt, 1998).

[65] Goodie Mob, "Black Ice (Sky High)," *Still Standing* (LaFace, 1998).

⁶⁶ Wade W. Nobles, "African American Family Life: An Instrument of Culture," in *Black Families*, third edition, edited by Harriette Pipes McAdoo (Thousand Oaks: Sage, 1997), 85.

⁶⁷ William Loren Katz, *Black Indians: A Hidden Heritage* (New York: Atheneum, 1997), 22.

⁶⁸ See Gregory Allan, "Silent Weapons for Quiet Wars: *An Introduction Programming Manual*," *The Lawful Path* <http://www.lawfulpath.com/ref/sw4qw/> accessed 18 August 2011.

⁶⁹ Gravediggaz, "Dangerous Mindz," *Wu-Chronicles: Chapter II* (Wu-Tang Records, 2001).

⁷⁰ Gravediggaz, "Dangerous Mindz.

⁷¹ Gravediggaz, "Dangerous Mindz.

⁷² Bob Marley and Peter Tosh, "Get Up, Stand Up," *Legend: The Best of Bob Marley and the Wailers* (1973; Def Jam, 2001).

⁷³ Marley and Tosh, "Get Up Stand Up."

⁷⁴ Mutabaruka, "Mutabaruka on Religious HardTalk," part 2 of 11, *YouTube* <http://www.youtube.com/watch?v=GzZYAZ3ngKk&NR=1> accessed 12 August 2011.

⁷⁵ Mutabaruka, "Mutabaruka on Religious HardTalk," part 1 of 11, *YouTube* <http://www.youtube.com/watch?v=IdAXGmYRSlY> accessed 12 August 2011.

⁷⁶ Mutabaruka, "Mutabaruka on Religious HardTalk," part 2 of 11, *YouTube*.

⁷⁷ Ismael AbduSalaam, "The RZA: Do the Knowledge (Tao of Wu)," Part 1, *All Hip Hop*, 15 October 2009 <http://allhiphop.com/stories/reviews books/archive/2009/10/15/21979105.aspx> accessed 16 August 2011. See also "religion" and its relationship to "rely," in *The American Heritage Dictionary of the English Language*, third edition, edited by Anne H. Soukhanov, et al. (New York: Houghton Mifflin, 1992), 1525.

⁷⁸ Wu-Tang Clan, "Impossible," *Wu-Tang Forever* (Relativity, 1999).

⁷⁹ Killarmy featuring Sunz of Man, "Wake Up," *Wu-Chronicles* (Priority, 1999).

⁸⁰ Killarmy featuring Sunz of Man, "Wake Up."

⁸¹ Gravediggaz, "Dangerous Mindz," *Wu-Chronicles: Chapter II* (Wu-Tang Records, 2001).

⁸² Gravediggaz, "Dangerous Mindz."

⁸³ Gravediggaz, "Dangerous Mindz."

⁸⁴ Gravediggaz, "Dangerous Mindz."

⁸⁵ Gravediggaz, "Dangerous Mindz."

[86] Malidoma Somé, *Of Water and the Spirit* (New York: Penguin, 1994), 232–233.

[87] OutKast, "Aquemini," *Aquemini* (LaFace, 1998); and Kelis, "Lil Star," *Kelis Was Here* (LaFace, 2006).

[88] Rakim, "Guess Who's Back," *The 18th Letter* (Universal, 1997).

[89] Rakim, "Guess Who's Back."

[90] Wakeel Allah, "It's Been A Long Time: Interview with Rakim Allah," *The A Team's Blog: My Space*, 23 January 2007 <http://www.my space.com/allahteam/blog/221128665> accessed 20 October 2012.

[91] Rakim, "Guess Who's Back."

[92] Rakim, "Guess Who's Back."

[93] Anthony T. Browder, *Nile Valley Contributions to Civilization: Exploding the Myths*, volume 1 (Washington, D. C.: The Institute of Karmic Guidance, 1992), 87.

[94] Browder, *Nile Valley Contributions to Civilization*, 87.

[95] Rakim, "Guess Who's Back."

[96] Zora Neale Hurston, *Dust Tracks on a Road* (1996; reprint, New York: Harper Perennial, 1942), 226.

[97] Toni Morrison, *Tar Baby* (1981; reprint, New York: Quality Paperback Book Club, 1987), 305.

[98] Sun Ra, *The Wisdom of Sun Ra*, 5.

[99] Sun Ra, *The Wisdom of Sun Ra*, 5.

[100] Lord Jamar, "The Sun," *Deep Space/The Corner, The Streets* (Babygrande, 2006).

[101] Lord Jamar, "The Sun."

[102] Gravediggaz, "The Night The Earth Cried," *The Pick, The Sickle, and the Shovel* (BMG Records, 1997).

[103] Digable Planets, "9th Wonder," *Blowout Comb* (Capitol, 1994).

[104] Erykah Badu, "On and On," *Baduizm* (Kedar/Universal Labels, 1997).

[105] Erykah Badu, "On and On."

[106] Erykah Badu, "Ye Yo," *Live* (Umvd Labels, 1997).

[107] Erykah Badu, "Ye Yo."

[108] Lord Jamar, "Deep Space," *The 5% Album* (Babygrande, 2006).

[109] Lord Jamar, "Deep Space."

[110] Lord Jamar, "Deep Space."

[111] Me'Shell NdegeOcello, "Shoot'n Up and Gett'n High," *Plantation Lullabies* (Maverick, 1993).

Works Cited

2 Chainz. "Birthday Song." *Based on a T.R.U. Story*. Island Def Jam, 2012.

AbduSalaam, Ismael. "The RZA: Do the Knowledge (*Tao of Wu*)." Part 1. *All Hip Hop* 15 October 2009. 16 August 2011 <http://allhiphop.com /stories/reviewsbooks/archive/2009/10/15/21979105.aspx>.

Allah, Wakeel. *In the Name of Allah: A History of Clarence 13X and the Five Percenters*. Atlanta: A-Team Publishing, 2007.

Armah, Ayi Kwei. *Two Thousand Seasons*. London: Heinemann, 1973.

Bambara, Toni Cade. "Broken Field Running." *The Sea Birds are Still Alive*. New York: Vintage, 1977. 43–70.

Badu, Erykah. "On and On." *Baduizm*. Umvd Labels, 1997.

-----. "Ye Yo." *Live*. Umvd Labels, 1997.

Bascom, William. *Sixteen Cowries: Yoruba Divination from Africa to the New World*. Bloomington: Indiana, 1981.

The Blues: Feel Like Going Home. Directed by Martin Scorsese. Narrated by Corey Harris. PBS, 2003.

Boston, Stephen W. "And God Said. . ." *The Reluctant Messenger*. 22 May 2011 <http://reluctant-messenger. com/and-God-said.htm>.

"Can't You Hear the Wind Howl?" The Life and Music of Robert Johnson. Directed by Peter Meyer. Narrated by Danny Glover. Winstar, 1998.

Caputo, Mat. "dead prez: Let's Get Free 10th Anniversary Feature." *Hip Hop DX*. 30 July 2010. 12 August 2011 <http://www.hiphopdx.com /index/interviews/id.1575/title.dead-prez-lets-get-free-10th-anniversary-feature>.

Chalie Boy. "I Look Good." Dirty 3rd Records, 2009.

Corbett, John. Introduction. "One of Everything: Blount Hermeneutics and the Wisdom of Ra." *The Wisdom of Sun Ra*. Compiled by John Corbett. Chicago: White Walls, 2006. 5–6.

D'Angelo. "Africa." *Voodoo*. Virgin, 2000.

-----. "Devil's Pie." *Voodoo*. Virgin, 2000.

Davey D. "Interview with Brother J of X-Clan." *Davey D's Hip Hop Corner: Anti Thug*. 10 August 2011 <http://www.daveyd.com/interview brotherj.html>.

dead prez. "Psychology." *Let's Get Free*. Relativity, 2000.

-----. "They Schools." *Let's Get Free*. Relativity, 2000.

De La Soul featuring Red Man. "Oooh!" *Art Official Intelligence: Mosaic Thump*. Rhino, 2000.

Digable Planets. "9th Wonder." *Blowout Comb*. Capitol, 1994.

Eminem featuring Bizarre. "Amityville." *The Marshall Mathers LP*. Interscope, 2000.

Fard, W. D. and Elijah Muhammad. "Lost-Found Muslim Lesson Number Two." *The Nation of Islam*. 20 February 1934. 19 December 2007 <http://www.thenationofislam.org/muslimlessontwo.html>.

Goodie Mob featuring Outkast. "Black Ice (Sky High)." *Still Standing*. LaFace, 1998.

Gravediggaz. "Dangerous Minds." *Wu-Chronicles: Chapter II*. Wu-Tang Records, 2001.

-----. "The Night The Earth Cried." *The Pick, The Sickle, and The Shovel*. BMG Records, 1997.

Holloway, Joseph and Winifred K. Vass. *The African Heritage of American English*. Bloomington: Indiana University Press, 1993.

Hurston, Zora Neale. *Dust Tracks on a Road*. 1942. New York: Harper Perennial, 1996.

Jay Z. "Can I Get A. . ." *Vol. 2 . . . Hard Knock Life*. Roc-a-Fella, 1998.

Karenga, Maulana. "The African Intellectual and the Problem of Class Suicide: Ideological and Political Dimensions." In *African Culture: The Rhythms of Unity*. Edited by Molefi K. Asante and Kariamu W. Asante. Trenton: Africa World Press, 1985. 91–106.

Katz, William Loren. *Black Indians: A Hidden Heritage*. New York: Atheneum, 1997.

Killarmy. "Allah Sees Everything." *Dirty Weaponry*. Priority, 1998.

Killarmy featuring Sunz of Man. "Wake Up." *Wu-Chronicles*. Priority, 1999.

Kelis. "Lil Star." *Kelis Was Here*. LaFace, 2006.

Knight, Michael Muhammad. *The Five Percenters: Islam, Hip Hop and the Gods of New York*. Oxford: Oneworld, 2007.

Level, featuring Mz. Trill. "Dumb Dick." *Street Credit 2: Disorderly Conduct (The Mixtape)*. Easy Hustle Entertainment, 2010.

Lil Kim. "Crush on You." *Explicit*. Big Beat/Wea, 1996.

Lomax, Louis E. *When the Word is Given. . .* New York: Signet, 1963.

Lord Jamar. "The Sun." *Deep Space/The Corner, The Streets*. Babygrande, 2006.

-----. "Deep Space." *The 5% Album*. Babygrande, 2006.

Marley, Bob and Peter Tosh. "Get Up Stand Up." *Legend: The Best of Bob Marley and the Wailers*. Def Jam, 2001.

Mason, John. *Orin Òrìṣà: Songs for Selected Heads*. New York: Yoruba Theological Archministry, 1992.

"Moorish Science Temple of America, Inc." *Moorish Science Temple of America, Inc.* 30 August 2008 <http://www.moorishsciencetempleof americainc.com/MoorishHistory.html>.

Morrison, Toni. *Tar Baby.* 1981. New York: Quality Paperback Book Club, 1987.

Muhammad, Elijah. "I Want To Teach You." *Our Savior Has Arrived.* Chapter 10. *Nation of Islam Settlement No. 1.* 31 July 2008. 10 August 2011 <http://www.seventhfam.com/temple/books/our_saviour/saviour 10.htm>.

Mutabaruka. "Mutabaruka on Religious HardTalk." Part 1 of 11. *YouTube.* 12 August 2011. <http://www.youtube.com/watch?v=IdAXGmYR SIY>.

-----. "Mutabaruka on Religious HardTalk" part 2 of 11. *YouTube.com.* 12 August 2011. <http://www.youtube.com/watch?v=GzZYAZ3ngKk&N R=>.

NdegeOcello, Me'Shell. "Shoot'n Up and Gett'n High." *Plantation Lullabies.* Maverick, 1993.

Nobles, Wade W. "African American Family Life: An Instrument of Culture." In *Black Families.* Third edition. Edited by Harriette Pipes McAdoo. Thousand Oaks: Sage, 1997. 83–93.

Ogundipe, Molara. "The Sacred and the Feminine: An African Response to Clément and Kristeva." In *The Sacred and the Feminine: Imagination and Sexual Difference.* Edited by Griselda Pollock and Victoria Turvey-Sauron. New York: I. B. Tauris, 2008. 88–110.

OutKast. "Aquemini." *Aquemini.* LaFace, 1998.

Rakim. "Guess Who's Back." *The 18th Letter.* Universal, 1997.

Reflection Eternal. "2000 Seasons." *Fortified Life/2000 Seasons.* Rawkus/UMGD, 2002.

Rich Boy, "Throw Some Ds." *Rich Boy.* Interscope, 2007.

The RZA. *The Wu-Tang Manual.* Penguin: New York, 2005.

Shange, Ntozake. *for colored girls who have considered suicide/when the rainbow is enuf: a choreopoem.* In *Totem Voices: Plays from the Black World Repertory.* Edited by Paul Carter Harrison. New York: Grove Press, 1989. 223–274.

Sun Ra. *The Wisdom of Sun Ra.* Compiled by John Corbett. Chicago: White Walls, 2006.

"Supreme Alphabets." *Black Apologetics.* 2007. 10 August 2011 <http://www.blackapologetics.com/mathdetail.html>.

"Supreme Mathematics." *Black Apologetics.* 2007. 10 August 2011 <http://www.blackapologetics.com/mathdetail.html>.

Scott-Heron, Gil and Brian Jackson. "Winter in America." *Winter in America*. 1974. Tvt, 1998.

Somé, Malidoma. *Of Water and the Spirit*. New York: Penguin, 1994.

Soukhanov, Anne H., ed. *The American Heritage Dictionary of the English Language*. Third edition. New York: Houghton Mifflin, 1992.

Thompson, Robert Farris. *Flash of the Spirit: African and Afro-American Art and Philosophy*. New York: Vintage, 1983.

Washington, Teresa N. *Manifestations of Masculine Magnificence: Divinity in Africana Life, Lyrics, and Literature*. Oya's Tornado, 2014.

-----. *Our Mothers, Our Powers, Our Texts: Manifestations of Àjẹ́ in Africana Literature*. Bloomington: Indiana University Press, 2005.

Wilson, August. "Preface." *King Hedley II*. New York: Theatre Communications Group, 2000.

Wright, Jeremiah. *Africans Who Shaped Our Faith*. Chicago: Urban Ministries, 1995.

Wu-Tang Clan. "Impossible." *Wu-Tang Forever*. Relativity, 1999.

-----. "Wu-Gambinos." *Wu-Chronicles*. Priority, 1999.

X Clan. "Grand Verbalizer, What Time Is It?" *To the East Blackwards*. 4th and Broadway, 1990.

-----. "Tribal Jam." *To the East Blackwards*. 4th and Broadway, 1990.

Iṣẹ́ Ògbóni

Asiri Odu

Everyone worked low to the ground and moved like old snakes in the underbrush. There were no marches, speeches, or protests. There was no hashtagging or social networking of any kind, not only because this Work was not about grandstanding, but also because information shared in cyberspace is information soon to be intercepted.

They silently amassed Ah stockpile and had a magnificent cache of weapons that ranged from Glocks, Tech 9s, Uzis and AK 47s to AR 15s, to 30-06s to 357s, 33s and 22s. The weapons they needed but could not attain without attracting attention to themselves, such as grenade launchers, hand grenades, ground to air missiles and launchers, they dreamt about. After his first dream about weaponry, Ra wrote down everything he recalled on his pillow case. He did not stop to think about his writing materials until he had sketched the last design. When Azure woke up and witnessed his epiphany, they began work on a forge.

The plan had backfired. Rather than keeping the inhabitants of Carvah isolated, ignorant, and susceptible to the penetration of the government and its officials, America's racism resulted in the creation of Ah fortress.

Azure, Alteveze, Saddiq, Sims, and Roper and many more Malare students and professors used their classes to network, organize, and strategize. While the community that had served as a buffer between Malare and Carvah looked the same, the interiors of the various abandoned homes were refurbished for the awakened brothers and sisters who poured in. These homes' electricity was supplied by a magnetic generator; the water was courtesy of Malare and rain. To avoid attention, the exteriors of the homes continued to sport falling porches, broken windows, and other signs of dilapidation.

Aint May, Chaka, and Jahmai came to Carvah and brought necessary healing and killing herbs and preparations. Wakynam and members of Kumba came to assist with the holistic healing of the addicts who deserved a chance to shine. Hawa and Danta taught the Carvah Nsibidi and Medu Netcher so that they could shield their writings and communicate freely.

In the midst of all the building, Vlady Cutlass, the VL's Polish coke supplier went missing. Mothers were selling greens and eggplant and corn at Farmer's Market and 3 police officers were found castrated and tied to a light post at the corner of 1st and Church. Relevant Reality was the largest underground hip hop act in the South and Midwest. AhTahn was the label and distributor, and everyone from Diddy to Dupri was seeking out the sextet. As Relevant Reality blew up, so did 20 police cars along with 40 *in situ* officers.

The drug trade spun back on Ogo as its offspring were now its main clientele. Carvah warriors flooded Caucasian suburbs with crack, heroin, and angel dust. Because Ogo manipulated the desegregation laws to Ogoize Nashville Central University (NCU), forcing the HBCU to become 50% Yurugu, it was easy for former gang-bangers to find Caucasian mules and dealers to purchase and then distribute the drugs where they were wanted most. The proceeds went to the fortification of Carvah and arms and ammunition.

Azure and Alteveze were sipping coffee while examining the blueprints for the Lair. When it was finished, the Lair would house the entire Wilson family along with Alteveze, Saddiq, Azure, Ra, Xavier and any Ah who needed a home. The Lair would have 5 stories and be equipped with 9 bathrooms, 16 bedrooms, a salon, a library, shrine, and a rec room for Ògúnian martial arts training and weightlifting. ¾s of the Lair would be underground. The exposed portions of the home would be impenetrable to battering rams and missile blasts.

The Carver collective was filled with carpenters, crafts and drafts persons, engineers, plumbers, electricians, and architects who had been unemployed and struggling long before the so-called great recession of 2008, so building, fortifying, and refurbishing were as effortless as taking a stroll in spring.

Their growth was so meteoric that Azure often felt she was living a dream. She put down her coffee cup and marveled at their power, "After all this time, all this struggle"

"after so many tears, so much sorrow:"

"The revolution is here!" she and Alteveze said at once; their eyes sparkled with dynamism.

"I am so honored to be here, to be alive and a part of this Work."

"This is a movement that so many thought would never come and that many more fought to keep from coming," Alteveze mused.

"And so many gave their lives for this struggle. Many millions gone. Millions upon millions. . ."

"We can finally avenge their deaths and resurrect them in a world worthy of their return. Worthy of their return."

The history of Ah-Tahn destruction over the millennia unfolded in the minds of the collective. Previous lessons largely focused on the achievements of the Ah; now it was necessary to show the hands, the hands of the Ah of Kng piled up at the sterns of small river boats. Hundreds of boats and thousands of hands: Each hand—a tax on inefficient rubber workers; the bodies of the survivors—a tapestry of wasted defiled lives twisted and shattered by the greed of Ogo.

The Tahn saw Yurugu armed to the teeth with weapons inspired by Chinese fireworks. Bullets too large for elephants were aimed at a procession of Zalah warriors. The warriors dance to a rhythm; their feet recall the last Jubah. They are armed with their melanin and their spears; it isn't enough. They are slaughtered. The rise up and are slaughtered again.

They travelled back centuries to Dah, where spiritual power rolled in vibrational waves like the ocean. Now see those who shine become the targets of those who do not. See thousands of mercenary women invade their peaceful neighbors—not to murder them—to steal them so their king can sell them.

Come see the coffles, hundreds of Ah deep. Witness the gory train of enslaved Africans trekking across the ravaged Continent, death marched to be sold like sacks of grain in Nashville, Meridian, Natchez, New York, Alapaha, Cap Haitian, Bahia, Paris, London, Sweden, Italy, Saudi Arabia, Fez, Tripoli.

Visit the leader of the free world and see its unique landscaping techniques: tree limbs blooming corpses with bursting eyes and split and oozing skulls; missing genitalia, fingers, and toes. Disembodied heads line streets. Testicles decorate fences. Mothers dangle from bridges. Fathers sway on light posts.

There are excised penises buried under hardened cement slabs. The sidewalks look innocent, even reassuring, but some of them are hollow, and their spaces contain tales that stones and earth are too ashamed to utter. Listen to the ancestors moaning beneath the streets in New Orleans. Listen to the royalty haggle with the factors at Gorée. Listen to our prices rise and fall with market speculations in London.

In the midst of capitalism's triumphant crushing of divinity, the skies are clouded with birds. Buzzards, Vultures, Black Birds, Jim and Jane Crows, Sparrows, Robins, Pigeons, Doves: See how high they fly! Reaching the stratosphere they resume their human shapes; in the ionosphere they are pure soul. Recharged by the cosmos and its inexhaustible wisdom, power, and purpose, Ah warriors, who are as necessary as the sun, return and continue the fight.

We have endured more than any organism to ever exist on this Earth: And we are still shining. You are complete and complex, not because I created you, my resplendent 1s, but because you used your creative forces to recreate yourselves. Yon, jealousy hates you, thievery slays you, and wickedness betrays you because they cannot *be* you. You are the cosmos: You are the Truth.

You are Tahn. Tahn is a Dah word. It means deceived, duped, seduced, decoyed, and it also means shining. You are shining. That is why so many ancestors have returned in the flesh to rejoin you, to become you. They could not have done otherwise, for your shining is visibly reflected in your melanin, but it is also in the vibrations of your language, your music, your textiles, all of your force. It summons; it embraces; it expands. Your soul is the only spontaneously regenerative force on this planet. Ah Jubah to all Tahn and Ah come and gone and come again. Mo Jubah to all Tahn!

Again and again cases were called and police officers, district attorneys, bailiffs, and judges positioned themselves in court to begin the lucrative racist dispensation of "justice." But where were all of the Black defendants? Why were there only 2 Black court officers present? Before eyes could narrow with consternation or widen with understanding, the courthouse collapsed and all that was within it was obliterated.

The destruction of the courthouse happened at the same time that the governor's mansion, 2 FBI offices, and 4 police stations were leveled in Nashville, Tennessee.

At 5:04 p.m. the previous day, 8 groups of 4 Tahn had maneuvered through underground tunnels to the 8 edifices of oppression. They had prepared the ammonia and fertilizer-based bombs and their computerized detonators 3 nights before. They set in place the exact amount of explosives necessary to implode the buildings so neatly that passersby thought they were witnessing government-authorized controlled detonations.

The CIA was dumbfounded, so they blamed al-Qaida and The Islamic State. Arab-looking people were profiled, detained, tortured, and, after several weeks, released. The general African American community went about its business with a sense of peace and purpose. The encoded 7th line of the song "Ọmọ Ògún" of *Iṣẹ́ Ògbóni* informed all Tahn to stay away from governmental institutions beginning 6 March because those institutions would cease to exist.

7 days after the bombings, every physician, researcher, and intern at Shinally Medical Center was found strapped to operating tables and

gurneys. Their bodies had all been dissected with laser-like precision: 9 body parts for the women; 7 body parts for the men. There was no blood.

Because there were no leads, motives, or explanations for the act or its remarkable meticulousness, officers set fire to Shinally and razed it to the ground. They attributed the deaths to the blaze and the blaze to faulty wiring. The public took great comfort in these lies.

The song "Authority Stealing 7" was written by Ra, encoded by Xaviah, and covertly installed on county jail and private, state, and federal prison computer networks around the world by Jah Sun. At 7 am and 7 pm every day for 7 months the 70 second song played and instructed wardens, parole board members, and corrections officers around the world to release Ah prisoners on July 7 at 7:00 am. With Bill Withers' "Lovely Day" booming from prison PA systems around the world, Gods emerged from dungeons, relocated to skill-specific cells, and went to Work.

The song "This Land Is Your Land," also on the album *Iṣẹ́ Ògbóni*, was encoded with instructions as to how to transform projects and other seemingly vulnerable dwellings into autonomous fortresses from which government overthrow could be affected.

Azure, Xaviah, Saddiq, Alteveze, Ra, and Dr. Sims began working with emerging sister sites in Chicago, Watts, Atlanta, Detroit, Brooklyn, DC, Oakland, LA, and Houston to assist in the mobilization of new sites and cells. The Carvah collective showed their comrades how to use their cities' existing tunnel or sewer and drainage systems to gain covert access to government buildings and police stations. The events that upended Nashville started occurring around the country, and, then, around the world.

The pope hanged himself. . . .

The Riot

Alieu Bundu

I dashed out of the Union Bank in Kaduna State and headed for my Benz that stood at the parking lot, which my father gave me as a gift on the day I graduated from the university five months ago. I eased into the driver's seat, started the car and sped out of the parking lot. Everywhere, people were running and dashing about as though they had gone mad and seeking refuge in whatever structure they could find.

Fifteen minutes before, my colleagues and I were busy tending to customers in the bank, when Hajara, my kid sister, and a fat dark-skinned woman dashed into the bank and told us that another riot between Muslims and Christians had just started. I froze. The first thought that flooded my mind and spilled from my lips when I heard what Hajara said was, "I have to go and save the life of Obinna and those of his family members." My hands were shaking as I put the money that was on the counter into my drawer and locked it.

"Why?" Sidiratu, my co-worker, asked.

My sister saw my anxiety mounting as she answered Sidiratu's question, "Because of what happened last month. Some Christians set a mosque on fire several metres near our school in retaliation for the bombing of the church that took place last month."

"*Yaa* Allah! I have to go and protect Obinna and his family members. The last time he told me some men he didn't know almost succeeded in killing him and his parents. Please, Sidiratu, take Hajara home for me in your car," I said as I fumbled for the car keys in my handbag.

"Sister, don't go! It's dangerous out there. You may run into the hands of bloodthirsty Christians," Hajara warned. Her voice was laced with fear and concern.

"My dear, I have to go. Obinna and his family members may need me. Don't worry. Allah will protect me, okay?" I said and dashed for the door.

Obinna was my boyfriend. We met and fell in love in Kaduna State University. I fell deeply in love with him not only because he always helped me out with my studies, but also because he made me laugh a lot by telling me jokes. Our days in Kaduna State University were full of fun and were still imprinted in my mind, I can still see us walking hand in hand on campus, studying together, attending university functions together. I see the face he made at me as I died with laughter after he finished telling me one of his jokes.

Obinna was an Igbo and a Christian; his parents came from the east and settled in Kaduna as traders. A month after we graduated, Obinna went to my father's house, despite the fact that his father wanted him to marry an Igbo girl, and asked for my hand in marriage.

"*Astagfirullah*[1]! Over my dead body! A *kaffir*[2] won't marry my daughter!" my father thundered.

I sank onto the ground. "Papa, please let me…"

"Get up before I curse you!" he said, snapped his fingers towards Obinna and yelled, "*O ya*, make you get out now before I chop off your head!" His eyes glinted with raw rage.

That evening, after Papa went for a family meeting, I went to Obinna's father's house at Jabu to beg him to forgive my father for treating him in such a despicable manner. When I arrived, I didn't meet him. Once Obinna's parents saw me, their faces grew dark with anger.

"*Ashewo*[3]! Why are you here?" they assaulted me with a chorus of contempt.

"I came to see Obinna."

"He is not at home. By the way, why are you pestering our child, she-goat?" His father said.

"I am not pestering Obinna. We love each other."

"*Tufia!*" Obinna's parents said, snapping their fingers.

"That's absolute nonsense! *Abi, you no dey shame*?! You and Obinna are not compatible. Your affair will bring nothing other than disaster. So leave him alone, okay. Now get out!" his father added. I could see his eyes narrowing with disgust.

"Sir, please. . ."

"Shut your filthy mouth and get out now!" he roared.

Our fathers' reactions strained our relationship, but that didn't stop us from seeing each other. Our love was too strong. In fact, when we met at Obinna's friend Emeka's house the following day, we swore to love and stay with each other forever.

"Please, come what may, don't let your father marry you off to someone else. Try to convince him to let us marry," Obinna said once we finished making our promise. I assured him that I would not marry anyone else, and

I promised him that I would do all I could to change my father's mind. I did stand by my words, but all my efforts were futile.

When I arrived at Obinna's, I shook my head clear of my father's disapproval. I parked the Benz on the road and rushed through the gate into the compound. What I saw once I entered it stopped me short. Bashiru, who was armed with a machete, and two other young guys armed with bayonets, stood staring at a man who was on top of Obinna's mother, raping her. His mother's agonizing moans tore at my soul. Obinna and his father knelt in front of them, their eyes glittered with tears, and their foreheads were creased with anguish.

I went cold. Bashiru was a classmate of mine in Kaduna State University. Shortly after Obinna and I started to date, Bashiru approached me in class one day and confessed his love for me. When I told him that I didn't love him in return and that I was already with someone else, he raged, "So you don't love me? You love that *kaffir* boy, *abi*? I promise you that infidel will pay some day!"

His words that filled my entire being with dread made me agitated, but nobody ever attacked Obinna. A couple of days after we graduated, Bashiru met me at home and told me that he would relocate to Lagos the next day to search for a job. I hadn't set eyes on him until today.

I charged at them like an enraged bull and tried to push the man that was raping Obinna's mother off her stomach. Bashiru pushed me, and I stumbled and fell to the ground.

"It's good you came! I am going to kill this thing in front of you," he sputtered and pointed at Obinna. His face was purple in rage. He laughed loudly. A shiver of revulsion racked my body.

"I came from Lagos three days ago mainly to fulfill my promise!" Bashiru grinned at me before turning his attention to the man raping Obinna's mother, "Man, make you fuck her hard and proper!"

"Please, I beg of you in Allah's name, have mercy," I pleaded as tears stung my eyes.

"No way! Obinna and his family members must pay for screwing you, our Muslim sister!"

"Muslim sister?" I asked myself. *What a phrase!*

Rage bubbled inside me. I had wanted to scream out that I am not a sister to a person who tortures and abuses innocent people for no good reason, but the fear of escalating Bashiru's rage restrained me. So, I begged him again. But it was fruitless. The man continued to rape Obinna's mother until he collapsed on top of her. Once he got up, Bashiru ordered another man to remove his trousers and rape her too. The man did as ordered without hesitation. After they all raped her, one after the other, Bashiru raised his machete and cut off Obinna's father's head in a swoop. The body fell on the ground with a thud and writhed about as blood pumped out like water out of a burst tank. Shocked, I sat transfixed and watched the head of Obinna's father roll across the compound.

Bashiru licked the blood on the machete and laughed. Goose pimples covered my entire body as my stomach flipped. Obinna retched and threw up. Bashiru stared at me and laughed again. His hoarse laughter bounced and resounded around Obinna's father's compound. He kicked Obinna under his belly once he recovered from his fit of laughter and roared, "You are not a good son at all! You knelt here and did nothing as your father and your mother were being tortured!"

He looked at me pointedly. His nostrils flared and his lower lip trembled. "See the person you shunned me for. He is not a man at all, but a sissy. What a shame!"

He stared at Obinna. "Since you don't deserve to be in this world, you are going to die now! Bid your mother farewell now!"

There was a pause. I could feel my heart thumping inside my ribcage. "You don't want to bid her farewell, *abi*? I see." He let out a heavy sigh. "Well, so be it!"

"No!" I roared, bolted onto my feet and rushed up to him as he raised his machete that glinted in the afternoon sunlight. I gripped his mouth with mine and kissed him intensely.

"Please don't kill him!" I pleaded after kissing him for a while. "To make up for shunning you, you can do whatever you want with me here!"

Bashiru's eyes glowed. "Really?"

"Yes."

"Well in that light, let me fuck you in front of your boyfriend. That's the only way to appease me," he said, dropping the machete and reached for the buckle of his trousers. Before the machete stopped clattering, I grabbed it and shoved it into Bashiru's belly.

"Die!" I roared as blood sprang out of his abdomen.

Bashiru gasped and his eyes bulged with horror. I removed the machete and flung it at Obinna who caught it by the handle. Obinna hopped up and whacked off the head of one of Bashiru's men. The other two men broke into a run and headed for the gate as the body of their colleague staggered about. Obinna ran after them but couldn't catch up with them, so he halted, turned and rushed to his father's corpse.

"Father, please forgive me. Bashiru was right . . . I am a useless son. I didn't do anything to save you and Mama," he said. His voice was thick with distress; his eyes gleamed with sorrow.

"Don't talk like that! You didn't do anything because your hands were tied. Get up let me drive you to the train station. You have to leave now before those guys return and kill you and your mother!" I said.

"Son, Laraba is right. You didn't do anything because your hands were tied. Let's get out of this place for good," Obinna's mother said. Her face was drenched in tears.

Obinna exhaled, stood up and we set out for my Benz. I drove towards the train station off Kachia Road. En route, we passed houses that were on fire. Outside some of these houses, dead bodies that were covered in blood were strewn about like piles of trash.

When we arrived at the train station, we met a throng of people struggling to board the train that was east bound. Some carried bundles while others did not. The bodies glistened with sweat, their foreheads creased with horror. Different phrases of the Igbo language pierced the air like gunshots. Once we got out of the car, Obinna flung his hands around me and gave me a tight embrace and said, "Thank you very much. May Jesus Christ bless you grandly; I will never forget you in my entire life."

"Me too, my dear," I said as tears misted my eyes. He kissed me intensely and muttered, "Bye. Hope to see you someday."

"You will soon see me. Where exactly are you heading to?"

"Mbanta, my paternal village."

"I will meet you there as soon as everything calms down, by the grace of Allah."

He smiled warmly at me. "I will be waiting for you, my love." There was a note of sadness in his voice.

He heaved a deep sigh, grabbed his mother's hand and pulled her along the platform. As they entered the train, Obinna halted, turned and waved at me. I waved in return with a smile as tears rolled down my cheeks. Obinna turned and disappeared into the train. Once he did, the engine puffed, and a huge cloud of steam billowed up. As the wheels glided against the tracks, I raised my hand and started to wave. I waved until the train became smaller and smaller, until it became a distant dot.

Notes

[1] [Editor's note: *Astagfirullah* is an Arabic expression that means "I seek forgiveness from Allah." As in the short story, "astagfirullah" is often uttered by someone who opposes or rejects something.]

[2] [Editor's note: *Kaffir* means "non-believer" in Arabic and refers to individuals who are not Muslim. In some regions "kaffir" has also come to signify "Black," and in some lands "kaffir" is the equivalent of "nigger."

See T. N. Washington, *Manifestations of Masculine Magnificence: Divinity in Africana Life, Lyrics, and Literature* (Oya's Tornado, 2014), 276–278.]

[3] [Editor's note: In Yoruba language, *aṣẹ́wọ́* literally means one who (*a*) makes (*ṣẹ́*) money (*owó*); idiomatically, it is translated as prostitute.]

The Wretched Being

Alieu Bundu

On the morning of the fifth anniversary of my Mama's death, while I was lying on my bamboo bed listening to the chirping of the early morning birds as cramps twisted at my stomach in knots, the door opened with a resounding crash. Tida rushed in with a face that was contorted with rage.

"Why are you still in bed?" she demanded in a voice that sent shivers through my entire body, "Have you forgotten what you have to do this morning?"

Tida was my stepmother. Papa married her six months after my Mama's death.

When I was ten, my Mama, a lovely woman died while bringing another life into this world. Before she died, she and I lived a pleasurable life in my Papa's six-roomed mud house, where my Papa, who was a hunter, constantly showered us with love. Each time he went to Makeni, a neighbouring town to sell chunks of meat from game that he had killed on his hunting trips, he would buy my Mama and me *lappas* and jewelry. At night as the moon glowed in the sky, he used to tell us folktales and also sing songs of praise about my Mama's beauty and mine. Unfortunately, everything that held us together fell apart after my Mama died, and my kind and caring Papa didn't only become withdrawn like a recluse but he also started to drink palm wine excessively and he stopped hunting.

Papa met and fell in love with Tida about two months after Mama's death at the wedding ceremony of one of our neighbours in Ropatefu, a neighbouring village two miles away from ours. Four months later, they got married. When Tida and her daughter, Vera, whom she had out of wedlock, came into Papa's household, things became worse for me because both of them started to treat me like a slave under my Papa's roof.

"No, I didn't forget. I can't go to the stream because my stomach aches terribly. My monthly flow started last night," I responded.

"Who cares?" she raged, clenching her fist and thrusting it into my belly. A bolt of pain shot through me and took my breath away. "Get up now and go and fetch the water before I skin you alive!"

I moaned as I climbed out of the bed and headed for our backyard. There, I found my Papa sitting on a wooden bench drinking palm wine.

"Good morning, Papa."

"Good morning, Ramata," I could not wait to complain to him.

"Papa, I am sick. Please tell Tida to send Vera to the stream."

"That will be over my dead body!" Tida, who was right behind me snapped and pushed me with all her might. I staggered and crashed onto the ground.

"Yes! Serves you right for your nerve!" she continued. "Who gave you the guts to tell this useless father of yours to ask me to send my precious daughter to the stream?" Her eyes glimmered with hot temper.

I remained absolutely silent.

She bent over me and said, "So, you want to try me in this house, eh?" Her breath hit my nostrils; it smelled like pus. "You better watch your footsteps. If not, you will follow your good for nothing mother to her grave!"

"Don't insult my mo—"

"Shut up!" Tida interrupted me with a slap.

"Tida it's—" my Papa started, but Tida interrupted him with her machete-sharp tongue. "Shut up you useless drunkard. You are the reason why this girl wants to grow wings in this house!"

She eyed him and faced me. "Make sure you fetch the water before my daughter wakes up!" Then she hissed and dashed back into the house.

I looked at my Papa who sat staring at me. He shrugged and resumed drinking his palm wine. I rose, took the bucket and headed for Bona Stream, where we laundered our clothes and fetched drinking water. The stream flowed along a steep and stony course about a mile away from our house. When I returned several minutes later, I met Vera sitting alone on the wooden bench Papa sat at earlier, holding a toothbrush and a cup.

"What kept you so long, you buffalo?"

I ignored her and put down the bucket. She jumped up, dipped the cup in the bucket and tossed the water over me.

"Answer me!" she roared.

Stunned, I stood rooted to the ground and stared at her. Vera grimaced at me and laughed. Her laughter, like her mother's, was witchlike.

"Yes. So much for your guts!"

Anger clawed at my insides like a cat in a sack. Vera took some water and made to go. I sprang up at her and slapped her. She dropped the cup and screamed. Her mother darted out of the house and asked, "What happened?"

"She slapped me," Vera screamed. Tida stepped forward and slapped me. A shower of stars danced before my eyes.

"What gives you the audacity to slap my daughter?" she demanded. Her eyes burned with raw anger.

"She started—"

"Shut up!" Tida interrupted me. "If you dare touch my daughter in this house again, I swear to God I will skin you alive . . . Goat!"

She walked up to Vera and consoled her. I rubbed my cheek that burned with pain, sighed, took the broom from the kitchen and started to sweep the compound. Afterwards, I prepared the breakfast and washed the dishes before setting off for school.

o o o

At the end of that school year, I came first in my class as usual. When I received my report card, I studied it eagerly before I left for home with a face that glowed like the moon. When I arrived home, I met Tida crocheting in the backyard.

"Why are you looking so happy?" she queried.

"I came first!" I beamed.

"Come, let's see."

I stepped forward and handed her my report card. She opened it and studied it for a while before she tore it up.

I stared at her in disbelief. "My God! Why did you tear my report card?"

"Because it is useless. It has no use since you will soon go to your husband's house."

I cocked my eyebrows. "My husband's house?"

"Yes. Your father and I have decided to marry you off before you become pregnant out of wedlock. Your husband to be is Kalilou."

Tida's words hit me like a blow in my stomach.

"What! Are you serious?"

Kalilou was the business man who owned a general store in our village. He was well-built with a pot-bellied stomach. Shortly after Papa married Tida, he started sending me to him to get provisions on credit, which Tida and her daughter would eat at night.

"Yes, my dear. Your father can't pay him the huge amount of money he owes him. So, I told him to give you to him in exchange. Two days ago, your father told Kalilou about it. He accepted at once. So get ready. Pretty soon you will go to his house as his wife," Tida explained with a smirk on her face.

As if on cue, once Tida finished explaining, my Papa burst in from one of the corners of the house, staggering. I rushed up to him pleading in a trembling voice, "Tell me it's not true, Papa. Tell me it's a lie!"

"What is it, my daughter?" His breath that reeked of sour palm wine struck my nostrils.

"Tida said you want to marry me off to Kalilou. Is it true?"

"Yes, dear," his face was distorted with sadness.

"Papa, please, I beg you in the name of God, don't let me stop going to school."

"No way!" Tida snapped. "Go and take off your uniform! I want to send you to the market."

I glared at her and stormed into the house.

On my way to the market, a voice inside my head told me to go to Mr. Kargbo and ask him to beg my father for me. Mr. Kargbo was my teacher. He and my father had attended the Roman Catholic Primary School together as boys.

"Yes, that's a nice idea. If Mr. Kargbo begs my father he might listen to him," I said with a smile.

After I bought all the condiments Tida had sent me for, I went to Mr. Kargbo's house.

"Ramata, what brings you here today?" Mr. Kargbo asked me after some pleasantries.

"Mr. Kargbo, I have a grave problem."

"What is it, my dear?"

"My father and my stepmother want to take me out of school."

"Why?" Mr. Kargbo asked with a worried look.

I took a deep, shaky breath and explained everything to him. Afterward, I begged him to go and plead with both of them to let me continue my schooling. Mr. Kargbo agreed at once and went off to make my case.

We met Tida and Papa sitting on the wooden bench.

"Yes Mr. Kargbo, what brings you here today?" Tida asked him after the preliminary greetings.

"I came to beg you and your husband to let Ramata continue with her schooling. She is a clever girl. Please let her finish her high school studies before marrying her off."

"We can't allow that. Things are hard for my husband and me. We can't afford her school expenses anymore."

There was a pause. Mr. Kargbo gazed at Papa.

"Yes Mr. Kargbo, my wife is right. We don't have any money to pay her school fees anymore. So, she has to stop going to school."

"Well if that's the case, let her be. I will take care—"

"Enough!" Tida cut Mr. Kargbo short. "We don't want to hear anything from you again, busy body. Please leave us alone and mind your own business!"

Mr. Kargbo looked at me sadly, shook his head and left.

"You dare bring that fool here to beg for you, eh!" Tida screamed as she stood up. She raised her hand and unleashed it on my back. Her slap felt like the stings of ten bees.

Five days after Tida broke the news of my impending marriage, Kalilou and his kinsmen came to marry me. Once the ceremony ended, I took my "Ghana Must Go"[1] bag that was filled with my worn-out clothes and went to my new husband's house.

When I arrived, Kalilou's two wives, Sukary and Digba stared at me with scorn and sucked their teeth. They glared at me with such fury that my blood turned cold and I shivered.

That night, Kalilou made love to me. When he thrust his big cock inside me, I felt as if a big hot iron rod had been shoved inside me repeatedly. I pleaded with him to stop, but he didn't listen. He continued to pump his big buttocks up and down until he discharged his sperm inside me.

"I am sorry, dear. I am so hungry for you! That's why I didn't listen to your cries," he said and rolled off me.

I covered myself with my wrapper as tears rolled down my cheeks. Soon, he started to snore heavily like a pig. I turned my back on him and continued to cry until I dozed off.

In the morning, when I woke up, Kalilou was not beside me. On the spot he lay, I saw a piece of paper that was covered with blue ink. The following words were written on it: "I have gone to Makeni to buy goods for my shop. If you need anything, ask my senior wives. See you soon." I hissed and tore the paper. Once I finished, the door opened and Sukary and Digba stormed in.

"Why are you still in bed? Do you think you have servants here? Get up and go and sweep the compound!" Sukary barked.

"All right, Ma."

I climbed out of the bed, reached for my clothes and put them on slowly.

"Hurry up, you fool. You are wasting our time!" Digba sneered as I got dressed.

o o o

Days and weeks dragged by. I continued to live in Kalilou's house in misery, because his wives ordered me about and often rained abuses on me.

At the end of my first month, I didn't get my monthly period. Worried, I told my husband about it.

Kalilou's eyes lit up and his face broke into a grin.

"Wow! This is great news! God, thank you," he looked up toward the ceiling and said.

"Why do you seem so happy?"

"My dear, you are pregnant."

He kissed me on my forehead and embraced me. Later, I told him to give me money to join a prenatal clinic in Makeni.

"No. That's not necessary. I have five children. All of them were born in this village. So, yours won't be an exception, okay?" he remarked.

A week later, my Papa died of malaria.

On my tenth month at Kalilou's, I went into labour. The moment my water broke, my co-wives and Aminata, a midwife in the village, took me into Kalilou's bedroom and tried to help me to deliver, but I couldn't. Several hours later, Kalilou took me to Makeni Government Hospital on a motorbike. The road that led to Makeni was brown, muddy, and filled with potholes. Each time the motorbike bumped into a pothole, a spear of pain would shoot through me. I thought the ride would never end.

When we arrived at the Government Hospital, Doctor Sheku examined me and explained, "She didn't give birth because her pelvis is too small. We must operate to save her life and that of the baby."

When I woke up from the operation the next day, I was drenched in urine.

"Doctor, what is wrong with me? Why am I soaked with urine?"

Doctor Sheku sighed and said, "I am sorry. You are suffering from fistula. During labour, the pressure of the baby's head that wedged deep in your pelvis smashed the delicate tissue at the base of your bladder and created a hole where urine currently escapes."

"My God! Am I going to continue like this?"

"I'm afraid so. Unfortunately I can't carry out a fistula operation on you because I am not a specialist. One more thing: your child didn't make it. He died during the operation," he added and walked out of the room.

His words shredded my heart into pieces. Tears stung my eyes and ran down my cheeks.

o o o

When I was discharged two weeks later, I went to Kalilou's house. To my dismay, when I arrived, I found out that my clothes had been moved to the storeroom, where household utensils and supplies were kept. When I asked why, Kalilou glared at me and said, "It's because I won't have anything to do with you again. Henceforth you cease to be my wife because you stink like a rubbish dump."

His words gnawed at my intestines like claws. My co-wives who stood nearby glanced at each other and laughed. Their laughter was coarse.

"Indeed, he is right. You stink of piss. Get out of our sight!" Sukary said.

I shook my head and headed for the storeroom as tears welled up in my eyes. There, I slumped down on the paved floor and cried until my eyes puffed up.

After eating in the evening, I went to the parlour to drink water. As I reached for the cup that was on the drinking bucket, Digba who was sitting crocheting barked at me.

"Ah! Don't touch it you stinking wretched being! Do you want to kill us with that sickness of yours? Get away from there now!"

I ignored her, took the cup and dipped it into the bucket.

"What!" Digba boomed as she stopped crocheting and stood up menacingly. She rushed up to me and snatched the cup. "How dare you defy my authority!" she said as she tossed the water over me. She shot me a nasty look and added, "In fact, you've contaminated this water. So, I am going to throw it out!" She grabbed the bucket and stormed out.

I went into the storeroom, took my bag and returned to my Papa's house.

"What have you come for?" Tida greeted me with a scowl when I arrived.

"I have come home for good. My husband said he wouldn't have anything to do with me because I have fistula."

"You are dreaming! You will never set your foot in this house again! You married your husband for better for worse. So go back to his house!"

I dropped down on my knees pleading. "Tida, I beg you in the name of God, don't do this to me. Kalilou and his wives no longer want to see me. So please let me in."

"No way! Leave this place, you stinking bitch!" she roared, spat at me before she rushed in and slammed the wooden door behind her.

I sank to the ground and contemplated what to do. After a while, I decided to go and stay at my Mama's farmhouse. I brushed my tears off my face, and hopped up. As I made my way to the dusty road that led to the farmhouse, the sun disappeared behind a thick, grey cloud.

When I arrived there a couple of minutes later, I sensed my Mama's presence throughout the farm. Everywhere I turned, her image would appear before my eyes. I saw her tilling the soil, weeding, cooking in the farmhouse, smiling at me and singing her favourite song "*Kurumasaba.*" Those images tugged at my heartstrings and huge tears poured out of my eyes and dripped down my cheeks.

I surveyed the small mud and thatch farmhouse that Mama used to store tools and resolved, "I can live here." There was nothing in the farmhouse but two hoes; two machetes, one of which was broken; and a small stool. "What am I going to do to feed myself? Even if I have enough strength to farm a small plot, food takes time to grow." I fell into despair and began weeping. After mulling through the night, I decided to beg: "I will use the money I earn begging to buy food," I wiped my face dry.

Shortly after dawn the next morning, I went and sat at the edge of the road and started begging passers-by. Some took pity on me and gave me coins, while others sneered at me and called me nasty names.

o o o

I continued to beg passers-by for coins as urine continued to pour out of me. One morning, as I sat by the edge of the road waiting for passers-by, I saw a white Pathfinder coming up the road. My heart did a little flop.

"Maybe if I succeed in stopping them, somebody in that car will give me one thousand Leone,"[2] I thought.

I got up and beckoned the car to stop with both my hands and my ingratiating beggar's smile. When the car stopped before me, my heart jumped into my mouth. As I began walking to the driver's door, the passenger door opened and Biba streamed out with a big smile. I froze. Biba was my best friend at my school. After she passed her National Primary School Examination, her parents sent her to Freetown to live with her aunt. I hadn't seen Biba in years. I smiled warmly at her still-slender frame and moon-round face.

"*Kushe,*"[3] Ramata," she greeted me in Krio.

"*Kushe o*! How are you doing?" I responded.

"Great, as you can see, my dear. I miss you so much. Give me a hug." Biba stepped forward with open arms to embrace me. I stepped backward.

The glow on Biba's face melted away. "Ramata, what is the problem? Why are you moving away from me?"

"Haven't you heard about my predicament?" I queried her.

The driver's door opened, and a pretty brown-skinned woman with thick eyebrows stepped out of the vehicle.

Biba's eyebrows rose, "What do you mean?"

"I don't want to embrace you because I am stinking of urine. My dear friend, I am suffering from fistula."

"My God!" Biba exclaimed. "How did it happen?" After suffering so much abuse, the genuine concern in her voice overwhelmed me.

As tears splashed down my face and onto the dirt road, I poured my story into the heart of my friend.

"Too bad!" Biba and the brown-skinned woman said in a chorus and shook their heads.

"Be courageous. By the grace of Allah, everything shall be all right. There is now a hospital in Freetown called Aberdeen Women's Centre. It specializes in curing fistula. Will you come with us for treatment?" the brown-skinned woman asked.

My eyes lit up and my heart puffed up with hope. Could my luck possibly change? "All right, Ma," I answered. "But are you sure the hospital will cure me?"

"Absolutely. You see, I was once a fistula patient. I developed it when ten rebels raped me five years ago. Aberdeen Women's Centre cured me."

"Oh, Ma, I am sorry o!" I wanted to hug her, but I was afraid I would soil her. "We thank Allah that you survived and are cured," I stared at the woman with amazement. She had suffered so much and was now cured and confident. . . But I checked my awe and insisted on facts, "How much is the surgery?"

"It is free. You won't pay a cent."

My face split into a wide grin, "Really?"

"Yes. By the way, my name is Angela. But you can call me Aunty Angie. Biba and I will go to the village to spend a couple of hours with our relatives. Gather your things. On our way back, we will pick you up and take you to the hospital."

Aunty Angie and Biba entered the Pathfinder and left me glowing in the red dust.

o o o

We arrived at Aberdeen Women's Centre, and it was jammed-packed with pregnant women and lactating mothers. The nurses welcomed us warmly with faces that were adorned with beautiful smiles. They ushered us into a waiting room that was laden with the sharp smell of antiseptic. Later, Doctor Williams, a plump light-skinned woman who was the surgeon specialist, examined me in her office and told me that I was suffering from obstetric fistula and that to cure me she would perform intravaginal surgery on me. She paused, looked at my ragged clothes and shriveled frame, and added, "It obvious you've gone through hell. By the grace of God, your misery will soon end. You only have to report here first thing on Monday morning for the operation, okay?"

On Monday, as the pink light of dawn rose over Lumley where Aunt Angie lived with her husband and Biba in a two-storied house, Aunt Angie came to the guest room and woke me up so I could get ready. When we arrived at Aberdeen Women's Centre, the nurses rolled me into the theatre on a gurney for the surgical operation. The last thing I remember is the kindness of the male nurse who placed an oxygen mask over my mouth and nose. When I came to later, I noticed that a catheter was inserted inside me. I could feel its pressure in my urethra. As I felt the sheets underneath me, my eyes locked with those of a nurse who smiled and patted my right foot. My dress and the bedspread were dry.

"Nurse, have I stopped leaking for good?"

The nurse looked at me with shining eyes and said, "We think so. Doctor Williams said your type of surgery has ninety-five percent success rate, and your operation went smoothly. You will need to use a catheter for the next two to three weeks." The nurse opened a box and said, "We have enough supplies here to take you through to your next appointment." The nurse then removed a flat oval bag and some tubes, "Okay, now I will show you how to remove and change your drainage bag."

When the nurse had finished, Aunt Angie and Biba arrived shining like stars. "Ramata," Aunt Angie, embraced me, "Congratulations! Welcome to the new you!"

Biba kissed my cheek and said, "You are brave, my sister! How are you feeling?"

"I am a little dizzy and sore, but I am so grateful!" Tears of joy flowed freely down my cheeks. It was as if they were washing away all of the suffering I had endured. I couldn't stop weeping, so I just let it all go. Aunt Angie and Biba held me tight.

Four weeks later, Doctor Williams examined me and removed the Foley catheter. After I got dressed, Aunt Angie and I entered the doctor's office.

"Congratulations!" Dr. Williams exclaimed, "You've healed perfectly. You will never leak again."

A wave of joy surged through me. I stood up and sank down to the tiled floor, "Thank you very much, Doctor Williams, for saving me from my woes. I will never forget you for what you did for me," I said while gripping her feet, my voice cracking with happiness.

"No, Ramata. Get up! You don't have to thank me; rather, thank God for restoring dignity to your life again. He is the one that cured you," Doctor Williams said with a smile.

"Doctor, you are right. Nonetheless, we must thank you for the instrumental role you play in healing us. We are truly grateful. May Allah bless and grant you all your wishes," Aunt Angie, who was standing beside Doctor Williams, said with a big smile.

"Ameen," Doctor Williams smiled.

Aunt Angie smiled at me and said, "I am so proud of you. You've become whole again." Her eyes were filled with love.

I ran, flung my arms around her, and gave her a tight embrace, "I owe you my life because you made me whole again. If not for you and Biba, I would not have seen this day." Tears welled up in my eyes. I thought of my friend Biba, who was taking her examinations, and I silently wished her luck.

Despite the clinic's strong cleansers and antiseptics, I caught a whiff of Aunt Angie's American Woman perfume. I inhaled deeply and smiled. Aunt Angie ran her fingers through my hair, which Biba had plaited for me, and said, "It's okay, Ramata. You don't owe me anything. I did what I did because I have to. By the way, I have a surprise for you."

"Surprise?" I asked.

"Yes. My husband and I would like you to live with us. We would like to send you to school. Would you like that?"

My eyes grew big in astonishment, "Are you kidding?"

Shafts of the afternoon sun flooded the room through the open windows.

"No, my dear. I am as serious as Ebola. In fact, we want to enroll you into Biba's school."

Oh, this is incredible!" I said and exhaled heavily. "Aunt Angie, may Allah bless you, your husband, and Biba greatly for everything you've done for me," I prayed.

"Aameen," Aunt Angie assented as she took my right hand in hers which felt as soft as a baby's. "It's high time we left for home," she added. We thanked Doctor Williams again before we made our way for the door.

Notes

[1] [Editor's note: Square-shaped woven plastic bags with zippers, handles, and plaid designs are made in China but earned the name "Ghana Must Go," when in 1983 Nigeria's head of state Shehu Shagari decreed that all foreign Africans without valid residence permits had to leave Nigeria. If they refused to leave, they would be arrested and deported. Ghanaians were the largest group affected by the order, and the aforementioned woven plastic bags were the cheapest and most convenient way to pack and

transport their belongings. Thousands of "Ghana Must Go" bags—loaded atop heads, lorries, and handlebars—came to symbolize the expulsion of Ghanaians from Nigeria.

Although West African countries enjoy better political relations at present, the name "Ghana Must Go" for the bags is enduring and is used in several African nations. For more on "Ghana Must Go" and expulsions of Ghanaians from Nigeria and of Nigerians from Ghana, please see Anne Chia's insightful article on the topic: <https://annechia.com/2015/04/20 /ghana-must-go-nigerias-expulsion-of-immigrants/>.]

[2] [Editor's note: The currency of Sierra Leone is the "leone." 1000 leone is about 0.25¢.]

[3] [Editor's note: "Kushe," is a Yoruba expression that means, roughly, "I greet you as you are working well." In Yoruba, it is spelled "Ku (i)ṣé."

Bundu's short stories, like those of Ishmael Beah and other Sierra Leonean writers, are sprinkled with Yoruba words which travelled throughout West Africa largely as a result of the abduction and enslavement of tens of millions of Africans from the 1400s to the 1800s, including millions of Yoruba who were trafficked from a region that Caucasian oppressors casually termed the "Slave Coast." After the British and some other European powers abolished the trafficking of human beings on international waters, boats found to be containing enslaved Africans were routed to Sierra Leone, a British colony, and there the Africans were freed. Many Yoruba stayed in Sierra Leone; some, like Fela Anikulapo Kuti's great, great grandmother Sarah Taiwo travelled back to Nigeria; some Yoruba settled in various West African lands.]

Straightened Hair as Social Currency

Morgan Miller

To be both Black and Woman, unapologetically, is a journey that taxes as much as it rewards. In a world where Black Women are constantly cheapened, devalued, and depreciated—where we are constantly reminded that our bodies are not our own, where our flesh is commoditized and capitalized for market consumption—to be both Black and Woman, unapologetically, is nothing short of revolutionary. Malcolm X poignantly stated that "the most disrespected woman in America is the Black woman. The most un-protected person in America is the Black woman. The most neglected person in America is the Black woman." However, such misogynoir, in fact, operates in an open economy that transcends borders and is exported and imported across seas, people, and time. We are taught to hate the color of our skin, the curve of our hips, the width of our nose, the fullness of our lips, and, particularly, the texture of our hair. Straightened hair monopolizes notions of beauty and self-worth and is always in constant demand. Straightened hair enjoys a sizable endowment of material privilege in the areas of employment and romance—while kinks, locs, and curls are lambasted with ridicule and hate. From the Dominican peso to the American dollar, straightened hair is a social currency of the highest value.

The initial intent behind my decision to go natural was practical rather than political. After arriving to college in a new city, I didn't have a trusted hair salon. As my roots began to grow, so did a newfound curiosity for what my natural hair would look like. Although I would sink my fingers into the grooves of my wave pattern in admiration, my hairstylist back home would suck her teeth in frustration, complaining about how "thick" (read: nappy) my hair was. Soon enough, I would truly begin to comprehend the truth behind Melissa Harris Perry's statement that "there are few follicles more politicized than the ones that grow out of a Black woman's head." This became painstakingly clear in a heated debate between my parents and me over my decision to wear my natural hair to a job interview at an eminent corporate law firm. With my mane of kinks sitting prominently atop my head, my parents proceeded to tell me that natural hair was unprofessional looking and unkempt. Straight hair was better, and would get me the job. With every "justification" they gave, I felt the spring in my curls deflate. I was devastated to know how they really felt about the hair that I had inherited from them both. "Ain't I enough?" I asked them with tears streaming down my face. Much to their chagrin, once I arrived at the interview, I was received by two Black women with bigger natural hair than I had. I felt my curls spring back into confidence. However, Melissa Harris Perry's statement still rang true. Nowhere did these follicles feel more politicized than during my time in the Dominican Republic.

I arrived in the Dominican Republic one year after my first visit and one month before the passing of *Sentencia* 168/13, a Supreme Court ruling that revoked the citizenship of Dominican residents whose parents were born outside of the country as far back as 1929, unless they could regularize their status. Just as the United States has yet to reconcile with its legacy of racism, the Dominican Republic has yet to reconcile with its own version of white supremacy, *anti-haitianismo*, and negrophobia. Behind the curtains of darker chapters in Dominican history lie an ultra-nationalism predicated upon *anti-haitianismo*, immigration policies of *blanqueamiento* (literally "whitening), the racism of dictator Rafael Trujillo, and the Parsley Massacre.

Although I had experienced some forms of discrimination during my first visit, having been denied entry to clubs and to the renowned Centro León museum, I noticed a heightened tension in race dynamics after *Sentencia* 168/13 was passed. There was a sort of thickness in the air that denoted angst. I came back to teach English as a professor in Santiago at Pontificia Universidad Católica Madre y Maestra. The city of Santiago, the country's second largest city, is situated in the northwestern region that is known as "El Cibao." Cibaeños are typically viewed as wealthier and phenotypically "whiter" than the rest of the country, which is largely owed to the fact that the region, especially Santiago, has historically been home to the Dominican oligarchy. This is compared to the capital city of Santo Domingo, once a major slave port on the island, that has a higher concentration of Dominicans with a visibly Black aesthetic. Over the first three days that I visited Santo Domingo, I saw more women rocking their natural hair than during the entire six months I had spent in Santiago. In fact, after returning to the States, I learned that there was a newly established natural hair salon called Miss Rizos, promoting the mantra "*yo amo mi pajón*" (I love my natural hair). Unfortunately, this nascent natural hair movement emerging in Santo Domingo had not yet reached Santiago.

In Santiago, I passed billboards depicting curly-haired women with the headline "your hair deserves better," and advertisements with sad-faced women sporting natural hair, juxtaposed with smiling women with fresh perms and lightened skin. As such, the decision to wear my *pajón* (afro) quickly became a source of anxiety. According to Ginetta E. B. Candelario, author of *Black behind the Ears: Dominican Racial Identity from Museums to Beauty Shops,* "for Dominicans, hair is the principal bodily signifier of race, followed by facial features, skin color and, last, ancestry." Little did I know, that I was about to experience race in a new way.

I lived only about five minutes from the edge of campus in La Lotería. Because of the proximity, I would make up to four trips daily between campus and home, returning for lunch at midday. However, these five minutes meant strategically maneuvering through an obstacle course of *piropos* (catcalls) and *puyas* (jibes). I learned to choose wisely which side of the street to walk on, after attempting to walk past a huddle of men unnoticed only to hear my halo of hair as the butt of a joke. I would breathe a sigh of relief once I reached the campus perimeter. From my fellow teachers and students, I received nothing but love. My students would often tell me how much they loved my hair, but I also believe that behind those compliments lied an admiration for the audacious decision to wear my natural hair in a place where such a high premium is placed on straightened, relaxed hair. I recall one student from San Francisco de Macorí recounting her own experience. One day she wore her hair curly to her elementary school only for her teacher to immediately call her mother, send her home and instruct her to come back when her hair was "fixed." Walking through the streets, I noticed that Dominican men sporting their natural hair were not subjected to the same level of derision that women were, marking the intersection between race and gender.

I slowly began to realize how naïve I had been in hoping that in the Dominican Republic I could escape the daily racism I experienced in the United States. As a Black American from the South, I openly welcomed the idea of living in a country where most people looked like my family members and me, considering the fact that the first Africans to arrive in the New World landed in Hispaniola. However, I soon began to learn that anti-Black animus, more specifically misogynoir, was everywhere, including in majority Black nations. I felt it in the looks of disdain I received for my venturing to wear my hair in its natural state. I felt it after a man in the club whispered in my ear for me to "fix" my hair. I felt it in conversations about *"pelo bueno"* (good hair) and *"pelo malo"* (bad hair), terminology that is also all too common within the Black American vernacular.

Peers suggested that had I worn my hair straightened, I would have been able to "pass" for Dominican. However, because of my afro, I was frequently mistaken as Haitian. This notion of racial passing was striking. One acquaintance I met from St. Kitts and Nevis had been living in the country for quite some time. She told me that she generally experienced no problems (read: she was accepted as Dominican) when she wore her hair straightened. But after getting box braids, she too began being mistaken as Haitian (read: she began to experience greater discrimination).

Despite these social pressures, I adamantly rejected the idea of straightening my hair as a form of escape. In the face of constant denigration, I chose to embrace the part of me that was subject to the greatest disparagement, growing deeper in love with myself in the end. I condemned this fixation with "fixing" what was never broken. I understood that these kinks possess a certain power that defies both gravity and conformity altogether while embodying the enduring resilience of our people. In a world where straightened hair is a social currency, to be both Black and Woman, unapologetically, is a revolutionary act that is priceless.

THE CONTRIBUTORS
PERMISSIONS
INDEX

THE CONTRIBUTORS

Tunde Adegbola is a research scientist, consulting engineer, and cultural activist. He holds a B.Sc. in Electrical Engineering, M.Sc. in Computer Science and Ph.D. in Information Science (with application in Linguistics). Prior to his present position as the Executive Director of African Languages Technology Initiative (Alt-i), he contributed to the development of Cellular Automata Transform (CAT) as one of the most advanced compression technologies employed on the global information infrastructure today. He has also made notable contributions in the design and installation of various audio and video production and post-production facilities as well as radio and TV stations in Nigeria and elsewhere in Africa.

Muhammad Ibn Bashir is the author of *Raw Law: An Urban Guide to Criminal Justice*, which should be considered required reading for African Americans. Mr. Bashir specializes in criminal and constitutional law and he is a motivational speaker and dedicated community servant.

Jacqueline Bediako is a school administrator, activist, and writer. Her work has been published by *Atlanta Blackstar*, *The San Francisco Bay View*, *Afrikan Heritage*, *Black Politics on the Web*, and *My Joy Online* in Ghana. Her work has also been featured in social media campaigns and on blogs. Currently, she writes about race, politics, and the education of students with disabilities. Jacqueline is also working on her first book of poetry, you can learn more about her work on her website: www.jacquelinebediako.com. The daughter of Ghanaian immigrants, Jacqueline was born and raised in London, and now lives in Brooklyn, New York. A graduate of the University of Bristol in England and Brooklyn College, she is currently working towards certification as a behavior analyst through an online program administered by the University of North Texas. Jacqueline is a committed volunteer with African Communities Together (ACT), and believes that as a Ghanaian it is her duty to support African immigrants seeking opportunity and civil rights in New York City.

Charlie Braxton is a poet, playwright, and essayist from McComb, Mississippi. He is the author of three volumes of verse: *Ascension from the Ashes* (Blackwood Press 1991), *Cinders Rekindled* (Jawara Press 2013) and *Embers Among the Ashes: Poems in a Haiku Manner* (Jawara Press 2016). His poetry has been published in various literary publications, such as *The Minnesota Review*, *Sepia Poetry Review*, *The Black Nation*, *Black American Literature Forum*, *Specter Magazine* and *The San Fernando Poetry Journal*.

Alieu Bundu is a Sierra Leonean writer. He holds a Bachelor of Arts degree in French from Fourah Bay College, University of Sierra Leone. He was the runner-up of April 2014 Africa Book Club Short Reads Competition. His stories have appeared on the Africa Book Club's website, and the *Kalahari Review*. His story "A Piece of Flesh" was published in *In the Belly of the Lion* an anthology of short stories from Sierra Leone. His story "Bintiya" was nominated for the 2016 Writivism Short Story Prize. You can contact him via email at alieubundu@gmail.com, or you can follow him via twitter at @alieubundu.

Baba A. O. Buntu is an activist scholar, consultant and trainer focusing primarily on Afrikan-centered education, leadership training, social development and community empowerment. Hailing from Anguilla in the Eastern Caribbean, he grew up in Norway and repatriated to Azania (South Afrika) in 2000. As a Pan-Afrikan practitioner and mentor, Baba Buntu has more than 30 years of experience in developing and contributing to community programs – in which the focus is to engage the Afrikan Family in decolonial transformation. He is the Founder and Executive Director of Ebukhosini Solutions, a community-based consultancy company in Johannesburg. Some of the programs he has developed include Afuraka (cultural community mobilization), SHABAKA – Men of Afrika (a men's program) and Street Academy (empowerment of young entrepreneurs).

Baba Buntu's academic background is in social work, group therapy and political science. He holds a Master Degree in Philosophy of Education from the University of South Africa and is currently a PhD Candidate in the same discipline. His works have been published in a number of international journals and anthologies, and he has been recognized by Afrikan communities in many countries as a dedicated servant-leader.

Contact and connect with Baba Buntu through the following channels:
- E-mail: buntu@ebukhosinisolutions.co.za
- Web page: www.ebukhosinisolutions.co.za
- YouTube: https://www.youtube.com/user/bababuntu
- Facebook: www.facebook.com/ebukhosinisolutions

Chinweizu is a Black Power Pan-Africanist. He has had a lifelong commitment to the redemption of the Black Race. After his education in mathematics and history, he chose to make his contribution by way of scholarship combined with public political education through journalism. He promotes of the ideology of Neo-Garveyism and advocates the creation of Garvey's United States of Black Africa, USBA, an economic and military superpower that will serve as the core state (leader and protector) of the Black race, of Black people wherever they may be in the world; just like China and Japan are the core states of the Yellow Race; and the USA and Russia are the core states of the White Race.

His published books include *The West and the Rest of Us* (1975); *Invocations and Admonitions* (1986); *Decolonising the African Mind* (1987); *Voices from Twentieth-Century Africa* (1988); *Anatomy of Female Power* (1990); *Caliphate Colonialism: The Taproot of the Trouble with Nigeria* (2015).

Because of his poor and declining health, he is praying to the gods and ancestors for just enough time to complete his last batch of Black Redemptionist works:

1. *Pan-Africanist Wisdom, 1791-2013: Selections from Pan-Africanist Thinkers since Boukman;*
2. *Ubuntology: Groundwork for the Intellectual Autonomy of the Black World;*
3. *Pan-Africanism Revisited, 1442-2002: A Maafacentric History;*
4. *On Niggerology: Investigations into the Origin and Possible Cures for the Maafa-Induced Nigger Mentality That's the Bane of the Black Race;*
5. *The Definitive Edition of The West and the Rest of Us, 1405-1991.*

In 2014 Chinweizu was given a Silverbird Lifetime Achievement Award.

Ricardo Cortez Cruz Stylin' and profilin', rocking cut n' mix, to explore the monstrous im/possibilities of creating a new black avant-garde aesthetic, Ricardo Cortez Cruz is the author of *Straight Outta Compton* and *Five Days of Bleeding*, novels short and funky. He has stitched together a third black body of (s)language—*Premature Autopsies: Tales of Darkest America*. His autobioGRAPHIC fiction, including that on Trayvon Martin, is a broken record. His creative work has appeared in numerous journals and anthologies such as *Mandorla: Nueva escritura de las Américas, Packingtown Review's* 2009 inaugural issue, *Fiction International's* abject/outcast issue, *African-American Review, Urban Reinventors, Crab*

Orchard Review, The Kenyon Review, The Iowa Review, Obsidian II: Black Literature in Review, Postmodern Culture, and Kevin Powell's anthology *Step Into A World.* His most recent publications include "Longing For Home" in the 2016 anthology *Proofread Or Die: Writings By Former Students & Colleagues of David Foster Wallace,* "Pieces Of A Man" in *Fjords Black American Edition* (guest edited by Geffrey Davis), and "The Get Outta The Ghetto Blues" in *Litscapes: Collected Writings 2015* (edited by Caitlin M. Alvarez and Kass Fleisher). Old s/kool, Cruz—reviewed by *The Nation, The Source* music magazine, *i-D Magazine* (London), *High Times,* etc.—has been teaching English at Illinois State University since the nineties.

Oyinlola Longe is a performer and lecturer in the department of dramatic arts at Obafemi Awolowo University Ile-Ife, Nigeria. She teaches media studies, communication theory, dramatic literature, theatre workshop, and theatre history. Her research interest includes making connections between fictional dramatic/narrative texts and lived experiences in Nigeria. She is presently writing about how the heterogeneous community where she grew up in Jos, Nigeria resisted the political, religious, and ethnic conflicts that devastated the city between 2001 and 2011.

Jumbe Kweku Lumumba serves as an advocate for homeless youth at Covenant House Georgia, Youth Commissioner for the World African Diaspora Union, radio journalist for *What Good is A Song? The Friday Night Drum* on WRFG Atlanta 89.3 FM, Media Relations Manager for House of Globalization, and founder and CEO of the Global Unity and Leadership Forum, Inc. He can be contacted by email at contact-@allafricans.org, or you can visit his website www.allafricans.org.

Morgan Miller is a native Houstonian who recently received her Master of International Affairs degree from Columbia University's School of International and Public Affairs (SIPA), concentrating in International Security Policy and specializing in both International Conflict Resolution and Latin America. She speaks both Spanish and Portuguese fluently and has elementary proficiency in Haitian Kreyòl and French. Prior to SIPA, she was a Chancellor's Scholar at Vanderbilt University, receiving her B.A. in Spanish and Medicine, Health, and Society in May 2013. After graduation, she taught Advanced Conversation and Academic Writing as an English professor at the Pontificia Universidad Católica Madre y Maestra in Santiago, Dominican Republic.

As a summer policy intern at Americas Society/Council of Americas, she wrote the most read article in the history of *Americas Quarterly (AQ)* magazine, entitled "My Struggle as a Black American in the Dominican Republic," which generated over 60,000 page views and more than 11,500 social media shares. Miller also researched and analyzed data for the new ethno-racial inclusion variable of Afro-descendants and Indigenous peoples for 17 Latin American countries for *AQ's* annual Social Inclusion Index.

Miller currently works as a graphic designer, and in 2009 she launched her own graphic design company, Noir et Blanc Productions (www.noiretblancproductions.com). In the fall, she will attend Cornell Law School to study public international law, critical race theory, and feminist legal theory. Her personal interests include travel, playing piano, producing music, and reading all things diasporic.

Asiri Odu is a Pan-Africanist and a political scientist. Odu's debut novel is entitled *Ah Jubah! APleaPrayerPromise*.

Chinwe Ezinna Oriji, a McNair Fellow and PEO Scholar, is currently a PhD Candidate in the African and African Diaspora Studies Department at the University of Texas at Austin. She completed her MPhil in Sociology at the University of Cambridge and is focused on a doctoral dissertation tentatively titled "We Remember Differently": Theorizing the Nigerian Diaspora within a Modern World System of Anti-Blackness. She is also the founder of the "Unispora.com" created to share narratives of immigrants and children of immigrants globally.

Kevin Powell, a native of Jersey City, New Jersey, is the author or editor of eleven previous books. Thanks to a college financial aid package, he studied at Rutgers University and has gone on to write for publications such as *The Huffington Post*, CNN.com, *Esquire*, *Rolling Stone*, the *Washington Post*, the *Guardian*, and *Vibe Magazine*, where he worked for many years as a senior writer, interviewing such diverse public figures as Tupac Shakur and General Colin Powell.

Powell is the author of twelve books, including his newest title, *The Education of Kevin Powell: A Boy's Journey into Manhood*. It is a critically acclaimed and brutally honest memoir about his life, including his youth. In 2018, he will publish a biography of Tupac Shakur, the late rapper and controversial American icon.

As a pop culture curator, Kevin produced the first exhibit on the history of hip-hop in America at the Rock and Roll Hall of Fame in Cleveland, Ohio, which toured America and overseas. As a humanitarian, Kevin's work includes local, national and international initiatives to end violence against women and girls (including a very well-regarded appearance on *The Oprah Winfrey Show* highlighting domestic violence); and he has done extensive philanthropic and relief work, ranging from Hurricane Katrina to earthquakes in Haiti and Japan, to Superstorm Sandy in New York, to his annual holiday party and clothing drive for the homeless every December since 9/11.

As an acknowledgement of Kevin's life of public service and his dedication to literature and the arts, Cornell University recently became the owner of The Kevin Powell Collection, documenting nearly 30 years of his work to date in print, photos, videos, books, handwritten notes, speeches, and select memorabilia.

Kevin routinely appears in interviews on television, radio, and in print and on the Internet discussing major issues of our time. As an activist, he is the president and co-founder of BK Nation, a new national, progressive, multicultural organization focused on such issues as education, civic engagement, leadership training, health and wellness, social media, arts and culture, and job and small business creation. Kevin was also a Democratic candidate for Congress in Brooklyn, New York, his adopted hometown, in 2008 and 2010. Visit www.KevinPowell.net and www.BKNation.org.

Blair Marcus Proctor is a Michigan State University doctoral candidate in African American and African Studies with a specialization in historical sociology and African Diaspora studies. His analysis and research methodology involve sociological, qualitative, and historical methods. Proctor's dissertation research focuses on how Blackness and spatial boundaries that are historically significant shape identity formation among South African Coloureds and New Orleans Afro-Creoles.

Proctor formerly worked for the MSU MasterCard Foundation Scholars Program for the Office for International Students and Scholars during fall 2013/spring 2014. He also formerly worked as a consultant for the MSU Writing Center and facilitated for the Writing Center satellite at the MSU Student Athletic Support Services during fall 2014/spring 2015.

Proctor is currently working as a lead tutor for Student-Athlete Academic Support Services at Georgia Institute of Technology. Proctor received both his B.S. in urban planning and masters of geographical sciences and environmental planning with a focus in community development, Arizona State University.

Ishola Akindele Salami is a lecturer in the Early Childhood Education Unit, Department of Teacher Education, University of Ibadan, Ibadan, Nigeria. He obtained his Bachelor's Degree in Early Childhood Education: Mathematics in the year 2004, his Master's Degree in Primary Mathematics Education in the year 2006, and his Doctorate in Early Childhood Education: Mathematics in the year 2014 all from the University of Ibadan.

He received three-month training on Preparation of Primary Mathematics Teachers at Kennesaw State University, Atlanta Georgia, USA. He has published several journal articles and chapters in books. His research interest tends towards primary education pedagogy and education of children with special needs. He is happily married with children.

Aseret Sin is a poet. You can read Sin's works in *Obsidian II*, *Eyeball*, *Phatitude*, and *FEMSPEC*. Sin's verses are featured in Asiri Odu's revolutionary debut novel *Ah Jubah! A PleaPrayerPromise*.

Teresa N. Washington vowed she would never edit an anthology for many reasons. . . . Then the myriad disconnects of the African World nearly electrocuted her while electrifying her political passions! Dr. Washington conceived of and compiled this anthology while on leave from her position as the Ann Petry Endowed Professor in English at Grambling State University in the hopes that the wisdom of the contributors could be used to further the African world's liberation, education, and elevation.

The liberation, education, and elevation of the African world consume Washington, and this is evident in her all publications, including the books *The Architects of Existence: Àjẹ́ in Yoruba Cosmology, Ontology, and Orature*; *Manifestations of Masculine Magnificence: Divinity in Africana Life, Lyrics, and Literature*; and *Our Mothers, Our Powers, Our Texts: Manifestations of Àjẹ́ in Africana Literature*. Contact and build with her: akeredun@yahoo.com.

Ayoka Wiles has over two decades of background experience in the arts, dance, culture, and education. Ayoka has had a long standing dance career starting at the age of four and she has traveled, studied, and danced with numerous companies and artists throughout the United States and in Africa. By age 16, she was teaching adults' professional dance. She danced with Maimouna Keita School of African Dance for 19 years and served as Assistant Artistic Director and Choreographer for 4 years. She was also a pre-professional African dance teacher/coach for an award winning youth ensemble that utilized the arts as a catalyst for social change.

Ayoka has worked with several community based organizations integrating the arts, literacy, spirituality and cultural education in programming for youth and adults. She served as the first Associate Director of Ifetayo Cultural Arts Academy, an Administrator for the Unitarian Society of Germantown and was a Business Manager for the Village of Arts and Humanities.

Ayoka received a B.A. in Economics from Mount Holyoke College and a Master's of Science in Nonprofit Management from The Robert J. Milano

Graduate School of Management and Urban Policy, New School University. She has also received numerous certificates of study including a Nonprofit Management certificate from Columbia Business School, Institute of Nonprofit Management and completed fieldwork in Buenos Aires, Argentina studying the Management of Socially Responsible Organizations in Latin America.

Ayoka's experiences with spiritual counseling, counseling, and personal growth work have varied in type and approach. While working for Ifetayo she provided counseling and served as a teacher to youth through their comprehensive rites of passage program. This program provides holistic social services to youth to support their personal, educational, emotional and social growth. Additionally, she has served as an Advisory member for the United Nations Committee on Spirituality, Values and Global Concerns-the Health, Transformation and Spirituality Working Group and spoke at their annual conference in October 2008. Ayoka's volunteer experiences vary widely and are focused on supporting spiritually and culturally centered organizations as well as organizations that support communities who are under-resourced or neglected. She is one of the founding board members of Egbe Omo Orisa, which is a weekend school that introduces children ages 2–12 to the basic elements of Yoruba religion, traditions, and practices and engenders them to have pride in their heritage. She is also a member of the Omo Obàtálá Egbe, Inc., a nonprofit cultural organization whose mission is to continue the veneration of Orisa and Yoruba culture. She served as a member of the American Women's Club of Lagos, Nigeria and served as the Chair of the Charity committee. She is currently an Advisory Board Member of Agbeti-Tree of Life, a nongovernmental organization that supports and provides health and wellness to under resourced communities in Ghana, West Africa. She hosted a monthly internet radio show that focuses on personal and spiritual development, is a spiritual life coach, and is the author of a book which was released in May 2010, entitled *I Hear Olofi's Song: A Collection of Yoruba Prayers for Egun and Orisa*. She is a 2010 recipient of an Art and Change grant from the Leeway Foundation to create a performance piece based on the narrative of her book. She is also a contributing author to *The Torch: Motherwit, Guideposts and Stories of Purposeful Womanhood* edited by Suzanne Henderson, 2015. In 2016, she served as a panelist at the *Art of Loving Your Mind, Body, Spirit and Soul* symposium hosted by The Caribbean Cultural Center and Center for Puerto Rican studies at Hunter College.

Ayoka has led a consulting firm that helps nonprofit organizations strengthen their organizational capacity by utilizing progressive models and practices. She served as the Director of the New Beginnings Nonprofit Incubator at Resources of Human Development, where she lead and provided technical assistance and capacity building to small and start up community-based programs. Services offered enabled organizations to grow, build their skill base, and maximize their impact through intensive, ongoing, individualized coaching, mentoring, and support aimed at building entrepreneurs' skills in: strategic planning and organizational development; fundraising; financial management; marketing; board, staff and volunteer management.

She currently works as the Associate Executive Director of Ifetayo Cultural Arts Academy and lives in New York with her supportive family.

PERMISSIONS

INDEX

www.ingramcontent.com/pod-product-compliance
Lightning Source LLC
Chambersburg PA
CBHW021843020426
42334CB00013B/173